THE SULTAN'S FEAST

THE SULTAN'S FEAST

A Fifteenth-Century Egyptian Cookbook

Ibn Mubārak Shāh

Edited, Translated and Introduced by
Daniel L. Newman

SAQI

To Nayla

إِلَى أَمِيرَتِي نائلة
مُوَدَّةً

SAQI BOOKS
26 Westbourne Grove
London W2 5RH
www.saqibooks.com

Published 2020 by Saqi Books

A full CIP record for this book is available from the British Library.

Printed and bound by Clays Ltd, Elcograf S.p.A

ISBN 978 0 86356 156 6
eISBN 978 0 86356 181 8

CONTENTS

PREFACE

WHEN, AS A STUDENT, I was making my first inroads into the wonderful world of the Middle East, I remember being struck by the uncanny similarity between one of the Babylonian words for 'doctor', *āshipu*, and the Persian word for 'cook', *āshpaz*. What made this even more interesting was the fact that the *āshipu* was actually a witch doctor, who employed magic in order to remedy the ills that bedevilled his patients. Later on, I found another tempting culinary cognate, *ashbū*, which, so my trusted dictionary told me, meant 'chafing-dish', or perhaps something closer to a magician's cauldron. What magic is this, I wondered? Were Babylonian cooks so skilled that, over time, they came to be known as magical doctors (of food), with the word travelling eastward to Persia, possibly along with some chafing dishes? The etymological conundrum became more interesting with the addition of another ingredient: the ancient Greek *mágeiros*, a relative of the word for magus (*mágos*), which at various points throughout history denoted butcher (originally of sacrificial animals), priest and cook (as it still does today).

The link between food, or rather the creation thereof, and magic seemed obvious to me, even then. It has never ceased to be so, particularly since I have gained theoretical knowledge and practical experience over the course of extensive travelling, and have delighted in the magic of seemingly random ingredients being transmogrified into succulent blends that are always much more than the sum of their constituent parts.

This book combines a number of my passions, as it is about language (Arabic, in particular), history, culture and food. It is a journey of pleasure through time, to the fifteenth century, to partake of the culinary joys from a distant past.

Food is, of course, much more than the act of eating, or a knowledge of ingredients. It is difficult to imagine anything more profoundly cultural and social than food, and it is often the first experience many of us have with the 'Other', in the broadest possible sense of the term.

Courtesy of our increasingly globalized world, what was once strange, exotic and even a little fearful, has now become an integral part of our daily lives. Nowhere more than in food does the diversity of our modern-day societies manifest itself on a daily basis. It is through food that relations and friendships are forged – over the breaking of bread, as the saying goes.

The study of food does not merely give us recipes, but also brings to light the interactions between peoples and changes in society, which, like cuisines, are enriched by extraneous additions that, just like ingredients, are mixed together to produce something exciting and new. When human beings travel, they do not take only their passports and belongings with them, but also memories of their native lands, of which culinary traditions are a major component. Food is a quintessential element in what Fernand Braudel called 'the repeated movements, the silent half-forgotten story of men and enduring realities, which were immensely important but made so little noise.'[1] It is these 'silent' stories that tend to speak the loudest.

A bite into a Turkish and Central Asian *manti* and *börek,* a Balkan *burek*, East European *pirogi*, Russian *pelmeni,* Greek *boureki*, Georgian *khinkali*, Indian *samosa*, Somali *sambuus*, or a Cornish pasty is to join a fascinating gustatory journey, which had its origins in a Chinese *jiaozi* (dumpling). All of these dishes consist of a (usually savoury) dough or pastry filled with meat and/or vegetables and spices. Their common precursor, and main conduit into cuisines across several continents, is the mediaeval Arab *sanbūsaj* (or *sanbūsak*) which started life in Baghdad, from where it travelled throughout the expanding Islamic empire, and beyond.

This book presents both a critical edition and translation of the last known mediaeval Arabic culinary text, entitled *Zahr al-ḥadīqa fī 'l-aṭʿima al-anīqa* (*Flowers in the Garden of Elegant Foods*), and will bring alive the smells and flavours of Mamluk Cairo, just a couple of decades before the region fell to the Ottomans.

On my journey, I have been fortunate to receive help when I needed it most, and I am pleased to be able to thank staff at the library of the University of Leiden (Netherlands), the British Library (London), the National Library of Medicine (Bethesda, MD), the Beinecke Rare Book & Manuscript Library (Yale University), the UCLA Louise M. Darling Biomedical Library, the National Library of Tunisia (Tunis), and the Bibliothèque nationale de France (Paris) for greatly facilitating my researches and their assistance in accessing the required manuscript sources. A special word of thanks is due to Ms Judith Walton and my friend Dr Mamtimyn Sunuodula at Durham University's Bill Bryson Library for their unstinting efforts to accommodate

[1] 1974: 15.

my often-complicated requests.

I should also like to express my gratitude to Durham University for granting me research leave, during which I was able to conduct part of the research that ultimately found its way into the book.

I benefited from the stimulating exchanges with those working in the same field, particularly in the context of papers delivered at the International Conventions on Food History and Food Studies, organised by the European Institute for Food History and Cultures (IEHCA) at the University of Tours.

And finally, as ever, this work would not have been possible without the unflagging support of Whitney Stanton, my most trusted and beloved companion on this journey – as on all others – who ensured that the authorial endeavour was accompanied by dishes recreated from the manuscript, and shared her vast culinary knowledge, which often provided invaluable insights.

NOTE ON TRANSLITERATION

THE TRANSLITERATION USED in the book is a 'narrow' scholarly one, with some minor amendments: initial *hamza* is not transliterated, no distinction is made between *alif mamdūda* and *alif maqṣūra*, both of which are rendered as *ā*. The *tā' marbūṭa* marker is not rendered, except when it occurs as the first element in a *status constructus* (the so-called *iḍāfa*).

ا	a, ā	ض	ḍ
ب	b	ط	ṭ
ت	t	ظ	ẓ
ث	th	ع	ʿ
ج	j	غ	gh
ح	ḥ	ف	f
خ	kh	ق	q
د	d	ك	k
ذ	dh	ل	l
ر	r	م	m
ز	z	ن	n
س	s	ه	h
ش	sh	و	w, ū
ص	ṣ	ي	y, ī
		ء	'

INTRODUCTION

The Mediaeval Arabic Culinary Tradition

Until relatively recently, Arabic culinary history enjoyed very little attention, and was the object of only a few studies.[1] This is all the more remarkable since it is the richest in the world in terms of the extant resources, which predate the earliest European recipe collections by several centuries. As one observer put it, 'from the tenth through the thirteenth centuries, Arabic speakers were, so far as we know, the only people in the world who were writing cookbooks.'[2] Even if in the meantime, the discovery of a collection of twelfth-century Latin recipes produced at Durham Cathedral Priory[3] vitiates part of this claim, it does not detract from the extraordinary history of the Arabic tradition, not least because of the sheer number of recipes, which number in the thousands.

The rise of this rich culinary tradition occurred during the Abbasid caliphate (750–1258 CE) and is thus another product of the so-called 'Golden Age' of Islam. The esteem in which the culinary art was held in the early Abbasid empire was such that among the authors of cook books we find several caliphs – Ibrāhīm al-Mahdī (d. 839 CE), al-Ma'mūn (d. 833 CE) and al-Wāthiq (d. 847 CE) – as well as famous scholars from various fields and disciplines. One culinary author provided his own explanation for the reason rulers, grandees and scholars started writing cookery books. Some chefs, he claimed, do not care about their work and are only interested in getting things done as quickly as possible and leaving the kitchen. Furthermore, they take little care and few precautions, which is why everything has to be explained to them and they need to be supervised: 'it is these flaws which have led caliphs and rulers to do the cooking themselves, to create dishes and compose many books on the subject.'[4] Cookery books were collected by the high and mighty. The owner of the earliest copy of the oldest work was the Ayyubid ruler of Damascus and

[1] For a survey of early studies see, for instance, Marín & Waines 1994: 11–17.

[2] *Wuṣla*, xvii.

[3] Gasper et al. 2014.

[4] *Andalusian*, fol. 22v.

	10th century	Author	Recipes
1.	*Kitāb al-ṭabīkh [wa 'l-'iṣlāḥ al-aghdiyya al-ma'kulāt wa ṭayyib al-aṭ'ima al-maṣnū'āt]*[a] *(A Cookery Book with the Best Food and Finest Preparations)*	Abū Muḥammad al-Muẓaffar Ibn Naṣr Ibn Sayyār al-Warrāq [Baghdad]	615
	13th century		
2.	*Kitāb al-ṭabīkh*[b] *(Cookery Book)*	Muḥammad Ibn al-Ḥasan Ibn Muḥammad Ibn Karīm al-Kātib al-Baghdādī (d. 637 AH/1239–40 CE) [Baghdad]	161
3.	*al-Wuṣla ilā 'l-ḥabīb fī Waṣf*	*anon.*[c] [Aleppo]	635

[a] The text has survived in three copies: Oxford, Bodleian, Huntington 187; Helsinki University Library, MS Coll. 504.14 (MS Arab 27); and Istanbul, Topkapi Saray, Ahmed III Library, 7322 A. 2143 (dated 696 AH/1297 CE). It was the second treatise (after al-Baghdādī's) to be published (Öhrnberg & Mroueh, 1987). It was also the subject of a second edition, by Iḥsān Dannūn al-Shāmīrī, Muḥammad 'Abd Allāh al-Qadaḥāt & Ibrāhīm Shabbūḥ (*Kitāb al-Ṭabīkh wa Iṣlāḥ aghdhiyyāt al-ma'kūlāt wa ṭayyib al-aṭ'ima al-maṣnū'āt*, Beirut: Dār Ṣādir li 'l- Ṭibā'a wa 'l-Nashr, 2012). The only complete translation is that by Nasrallah 2007. Translated extracts can be found in Waines 1989 (French trans., Marie-Hélène Sabard, *La Cuisine des califes*, Arles: Sindbad/Editions Actes Sud, 1998); Zaouali 2007 [twenty-four recipes]; Salloum et al. 2013.

[b] In addition to the autograph manuscript (Istanbul, Süleymaniye, MS Ayasofya 3710, dated 623 AH/1226 CE), there is only one other known (undated) mss copy (British Library MS Or5099). The text has been edited several times, by Dāwūd al-Jalabī (*Kitāb al-ṭabīkh*, Mosul: Maṭba'at Umm al-Rabī'ayn, 1934), Fakhrī al-Bārūdī (*Kitāb al-ṭabīkh wa dhayl 'alayhi al-ma'ākil al-Dimashqiyya*, Damascus: Dār al-Kitāb al-Jadīd, 1964), and Qāsim al-Sāmarrā'ī (*Kitāb al ṭabīkh*, Beirut: Dār al-Warrāq li 'l-Nashr, 2014). All of the editions rely solely on the Istanbul autograph. It has been translated into English several times (Arberry 1939; Perry, in Rodinson et al. 2001: 19–90; Perry 2005), and in Italian (Mario Casari, *Il cuoco di Bagdad. Un antichissimo ricettario arabo*, Milan: Guido Tommasi Editore, 2004). Some of its recipes are extracted in Waines 1989; Salloum et al. 2013; Sa'd al-Dīn 1984.

[c] The text was clearly a bestseller as it has survived in no fewer than fifteen mss copies, the oldest of which dates back to the early fourteenth century, though not all of them are complete: Aleppo, Aḥmadiyya (later Waqfiyya) library, No. 1678; London, British Library, Or6388; London, School of Oriental and African Studies Library, ms. 90913; Oxford, Bodleian, MS. Huntington 339; Damascus, Ẓāhiriyya library, Adab 3259; Istanbul, Topkapi Saray, Ahmed III library, 157 2088 [dated 30 October 1330]; Cairo, Dār al-Kutub, Taymūr 75; idem, Ṣinā'a 74 (703 AH/1303–4 CE); idem, Lām 5076; Istanbul, Süleymaniya library, MS Fatih 3717 (dated Rabī' II, 873 AH/October 1468 CE); Paris, BNF, Arabe 4938 [dated Rabī' II 1126 AH/April 1714 CE]; Berlin, Staatsbibliothek WE 5463 [extract]); Patna, Bankipore Khuda Bakhsh Oriental Public Library, 2193: 259/1; idem, 96/4; Bursa, Inebey medresi. Another known manuscript (dated 979 AH/1571–2 CE), held in Mosul (Madrasat al-Ḥājjīyāt), appears to have

	al-ṭayyibāt wa 'l-ṭīb[d] *(Reaching the Beloved through the Description of Delicious Foods and Flavourings)*		
4.	*Kitāb al-ṭabīkh*[e]	*anon.* [al-Andalus]	472[f]
5.	*Fuḍālat al-khiwān fī ṭayyibāt al-ṭaʿām wa 'l-alwān*[g] *(Delicacies*	Abū 'l-Ḥasan ʿAlī Ibn Muḥammad Ibn Razīn al-	428

---

been lost (see *Wuṣla* 1986, II: 334). The text was first edited by Sulaymān Maḥjūb and Durriyat al-Khaṭīb (Aleppo: Maʿhad al-Turāth al-ʿIlmī al-ʿArabī, 2 vols, 1986), and then with accompanying English translation by Charles Perry (2017). References will be to the latter edition (hereinafter referred to as *Wuṣla*). For a discussion of the manuscripts, see *Wuṣla* 1986: II, 415–447 and *Wuṣla* 2017: xxxix–xl.

[d] The editors of the 1986 edition attributed the text to Kamāl al-Dīn ʿUmar Ibn Aḥmad Ibn al-ʿAdīm (1192–1262). However, since then the authorship has been called into question; for a discussion, see *Wuṣla*, xxxvii–viii.

[e] Until recently, this cookbook was thought to have survived in only one manuscript (BNF Ar7009), which was completed on 13 Ramaḍān 1012 AH/14 February 1604 CE. It was first edited by A. Huici Miranda, 'Kitab al tabij fi-l-Magrib wa-l-Andalus fi 'asr al-Muwahhidin, li-mu'allif mayhul (Un libro anónimo de la Cocina hispano-magribí, de la época almohade)', *Revista del Instituto de estudios islámicos*, IX/X (1961–62) 15–256 [= *La cocina hispano-magrebí en la época almohade según un manuscrito anónimo. Edición crítica*. Madrid: Impr. del Instituto de estudios islámicos 1965]. Catherine Guillaumond's unpublished PhD dissertation, *La cuisine dans l'occident arabe médiévale* (Université Jean Moulin-Lyon III de Lyon, 1991) included a critical revised edition, as well as a French translation. In the early 2000s, the Moroccan scholar ʿAbd al-Ghanī Abū 'l-ʿAzm discovered another copy of the same text (477 recipes), completed on 18 Dhū' l-Qaʿda 1272 AH/21 July 1856 CE and entitled *Anwāʿ al-ṣaydala fī alwān al-aṭʿima* ('Pharmaceuticals in Food dishes'), which he edited and published in 2003 (Rabat: Markaz Dirāsāt al-Andalus wa-Ḥiwār al-Ḥaḍārāt bi 'l-Ribāṭ [repr. 2010, Rabat: Mu'assasat al-Ghanī li 'l-Nashr]). The BnF mss was first translated by A. Huici Miranda (*Traducción española de un manuscrito anónimo del siglo XIII sobre la cocina hispano-magribi*, Madrid: Maestre, 1966; 2nd ed. *La cocina, hispano-magrebí durante la época almohade*, 2005, Madrid: Trea). Charles Perry translated it into English under the title *An Anonymous Andalusian Cookbook of the 13th Century,* but to date it has only appeared on line (http://www.daviddfriedman.com/Medieval/Cookbooks/Andalusian/Andalusian_contents.htm) [519 recipes], with a revised (and augmented) version being made available by Candida Martinelli et al. (http://italophiles.com/al_andalus.htm). Guillaumond published a French translation: *Cuisine et dietetique dans l'occident arabe medieval d'après un traité anonyme du XIIIe siècle. Étude et traduction française*, Paris: L'Harmattan, 2017. The text will be referred to hereinafter as *Andalusian*, with references to the Arabic text being to the BNF manuscript, whereas Abū 'l-ʿAzm's edition will be referred to as *Anwāʿ*.

[f] This number excludes the descriptive entries on herbs and spices, as well as the appended list of fifty-seven medicinal syrups and electuaries (fols. 76–83).

[g] In addition to mss copies in the Royal Academy in Madrid (Galuengos 16) and Tübingen University (Ar. 5473), there is also one held in a private collection. It was first studied by Fernando de La Granja y Santamaria (*La cocina arábigo-andalusa según un manuscrito inédito*, unpubl. PhD diss., Madrid, 1960). The edited text by Muḥammad Ibn Shaqrūn and Iḥsān ʿAbbās (Beirut: Dār al-Gharb al-Islāmī, 1984, repr. 2012) relied on all three manuscripts, whereas

	of the Table as regards the Finest Foods and Dishes)	Tujībī [al-Andalus, Tunisia]	
6.	*Kanz al-Fawāʾid fī tanwīʿ al-Mawāʾid*[i] *(Treasure of Benefits in the Variety of Dishes)*	*anon.* [Egypt]	750/79[h]
7.	*Taṣānīf al-aṭʿima (Classification of Foods)*[j]	*anon.*	171
	14th century		
8.	*Kitāb Waṣf al-aṭʿima al-muʿtāda*[k]	*anon.* [Egypt]	480

Ibn Shaqrūn's earlier edition (Rabat, 1981) was based only on the privately held one. The present author has identified another manuscript copy of al-Tujībī's text in a British Library manuscript collection of several medical treatises (Or5927, fols. 101r.–204v.). Unfortunately, none of the extant versions are complete as there are eight chapters missing (six from the seventh section, and two from the tenth). There are two complete translations, one in Spanish (Manuela Marín, *Relieves de las mesas, acerca de las delicias de la comida y los diferentes platos,* Madrid: Trea, 2007), and one in French (Mohamed Mezzine & Leila Benkirane: *Fudalat al-Khiwan d'ibn Razin Tujibi*, Fez: Publications Association Fès Saïss, 1997), with extracts (fifty-three recipes) appearing in Zaouali 2007. Also see Ibn Sharīfa 1982; Heine 1989.

[h] It has survived in six manuscripts: Dublin, Chester Beatty Library No. 4018; London, Wellcome Library WMS Arabic 260; Cambridge University Library, No. 192; Cairo, Dār al-Kutub, Ṣināʿa 18; Gotha Orient A 1345 (Arab 117); Patna, Bankipore Khuda Bakhsh Oriental Library, No 2. The sole critical edition is by Manuela Marín and David Waines (Beirut/Stuttgart: Franz Steiner Verlag, 1993), with an English translation by Nawal Nasrallah, *Treasure Trove of Benefits and Variety at the Table: A Fourteenth-century Egyptian Cookbook*, Leiden: Brill, 2018 (unfortunately, I was not able to access this work during the preparation of the present book). Zaouali 2007 also includes thirty-seven recipes from the book. It will be referred to hereinafter as *Kanz*. All the references in the text are to the Marín and Waines' edition.

[i] The second number refers to recipes placed in the Appendix of the published edition, since they were not found in the Cambridge manuscript the editors used as their basic text, but only in the Chester Beatty or Cairo manuscripts. Most of them are from the latter, with four occurring in both the Chester Beatty and Cairo mss. (Nos. 37, 38, 40, 46) and four only in Chester Beatty (Nos. 42, 43, 44, 45).

[j] Wellcome, WMS Arabic 57, Fols. 48r-112v. It does not appear to have been identified as a culinary treatise, and is part of a collection that also includes a treatise on simple medicines (*al-adwiya al-mufrada*) by the Andalusian polymath Abū 'l-Salt (1068–1134), who was not, however, the author of the cookbook. The origin of the text is unknown, as is the date. The only factual clue as to the origin of the manuscript copy is that it was written in the Maghribi script. It has speculatively been placed in the 13th century since the types of recipes are closer to those found in other treatises of the period. Secondly, there are similarities with the work of the eleventh-century pharmacologist Ibn Jazla (see below), and recipes found in al-Baghdādī and *Waṣf.* This would support the hypothesis that the manuscript was copied in the Muslim West, but produced in the East. The present author is preparing a study and edition of the work where these issues will be further elaborated.

[k] There are only two extant manuscript copies, both held in Istanbul (Topkapi Saray Library, 62 Ṭibb 1992 and Ṭibb 22/74, 2004 (dated 13 Jumādā II 775 AH/30 November 1373 CE), cop-

	(The Book of the Description of Familiar Foods)		
	15th century		
9.	*Kitāb al-ṭibākha*[l]	Jamāl al-Dīn Yūsuf Ibn Ḥasan Ibn ʿAbd al-Hādī al-Ṣāliḥī, Ibn Mubarrad (Mibrad) (1437–1503) [Damascus]	55[m]
10.	*Zahr al-ḥadīqa fi 'l-aṭʿima al-anīqa (The Flowery Garden of Elegant Food)*[n]	Shihāb al-Dīn Aḥmad Ibn Mubārak Shāh (1403–1458) [Egypt]	332
		TOTAL	**4,178**

ies of which can also be found in Cairo, Dār al-Kutub (Ṣināʿa 51 and Ṣināʿa 52, respectively). An English translation was made by C. Perry, 'The Description of Familiar Foods', in Rodinson et al. 2002: 273-466 (hereinafter referred to as *Waṣf*).

[l] It was edited by Ḥabīb al-Zayyāt (*al-Mashriq*, vol. 35, 1937, pp. 370–376), with an English translation by C. Perry, '*Kitāb al-ṭibākha*: A Fifteenth-century Cookbook', in Rodinson et al., 2000, pp. 467–76 (= *Petits Propos culinaires*, 21, pp. 17:22). For details on Ibn Mubarrad, see Richardson 2012: 97–104.

[m] This number takes into account variants in individual entries (= 44) in the edition.

[n] Henceforth referred to as *Zahr*.

Egypt, Najm al-Dīn Ayyūb (d. 1249 CE).[5] The culinary appreciation of these recipe books amongst the wealthy continued well past the Abbasid caliphate into the Ottoman Empire. The Sultan himself commissioned an ornate copy of al-Baghdādī's cookery book, complete with magnificent gold-leaf headings.[6] A Turkish translation was made of the same book in the 15th century, by a certain Maḥmūd Shirvānī (Mehmed Chirvani), who added over ninety recipes of his own, thus producing the first Ottoman cookery book.[7]

The table above lists the ten cookery manuals that are known to have survived. They span a period of five centuries (tenth to fifteenth) and represent a geographical area extending from al-Andalus (Muslim Spain) to Tunisia, Egypt, Baghdad and Aleppo. Another forty or so are known by their titles only.[8]

The history of the Arab culinary tradition is wrapped in mystery. The first is that, based on current evidence, it burst onto the scene fully formed, without any apparent evidence of gestation stages. That is, if we accept the consensus view that the treatise considered the oldest actually deserves this epithet, despite the fact its oldest dated manuscript is from the late 13th century (1297 CE) – over seventy years after al-Baghdādī's autograph (the only one among the texts) from 1226 CE. Combined with a relatively small number of works across half a millennium, this complicates attempts at identifying trends and periodization.

The issue of authorship – or, to be more precise 'ownership' – of the recipes is a highly challenging question. For a start, at least half of the treatises have no, or dubious, authorship, whereas in many – if not all – cases, it is unlikely that one is dealing with a wholly self-contained collection, but rather, for the most part, a sample from a historical pool of recipes.

According to Maxime Rodinson, the author of the first study of Arabic culinary writings,[9] by the end of the Abbasid Empire, the books had ceased 'to be a princely amusement, a distraction for the highborn courtier, earning him a reputation for good taste and fine manners', and became the preserve of 'obscure scholars, part-time epicures who wish to preserve for themselves

5 Nasrallah [al-Warrāq 2007]: 7–8.

6 This copy is currently held at the British Library, Oriental MSS 5099.

7 Yerasimos 2001: 11–3.

8 For a list and discussion see al-Warrāq 1987: V–VII; Nasrallah [al-Warrāq 2007]: 15–22.

9 'Recherches sur les documents arabes relatifs à la cuisine', *Revue des études islamiques* 17, 1949, pp. 95–165 (English translation: 'Studies in Arabic Manuscripts Relating to Cookery', in Rodinson et al. 2001: 91–164).

recipes of dishes they have enjoyed so that they can have their servants prepare them on demand. In short, they are simple recipe notebooks for home use, like the part devoted to cookery in the *Menagier de Paris*.[10] Such books are not often copied, but the successive owners of each manuscript tend to add further recipes in the margins thus increasing their utility.'[11]

Unfortunately, the reference to a 'golden age' in culinary writing is based solely on references to works that have not survived, whereas the description of the 'post-classical' group – thirteenth century onwards – is somewhat oversimplified in light of the extant manuals.

In terms of genres, it is possible to divide the corpus into two broad categories: works that consist solely of recipes, and those that have literary aspirations and include poetry, as well as dietetic information. The latter group may conveniently be considered a type of *adab* literature, which refers to works of *savoir-vivre* produced for the cultured elite and contained a collection of prose, poetry and anecdotes. Al-Warrāq's book exemplifies this genre, with its numerous poems, the frequent use of a high-literary register, complete with rhymed prose (*saj'*) in titles, and attention to dining etiquette, not found in any of the other works. However, one single treatise does not a genre make, and in the absence of any other, it is not possible to extrapolate its features to works of which we only know the title.

The second biggest group consists of recipe collections, which may, however, contain some dietetic elements, as well as medical preparations, but whose features do not comply with high literary conventions of the time. The fact that these were intended for use by people who knew their way around a kitchen – or used it to instruct their servants (as in the case of *Zahr*) – explains why recipes generally provide little detail on quantities and exact preparation methods and timing. Similarly, the fact that, like today, they would have been used in a kitchen environment, which is not conducive to the preservation of paper, explains the relative dearth of surviving copies.

Geographically, we can divide the existing books into two categories, those produced in the Near East, and those from the Muslim West, i.e. al-Andalus and North Africa.

One thing all treatises, except Ibn Mubarrad's, have in common is that they for the most part reflect a cuisine enjoyed by gatherings of the elite.

---

[10] A 'housewife's guide' from 1393 which also contains a large number of recipes (over 350). See Greco & Rose, 2009.

[11] Perry et al. 2001: 102.

This is evident from the technical complexity of the dishes, the equipment required, and the preciousness of some of the ingredients. Equally significant is the fact that the books were produced in the centres of power and culture of the time (Damascus, Aleppo, Cairo, Tunis), where potential patrons could be found. One should be wary, therefore, of using the books as a mirror of mediaeval Arab societies, since, for the most part, they say very little about the daily lives of the vast majority of the population.

What is known about the authors, and why and how did they write the books? They include a bookseller (al-Warrāq), a government scribe (al-Baghdādī), a religious scholar (Ibn Mubarrad), a poet (Ibn Mubārak Shāh), and a government official (al-Tujībī). The motive for writing is rarely made explicit. Exceptions include al-Baghdādī, who states he composed the book for himself 'and whomever may want to use it in the making of dishes',[12] whereas the author of *Wuṣla* invoked religious motives as 'consuming good foods strengthens adoration in God's servants and draws pure praise from their hearts.'[13]

There is no direct evidence that any of the authors was a professional cook, and in some cases their experience may have been limited to eating the dishes. However, some went well beyond that, and the author of *Wuṣla* proudly stated: 'I have included nothing without having tested it repeatedly, eaten it copiously, having worked the recipe out for myself, and tasted and touched it personally.'[14] As a result, the comment by Perry[15] that 'it is clear that scribes were uniformly ignorant of cooking,' and that '[a]s a result, cookery manuscripts tend to be marred by a remarkable number of errors' is somewhat tenuous.

An obvious corollary of the above is that it is more accurate to talk of compilers rather than authors. Their sources no doubt included professional cooks' recipe collections, as well as other compilations. Al-Warrāq, for instance, mentions a large number of authors – twenty in total – whose works he consulted and who included physicians, dignitaries and caliphs, like the afore-mentioned gastronome Ibrāhīm Ibn al-Mahdī. It is relatively rare to find references to specific works. Exceptions include the anonymous *Andalusian*, whose author mentioned one of the other extant treatises (al-Baghdādī's),[16] as

[12] Al-Baghdādī 1964: 10 (trans., 26).

[13] *Wuṣla*, 4–5.

[14] Ibid.

[15] *Wuṣla*, xxxviii.

[16] *Andalusian*, fol. 27r.

well as Ibrāhīm Ibn al-Mahdī's *Kitāb al-Ṭabkh*[17] and even a solitary Persian source.[18]

Slightly less rare are the attributions – often putative – to individuals who allegedly invented the dish (which may be named after them), or even taught it to the author. For instance, in *Wuṣla* there are references to a cake made by a maidservant (*jāriyya*) of al-Malik al-ᶜĀdil al-Kabīr,[19] 'an elegant and extraordinary gourd recipe [learned] from the daughter of the governor of Mārdīn,'[20] and one 'learned from the domestic servants of al-Malik al-Kāmil.'[21] Probably the most famous example is that of the *Būrāniyya*, named after Būrān, the caliph al-Ma'mūn's wife, who, according to tradition, was an accomplished cook, renowned for her fried aubergine dishes. References to chefs are rare and they, like most craftsmen in history, generally remain anonymous.[22] Whilst the kitchens in the grand households would also have included women, the authors of cookery books are all men.

Turning briefly to the organisation and content of the cookery books, it is possible to identify a number of common features. With the exception of Ibn Mubarrad's manual, where recipes are organized in alphabetical order, the other treatises tend to group dishes together in chapters, according to cooking methods (fried, oven dishes) and/or main ingredient (e.g. fish, chicken), flavours (sweet, sour), or the type of dish (vegetarian, condiments, pickles, beverages, sweets, cold dishes). Some, like *Wuṣla*, have an overarching structure in that they broadly follow the various stages of the banquet.

The modern concepts of breakfast, lunch and dinner did not exist, and the cookery manuals provide no details about such divisions, or when dining should occur. In fact, there is little information anywhere about this aspect. One of the few sources to address this was the fifteenth-century author al-Aqfashī, who stated that 'for the Muslim the time of lunch (*ghadā'*) began at dawn and lasted until midday. Afterwards the time of supper (*'ashā'*) started, which lasted until midnight.'[23] This may be compared to practice in the early nineteenth century in Egypt, where supper was always the principal meal and

---

17 Ibid., 48r. ff.

18 *Andalusian*, fol. 24r.–v.

19 *Wuṣla*, No. 7.99.

20 *Wuṣla*, No. 8.37.

21 *Wuṣla*, No. 8.52.

22 See Yungman 2017.

23 Lewicka 2011: 414.

it was 'the general custom to cook in the afternoon; and what remains of the supper is eaten the next day for dinner, if there are no guests in the house. Evening meal is before the evening prayer.'[24]

While Ibn Mubarrad's collection is the only one that provided recipes of everyday food, some of the others occasionally included recipes that were inspired, and enjoyed, by the common folk.[25] The *Andalusian*, for instance, includes two dishes eaten by 'shepherds in the countryside of Cordoba', a 'servant's recipe', as well as several for slaves,[26] whereas al-Tujībī's choice of ingredients (e.g. tripe) and references to food being cooked in the communal oven also reflect a less high-brow cuisine.

Even a cursory examination of the manuals yields a number of overlaps, between, on the one hand, the Near Eastern works (excluding Ibn Mubarrad), and those from North Africa and al-Andalus. In addition to overlaps between *Kanz* and *Wuṣla* (e.g. mains,[27] desserts,[28] condiments,[29] hygiene compounds,[30] incense[31] and perfumes[32]), there are similarities between al-Warrāq, al-Baghdādī and *Kanz*. In some cases, the relationship is much more direct, as in *Kanz/Zahr* and al-Baghdādī/*Waṣf*. The varying degrees of relationship or influence (sometimes just a couple of recipes) may be tentatively represented in the chart on the facing page.

The state of present research – not least in terms of dating and authorship – makes it very difficult to trace the direction of the borrowing and, indeed, of the sources. If anything, the gaps in the current knowledge support the hypothesis of other 'donors' that have since then been lost. The fact that multiple recipes have identical names, even within one and the same cookery book, but diverge in terms of ingredients and/or instructions, also lends support to the idea that recipes were gleaned from different sources.

---

24 Lane 1923: 145.

25 On the food of common people in the mediaeval Near East, see Ashtor 1968; *idem* 1970; Levanoni 2005.

26 *Andalusian*, fols., 37r., 46v., 47v., 49r.-v., 59v.

27 *Kanz* Nos. 34 (*mawziyya*, lamb with bananas; *Wuṣla*, No. 6.138), 96 (*lūbiya*, bean stew; *Wuṣla*, No. 6.86), 144–45 (preserved sparrow; *Wuṣla*, Nos. 8.62–3), 260–61 (salted fish, *Wuṣla*, Nos. 8.59–61); 610 (mashed chickpeas; *Wuṣla*, No. 8.130).

28 e.g. No. 293 (*jūdhāb al-qaṭā'if*, crêpe drip pudding; *Wuṣla*, No. 7.39).

29 No. 486 (*sals* with verjuice; *Wuṣla*, No. 8.75); *Kanz*, No. 543 (= Wuṣla, 8.5): Greek turnip pickles.

30 e.g. *Kanz*, Nos. 639–640 (*ushnān*, 'handwash powder'; *Wuṣla*, No. 9.2, 9.4).

31 e.g. *Kanz*, No. 665 (*Barmakiyya*, 'incense tablets'; *Wuṣla*, No. 1.15).

32 e.g. *Kanz*, No. 660 ('*dawā 'araq*', 'sweat medicine', i.e. deodorant; *Wuṣla*, No. 1.25).

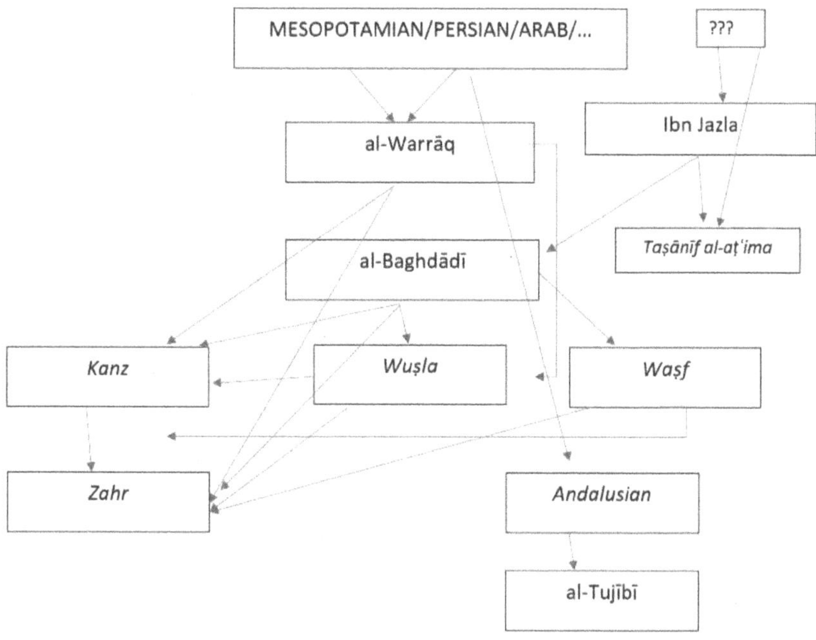

In line with the occasions at which they were served, the dishes were intended to impress at every level and appeal to all the senses by presentation, ingredients, smell or colour.[33] Meat reigned supreme. Although some of the cookery books contained vegetarian dishes, these were often deemed fit only for sick people and Christians during Lent. Probably the most grotesquely carnivorous recipe is one allegedly made for the Governor of Ceuta (Morocco), and involves an oven-roasted lamb that has been gutted and then filled with a sparrow inside a starling inside a pigeon inside a chicken inside a goose.[34] Clearly not a dish for a household oven.

Like meat, sweets were associated with 'the upper classes [and] were identified with the food of kings.'[35] However, the most valuable commodity in the dishes were rare and exotic ingredients (especially spices), and so the culinary writings reveal a great deal about international trade at the time, too.

---

33 See, for instance, Marín, 'Beyond Taste: The Complements of Colour and Smell in the Medieval Arab Culinary Tradition', in Tapper & Zubaida 1994: 205–14; Aubaile-Sallenave, 'Parfums, épices, et condiments dans l'alimentation arabe médiévale', in Marín & Waines 1994: 217–49.

34 *Andalusian*, fol. 5v.

35 Levanoni 2005: 215.

From within the Muslim empire, there came yoghurt, dates, leeks, pomegranates, rice and roses from Persia; quince and apples from Iṣfahan; fruit syrup from Shiraz; pears from Sijistan; grapes, rhubarb, raisins and sumac from Khorasan; saffron and olive oil from North Africa; melons from Samarqand; leek and mulberries from Syria; and agarwood from Socotra. Many ingredients were sourced from farther afield, as well, and the author of the oldest extant geographical manual, Ibn Khurradādhbih (d. 912 CE), described the activity of Arab merchants who returned from China with silk, musk, agarwood, coconuts, cassia, cinnamon, galangal, sandalwood, agarwood, camphor, cloves and nutmeg.[36] In the case of cassia, its Arabic name, *dār ṣīnī*, reveals both its origins and journey, as it goes back to the Persian *dār chīnī*, meaning 'Chinese wood, or bark'.

Very early on, the spice trade was firmly in Arab-Muslim hands, and the ninth-century *Akhbār al-Ṣīn wa 'l-Hind* ('News from China and India') informs us that there was already a Muslim community in Khānfū (the modern Guangzhou) at this time. The Chinese emperor even appointed a representative in Khānfū, who settled disputes arising between them and locals, served as imam, and 'prayed for the sultan of the Muslims.'[37] As for the route, cargo was hauled from Basra, Oman and elsewhere to the port of Siraf (Iran), where it was loaded onto ships bound for China.

The tenth-century geographer and encyclopaedist al-Mas'ūdī reported that agarwood, cloves, aromatics, saffron musk and all perfumes came from India; camphor, sandalwood, nutmeg, cardamom and cubeb from present-day Vietnam; and amber, saffron and ginger from Spain.[38] The same author provided a list of some twenty-five aromatics that were available in his day; in addition to those already mentioned, it includes costus, lentisk gum, ladanum and storax gum.[39] Surprisingly, there is no reference to the oldest and one of the most-utilised spices, pepper, which, according to Ibn Khurradādhbih, was sourced from Kīlah (identified as Kra, in the Malay Peninsula).[40] Equally interesting is the absence of references to the banana, which was known very early on, as it appeared as an ingredient in al-Warrāq's treatise (in a drip

---

[36] Ibn Khurradādhbih 1889: 70–1 (trans., 49).

[37] Mackintosh-Smith & Montgomery 2014: 7–8.

[38] al-Mas'ūdī 1861–77: I, 61, 341, 367.

[39] *Ibid.* I, 367.

[40] Ibn Khurradādhbih 1889: 70–1 (trans., 49); Dalby 2003: 65.

pudding), and in a few more recipes in *Kanz*[41] and *Wuṣla*.[42]

Besides the specialised treatises, information about food and dishes can be found in a variety of other sources, such as manuals composed for market inspectors (*muḥtasib*), for whom monitoring the production of food and purity of ingredients was a key responsibility. And in a culture that appreciated good food, it is not surprising that it played an important part in literary works, too.[43]

Arabic culinary literature may appear to have burst on the scene out of nowhere, but nothing emerges out of a vacuum, of course, especially if it is related to something as vital as food and drink. Although evidence is sometimes thin on the ground, it is possible to identify some antecedents of mediaeval Arab cooking.

Rather unsurprisingly, the oldest inspiration comes from within the Near East, in ancient Mesopotamia, for which evidence has survived in the form of three cuneiform tablets containing a total of some thirty-five ancient Babylonian recipes, dating from 1700 BCE.[44] There are a number of similarities with mediaeval Arab recipes, first and foremost in terms of the ingredients. Many of the future staples, such as honey, vinegar, cumin, mint, coriander, garlic, onions and leeks are already here. The amounts of seasonings used also sound familiar, with up to ten condiments in one dish, some of which are cooked in the broth, others added at the end. As for ingredients, most of the recipes are meat based (including grasshoppers), though there is also a green wheat porridge (which would become a *harīsa* later on). There is already sheep's tail fat (added after boiling), the use of multiple meats in one dish, or breads baked along the wall of an oven. In terms of techniques, most of the dishes are stews or broths, though there are some pickles as well.

One of the most interesting dishes is a lamb broth, which besides fat, onion, coriander, cumin, leek and garlic, calls for 'crumbled cereal-cake'. This bears an uncanny resemblance to one of the few dishes attested in pre-Islamic Arabia and famous still today – the *tharīd* (bread sopped in a thick meat and vegetable broth), which was basic fare among Bedouin and allegedly a favourite of the Prophet, himself.

Ancient Greece and Rome is another connection worth exploring, and the

---

41 24–5 (No. 34).

42 Nos. 6.136–8.

43 For food in Arabic literature, see van Gelder 2002.

44 For a discussion and translation of the recipes, see Bottéro 1987, 1995, 2004. Also see Nasrallah [al-Warrāq 2007]: 45–55.

medical and pharmacological works, such as those by the botanist Dioscorides (first century CE) and the physician Galen of Pergamon (d. *ca* 216 CE), contain a lot of information about foods and ingredients.[45] However, when it comes to cookery books, the sources all but dry up. The genre appeared in the 5th century BCE but most of the works are lost, with only fragments remaining. Another, equally scanty source are the occasional references to food and matters culinary in Greek literature, for instance in gastronomic poetry and comedies.[46] This dearth of sources is all the more disappointing as there emerged a culture of gastronomy which used exotic spices and fruits, many of them introduced as a result of Alexander's campaigns. Greek cooks already made use of saffron, sumac, coriander and cumin, albeit in relatively low quantities as they were thought by some scholars to ruin the taste of the food, and should more appropriately be used in wine. Vegetables were not part of dishes, but were eaten as a side, with bread.

The Romans developed gastronomy to new levels of sophistication and extravagance, as shown, for instance, in Petronius' *Satyricon* (first century CE). It is in fourth-century Rome that 478 recipes were gathered in a book called *De Re Coquinaria* (*On the Art of Cooking*), which has been attributed to Caelius Apicius, and is the only extant complete cookery book before the Arabic treatises.[47] Like in the mediaeval Arabic tradition, the recipes reflected dishes of the higher classes, and revealed a high degree of technical proficiency in the kitchen, with numerous ingredients (often more than ten), including many of the same spices found in Arab cooking, and specialised equipment.

Most of the dishes involve meat, but there are several for fish, as well, and all were served slathered in sauce. Similarities with later Arab cuisine include preserves, salted meat and fish, and especially the use of hitherto unknown aromatics like asafoetida and spikenard as a result of the expansion of Roman trade. The abundant use of spices like cumin, coriander, rue and pepper means that someone dining in Baghdad in the tenth century would probably have had a sense of '*déjà-goûté*' with many of Apicius' dishes.

One of the key ingredients in Roman cuisine, particularly as a sauce base, was a condiment already used by the Greeks. Known as *garum* (Greek *garos*),

---

45 See, for instance, Grant 2000.

46 On ancient Greek food, see Dalby 1996; Dalby 2003: *passim*; Wilkins & Nadeau 2015; Wilkins & Hill 2006. On food references in Greek comedy, see Wilkins 2000.

47 The most recent (and best) translation (with accompanying Latin edition) is Grocock & Grainger 2006. On Roman cooking, also see André 1961.

or *liquamen*, it denoted fermented fish, which served to provide the salty flavour.[48] The sources also mention *muria*, which was brine, or the liquid in which fish, vegetables, etc. have been pickled. Etymologically, the latter would appear to have much in common with a substance the Arabs referred to as *murrī*, a condiment resulting from an elaborate process of rotting and fermenting some cereal grain (often barley), though a few recipes (mainly from the Muslim West) called for fish.[49] David Waines made a case for the existence of two distinct types of *murrī*, at least in al-Andalus and North Africa: one based on cereal (probably pre-Islamic), and another on fish (similar to *garum*).[50] In terms of usage, it is worth noting that the Arab *murrī* is found only in savouries, while the Romans used *garum* in both savoury and sweet dishes. A modern recreation of *murrī* revealed that it tastes like soya sauce, which, of course, is also the result of mould and fermentation.[51]

We are on much more stable ground with a potential Persian (Sasanid) influence on mediaeval Arab cuisine, even if no cookery manual has survived that predates the Arabic works. The evidence, some of it circumstantial, is both culinary and lexicological.

The earliest source can be found in Middle Persian (Pahlavi) wisdom literature and involves a story from the late sixth or early seventh century, entitled *Khusraw ī kawādān ud rēdak-ēw* (*Khosrow son of Kavād and the Page*). It comprises a dialogue between the king and a page, who is questioned about his knowledge of various aspects of cultured life.[52] It is the questions on foods and wines that most concern us, and they provide a great deal of information about the courtly culinary culture of the day. The similarities with the mediaeval Arabic works include the use of certain ingredients (e.g. types of meat), condiments, dishes and the use of sugar in savoury foods.

The Muslim conquest of Persia and the fall of the Sasanid Empire did not result in the loss of its culture. Not only was Iran never 'Arabized', its contribution on all levels, whether, political, religious (e.g. Shiism), cultural or literary, remained substantial, particularly during the Abbasid caliphate. And when it came to food culture, Persian sophistication was both an inspiration and

48 See Corcoran 1963; Curtis 1978.

49 al-Tujībī 2012: 262–70; al-Warrāq 1987: 46 (trans., 136); Bolens-Halimi 1991; Perry 1983; *idem*, 1988; *idem*, 1999; Weingarten 2005.

50 Waines 1991.

51 Perry 1998.

52 See Unvala 1921; *Encyclopedia Iranica*, s.v. 'cooking' (Nancy Hatch Dupree). On Persian cooking see also Sancisi-Weerdenburg 1995.

an aspiration, and the above-mentioned story was even translated into Arabic by the (Persian-born) anthologist ʿAbd al-Malik al-Thaʿālibī (961–1038).[53]

Stews (*khōresh*),[54] a mainstay of Sasanid cooking as well as in modern Iran, were taken to with gusto by the Arab conquerors, and make up more than half of the cooked dishes in the treatises. The Persian influence in the culinary lexicon appears in the names of ingredients and dishes, such as *sikbāj* (> *sik*, 'vinegar'; *bāj*, 'stew') and *zirishk* ('barberries').

Despite the fact that no Persian cookery book remains today, some were in circulation as the author of the *Andalusian* treatise excerpts some details about hygiene and cooking taken from a book written by the Sasanian King Anushirwān (d. 579 CE).[55]

The Mongol conquest and rising influence of the Turks in the region from the thirteenth century onwards also led to food transfers, and in the present book one finds, for instance, *tuṭmāj* (a type of pasta), *yāghurt* (a yoghurt dish), and *qāwūt* (a nut confection).[56]

Another influence on mediaeval Arab cuisine, which has hitherto received little attention, comes from India. Yet the connection would appear to be an obvious one, if only because of the intense trading contacts and the sourcing of many spices and plants. Unfortunately, little evidence is available. Linguistically, there are the borrowings from Sanskrit, such as *nārjīl* (*narikela*, 'coconut', also known in Arabic as *jawz Hindī*, 'Indian walnut'), *kurkum* (*kuṅkuma*, 'saffron, turmeric'), or the rice dish known as *bahaṭṭa* (from the Hindi *bhat*, 'boiled rice')[57] for which a recipe is found in a number of cookery books, including *Zahr* (No. 72).

Additional information is provided by the oldest extant source on Indian cooking in the Middle Ages, the so-called *Mānasollāsa* (*Delight of the Mind*), a Sanskrit text completed in 1129–30 by the South-Indian king Someśvara III. This encyclopaedic work is a valuable source for eleventh–twelfth-century Indian culture as it discusses a large number of subjects, including politics, astronomy, painting, medicine and poetry. The third book is devoted to food and dishes, some of which are somewhat similar to Arab dishes, such as meat

---

53 1900: 705–11. Also see Rodinson et al. 2001: 99–100.

54 Also *khōresht*, which translates as 'food' in the sense of 'eating and drinking', thus showing the importance of this type of dish in the diet. Steingass 1892: 484.

55 fol. 24r.–v.

56 Also see Buell & Anderson 2010.

57 Perry ([al-Baghdādī 2005]: trans., 50, note No. 1) recommends reading the word as *bihaṭṭa*, 'indicating a pronunciation even closer to the Punjabi *bhatt* (Urdu *bhāt*).'

cooked in sour fruit juices, rice beverages, fermented cereals and milk-based sweets.[58] The mixture of spices also yields some interesting findings, such as the combination of betel leaf, nutmeg, mace, cloves and cardamom of the post-prandial *paan*, which are also the basis for a popular Arab spice mix, *aṭrāf al-ṭīb*, to which we shall return later.

Mediaeval Islamic medicine, like Greek medicine before it, took a holistic and preventative approach to health, within which food occupied a central place as ingredients and dishes alike also served as remedies. The theoretical framework that governed the body is known as 'humorism', which Muslim scholars inherited from the Greeks, particularly Hippocrates (ca. 460–ca. 375 BCE) and the already-mentioned Galen.[59]

It was based on four humours, rendered in Arabic as *khilṭ* (pl. *akhlāṭ*), which were fluids – blood, phlegm, yellow bile and black bile – regulating body and health. The humours were also linked to the four elements that make up all things: air, water, fire and earth. Each of them was linked to two of the so-called primary qualities – hot (*ḥārr*)/cold (*bārid*) and moist (*raṭb*)/dry (*yābis*): fire is hot and dry; air, hot and moist; water, cold and moist; earth, cold and dry. The elements are concentrated in the humours: air in blood (*dam*); water in phlegm (*balgham*); fire in yellow bile (*mirra ṣafrā'*); and earth in black bile (*mirra sawdā'*).

The humours were also endowed with the primary qualities associated with the element: blood was considered hot and moist; phlegm was cold and moist; yellow bile was hot and dry; and black bile was cold and dry. Finally, there was a connection between the humours and the season: blood with spring, yellow bile with summer, black bile with autumn, and phlegm with winter.

A person's physical health and personality were linked to the balance of the humours – also known as the 'temperament' (*mizāj*); if black bile, for instance, predominates, the individual has a cold and dry (or melancholic) temperament, which is prone to sadness. Illness was viewed as the result of an imbalance in the humours, with balance being restored through medical treatment and/or diet as foods were linked to varying degrees (up to four) of the primary qualities. The need for equilibrium also manifested itself in a recommendation of temperance over excess not just in ingredients, but also in food, in general.

---

58 Achaya 1994: 89–91, 96; *idem* 2012: 108–11; Sen 2015: 165.

59 See, for instance, Ullmann 1970: 97–100; Conrad et al. 1995: 23–5, 99–104; Jouanna 2012: 335–59.

The identification of the temperament of foodstuffs was not a precise science and there is a great deal of variation in the medico-pharmacological literature, not just in the intensity of the quality, but the qualities themselves. For instance, rice was considered cold and dry in the second degree by some, but hot (in the first degree) by others, whereas onions appear as hot (third or fourth degree) and dry (third or fourth degree), or moist (third degree). Varieties of the same substance could also demonstrate different temperaments; sweet pomegranates were cold and moist, while sour ones were cold and dry. In practice, this meant that, say, an individual with an excess of phlegm (cold and moist) would be prescribed hot and dry foodstuffs (e.g. pepper) in order to counteract the properties and restore balance. Ideally, the food should be suited to the temperament, age and state of the diner, and the season.

Cooked dishes were also associated with the primary qualities, and thus had therapeutic properties. However, here, too, there was considerable variation in the alleged properties. In most cases, there appears to be no obvious cumulative effect as the medicinal effects of a dish were often unrelated to those of its constituent components.

In the cookery books there is sometimes ambiguity as to whether a recipe should be considered medicine or food, as preparations originally designed as a medicament were eaten for pleasure as well, such as stomachics (digestive medicine).[60]

An examination of the medical references across the manuals reveals that al-Warrāq's is the odd one out by the amount of dietetic content. However, it is important to add that none of it was original and was copied for the most part from medical works, such as the *Kitāb al-Manṣūrī fī 'l-ṭibb* by al-Rāzī (d. 925 CE), who gained fame in Europe as Rhazes.[61] The next attested treatise, by al-Baghdādī, contains none whatsoever. The same is true for *Waṣf*. The other works that include medical information are the *Andalusian*, *Kanz* and *Zahr*, which, in addition to specifying the medicinal properties of some recipes (e.g. aphrodisiacal or anti-emetic effects), includes the humoral properties of some key ingredients.

The earliest dated culinary information – though not actual recipes – can be found in medical and pharmacological works. There is, however, one

60 See Marín & Waines 1989.

61 al-Rāzī 1987: 109–65; al-Warrāq 1987: 21–63 (Chaps. 8–26); al-Samarqandī 2017: 4 (note No. 13).

source that includes a substantial number of recipes. The *Minhāj al-bayān fīmā yastaʿmiluhu al-insān* (*The Pathway of Explanation Regarding that which Human Beings Use*) by the Baghdad physician Ibn Jazla (d. 1100 CE) is a pharmacological dictionary containing over 2,200 entries, most of them plants and drugs, as well as over 200 food recipes.[62] It is particularly significant since the earliest copy can be reliably dated to Rajab 489 AH (June–July 1096 CE),[63] whereas the oldest cookery book manuscript (al-Baghdādī) dates from 1226 CE. The book was quite the bestseller in its time, as around fifty manuscript copies have survived to the present day.

It is safe to hypothesize that Ibn Jazla was not the creator of the recipes, but that they were culled from as yet unknown – and probably lost – sources (culinary and/or pharmacological), which may have constituted an immediate precursor, or the missing link, in the early history of the cookery books and thus, in a way, reversely mirror the food–drug continuum in which food became medicine. In parallel – or in a subsequent stage – there would have been the addition of *adab* elements (as in al-Warrāq), followed by the final stage of the recipe book. The *Taṣnīf al-aṭʿima* could well be another example of this additional stage in the early development of the culinary writings.

Evidence of the hypothesis is provided by al-Baghdādī's autograph manuscript. Firstly, there are a number of extracts from the *Minhāj* added by another hand (and at a later date) in the margins of many of al-Baghdādī's recipes.[64] The marginalia include recipe variants, dietetic information about recipes or ingredients, and even entire recipes, as in *amīr bārīsiyya* (barberry stew)[65] and *ḥasāʾ* (soup).[66]

However, the influence far extends the margins as in a number of cases the recipes are near-identical, with only minor differences in, for instance, the title of the recipe, the sequence of instructions, or proportions of ingredients. In one case (*khabīṣ*), three of al-Baghdādī's recipes appear under one entry in

---

62 See Graziani 1980; *EI²*, s.v. 'Ibn D̲jazla' (J. Vernet); Chipman 2009: 30–1. The present author is currently preparing a critical edition and translation of the *Minhāj*.

63 British Library, Or.7499, fol. 239v. The transcription of the copyist (Hibat Allāh Ibn al-Ḥasan) was endorsed by Ibn Jazla, himself (fol. 13r.).

64 fols. 5r., 5v., 6v., 7v., 8r., 8v., 9r., 9v., 10r., 10v., 13v., 16r., 16v., 18r., 19r., 19v., 20r., 21r., 21v., 24v., 25v., 27v., 30v., 31r., 31v., 32r., 34v., 35r., 36v., 37r., 37v., 38v., 40v., 44r., 46r., 46v., 47r., 48r., 48v., 49r., 50r., 51v., 52v., 53v.

65 al-Baghdādī mss. fol. 10r.; Ibn Jazla, fol. 27r. (where it is called *ʿanbar bārīsiyya*). Also see recipes Nos. 19, 284.

66 al-Baghdādī mss., fol. 53v.; Ibn Jazla, fol. 71v.

Ibn Jazla.[67] In other cases, the borrowing is only partial. The recipes borrowed are predominantly (sweet) puddings, as well as some meat dishes. Although al-Baghdādī at no point acknowledged his source, the origin ('*Minhāj*') is mentioned at the end of each of the marginal additions, some of which include elements not copied from Ibn Jazla's recipes, thus 'restoring' them to their original form.[68] The most salient feature is the omission of the medical information which prefaces Ibn Jazla's recipes. The two texts also share a number of other dishes with identical names but different cooking instructions, such as *akāriʿ* (trotters),[69] *sikbāj*,[70] *shīrāz buqūl* (a type of condiment),[71] *samak musakbaj* (fish stewed in vinegar),[72] and *samak mamlūḥ mamqūr* (salted fish dish).[73]

While it is likely that al-Baghdādī borrowed the recipes directly from the *Minhāj*, not least because of the popularity of Ibn Jazla's text and the fact that both men were from the Baghdad, it is, of course, possible that both copied from another, hitherto unidentified source.

The link between food and religion is an important one in Islam, and there are numerous references in religious texts, whether it be the Qur'ān or hadiths.[74]

The prohibition of certain foods in Islam is widely known, whether it is the unlawfulness of pork and alcohol, or the abstention from food in general between sunrise and sunset during the holy month of Ramadan. Less familiar to us today, perhaps, are the food prohibitions common amongst mediaeval Christians, whose diet was subject to religious stricture, not least that enjoying food was synonymous with gluttony, which was considered the sin committed by Adam and Eve and led to the Fall. As a result, restraint (often in the form of fasting) was the road to godliness and salvation. Things were different for the mediaeval Muslim, who was encouraged to enjoy the bounty provided by Allah (e.g. Qur. 7:32, 2:57), albeit without excess (7:31). Several of the cookery authors preface their books with a disclaimer and include the religious injunctions to endorse the enjoyment of their recipes. Al-Baghdādī, for instance, referred to wholesome food and drink as Allah's graces, as well

---

67 al-Baghdādī 1964: 73–4 (trans., 96–7); Ibn Jazla, fol. 80v.

68 Most notably in the case of *jūdhābs* and *khabīṣ*; Ibn Jazla, fols. 57r.–58v.

69 al-Baghdādī 1964: 55 (trans., 75); Ibn Jazla, fol. 26r.

70 al-Baghdādī 1964: 55 13–4 (trans., 30); Ibn Jazla, fols. 124v.–125r

71 al-Baghdādī 1964: 64 ('*shīrāz bi-buqūl*'; trans., 88–9); Ibn Jazla, fol. 140v.

72 al-Baghdādī 1964: 61 (trans., 82); Ibn Jazla, fol. 127v.

73 Ibid.

74 For a brief discussion, see Waines, in Mcauliffe 2001–6: II, 216–23.

as being 'the foundation of the body and the essence of life.'[75]

When it comes to religious prohibitions, references in the cookery books are few and far between. They tend to involve instructions not to let people who are in a state of ritual impurity touch certain dishes when they are being prepared. This usually referred to women on their period, but also includes touching something impure (e.g. blood, semen, faeces) beforehand, without washing, or being a non-Muslim. Interestingly enough, the dishes in question share the fact that they involve pickling or fermentation, as in a recipe for *murrī* in *Zahr* (No. 91).[76]

References to the religious status of wine (*khamr*), on the other hand, are conspicuous by their absence. This is particularly interesting because wine was frequently served at banquets, while both pre-Islamic and classical Arabic literature include numerous references to wine, which is the object of a special genre in poetry known as *khamriyyāt*.[77] Leaving aside wine vinegar, which is not alcoholic, references to wine in the cookery books are extremely rare, irrespective of the context. In fact, there are only two in which wine is an ingredient, both of which are found in culinary treatises from the Muslim West; one is a recipe for a 'fish *murrī*'[78] and the other, a 'chicken *khamriyya*', which calls for about a pint of wine, which can be replaced, however, by the same quantity of honey.[79] In the present text, unadulterated wine (*sharāb ṣirf*) is an optional ingredient (to lemon juice) in the preparation of a fish paste (No. 136). The treatise by al-Warrāq stands out by the fact that it has several recipes for making the beverage,[80] but none that actually requires it.

Wine also received the attention of physicians and pharmacologists, such as the Andalusian botanist Ibn al-Bayṭār (d. 1248 CE) and al-Rāzī, who discussed both the beneficial and harmful effects of the beverage, without making any reference to its religious prohibition.[81]

Related to a verb meaning 'to ferment' (*khammara*), the word *khamr* is

---

[75] al-Baghdādī 1964: 9 (trans., 25–6). Also see al-Tujībī 2012: 29; *Wuṣla*, pp. 2–5.

[76] Also see al-Tujībī 2012: 264, 258 (preserved limes), 256 (preserved olives, with an explicit reference to 'both men and women who are impure').

[77] On this genre, see F. Harb, in Ashtiany et al. 1990: 219–34; Kennedy 1997.

[78] al-Tujībī 2012: 270.

[79] *Andalusian*, fol. 48r.

[80] al-Warrāq 1987: 302–3 (trans., 460, 462).

[81] Ibn al-Bayṭār 1992: II, 341–9 (trans., II,46–55); al-Rāzī 1881: 16–7. On the various aspects of wine, see Heine 1982; Kueny 2001; Waines, 'Abū Zayd al-Balkhī on the Nature of Forbidden Drink: A Mediaeval Islamic Controversy', in Waines 2002: 329–44; Hernández López 2013; van Gelder 1995; Lewicka 2011: 483–550 (on the alcoholic drink scene of mediaeval Cairo).

probably of Aramaic origin. In pre-Islamic Arabia, wine was mostly made from dates, or from raisins, honey, wheat, etc., and was traded predominantly by Jews and Christians.

Another word for wine, *qahwa*, related to a verb meaning to lose appetite, would become more famous since it came to mean 'coffee'. When the bean was introduced in the Peninsula in the fourteenth century, it acquired its name from the fact that its colour resembled that of *qahwa*. For their part, Arabic lexicographers, such as Ibn Manẓūr (d. 1313 CE), the author of the famous *Lisān al-ʿArab* (*The Tongue of The Arabs*), attributed the semantic shift to the fact that both wine and coffee suppress the appetite.

In the Qur'ān, the views on wine vary significantly. In verse 16:67, there are no issues with wine; in fact, it is praised as one of the signs of God's grace: 'And from the fruit of the date-palm and the vine, you get out wholesome drink and food: behold, in this also is a sign for those who are wise.' This is corroborated in 16:69, where it is said to be healing to human beings. There is a slight shift in verse 2:219, which has an admonishing tone: 'They ask you concerning wine and gambling. Say: "In them is great sin, and some profit, for men; but the sin is greater than the profit."' In other words it is sinful, yet contains some benefits. In the hadith literature, the change is said to have occurred as a result of the Prophet witnessing the effects of drunkenness, such as his uncle mutilating ʿAlī Ibn Abī Ṭālib's camels, and believers performing their rituals badly when in their cups. Reference to the latter appears in verse 4:43: 'do not approach prayer while you are intoxicated until you know what you are saying or in a state of *janāba* (major ritual impurity)'. Through a principle known as abrogation, the verse (5:90) that supersedes the others is one that refers to *khamr* (together with gambling, making sacrifices to idols and divining arrows) as a satanical abomination. This is also the line that is consistently found in hadith, where the drinking of wine is adjudged one of the major sins.

There existed yet another word for wine, *nabīdh*, which is not mentioned in the Qur'ān, and applied to any kind of intoxicating drink, irrespective of the substance that was left to steep in water until it fermented.[82] Unlike *khamr*, which still means 'wine', *nabīdh* has maintained its general meaning and in some vernaculars still refers to any kind of alcoholic drink. In others (for instance, Egypt), *nabīdh* and *khamr* are synonyms.

In the culinary tradition, only al-Warrāq mentions *nabīdh*, as an

82 See Waines, ibid.

ingredient,[83] as well as several recipes to make the beverage itself.[84] The absence in later manuals may reflect a change in attitude and a departure from the 'old' Abbasid banquets where wine flowed freely.

To most Muslim scholars, the (un)lawfulness of 'wine' is related to whether or not it has been fermented outside for more than three days. When a drink is made through boiling, rather than fermentation, it was also allowed.[85] This explains why wine vinegar, which is the usual type of vinegar used in culinary treatises, was lawful.

This also covers another substance, a kind of beer known as *fuqqāʿ*, of which there are several recipes in most of the cookery books, including *Zahr* (Nos. 166–8). It involved a heavily spiced drink (based on, for instance, a cereal, rice, or honey) that was allowed to ferment for no more than one day, and is thus not intoxicating.[86] Though limited, the fermentation aspect did continue to cause disagreement among scholars. Al-Rāzī listed it among the 'non-intoxicating beverages', together with oxymel and honey water, but stated that it 'rushes to the head (*kathīr al-ṣuʿūd ilā 'l-ra's*).'[87] The issue of the lawfulness of *fuqqāʿ* never reached the Muslim West as there are no references to the beverage in the *Andalusian* or al-Tujībī.

Mediaeval Muslim society was a true melting pot of ethnicities and religions, which made for a rich environment for exchanges of all sorts, including food. Jews and Christians were found at all levels of society; indeed, many of the physicians were from those backgrounds.

What do the culinary treatises say about this diversity? Perhaps surprisingly, there are only two treatises, one from either side of the Muslim Mediterranean, that contain dishes that are identified as being Jewish.

The Near Eastern *Waṣf* contains a recipe for Jewish meatballs (*makābīb al-Yahūd*), which are made with lean meat, pistachios, cassia, pepper, salt, parsley, mint, celery leaves and eggs.[88] Interestingly enough, the only other copy of the treatise names the recipe 'Meatballs cursed by the Jews'.[89] There does not appear to be anything identifiably Jewish about the dish, whether

---

83 al-Warrāq 1987: 101 (trans., 207), in a relish of crushed condiment; 153 (trans., 276), in a *zīrbāja* stew.

84 al-Warrāq 1987: 302–3 (trans., 461–3), 308–10 (trans., 468–70).

85 See Nasrallah [al-Warrāq 2007]: 552–3 (*khamr*), 554–5 (*nabīdh*).

86 On this beverage, See Lewicka 2011: 465–84.

87 al-Rāzī 1881: 20.

88 *Waṣf*, 379; Dār al-Kutub, Ṣināʿa 51, pp. 187–8.

89 Dār al-Kutub, Ṣināʿa 52, pp. 158–9.

it be the ingredients or preparation. The fact that the tendon (*ʿirq*) should be removed from the meat led Perry to suggest a connection with Jewish dietary law (*kashrut*), which proscribes the sciatic nerve.[90] This might have been a viable hypothesis, if it were not for the fact that other Arabic cookery books (*Zahr*, *Kanz* and al-Baghdādī) recommended removing tendons before cooking meat. And what about the alternative name of the dish being 'cursed by Jews'?

In the Islamic West, the anonymous *Andalusian* treatise contains six purportedly 'Jewish' recipes : (stuffed) 'Jewish partridge' (*ḥajala yahūdiyya*); 'Jewish hen' (*farrūj yahūdī*); two 'Jewish partridge' (*ḥajala yahūdī* [sic]) dishes; 'stuffed, buried Jewish dish' (*lawn yahūdī maḥshū madfūn*); and 'stuffed aubergine with meat' (*bādhinjān maḥshū bi-laḥm*).[91] Other than the name, there do not appear to be any identifiably Judaic features, either in the ingredients, or references to the use of the dishes in, for instance, religious rites or feasts. The only things the recipes have in common is that they tend to require lamb or poultry and all of them involve stuffing. None of this, however, sets them apart from the other recipes, either in the *Andalusian* manual, or any other for that matter. And then there is the fact that the first three recipes and the fifth all end with 'and serve it *in shāʾ Allāh* ('Allah willing').'

Guillaumond[92] reported that the editor of *Anwāʿ al-ṣaydala* (a renamed copy of the anonymous Andalusian manual) suggested, presumably on the grounds of the 'Jewish' recipes, that the author was either a chef or a Jewish physician. Basing this hypothesis on little more than the mere inclusion of the word 'Jewish' in six recipes (out of a total 472) is fanciful to say the least, particularly since there is more evidence to gainsay any 'Jewish' connection. Furthermore, the presence of dietetic and medical information in the treatise does not necessarily point towards a physician chef, but, as we have seen, is perfectly in line with several of the other culinary writings.

The absence of more references to Jewish food is striking not only in light of contacts between the communities, but also because one would have imagined the dietary restrictions to have been of interest to cooks. Even more striking is that nothing is found in this regard in the medical works of leading Jewish physicians of the Muslim world. Perhaps the conclusion is a simple one: food was the same, except for religious events, and thus there was no need for strictly 'Jewish' dishes.

---

90 *Waṣf*, 379.

91 *Andalusian*, fols., 17r., 17v., 18r., 19v.-20r., 20v.-21r., 70v.

92 2017: 27.

When it comes to 'Christian' dishes, the sources provide some interesting information. For a start, there are the vegetarian recipes, which are called 'counterfeit' or 'simulated' dishes (*muzawwarāt*)[93] and often bear the same name as their meat (or fish) counterparts, the idea being that it would entice the diner to eat them. These were commonly associated with Christians, due to restrictions related to festivals (such as Lent), as well as invalids.

Al-Warrāq included a chapter from the 'Treatise on the treatment of illnesses afflicting monks living in a monastery or far from towns' (*Maqāla fī tadbīr al-amrāḍ al-ʿāriḍa li 'l-ruhbān al-sākinīn fī 'l-dayr wa min buʿd ʿan al-madīna*), written by al-Mukhtār Ibn al-Ḥasan Ibn ʿAbdūn Ibn Saʿdūn (1001–1038 CE), better known as Ibn Buṭlān, one of the leading physicians and pharmacologists of his age.[94] A Nestorian Christian working in Baghdad, he is most famous for his health almanac (*Taqwīm al-ṣiḥḥa*), which became a standard reference work in European medicine through its Latin translation *Tacuini sanitatis*. Some twenty recipes (both savoury and sweet) from the same source were also extracted in *Waṣf*.[95]

Al-Warrāq specifically states that these dishes were eaten by Christians during Lent (*fī 'l-ṣiyām*)[96] or for the nourishment of the sick.[97] Other Ibn Buṭlān dishes in al-Warrāq's treatise include a rice porridge (*harīsa*),[98] but also a meat dish (a 'Syrian *tharīda*') eaten by some Christians.[99] The only somewhat unusual thing is that it is cooked with cheese, but this is hardly linked to Christians as cheese is also found in other recipes.

There are fewer *muzawwarāt* in *Zahr*, but this may be due to the fact that there was a belief, reported by al-Masʿūdī, that Egyptian Christians are the

93 On these dishes, also see: Waines & Marín, '*Muzawwar*: counterfeit fare for fasts and fevers', in *idem* 2002: 303–15.

94 Ibn Buṭlān 1968: 413ff. Nasrallah ([al-Warrāq 2007]: 238, 521) erroneously identifies 'Ibn Abdun' as ʿAbdūn al-Naṣrānī ('the Christian'), 'the brother of Saʿīd bin Mukhallad, vizier of the Abbasid Caliph al-Muʿtamid (d. 892)', and the title of the book as *Mā ya'kulū al-marḍā wa 'l-ruhbān wa 'l-Naṣārā* (*Foods That Sick People, Monks, and Christians Eat*).

95 *Waṣf*, 443–450. Perry incorrectly identifies the chapter as No. 14, rather than 41.

96 al-Warrāq 1987: 119–24 (trans., 238).

97 al-Warrāq 1987: 281–4 (trans., 433–7). This chapter (105) has the same title as *Kanz* chapter 8 (Recipes Nos. 204–227): *fīmā yataghaddī bihā al-ʿalīl min muzawwarāt al-buqūl* ('Healthy vegetarian dishes with which the sick feed themselves'). Four recipes (Nos. 205, 206, 207 and 224) are identical to those found in al-Warrāq. *Kanz*, 81–2 (No. 204), on the other hand, is identical with *Waṣf*, 443–4.

98 al-Warrāq 1987: 123–4 (trans., 238).

99 al-Warrāq 1987: 206 (trans., 340).

only ones who eat meat.[100]

The familiarity with some 'Christian' dishes can partly be explained by the close intercourse between the religious communities, but also, and more particularly, by the fact that many physicians in the early Abbasid Empire were (Nestorian) Christians.

There are also some less direct references, such as the mention of Coptic months in *Zahr* (No. 25). In other cases, we find examples of dishes borrowed from the Crusaders. *Wuṣla*, for instance, contains a 'Frankish roast (*shuwā' Ifranjī*)', which was fatty lamb rubbed with salt, sesame oil and rose water before it was skewered on a pole and slow-roasted over a fire.[101] Several cookery books include a number of *ṣalṣ*, which betrays its Romance origins (*salsa*) and involved a condiment usually of ground nuts, herbs and a souring agent (vinegar, lemon juice), sometimes even with fried fish.[102] One of them requires sour yoghurt and garlic, which results in something most people today would recognise as *tzatziki*.[103]

In the Muslim West, in al-Andalus, references to Christian dishes are equally sparse. The anonymous *Andalusian* refers to a dish 'eaten by Christians', a stuffed fish, baked in a casing of bread, somewhat similar to a *papillotte*.[104] Elsewhere, there is mention of a 'Christian practice' to sprinkle ground pepper over the food when it is cut for eating.[105] In al-Tujībī's treatise, the evidence is more circumstantial, ranging from a dish for monks (*rāhibī*), to the use of parsley, which is used in two meat dishes (meat and rabbit) and one fish dish.[106] This is significant as parsley was considered a 'Christian' herb in al-Andalus, just as coriander was considered a 'Muslim' herb by Iberian Christians.

As the surviving mediaeval Arabic culinary writings come from two distant regions, it is not surprising that the geographical split between East and West also resulted in a culinary split. Even though they shared common ancestors, and a fair number of dishes, they each developed in different directions as they were subject to local influences (e.g. Berber in North Africa), and there are differences in terms of produce, cooking methods, utensils, as well as, of course, taste preferences.[107]

---

100 al-Masʿūdī 1861–77: II, 303.

101 *Wuṣla*, No. 6.13.

102 *Waṣf*, 388–9, 392; *Wuṣla*, Nos. 8.67–77.

103 *Wuṣla*, No. 8.67.

104 *Andalusian*, fol. 54v.

105 Ibid., fol. 23v.

106 al-Tujībī 2012: 101–2, 142, 201–2.

107 On the culinary tradition in the Western Muslim Mediterranean, see Rosenberger 2003,

In fact, some authors were aware of differences between the two regions. The most extensive information comes from the anonymous *Andalusian*,[108] according to which the people of Yemen prefer to cook with dates; the Persians like rice with sumac; Egyptians in the Nile Delta cook fresh fish the way they do their meat, and like *maḍīra* (sour stew)[109] and *marwaziyya* (sweet lamb stew),[110] which is abhorred by Iraqis who consider it a medicine because it contains pears, jujubes and oil. As for Bedouins, they have a liking for *malla* (unleavened bread cooked under hot embers),[111] which is hated by city dwellers.

More frequently, however, it is the recipes and ingredients that speak the loudest. Rice, for instance, was not used much in the Western Muslim Mediterranean, mainly due to the fact that it was not a commonly cultivated crop, and one author specified that it was only grown in Murcia and Valencia.[112] Indeed, to this day, rice is rarely used in North African cuisines in general, where couscous and bread are king.

Although meat reigned supreme on either end of the Mediterranean, the Western treatises include a lot more fresh fish than those produced in the East, where it appears sparingly, in salted varieties, or in condiments. In addition to reasons of access in some cases, fresh fish was not considered a luxury item, besides being harmful to one's health.

A number of spices frequently found in Eastern manuals were markedly less used in the West. Examples include sesame and sumac. The latter, in particular, was exceedingly popular in the East, where a stew soured with sumac (*summāqiyya*) was said to be the favourite food of the Abbasid caliph Hārūn al-Rashīd (d. 809 CE) of Arabian Nights fame. By contrast, it is found

---

2014; Marín 1997; *idem*, 'Pots and fire: the cooking processes in the cookbooks of al-Andalus and the Maghreb', in Waines 2002: 299–302; Bresc 1997; Waines 1992; Grewe 1992; Guichard 2008.

108 *Andalusian*, fols. 21v.–22r.

109 See below, recipe No. 248.

110 For recipes, see *Kanz*, No. 65; *Andalusian*, fol. 8r. (where it is also listed as a dish from Ifrīqiya, which roughly corresponds to present-day Tunisia); al-Tujībī 2012: 97. This dish is associated with Western Arab cuisine, even though its name is derived from the Persian city of Merw. In Andalusian Arabic, it was more usually known as *murūziyya*. According to Dozy, who writes it as *murūziyā*, it was a dish called *al-ʿāṣimī* in Granada and made with meat, salt, coriander, oil, honey and starch. He refers to a contemporaneous Moroccan dish *murusiyya* (meat boiled with honey, almonds and raisins), linking it to the Latin *amorusia* (broth). In modern Morocco, *murūziyya* denotes a very sweet meat jam. See Oubahli 2008: 135–7; Corriente 1997: 498; Paavilainen 2009: 647; Dozy 1877–91: II, 585–6; Zaouali 2007: xvi.

111 Waines 2011: 164.

112 al-Tujībī 2012: 62.

in only one of al-Tujībī's recipes, in a dish that was clearly imported from the East,[113] whereas in the *Andalusian*, there is one mention of it, or rather its juice, for colouring *zulābiyya* (fritters).[114]

In terms of fruit, lemons and verjuice are absent from al-Tujībī's treatise, while dates and raisins appear only rarely in the two Western manuals. Cherries, too, are conspicuous by their absence. Unsurprisingly, olives are used far more in the Muslim West than in the East, often also to decorate dishes, or in the stuffing of meat dishes. The vegetable that stands out is the aubergine, even though it would become a 'Jewish' vegetable in Spain; it is used in three times as many recipes in the *Andalusian* as in the Eastern manuals, with the exception of al-Baghdādī (where it is called for in about 10% of the dishes).

As regards condiments and oils, treatises from the Muslim West do not mention dried yoghurt (*kishk*), which appears in every Eastern cookery book.

In the East, clarified butter (*samn*), a staple all over the Arab world today, was preferred to fresh butter (*zubd*), which occurs only once (in a rice porridge) in al-Warrāq, and not at all in al-Baghdādī and *Waṣf*. The anonymous author of the Andalusian manual explained that clarified butter 'is not used in dishes, but only in various kinds of flatbreads and in some *tharīds* and other food for women. It is needed for oil when there is excessive dryness and for pungent and pickled things in order to curb their sharpness and make them soft.'[115]

The biggest difference occurs in the use of olive oil, which is encountered relatively little in most Eastern treatises, and not at all in al-Baghdādī. When it does appear, it is usually in conjunction with another oil, such as (toasted) sesame oil. In contrast, it is required in nearly all of al-Tujībī's recipes. Wine vinegar, too, deserves a mention, as it is frequently used in the East, but absent from the Western manuals.

Milk is used more in the Muslim East than in the West; conversely, cheese is more associated with Andalusian and North African cuisine, where eggs were also much more used, 263 times to be precise in the *Andalusian*, for instance, with no fewer than thirty dishes requiring poached eggs to float on top.

Among the 'Western' ingredients unknown in Eastern recipes, one may cite *ḥalḥal* (lavender),[116] or the somewhat mysterious *banj* (a type of millet)

---

113 al-Tujībī 2012: 161.

114 *Andalusian*, fol. 69v. For the *zulābiyya*, see recipe No. 150 below.

115 fol. 23v.

116 *Lavendulan stoechas*; Dozy 1877–91: I, 315; Corriente 1997: 135 ('grape hyacinth [*Muscari botryoides*]; a kind of cultivated flax; French lavender').

and *zanbūʿ* (a kind of citrus) which are mentioned only in al-Tujībī's treatise.[117]

The discrepancies in the terminology of dishes and ingredients is also revealing. For instance, fennel is *rāziyānaj* in the East, but *nāfiʿ* and *basbās* in the West; sesame is *julajān* in the West but *simsim* in the East.

Quite a few dishes are found only in Western manuals, such as *mujabbanāt* (deep-fried cheese balls).[118] In other cases, the dishes are the same, but with different names, with the Maghribi flatbread *rafīs*[119] or sausages *mirqās* (the lexical ancestor of the *mergues*)[120] corresponding to the Eastern *raghīf* and *laqāniq*, respectively. The Eastern *tharīd* was (and still is) a savoury dish with bread, vegetables and meat; in the West, it could also denote a pudding similar to what in the Eastern cookery books would have been known as a *khabīṣ*. The *jūdhāb(a)* was a drip pudding in the Near East but was re-invented in the West as a lamb-mince pie, or custard and almond pastry.[121] And then there is the verb *khammara*, which in the East only refers to fermentation, but in Andalusian Arabic culinary jargon denoted crusting a dish with eggs, bread crumbs and spices.

Some of the cookery books, especially those from the Western Mediterranean, refer to intra-regional origins of certain dishes, as in those associated with Berber tribes, such as the Ṣanhājī or the Kutāma.[122] Local differences in terms of cooking are also found. For instance, the people from Bougie preferred making *kunāfa* with butter and clarified butter, rather than with olive oil.[123] As for *balāja*, a mutton pie, it was the speciality of the towns of Cordoba and Marrakech, and those in between.[124]

The Text

In Egypt, the fifteenth century brought little solace from the tragedies that had befallen the country during the turbulent fourteenth century. The Mamluk dynasty of former slave soldiers was under threat from the Mongols and became embroiled in a war of attrition with the Ottomans, which ended with

---

[117] al-Tujībī 2012: 37, 101. On the *zanbūʿ* (Corriente 1997: 235), see the study by Aubaile-Sallenave 1992. In modern Arabic *zanbāʿ* denotes grapefruit.

[118] *Andalusian*, fols. 63v.–64v.; al-Tujībī 1992: 82–5. For more examples, see Marín 1997.

[119] al-Dabbābī 2017: 117–120; *Andalusian*, fols. 60v., 64v.–66r.

[120] al-Tujībī 2012: 144–146, 234.

[121] al-Tujībī 2012: 67–8, 74; *Andalusian*, fol. 63r.; Corriente 1997: 107.

[122] *Andalusian*, fols. 2v.; 51r.–v., 65r.–v., 59v.; al-Tujībī 2012: 193–6.

[123] *Andalusian*, fol. 63r. For a *kunāfa* recipe, see below No. 141.

[124] al-Tujībī 2012: 127; *Andalusian*, fol. 11r.; Marín 1997: 15.

Sultan Selim I (1470–1520) capturing Cairo in 1517 CE. Egypt's economy was in free fall, and its people were intermittently attacked by the plague, which reared its head every eight to nine years after the worldwide epidemic of 1347 CE, and killed an estimated forty per cent of the population.[125] The splendour of the Golden Age of the Abbasid Empire, whose capital Baghdad had been sacked by the Mongols in 1258 CE, was but a distant memory.

It is in these troubled times that the author of the book, Shihāb al-Dīn Aḥmad Ibn Muḥammad Ibn Ḥusayn Ibn Ibrāhīm Ibn Sulaymān al-Miṣrī (or al-Qāhirī) al-Ḥanafī (al-Ṣūfī), known as Ibn Mubārak Shāh was born in Cairo in Rabīʿ I of 806 AH/September 1403 CE, and would also die there in Rabīʿ I, 862 AH/January 1458 CE.[126]

Very little is known about Ibn Mubārak Shāh, although he was held in great esteem in his lifetime. The sources all describe him as a poet and scholar, conversant in many arts and sciences. He was famous, however, not for his own output, but as a collector of poems. His magnum opus in this field is a so-called *tadhkira* (poetry compilation), entitled *al-Safīna* (*The Ship*), which runs to a staggering fourteen volumes, an autograph copy of which is part of the Feyzullah Library in Istanbul. It is of significant value as a historical document as it comprises a number of materials not found elsewhere, such as unknown *zajals* (strophic poems in the colloquial) by the originator of the genre, the Andalusian poet Ibn Quzmān (d. 1160 CE), and others.[127]

The historical context in which the culinary treatise was written may shed some light on why someone like Ibn Mubārak Shāh, who was not a chef, should have committed these recipes to paper. These were not the times of opulent banquets and courts requiring elaborate recipes to impress diners. In light of the highly eclectic selection of dishes, he was one those 'obscure scholars [and] part-time epicures', as Rodinson put it, compiling a private recipe book for dishes to be prepared in the household. Then again, one may draw a parallel with his interest in preserving poetry, and imagine his conceiving of the book as an anthology of sorts, recorded for posterity.

He was a member of a group of contemporaneous scholars and poets that were known as the 'Seven Shooting Stars', in reference to the fact that they

---

125 Dols 1979.

126 al-Ziriklī n.d.: I, 229; Brockelmann 1937–49: *Sup*. II, 1032; Kaḥḥāla 1992: I, 235; Ḥājjī Khalīfa n.d.: I, 384; al-Sakhāwī 1992: II, 65 (No. 200); al-Baghdādī 1951: I, 132; al-Ghazzī 1983: II, 42–3; al-Suyūṭī 1922: 54–7 (No. 37).

127 Hoenerbach 1950: 267; *idem*, 1952: 271; *EI*², s.v. 'tadhkira' (W. F. Heinrichs).

all bore the honorific *Shihāb al-dīn* ('Shooting Star of the Faith'). The others included such famous literati as Shihāb al-Dīn Ibn Ḥajar al-ʿAsqalānī and Shihāb al-Dīn al-Thaʿālibī.[128]

The translation is based on the sole known extant manuscript of the text, held at the Gotha Library in Ehrfurt (No. 1344, formerly arab 668, Stz. Kah. 1170).[129] The manuscript counts thirty-eight folios (1r.-38v.), with leaf sizes measuring 17.5cm × 32.5cm, each bearing twenty-one lines of text in black ink, with rubricated headings. There is foliation in grey pencil, with Arabic numerals, in the upper left-hand corners of the rectos.

Each folio has a catchword, with very occasional marginalia.[130] It is written in a legible *Naskhī* script. Despite some foxing and water staining, it is a good readable copy. There is some damage and patching on fols. 37r. (most of lines ten and eleven are illegible), 37v. (multiple words in line ten are illegible), 38r. (line eleven illegible), 38v. (most of line eleven illegible). It was acquired by the German explorer Ulrich Jasper Seetzen (1767–1811) in 1808.

The manuscript is not dated, and the only indication of its chronology is that it was copied after the death of the author Muḥammad Ibn Mubārak Shāh, whose name on the cover sheet is followed by the customary formula, 'May God have mercy on him' (*raḥimahu Allāh*). The name of the copyist appears as Muḥammad ʿAbd Allāh al-ʿUmarī in the colophon.

An edition of the manuscript was published by Muḥammad ʿAbd al-Raḥmān al-Shāghūl in 2007.[131] Unfortunately, this is a highly defective text with numerous misreadings and misidentifications. In places the text is simply unintelligible and thus a new edition was sorely needed.

Ibn Mubārak Shāh has been somewhat neglected by specialists in Arab mediaeval culinary culture. Extracts of the book were first published by the German Arabist Adam Metz in his 1902 edition of the tale *Ḥikāyat Abī 'l-Qāsim al-Baghdādī* (*The Tale of Abū 'l-Qāsim al-Baghdādī*),[132] by the eleventh-century author Muḥammad Ibn Aḥmad Abū 'l-Muṭahhar al-Azdī. It would take nearly half a century for *Zahr* to be mentioned again, albeit tangentially, in Rodinson's seminal study.[133] Some years later, the same scholar

128 Richardson 2012: 57–9.

129 Pertsch 1859–1893: III:3 (1881), 15–6.

130 Fols. 2r. 3., 4r., 5r., 8v., 9r., 11r., 17r., 17v., 19r., 20r., 26r., 28r., 32v., 36r., 37r.

131 Cairo: al-Maktaba al-Azhariyya li 'l-Turāth.

132 1902: XXIX.

133 Rodinson et al. 2001: 103, 135, 141.

First page of Gotha Ms. orient. A 1344.

brought the text to his colleagues' attention again when discussing the development of the *ma'mūniyya* dish.[134]

Later references to *Zahr* are not only few and far between,[135] but also confusing in terms of its origins, by considering it a 'Western' (Maghrebi-Andalusian) text,[136] or its relationship with other treatises.[137] It is, to say the least, odd that the book goes unmentioned by the editors of *Kanz*, on which, as we shall see, the author of *Zahr* relied extensively.

The language of the manuscript provides a number of interesting clues about its aims, origins and authorship. Like many of the culinary treatises, the language can best be described as 'Middle Arabic', that is to say, a generally 'standard', classical Arabic register, interspersed with informal and/or dialectal usage as regards spelling, lexis and morphology.[138]

On the one hand, the linguistic lapses are somewhat at odds with an author who, as we have seen, was a renowned scholar and poet. On the other hand, it is perfectly in keeping with a *divertissement,* not intended for circulation. In any event, as no autograph exists, it is, of course, impossible to establish the extent to which the linguistic lapses are the author's, or whether they are the result of the copyist's inadequate linguistic skills.

The following features can be highlighted. Firstly, in terms of spelling, there are a number of missing diacritic dots in consonants, such as *tā' marbūṭa* (ة), *thā', dhāl* or *shīn*. Generally, the *hamza* tends to be elided. As mentioned, there are only a few vowelling marks. There is considerable inconsistency in spelling: e.g. *naʿnaʿ/naʿnāʿ* (mint), *kuzbara/kusfara* (coriander), *ṭājīn/ṭājin* (pan), *salaqa/ṣalaqa* (to boil). There is also lexical inconsistency in the names of substances, such as *qarʿ/yaqṭīn* (gourd) or *qamḥ/ḥinṭa* (wheat).

The dialectal influence manifests itself in a number of Egyptianisms in vocabulary.[139] In grammar there is, for instance, the absence of definite articles in the genitival *iḍāfa* construction (e.g. *aṭrāf al-ṭīb* alongside *aṭrāf ṭīb*). The

134 'La Maʿmūniyyat en Orient et en Occident', *Études d'Orientalisme dédiées à la mémoire de E. Lévi-Provençal*, II, 1962, Paris: Maisonneuve et Larose, pp. 733–747 (English translation: 'Maʿmūniyya East and West', B. Isnkip in Rodinson et al., 2001: 183–197).

135 Perry, 'Medieval Arab Fish: Fresh, Dried and Dyed', and 'A Thousand and One "Fritters": the food of the Arabian Nights', in Rodinson et al. 2001: 477–86, 487–96.

136 Perry 1981: 102, note No. 1; Laurioux 2005: 309.

137 For instance, Perry (2001: 480) described it as a collection of recipes from al-Baghdādī and *Wuṣla*.

138 For an overview with key bibliography see, for instance, J. Lentin, in Versteegh et al. 2006-2009, III, 215–24.

139 See for instance Nos. 142, 150, 248.

latter is also sometimes replaced by the dialectal analytical genitive exponent *mtāʿ*, which is today primarily associated with North African dialects. The classical Arabic rules governing agreement between the noun and its adjective are frequently influenced by vernacular usage, as in the case of *qudūr judud* (for *qudūr jadīda*), 'new pots'.

Verb morphology is equally inconsistent and in one and the same recipe, there are shifts between the use of the imperative, passive, or second and third persons of the imperfect, while the third person plural ending *-ūna* appears in its dialectal clipped *-ū* form.

In the Arabic edition of the text, obvious spelling mistakes and missing diacritics in the manuscript have been corrected, as well as conventional *hamza*, *tashdīd* and indefinite accusative markings added. However, most of the above-mentioned morphological and lexical inconsistencies and idiosyncrasies have been reproduced. In the source text, round brackets denote editorial additions, while in the translation these are marked by square brackets.

The content and structure of the text reveal a number of issues, such as missing chapter headings, incongruous recipe juxtapositions, not to mention incomplete recipes.

Closer examination reveals some method in the chaos, though. For a start, the book is, to some extent, an abridgement of *Kanz*. The two works have 228 recipes in common, meaning two-thirds of the total recipes are partly or wholly borrowed, with varying degrees of adaptation. This amounts to a little over one quarter of the total number of recipes (829) included in the *Kanz* manuscripts that were used for the 1993 edition. As *Zahr* includes nearly forty per cent of the *Kanz* recipes found only in the manuscript at the Egyptian National Library (Dār al-Kutub) in Cairo, one may presume that Ibn Mubārak Shāh used this recension (perhaps even the same copy).

To illustrate the similarities, the table overleaf provides an overview of the chapters in both texts. It shows the eclectic way, to put it mildly, in which the author selected the *Kanz* recipes and supports the fact that it was very much a personal recipe book.

The changes can be put under a number of headings. Firstly, those affecting the order of the chapters, with *Zahr* reversing chapters 5 and 6, and 8 and 9 from *Kanz*. Chapter breaks are inconsistent and three chapters are untitled (Nos. 11, 12 and 16). The numbering of the chapters is absent from all but the first two chapters in the manuscript.

Secondly, the 'cutting and pasting' of recipes, with chapter 10 including recipes from *Kanz* chapters 13 and 14. Chapter 3, on the other hand, corresponds to two chapters in *Kanz* (3 and 4), but in *Zahr* the second is included as a section (*faṣl*). The order of recipes is regularly jumbled up and, for instance, numbers 165 and 166 in *Zahr* are 371 and 365, respectively, in *Kanz*.

The omission of recipes from certain chapters is often the result of personal preference but may also reflect a more general change in palate. From chapters 13 and 14 in *Kanz*, only one recipe is excerpted from each – one for macerated apricots (out of six) and one anti-emetic (out of twenty-six) – and placed at the end of the chapter on beverages (No. 10). Rather than the result of mere personal preference, the omission of the medical preparations can perhaps be viewed within a more general shift away from dietetics in the later development of the culinary writings.

For the sake of readability and reference, the recipes have been numbered in both the translation and the edition. In some cases, missing chapter breaks and headings have also been added.

The table provides only part of the story of *Zahr* as there are a number of overlaps with other sources, too. These can be divided into two groups: those that also involve *Kanz*, and those that do not. In the former group, we find the following combinations: *Zahr* and *Kanz* only (one hundred and eighty-nine recipes); *Zahr, Kanz* and al-Warrāq (e.g. chapter 3); *Zahr, Kanz*, al-Baghdādī and *Waṣf* (six recipes); *Zahr, Kanz*, and *Waṣf* (fifteen recipes); *Zahr, Kanz, Wuṣla*, and *Waṣf* (one recipe); and *Zahr, Kanz*, and *Wuṣla* (sixteen recipes). The second group includes *Zahr* and *Waṣf* (one recipe), and *Zahr* and *Wuṣla* (forty-two recipes).

The link with *Wuṣla* is quite interesting. If we include recipes that are in common with some of the other sources, the proportion of recipes found in both *Zahr* and *Wuṣla* amounts to almost eighteen per cent. The location of the shared recipes is not always haphazard, but clustered. For instance, the recipes shared between *Zahr, Kanz*, and *Waṣf* are concentrated between Nos. 10 and 30, the *Zahr–Kanz–Wuṣla* recipes occur essentially from No. 138 onwards (except for a few earlier outliers), while those found only in *Wuṣla* start at recipe No. 221 and continue more or less until the end. In other words, the author simply put down *Kanz* and then started selecting recipes from *Wuṣla*, proceeding in the same way, randomly copying recipes that tickled his fancy, jumping to and fro between chapters. In a number of cases, this included variations of existing recipes.

If we deduct all of the recipes shared with other treatises, the number of

	Zahr		*Kanz*	
Chapter	**Title**	**Recipes (Nos.)**	**Title**	**Recipes (Nos.)**
1.	What a cook should know	—	Instructions that a cook must know	—
2.	Bread making	1–9	On breads, the way to knead and bake them, and how to make aromatic, seeded, salted, etc. loaves	1–6
3.	Drinking water	—	On organizing drinking water with crushed ice	—
4.	Dishes	10–90	On the quality of air-cooled water and what physicians have said about it	—
5.	Making *murrī*	91–99	On types of dishes	7–149
6.	Making omelettes and other things	100–115	On making *murrī* and storing verjuice and lemon juice	150–165
7.	Counterfeit dishes	116–125	On making eggs into omelettes, etc.	166–203
8.	Fish	126–141	On vegetarian counterfeit dishes to feed to the sick	204–227
9.	Sweets	142–165	On making dishes with various types of fish	228–264
10.	Beverages like *fuqqāʿ* and *sūbiyya*	166–172	On types of sweets	265–346
11.	*Untitled* [mustard]	173	On stomachics, electuaries and beverages which are served before and after food	347–391
12.	*Untitled* [sauces]	174–177	On making *fuqqāʿ* On making *aqsimāʾ*, *fuqqāʿ* and barley water	392–403, 404–434

13.	Dairy dishes	178–190	On macerated apricots	435–440
14.	Pickles	191–226	On making anti-emetics	441–467
15.	Storing fruits and keeping them when they are out of season	227–232	On making mild, hot and tart mustards	468–484
16.	*Untitled* [dishes]	233–321	On sauces	485–499
17.	Cold dishes	322–325	On making dairy dishes such as *kawāmikh*, *jājaq*, with capers and thyme, *birāf*	500–533
18.	Toothpicks	326	On all types of pickled turnips, onions, fruit, vegetables, and the salting of lemons, *kabbād*, etc.	534–609
19.	Fragrances	327–332	On making cold dishes	610–637
20.			On aromatics, toothpicks made out of willow wood and of chalef twigs	638–654
21.			On fragrant incense, which invigorates the soul and heart, and aromatic pills, deodorants, etc.	655–673
22.			On royal perfumed powders	674–717
23.			Storing fruit when it is out of season	718–750

recipes that are found only in *Zahr* amounts to forty-nine, that is to say around fifteen per cent, and includes a wide variety of dishes, except fish and sweets. Significantly, they are concentrated in the final third of the text.

The recipes reveal the cosmopolitan and diverse character of the cuisine and the culture in which it developed. One sauce recipe (No. 175), for instance, advises that 'if it's made for a Turk, then add garlic steeped in olive oil.' The reference here is, of course, to a member of the Mamluk ruling class, many of whom were Turks. In addition, there are a number of recipes where a Turkish influence can be observed in the names of ingredients (Nos. 143, 184, 186, 188). Other parts of the Muslim empire are also represented, such as the North African couscous (No. 86), while several recipes call for foreign ingredients, including Syrian leeks, coriander and cheese, Nisibin roses, or Iraqi rosebuds.

Somewhat less expected are non-Muslim references, for instance, to the Coptic months, or the Gregorian calendar with the use of the word *Nuwanbar* for November.

The names of the recipes reveal common features with those in other cookery books, and can be put into a number of categories. Those that are named after the key ingredient (e.g. *laymūniyya*, *labaniyya*); an aspect of their appearance (e.g. *narjisiyya, rukhāmiyya, yāqūtiyya*); the preparation or cooking methods (e.g. *mudaqqaqa, tannūriyya*); geographical origin (e.g. *Jurjāniyya*); famous people, usually rulers from the Abbasid Golden Age (e.g. *Ma'mūniyya*), or purported originators of the dish (e.g. *Būrāniyya*).

There are quite a few recipes with identical names, which are often variations but may also reflect different sources: *narjisiyya* (Nos. 62, 256, 357), *mudaqqaqa* (Nos. 25, 28. 85, 130), *sikbāj* (Nos. 10, 239), *mulūkhiyya* (Nos. 46, 57, 88, 240, 300), *fustuqiyya* (17, 39, 47, 317), *ma'mūniyya* (Nos. 53, 55, 313), *zīrbāj* (Nos. 16, 36, 49, 124, 236, 285). However, in some cases (e.g. Nos. 44 and 52), a much-abridged homonymous variant precedes the full recipe, without which it is impossible to cook the first one.

Though for the most part representing courtly food culture, the text includes references to adapting recipes 'for the common man' (No. 174), or the author's 'meagre income' (No. 173). The recipes also provide practical information about everyday culinary practice at the time, with, for instance, a reference to purchasing ready-made ingredients, such as rose-water syrup, in the market. Or the advice (No. 143) to have the flour roasted at the roasted-chickpeas stall. Conversely, pulses should be macerated and sieved at home, rather than purchased ready-made from the market.

Though not a chef, the author had considerable interest and expertise in the culinary arts and was keen on imparting it, with some useful tips, and personal recommendations on alternative ingredients, or how to improve one's ability by being creative 'to become proficient by experimenting with things that have not been mentioned' (No. 79). And when one finds something that is good, one should 'stick to it.'

The target audience was expected to be familiar with the basics and things are often taken for granted; for instance, the absence of cooking instructions for dishes that are 'well known', or ingredients, as in the *tuṭmāj* noodle dish (No. 75), where there is no mention about how to make the principal element. In other cases, things are a bit more mysterious, such as in the cumin stew (*kammūniyya*) without cumin (No. 60) or a pistachio stew (*fustuqiyya*) without pistachios (No. 39).

The format of the recipes, too, bears the audience in mind as they often list the required ingredients at the start ('You need...' or 'Take...'), followed by the actual instructions, and are thus not that different from recipes in modern cookery books. The author also becomes visible in other comments, as many recipes are 'extremely delicious' or 'fit for caliphs.'

Even though dining etiquette is not specifically discussed, there are some non-food recipes (eight in total) that would have been relevant to guests both during and after the meal, such as a nausea medicine (No. 172), perfumes (Nos. 327–32), and toothpicks (No. 326). After deducting these and some others that are not, technically, food recipes (e.g. Nos. 65, 119), we arrive at a total of around three hundred and fifteen.

Many of the recipes will appear very alien to the modern reader, whether Arab or not, and most of the mediaeval classics (especially the stews) have not survived. The modern palate no longer appreciates the sourness that often marks the dishes, or some of the more unusual ingredients and spices, such as rue, ambergris, mastic or spikenard. Not long after its author died, the discovery of a faraway continent would lead to the introduction of many new ingredients, courtesy of the Columbian exchange, which would fundamentally change Arab cuisine. The popular Near Eastern dip *muḥammara* is a good example of old meeting new, as it combines the mediaeval love of nuts (in this case walnuts) with peppers, a native of the Americas.

However, some of the *Zahr* dishes will sound familiar to modern Arab ears, such as the Jew's mallow stew *mulūkhiya, tharīd, harīsa, shīshbarak, sanbūsak, kabāb*, or couscous and *mufalfal* rice, and sweets like *qaṭā'if, muhallabiyya* and *khabīṣ*. In some cases, the preparation methods have of course changed over the centuries, and the *kammūniyya* (cumin stew) is now usually made with fish, rather than meat. Pickled condiments, which were very popular, also appear quite modern, as do flavour combinations such as mustard with honey.

There is considerable complexity in the preparation of the dishes; a total of one hundred and eighty ingredients occur, with an average of seven being required in the recipes. This is not a kitchen of 'less is more', but one where, as the author puts it, 'those who have the acumen to increase flavours have infinite perspicacity and intelligence.'

In keeping with the other cookery books, the dishes in *Zahr* are quite meat heavy. Nearly half of the dishes require meat or chicken, with the flavours being predominantly sweet (often through cassia) and/or sour. The fish dishes (thirteen) barely outnumber the vegetarian ones (ten).

Contrary to modern practice, the term 'meat' remained for the most part cloaked in mystery in recipes and could, in theory, refer to any kind, except poultry. Of the one hundred plus recipes that require meat, only two refer to lamb as an option (Nos. 180, 168), and a further two to beef (Nos. 67, 68). The only other specification that is sometimes offered is that the meat should be lean or fatty. Chicken is the preferred meat in some fifty dishes, mostly sweet or sweet-and-sour stews, and has a frequent affinity with sugar, almonds, mint, pistachios, or rose water/syrup. Conversely it never appears with turnips, aubergine, carrots or Jew's mallow. The preparation of meat and chicken is somewhat different from today and they are often boiled, to tenderise them, before frying and/or stewing. As chickens were slaughtered as and when required, the instructions include scalding. Furthermore, the author recommends that prior to killing the chickens they should be fatigued by making them run (and also feeding them vinegar and rose water) to make the meat more tender. The ingredients most often used with meat are onions, pepper, salt, cassia, coriander, garlic or cinnamon.

Although many of the spices will be familiar to today's reader, others, such as black cardamom, musk, mastic or agarwood, will sound more exotic. The way in which the spices were used does not differ that much from contemporary practice, either; most of them are pounded or crushed before being put in, usually in the first batch of ingredients. Often, additional spices are added in subsequent cooking stages, but the author of *Zahr* recommends adding salt at the end since it can slow down the cooking time of other ingredients.

The various spice combinations tell us a great deal about dominant flavours in dishes. For instance, salt is used in one quarter of the meat recipes, and is mostly found with olive oil, onions, meat, dried coriander, garlic, mint, cassia or pepper.

Many of the recipes use generic terms as well as spice mixtures. Among them we find *abāzir*, which denoted spices and condiments, whether dried or fresh, whereas *tawābil* (singular *tābil*) are dried seasonings.[140] Whilst al-Rāzī[141] did not distinguish between the two, the thirteenth-century Andalusian pharmacologist Ibn Khalṣūn[142] identified the following as *abāzīr*: pepper, ginger, cassia, cloves, saffron, cumin, caraway, spikenard, fennel, aniseed, nigella, coriander and mastic.

More specific terms are *ṭīb* and *afāwīh*, both of which refer to aromatic spices. The former, which has the cognate verb *ṭayyaba* (to add aromatics to food), means perfume as well, in which case it is used interchangeably with *ʿiṭr*.[143] The term *afāwīh* is a near-synonym of *ṭīb* as its meaning also resides on the cusp of food flavouring and perfume and denotes any kind of odoriferous substance. One of the cookery books (*Kanz*) helpfully provides a list of *afāwīh* for cooking: cloves, cardamom, spikenard, cassia, ginger and saffron.[144]

We find the combination of *ṭīb* and *afāwīh* in the most commonly used spice mixture, *afwāh al-ṭīb*, which usually occurs as *aṭrāf al-ṭīb*, and comprises spikenard, betel leaf, bay leaf, nutmeg, mace, cardamom, cloves, rosebuds, ash tree fruit (*lisān ʿuṣfūr*), long pepper, ginger and black pepper.[145] In *Zahr*, the mixture is used in about ten per cent of dishes, often alongside mint, rue or saffron. It is not usually called for in meat or fish dishes; instead, it is found in beverages, sweets, pickles and fragrances.

In many cases, the stalks and leaves of vegetables are used in recipes, but in the case of the variety of celery that was available, only leaves were eaten as the stalks were too bitter. The text reveals the predilection for onions as they occur in almost one-fifth of the recipes, but also includes a number of vegetables not often found in other cookery manuals, such as taro, snake melon and capers. Conversely, cowpeas and cucumber, which are used quite

140 The singular is *bizr*, 'seed', but also 'seeds used in cooking for seasoning'. The plurals are *abāzīr* and *abzār*, the latter of which is actually a borrowing from the Persian *afzār*, 'seasonings', which may be related to Middle Persian *afshārdan*, 'to crush'. The Arabic expression *bazara al-qidr* means 'to season the pot'. See Lane 1863–74: IV, 199; Nasrallah [al-Warrāq 2007]: 643; *EI²*, s.v. 'ghidhā'' (M. Rodinson); Steingass 1892: 82, 272; Mackenzie 1986: 5.

141 1882: 40–2.

142 1996: 163–4 (trans., 92–3).

143 Dozy 1877–81: II, 77; Lane 1863–74: V, 1901. Ibn Khalṣūn's list of *ṭīb* reflects these two aspects as it includes saffron, amber, liquorice, narcissus, camphor, sandalwood, musk, rose, violet, nenuphar, myrtle, agarwood, nutmeg, spikenard, white musk rose, camomile and cloves (1996: 164; trans., 93).

144 *Kanz*, 146: No. 391. The word is the plural of *afwāh*, which is itself the plural of *fūh*, 'mouth'. See *EI²*, s.v. (A. Dietrich); Lane 1863–74: VI, 2465–6.

145 See recipe No 170, below; *Wuṣla*, No. 4.4.

often in contemporary Middle Eastern cuisine, appear in only six and three recipes, respectively.

The recipes call for a total of eighteen fruits, including various types of citrus fruit, pomegranate, dates, quince, grapes, figs, melon and mulberry. However, the biggest food group is made up of nuts (almonds, pistachios, walnuts, and hazelnuts, in order of importance), which are used in half of all the recipes, and often multiple varieties are required. The instructions usually specify that the nuts need to be peeled or skinned, and blanched. They are generally ground, except when used for decorative purposes, and are often found together with rose-water syrup or sugar. One recipe calls for musk-infused pistachios.

Many of the sour dishes include the juice of sour grapes (verjuice). Sometimes, sour grapes were dried and then soaked in hot water before use in cooking. Sweet grapes are only mentioned in regard to storage, but never as ingredients.

In the majority of cases where citrus fruits are used, it is the pulp and juice that is called for. Citron peel was rarely used in cooking, but it is sometimes found in fragrance and incense recipes. Orange peel, in particular, was deemed unsuitable (due to its extreme bitterness), and recipe No. 20 specifies that the person peeling sour oranges should not be the one who squeezes them.

When milk is added (often in meat dishes), the type is never qualified, but would in most cases have been from sheep or cows, although one recipe (No. 188) gives buffalo milk as an option. A more unusual dairy item is sheep colostrum, which is praised for its nutritional properties and appears in three recipes (Nos. 179–81). It is usually mixed with milk or egg whites or, in a particularly rich combination (No. 180), with egg whites, while a yolk is added at the end.

Cheese also tends to be unspecified, except for its geographical origin ('Syrian cheese'), and when used in stews is usually added at the end. *Zahr* is one of the few cookery books where cheese is mentioned as a side, despite its harmful qualities, with the author explaining that 'there are people who do not enjoy their food unless there is cheese on the table' (No. 182). One recipe uses *ḥālūm* cheese, preserved with orange leaves and boiled milk (No. 186).

In a cuisine noted for being sweet and sour, it is unsurprising to find a high proportion of sweeteners in the recipes. Sugar heads the list as it appears in almost one hundred recipes, followed by honey, rose water, rose-water syrup and *dibs* (date syrup).

Often, multiple sweeteners were used, and rose water was commonly used at the end of the cooking process when it was rubbed along the sides of the pot. *Dibs* tends to be an alternative to honey or sugar, while half of the recipes that require it also have jujube or rice.

The recipes also reveal a very oil and fat heavy cuisine. Like in the other Near Eastern cookery manuals, butter is a relative rarity. Clarified butter is found in fewer than ten recipes, fresh butter in only two bread puddings. Where once sheep's tail fat had been the main oil for frying and cooking, in *Zahr* sesame oil is used in a quarter of the recipes, and is also recommended for cleaning clay jars. Tail fat is required in less than ten per cent of the dishes, and is usually rendered before use. Prior to adding it to the pot, the tail fat might also be rubbed with a number of spices, such as mastic or cinnamon, as well as lime juice (e.g. No. 5). Although it is not always specified, the scum resulting from the rendering would have to be skimmed off.

In cooking oils, olive oil comes a close second to sesame oil, and tends to co-occur with salt, garlic, coriander, cinnamon, or mint. It was also commonly used to seal liquids during storage. Almond oil was toasted, and added for additional flavouring at the end of the cooking process. Pistachio oil appears only once, in a shredded chicken dish. Sometimes, identifying the kind of fat or oil is not straightforward, for instance in the case of *duhn*, which can refer to fat or oil, depending on the context.

Vinegar is one of the emblematic ingredients in mediaeval Arab cuisine and greatly contributed to its distinctive flavour. The author of *Zahr* even advises pouring vinegar on all ingredients! Besides the usual wine vinegar, *Zahr* contains recipes calling for lemon or grape vinegar. Though it is a frequent ingredient in meat dishes, it occurs in only two chicken recipes.

The book contains thirteen fish recipes, all of which rely on fresh fish. Its usual accompaniments are black pepper, salt, olive oil and garlic. Various kinds of nuts, too, are a regular feature, and are called for in a quarter of the fish recipes. More unusual perhaps is the use of raisins, dates or dried yoghurt (*qanbarīs*) in fish dishes.

The book provides a great deal of information about the way in which food was processed, including hygiene, kitchenware, cooking methods, and measures, which will be discussed briefly now. It opens with a set of guidelines the responsible cook should follow, ranging from appearance, personal hygiene and cleanliness of the workspace to the use of the various utensils.

The terminology shows the technically advanced culinary practice, and precise information is given on how ingredients should be pounded or crushed, the intensity of the fire, even if the length of time was much less precise, with 'for an hour' often just meaning 'for a little while'. Equally vague is the use of generic verbs like *'amala* or *ja'ala*, both meaning 'to make', which often have to be translated as 'cook' or 'add'. Somewhat confusing is that *maḥshī* can refer either to stuffing (especially for chickens and sweets) or dousing with a sauce (in fish recipes, but also in vegetable ones). In fact, the very word for 'recipe' is also unusual and appears as *lawn* (colour) or, more often, *ṣifa* (method).

More than two-thirds of the recipes require boiling, which sometimes also means 'cooking' or 'stewing'. Frying is involved, usually as one of the stages, in about one hundred recipes. Toasting is often applied to almonds, coriander, walnuts, hazelnuts, sumac, caraway seeds and flour.

One of the principal kitchen appliances in the mediaeval kitchen was the *tannūr*, the dome-shaped oven. The *tannūr* was the typical bread oven in ancient Babylonia, and was known in Akkadian as *tinūrū(m)*, which gave rise to the Persian *tanūr*, 'clay oven'.[146] In the Qur'ān (11:40, 23:27), it appears in the story of Noah where the boiling (*fāra*) of the *tannūr* announces the flood. Flat bread loaves were inserted through the hole at the top and then stuck to the sides for baking. As a result, bakers were required to clean the insides before baking the bread.[147] Besides bread, the *tannūr* was also used to cook pot dishes (*tannūriyyāt*). The already-mentioned *jūdhāb*, which involved roasting a chicken over a pudding (usually containing fruit), was also made in it. In pre-modern times, the oven could only be found in the homes of the wealthy, with the general population using communal ovens that catered for the local community, a practice which can still be found in some countries in North Africa (especially Morocco) and the Near East today.

The use of the *tannūr* appears to have declined over the ages and is mentioned only once in *Zahr*, in a recipe requiring food to be hung inside it (No. 295), as compared to thirty times in al-Warrāq's treatise. Conversely, the other type of mediaeval oven, the wood-fuelled brick *furn*, is called for in some ten recipes (as opposed to only seven in al-Warrāq). It was (and still is) used typically for breads, but in *Zahr* serves to cook a variety of dishes, ranging from *murrī* to omelettes and fish.[148]

The *batterie de cuisine* was quite extensive, with a wide range of pots, pans

---

146 See McCauliffe 2001–6: II, 219; Jeffery 2007: 92–5 (who traced the word back to a pre-Semitic and pre-Indo-European etymon); Nasrallah [al-Warrāq 2007]: 35–46; Waines 2011: 148–9; Salonen 1964; Balossi Restelli & Mori 2014: 46.

147 Buckley [al-Shayzarī] 1999: 47; al-Warrāq 1987: 12, 34 (trans., 88–9, 119).

148 For discussions of *tannūr* and *furn* see: *EI*², s.vv. 'khubz' (Ch. Pellat), 'maṭbakh' (D. Waines); Waines 1987: 255–85; al-Isrā'ilī 1992: 197–202; Mielck 1913: 53–65.

and implements. The list on the following pages contains those that appear in the present text, with some of their uses.

Then, as now, implements often came in different specifications, and recipes sometimes require a fine-mesh (or flour) sieve (*ghirbāl/munkhal ṣafīq*).

The material out of which pots and other cooking vessels were made also mattered. In *Zahr*, the best cooking pots are said to be of soapstone, followed by earthenware; copper is discouraged, unless the containers are tinned. Although iron is not specifically mentioned here, it was often used for cooking pots, provided they were maintained well (to avoid rust), hence the call to use new pots in recipes. Lids are not mentioned separately, but gypsum or clay are often used to seal the pot.

There is only one example of the use of glass in *Zahr*, for a specially-made glass pot filled with water in which sparrows are cooked in front of the diners.

Despite their impressive arsenal, the mediaeval chefs often came up with more creative methods to prepare food, such as in the preparation of 'fake marrow', which involved boiling liver in long copper pipes to provide not only the taste, but also the colour of marrow (No. 298). Similarly, they were not averse to decamping to locations not usually associated with cooking. One recipe (No. 231) suggests reviving rosebuds in the water storage tank of the Turkish bath (hammam)!

The weights (*wazn*; pl. *awzān*) and units of capacity (*mikyāl*; pl. *makāyīl)* used in food recipes often pose a challenge for a variety of reasons. Firstly, there was a multitude of systems across regions, or even towns, with identical terminology denoting a wide array of weights and measures. For instance the Egyptian *qinṭār* varied in weight between 45kg, 62kg, 81.25kg or 96.7kg, whereas in Damascus it was 185kg.[149] The author of *Zahr* clearly recognised this fact and in one recipe explains that 'the weight of one Damascene *mudd* is equivalent to ten Egyptian *raṭls*' (No. 210).

Secondly, measures and weights often underwent changes over time. Thirdly, the same measure could denote different weights depending on what was being weighed.[150] These differences may also explain the occasionally dramatic discrepancies in portions between similar recipes in the text.

Rather than converting weights and measures into modern equivalents,

149 Hinz 1955: 24–26.

150 For more details on the various measures and their development, see Hinz 1955; *EI*², s.v. 'makāyīl' (E. Ashtor); Rebstock 2008; Nasrallah [al-Warrāq 2007]: 800–1. For al-Andalus, see Rodríguez Lorente 1988); Vallvé Bermejo 1976, 1977, 1984.

Implement	No. of Recipes	
barniyya (pl. *barānī*)	9	Wide-mouthed (earthenware or glass) jar.[a] Used for storing fruit and pickled vegetables, and is sometimes scented, with agarwood and ambergris (No. 218).
bilāṭa	3	Tile, slab. In the text, it is used for a variety of things, including fish, meat or even paste (No. 146).
burma (pl. *birām*)	4	Stone (especially soapstone) cooking pot.[b]
bustūqa (*bastūqa*)	1	In the Muslim East, this denoted a narrow-necked earthenware jar, whereas in al-Andalus it was a glazed earthenware pot. In the text, it is used to store meat, though it would usually have been for liquids or butter.[c]
dann	2	'Large cylindrical earthenware vessel or cask, which tapers into a rounded bottom.'[d] In the text it is used for storing pickles or grapes.
dast (*dist*; pl. *dusūt*)	7	'A flat-bottomed utensil with inward-sloping sides several inches high'[e] or 'copper (or brass) cooking pot wide at the bottom, contracted at the mouth, and more contracted a little below the mouth.'[f] Today, it most commonly refers to a (copper or brass) cooking pot.[g]
furn (pl *afrān*)	10	Brick oven.
ghaḍāra	1	A large green-glazed bowl, [h] similar in size to a *qaṣ'a* (see below).

[a] Nasrallah [al-Warrāq 2007]: 680; Corriente 1997: 49; Lane 1863–74: I, 196 (vessel of baked clay, or glass 'big, bulky and green', similar to a *qārūra*. As it is a cognate of a word denoting a type of dates (*barnā*), it may not be too far-fetched to imagine that the container was originally used to store this particular fruit.

[b] Lane 1863–74: I, 195; Nasrallah [al-Warrāq 2007]: 680–1.

[c] Nasrallah [al-Warrāq 2007]: 681; Corriente 1997: 51.

[d] Nasrallah [al-Warrāq 2007]: 681. According to Lane (1863–74: II, 918), it was a wine jar, often smeared with pitch on the inside, tapering to the bottom.

[e] *Waṣf*, 286.

[f] Lane 1863–74: I, 878.

[g] Hinds & Badawi 1986: 288; Wehr 1993: 324.

[h] Nasrallah [al-Warrāq 2007]: 411, 680. The word *ghaḍār* denotes 'green clay' as well as porcelain; Lane 1863–74: VI, 2266; Dozy 1877–81: II, 216.

ghirbāl (pl. *gharābīl*)	13	Sieve.
ḥantam	1	Green-glazed jar.[i]
hāwūn (pl. *hawāwīn*)	10	Mortar.
ḥuqq(a) (pl. *ḥuqaq, ḥiqāq*)	1	'Receptacle of wood, or ivory; small round box for unguents and perfumes, a small cocoa-nut used as a box for snuff, etc.; a receptacle for wine.'[j] In the text (No. 207), it is used for pickles and would appear to be closer to a bowl.
ijjāna	1	Tub, usually used for kneading dough.
inā' (pl. *awānī'*)	29	Glass or earthenware jar. When used for ermenting was also sometimes smeared with pitch (*muzaffat* < *zift*) [Nos. 134, 223].
isṭām, iṣṭām[k]	4	Paddle.
jafna (pl. *jifān, jafanāt*)	1	Bowl, often used for kneading.
jarr(a) (pl. *jirār*)	3	Earthenware jar.
jirāb (pl. *ajriba, jurub*)	1	Knapsack.
jumjuma[l] (pl. *jamājim*)	1	Wooden bowl.
jurn (pl. *ajrān*)[m]	3	Mortar.
khābiya (pl. *khawābī*)	3	Big earthenware cylindrical jar with a tapering rounded bottom.[n] Though usually used for liquids (especially wine), in the text it serves mainly for storing fruit and pickled items.
khirqa	13	Cloth for making a herb or spice sachet.

[i] Lane 1863–74: II, 655. The *ḥantam* was originally used in wine production.

[j] Lane 1863–74: II, 608. Nasrallah ([al-Warrāq 2007]: 682) defines it as 'small rounded bowl made of carved wood, ivory, glass, brass or copper, used in recipes for making moulded cookies.'

[k] A cognate of the Classical Arabic *siṭām*, 'sword edge', which in Modern Standard Arabic means 'stopper'.

[l] Measure for corn, etc., or a wooden bowl (whose capacity originally was that of the measure); Lane 1863–74: I, 450.

[m] In contemporary Egypt, it also denotes a 'threshing floor'; Hinds & Badawi 1987: 157. Originally, it denoted a (usually stone) basin, which explains why it is also used for (baptismal) font.

[n] Nasrallah [al-Warrāq 2007]: 685.

khiwān (*khuwān*, pl. *khiwan, akhwina, akhāwīn*)[o]	1	Traditional low dining table or large tray.
lawh (*khashab*)	3	Wooden board.
mājūr (pl. *mawājīr*)[p]	1	Earthenware bowl.
maṭar[q]	4	A container made out of leather for liquids; jar, vase. Recipe No. 179 specifies that it is wide with a narrow mouth.
miʿṣara (pl. *maʿāṣir*)	1	Press, juicer for fruit (e.g. lemons) and olives.
midaqqa (pl. *midāqq*)	1	Pestle (wooden).
mighrafa (pl. *maghārif*)	7	Ladle.
mihḥakka	1	Grater.
mihrās (pl. *mahārīs*)	1	Mortar.
miqlā (pl. *maqālin*)	3	Frying pan, made of iron, and sometimes tinned.
misalla (pl. *masāll*)	3	Needle.
miṣfā (pl. *maṣāfin*)	3	Strainer.
munkhal, munkhul (pl. *manākhil*)	18	Sieve.
naʿāra	1	Jug (earthenware).
qarrāba (pl. *qarrābāt*)	1	'A large flagon or vessel having two handles and a spout (made of glass, in which wine is left standing forty days in order to refine).'[r]

o > Persian, where it denoted 'a table, covered table, and the meat upon it; a spacious tray'; Steingass 1892: 481.

p Dozy 1877–81: II, 569 (also 'flower vase').

q Its etymon is the Greek liquid measure *metrētēs*. The cognate *maṭāriyya* denoted a long-necked earthenware pot. Dozy 1877–81: II, 600; Liddell & Scott 1940: 1122.

r Steingass 1892: 961. According to Dozy (1877–81: II, 323), it is 'a type of box for transporting apples.'

qārūra (pl. *qawārīr*)[s]	1	Wide-mouthed (glass) bottle.
qaṣʿa (pl. *qaṣaʿ*, *qiṣaʿ*, *qiṣāʿ*)	1	Wooden bowl (large).
qaṣriya (pl. *qaṣārin*)	6	Large bowl.
qaṭramīz[t]	5	Large glass jar used to store fruit and pickled vegetables.
qidr (pl. *qudūr*)	93	General word for cooking pot. It could be made of (glazed) clay, copper, iron or stone.
qinīna (pl. *qanānin*)	2	Glass bottle.
qirba (pl. *qarārīb, qirab*)	1	Leather bag for storing and carrying liquids.
qirma (pl. *qiram*)	1	Wooden cutting board for meat.[u]
qiṭāf	1	Hook (iron), used to hang food on for roasting in the *tannūr*.
quffa (pl. *qufaf*)[v]	3	Basket.
rāwūq[w]	1	Strainer.
saffūd (pl. *safāfīd*)[x]	1	Skewer, made out of wood or iron.
ṣaḥfa (pl. *ṣiḥāf*)	1	Bowl, dish. According to Nasrallah,[y] it is a shallow serving bowl. While this is probably the case in the present text (No. 229), it must have also denoted a deeper vessel since in some manuals (e.g. al-Tujībī) it is used to crack and beat an egg in.

[s] The word is derived from the verb *qarra* ('to be cool' – cf. *qarr*, 'chilly, cool'), in reference to the properties of the bottle to keep liquids cool.

[t] From the Greek *kéramos*, 'wine jar'. Dozy 1877–81: II, 366 ('a type of vase with a short neck and wide mouth').

[u] From the Greek *kormós*, 'trunk of a tree with the boughs lopped off', 'log'. Dozy 1877–81: II, 337; Liddell & Scott 1940: 981. In contemporary Egypt, *qurma* still means 'log, tree stump', as well as 'chopping block'. Wehr 1993: 889; Hinds & Badawi 1987: 696.

[v] The word goes back to the Akkadian *quppu* and has also been used in maritime terminology to denote a coracle; Agius 2008: 130.

[w] From the verb *rawwaqa*, 'clarify', 'filter'. Lane 1863–74: III, 1192.

[x] The noun is derived from the meaning of the verb *safada*, 'to cover, mount' (female animals).

[y] [al-Warrāq 2007]: 818.

ṣaḥn (pl. *aṣḥun, ṣuḥūn*)	9	Plate.
salla (pl. *silāl*)	1	Basket.
sāṭūr (pl. *sawāṭīr*)	1	Cleaver.
sīkh (pl. *asyākh*)	2	Skewer.
ṣurra (pl. *ṣurar*)	1	Parcel (used with citron leaves, for instance, to infuse the dish).
ṭabaq (pl. *aṭbāq*) to	5	Tray, platter. It was used to serve foods that need be spread out.
ṭājin (pl. *ṭawājin*)[z]	14	Shallow earthenware stewing pan (also references to it being hung over a fire).
tannūr (pl. *tanānīr*)	1	Clay oven.
wiʿā (pl. *awʿiya*)	29	General word for container, vessel. In the text, however, it sometimes denotes a platter (e.g. Nos. 131, 153).
zubdiyya (pl. *zabādī*)	6	Porcelain bowl.[aa] Used to serve a number of dishes, ranging from fish, chicken and condiments.

[z] This is related to the verb *ṭajjana*, 'to roast, grill', which, in turn, goes back to the Greek *tágēnon* (or more commonly *tēganon*), 'frying pan', 'gridiron'. Dozy 1877–81: II, 27–8; Liddell & Scott 1940: 1786.

[aa] In contemporary Egypt, the *zibdiyya* is a crock used to store liquid dairy; Hinds & Badawi 1987: 364.

the translation retains the original Arabic terms. The table on the following page provides approximate equivalents for the measures that appear in the text.

In cooking, a frequent – and far more intractable – problem is the absence of precise portions. Most of the time, the reader is given the briefest of instructions, including indefinite measures: a bunch (*jurza*), handful (*kaff*), a lot (*kathīr*), a little (*qalīl/yasīr*), a spoonful (*mil'aqa*), or a fistful (*qabḍa*). In other instances, even this cursory advice is dispensed with, and the cook is told, simply, to add 'enough to make it taste like . . .', or 'enough to increase (or temper) the sourness (or sweetness)' of the dish. The proof of the pudding is in the eating, indeed!

Whilst making things challenging for the modern cook, the lack of precise measures is not at all surprising since, as we have seen, the manuals tended to be written for cooks, who can be trusted to rely on their professional expertise and do not require everything to be quantified in every jot and tittle.

Measure	**No. of Recipes**	
raṭl[a] (pl. *arṭāl*)	62	450g
ūqiya[b] (pl. *awāqin*)	24	37.5g
dirham[c] (pl. *darāhim*)	12	3.125g
qadaḥ[d] (pl. *aqdāḥ, qidāḥ*)	11	(liquid measure) 0.94l (small) or 1.88l (large); (dry measure) 716.83g (small) or 1.43kg (large)
mudd[e]	4	2.5l or 900g
dāniq[f] (pl. *dawāniq, dawānīq*)	2	*ca* 0.52g [1/6th of *dirham*]
mithqāl (pl. *matāqīl*)	2	4.68g
qinṭār (pl. *qanāṭīr*)	2	*ca* 44kg[g]
qīrāṭ (pl. *qarārīṭ*)	2	0.2004g or 0.064l
rub' ('one quarter' [of *qadaḥ*])	2	0.516l or 101g[h]
thulth ('one third' [of a *qadaḥ*])	2	0.31l
kayl(a) (pl. *akyāl*)	1	7.5l[i]
ghumra	1	4–6l[j]

[a] The Aramaic form of the Greek *lítron*. This is the Egyptian measure; in Damascus, it was 1.85kg, and in Jerusalem 2.5kg. Hinz 1955: 29.

[b] From the Latin *uncia*.

[c] From the Greek *drachme*.

[d] The literal meaning is 'goblet' and originally denoted the quantity it could hold.

[e] The Roman *modius*.

[f] From the Persian *dānak*, 'a small grain; *dānk, dānug, dāng*, the fourth part of a dram; a sixth of anything' (Steingass1892: 501).

[g] Hinz 1955: 24–5.

[h] *Ibid.*, 50.

[i] *Ibid.*, 40.

[j] The word *ghumr* originally denoted a small cup. The above estimate is based on Lane's statement that it was two or three times the amount of a *kaylaja*, which is around 2 litres; Lane 1863–74: 2292; Hinz 1955: 40–41.

THE BOOK OF FLOWERS IN THE GARDEN OF ELEGANT FOODS

written by the most unique, virtuous and erudite Imam, Shihāb al-Dīn Aḥmad, son of the late lamented Mubārak Shāh al-Ḥanafī, may Allah the Almighty have mercy on him!

IN THE NAME OF ALLAH, THE COMPASSIONATE, THE MERCIFUL

Shaykh Shihāb al-Dīn Aḥmad Ibn Mubārak Shāh – may Allah have mercy on him! – says: 'Praise be to Allah, Lord of the Two Worlds, may God facilitate the completion of the task for the sake of the Prophet Muḥammad and his family.'

ONE

Useful Things That a Cook Should Know[1]

A COOK SHOULD:

- Avoid contact with dirt and filth since that will turn people away from his food.
- Take care of his personal hygiene, have an intelligent disposition, pared nails, and clean clothes since these are attractive to people.
- Know that the best cooking pots to choose are those made out of soapstone, followed by earthenware. Copper [containers] are bad and must be tinned.
- Choose wood that is dry and does not produce visible smoke because it is damp. If you cook with it one day and it does not smoke, continue using it. I have cooked with dried date palm branches and found its smoke to be highly fragrant.
- Use rock salt;[2] if it is not freely available, take pure white salt, devoid of dust and rock.
- Use the best vegetables and spices; he should find out which is the best of things he has no knowledge about so he may increase his expertise.
- Know that fresh pepper is better than old pepper and the best ginger is that which is not worm-eaten.
- Take great effort at cleaning spices and should only grind what he will use so as not to dilute the strength of the spice.
- Wash the cooking vessels with hot clay, saltwort,[3] dried roses, and

---

[1] Variations of this section can be found in al-Baghdādī 1964: 11–12 (trans., 28–9); *Waṣf*, 302–5; *Kanz*, 5–10.

[2] *milḥ andarānī*, which was considered one of the finest varieties of salt. Nasrallah ([al-Warrāq 2007]: 579) traces it to '*dhar'anī*, derived from *dhur'a*, excessive whiteness,' whereas Perry ([al-Baghdādī] 2001:.28) links it to the town of Andaran, near Nishapur.

[3] *ushnān*; a borrowing from Persian, it was also known as *ḥurḍ*, *qillī*, and *ghāsū*. It refers to soda from the ashes of the weed which served as a hand-washing powder. According to Ibn Jazla, the bulbs are dried in the shade, and then ground and kneaded with rose water. Then, the mixture is fumigated with aromatics before being re-ground to harden it. Ibn Jazla, fols. 13v.–14r.; Ibn Sīnā 1999: I, 361–2 (trans., 61–2); Nasrallah [al-Warrāq 2007]: 778 ('alkali pow-

> fumigate porcelain bowls with mastic[4] and agarwood[5] before putting food in them. After washing the pots, wipe them down with rubbed dried sour orange or citron leaves.

For pounding meat, choose a mortar made out of stone, and for spices one made of copper. When cooking meat, remove the scum, froth and any other dirt that may float on the surface after boiling. So, before cooking meat, wash it with hot water and salt, and remove the glands, tendons, membranes and other waste that is not meant to be eaten. Remove grilled meat when it still has moisture left in it. When cooking lean meat, make sure to smear it with oil it before grilling.

The cleavers and knives should be sharpened, and the onion knife should only be used to cut onions, nothing else. Maintain the serving tray with mustard seeds.[6] When there are several dishes, each pot must have its own ladle. Prepare hot water in a pot in case it needs to be added to a dish during cooking. Do not grind spices in a mortar that contains traces of the liquid or sap of others.

Do not ladle food from a pot until it has stopped boiling, and the flames and bubbling have died down. When the pot is smoking, throw in hazelnut husks. Smoke will also intensify if the meat is rotten. When preparing tripe, sprinkle lime on it and strip it as this will expel the dirt.

The cook should wash his hands before ladling food, and sanitize them

---

der'); Steingass 1892: 67.

4 *maṣṭikā* (> Greek *mastíkē*). Possibly the world's oldest chewing gum, mastic is the aromatic dried resin of the pistachio tree. In classical Antiquity, as now, mastic was associated with the island of Chios as the only place where it could be obtained. In Arab cooking, mastic was used in a variety of dishes, including fruit stews and sweets. The other main area of application was in perfumes, as well as being used as a breath-sweetener and teeth cleanser. Ibn al-Bayṭār 1992: IV, 448–50; Ibn Jazla, fol. 215v.; Ibn Sīnā 1999: I, 553–4 (trans., 438–40); Lev & Amar 2008: 203–5; Dalby 2003: 85, 209–10.

5 *'ūd*; meaning 'wood', 'rod' or 'stick', it refers to agarwood (grown in India, China and Yemen), or its resin extracts. Despite its alternative name of 'aloeswood', it should not be confused with 'aloes', which is known in Arabic as *ṣabir* (*Suquṭrī*), and refers to the sap of an aromatic plant associated with the Island of Socotra. In the Arab world, agarwood has been mainly used in incense preparations, as well as for fumigating receptacles to remove unpleasant odours. It is found in cooking as an ingredient in some dishes (e.g. stews), in which case it was ground. Ibn al-Bayṭār 1992: III, 194–5 (trans., II, 484–5); Lev & Amar 2008: 97–8.

6 The mustard (whether seeds or powder) helps remove the smells from the wood.

with onions. If you want to thoroughly cook the meat,[7] then put borax,[8] wax, a bunch of watermelon veins – or its peel – in the pot.

When cooking syrups,[9] prepare a receptacle with water, and use a clean white rag to wipe down the edge and sides of the copper pot whenever you observe a change [in colour]. This will prevent discolouration and burning. As for wide-mouthed earthenware jars, these should be wiped with sesame oil, while cleaning the area where your sweets have been prepared. Then place on the ground so as to protect them from ants.

Do not prepare *harīsa*,[10] *aruzziyya*[11] and *farīkiyya*[12] together, except if you use fat, the best of which is that from a hogget.

Garlic draws forth the aromas of oils in broths, seeds and vegetables, and enhances their flavour. Pepper is used in most great dishes and seed dishes. It is also used in dishes in order to reduce the flavour of cassia and galangal; it has a powerful effect and enhances the smell of the food. You do not need a large quantity of it.

As for ground gum Arabic,[13] rice flour and chickpea flour, these thicken food. If you are cooking seeds, continue stirring until you lift the dish from the fire so that they do not burn.

Do not pour oil or anything like it into the pot before removing any

---

7 *Kanz* adds 'quickly'.

8 *bawraq* (< Persian *būrah*), a mixture of salt and soda mined in the Egyptian desert, especially in Wādī al-Natrūn (northeastern Egypt). It was also commonly known as *naṭrūn* (< Greek *nitron*) and, dissolved in water, was used as a glaze for bread. It was also used as a leavening agent in dough (e.g. *Wuṣla*, Nos. 5.76, 7.77; *Waṣf*, 460) or, more rarely, as a food ingredient (e.g. a *maḍīra* in *Waṣf*, 321). Al-Tujībī employed it in a handwash (2012: 279). Ibn al-Bayṭār 1992: I, 195–6 (trans., I, 288–90); Renaud & Colin 1934: 42 (No. 92), 173 (No. 401).

9 *ashriba* (sg. *sharāb*). This can refer to beverages in general but often denoted syrup, made from a wide range of sweetened fruits and vegetables. According to Ibn al-Quff, the term is synonymous with *khamr* (wine) in the medical literature. Ibn Sīnā, for his part, equated it with *qahwa* (see Introduction). It is the etymon of the English *sherbet*. Lev & Amar 2008: 567; Ibn Sīnā 1999: I, 685; Kircher 1967: 234.

10 See recipe No. 67 below.

11 A milk-based rice porridge, which could be either savoury (with meat) or sweet. It was also known as *harīsat al-aruzz:* al-Warrāq 1987: 142–4 (trans., 261–3); al-Baghdādī 1964: 52–3 (trans., 72–3); *Waṣf*, 367 (where it appears with the alternative name of *'ursiyya*, presumably because it was often served at weddings, *'urs*).

12 See recipe No. 66 below.

13 *ṣamgh 'arabī*; a resin harvested from the acacia tree, varieties of which are found in (sub-Saharan) Africa and the Near East. The Egyptian gum was particularly prized. In cooking, it was used ground as a thickener, or dissolved in water for use in batters. Powdered gum Arabic was used in toothpastes. Ibn Sīnā 1999, I: 639–40, II: 734 (trans., 361–2); Ibn al-Bayṭār 1992: III, 114–15 (trans., II: 376–7).

froth or foam. If there are some remnants of cooked meat [in the pot], apply some borax or ground dried melon peel. If the meat has changed (i.e. gone off slightly) and become greasy, take finely ground walnuts and knead them thoroughly into the meat, and then throw both into the pot. This takes away the rancidness and grease, while their oil will improve the aroma of the meat. Do not put the lid on the pot until the flames underneath it have subsided and all that remains are smooth embers, and until it is smoking. Throw the salt in after the last ingredient that requires cooking, especially grains, since salt slows down their cooking time. Vinegar should be poured on all of the ingredients, even cooked broad beans. If you make a cold dish with them, and pour some vinegar on them before eating, they become hard, as if they were raw. Alternatively, pour [the vinegar] on at the time of eating.

Dishes that have too much liquid need to be dried out, by increasing the heat; those that are dry require more hot water in a quantity to be decided by the cook. However, if water is added to *harīsa*, rice, beans, certain types of seeds and any legumes at the end of the cooking, it will ruin them in all instances; the flavours will disappear even if they were exquisite previously. That is why the cook should estimate the required quantity of water to be used in order to avoid having to add any afterwards.

The guiding principle of cooking is a sound combination of flavourings[14] in a dish so that none dominates and there is an equilibrium of flavours.

The best way to deal with cut onions in most dishes is to wash them thoroughly in water after having cut them, and then to add them to the pot. Also, wipe the knife that is used only for onions or for garlic with high-quality olive oil.

Make sure that the knives used for chopping are sturdy, whereas those for slicing should be thin and sharp, and fit for purpose.

Aubergines and gourds must be put in water for a good hour after they are cut before they can be put in the pot [for cooking]. When aubergines are added to white [i.e. milk-based] dishes[15] such as *maḍīra*[16] or *ḥisrimiyya*,[17] it

[14] *ḥawā'ij*; the plural of *ḥāja*, which simply means 'thing', it often denoted 'seasoning' in general, or, in some cases, vegetables (e.g. No. 243). Also see Lane 1863–74: II, 663–4.

[15] The most common category of 'white dishes' are *isfīdhbāj(a)* (< Persian *isfīdh*, 'white' and '*bāj*', 'stew, broth'), in reference to the original use of cheese (though there are also examples of non-white *isfīdhbājāt*). For recipes, see: al-Baghdādī 1964: 31–2, 51 (trans., 50–1, 70); *Waṣf*, 336 (*isfīdhbājiyya*), 446; al-Warrāq 1987: 159–60 (trans., 282–4); *Taṣānīf al-aṭ'ima*, fol. 66v.

[16] See recipe No. 248 below.

[17] See recipe No. 70 below.

is important to remove the outer peel and ends before throwing it in water and salt. The cook must use a separate ladle for each dish, and not use the same ladle for different dishes.

The best *tharīd*[18] is one with a sweet-and-sour broth and *ruqāq*,[19] *jardaq*,[20] *kaʿk*[21] or clean bread.[22] The quantity [of bread] should be sufficient to absorb the liquid. Push the centre [of the bread] down with a scoop and pour fat in. If the *aruzziyya* gets burnt, add rue to it and the smell will disappear. If Jerusalem cowpeas get burnt, fumigate them with a woollen cloth underneath to get rid of the smell.

If you smell an offensive odour emanating from the cooking pots, add a walnut or two, and leave for an hour; they will dry out the stench. The proof is that when you take the walnuts out, you won't be able to bear their foul odour.

If you soak a cloth in water and hang it in the pot, it will absorb salt, as does bran. Similarly, if you heat up a scoop until it becomes red hot and hang it in the pot, it will also absorb its salt.[23]

If you want to cook chickpeas quickly, add a bit of mustard seeds to the pot.

If you want to keep meat tender for as long as you want, take meat from the thigh and remove the fat and bones; slice and salt well, and then leave overnight. The following morning, thoroughly clean the meat with water. Spread it out until it is dried, then rub with fat and place in a jar. Pour fat on top until it covers the meat and then put the lid on the jar. Put the quantity you like and then take it out when required. You will find that it is fresh when it is very hot, without having to use salt. Then, take the meat, and hang it from a fork lowered in a well, near the surface of the water, until it almost

---

18 The word is derived from the verb *tharada*, 'to crumble and sop (bread)'. For recipes in the cookery books: al-Warrāq 1987: 204–9 (trans., 373–43); *Andalusian*, fols. 20v., 46v., 56v.–58r., 60r.–61v. (some thirty recipes in total); al-Tujībī 2012: 39–57 (27 recipes); *Taṣānīf al-aṭʿima*, fol. 68r.–v. In medieval Cairo, *tharīd* was prepared and sold by the dealers of cooked sheep's heads (*rawwāsūn*), some of whom would corrupt the dish by adding to it oil dripped from the roast meat, and mixing it with oil from the trotters; Buckley [al-Shayzarī] 1999: 56; Lewicka 2011: 161–2. According to Ibn Khalṣūn, *tharīd* is quickly digested, but fattening (1996: 157/ trans., 82). Also see al-Dabbābī 2017: 103–16.

19 The singular (unit noun) is *ruqāqa*; a thin bread loaf, which could also serve as a plate (analogous to the *trauncher* of medieval England).

20 A thick round type of bread or cake, etymologically linked to the Persian *girda* (Steingass 1892: 1081).

21 See recipe No. 5.

22 According to *Kanz* (p. 8), the bread should also be stale, which makes more sense in terms of the dish.

23 This section is heavily corrupted in the manuscript and was corrected with the text in *Kanz*, 9.

comes into contact with it.[24] Take it out when needed and you will find that it has remained fresh.

If the meat has started to rot and its odour has changed [but] you still want to cook it, then hang two whole walnuts in the cooking pot after piercing the shells all the way to the kernel. The bad smell will be absorbed by the nuts, the inside of which will smell more putrified than a cadaver. If you break an egg inside the pot, the putrid smell will also disappear. If a small quantity of fenugreek is boiled with the meat, after the water is removed and fresh water added, the smell of putrefaction will disappear. The flavour will be such that it is impossible to tell whether the meat was rotten or fresh.

If the meat smells off, cut it up and put it in a pot with ground hazelnuts, which will remove the odour.

If you want food to cook quickly, take the peel of green melon, dry it, pulverize it and then keep. If you need to cook food quickly, just add a little bit of the melon grounds.

If you do not want garlic to go off, then burn the spathes that are on it, and it will keep until you want it, and will not shrink or become spoilt.

If you want to make sure that no bones remain in a Nile carp, then take betel nut,[25] and pound. Split the carp on each side and insert the crushed betel. When grilling the fish, all the bones will fall apart.

If at any point you want to boil broad beans, wild mustard seeds, cabbage or fresh chard, add a little of natron in the pot with the water. Boil the water until the natron breaks up and then put the desired ingredient(s) inside the pot. Once you throw them in the pot with boiling water, do not cover with a lid since that would make everything inside turn yellow. Make sure not to overcook the ingredients, but to take them out [of the pot] while they are still firm, as this is better.

If you boil spinach, wash it with water and place in a pot, but do not add any water because the vegetable will release a great deal of liquid when it is heated by fire.

Similarly, when cooking Jew's mallow, do not put a lid on the pot or put it over a blazing flame. Do not overcook it by leaving it on the fire for too long.

If you want to cook pulses, such as lentils, peas, grass peas, broad beans,

---

24 The text omits part of the instruction as according to *Kanz* (p. 9), it is in order to keep the meat fresh without adding salt in times of great heat that one should hang it from a fork, etc.

25 The text has *fūl*, which translates as 'broad beans'; however, as this does not make any sense in the context, it has been corrected to *fawfal*, which is the word found in *Kanz* (p. 9).

or chickpeas, do not buy them macerated from the market. Rather, buy them whole and then macerate and sieve them yourself at home. Add the required quantity of saffron and then let them dry. If you then want to cook some, boil water with a little bit of salt. Once it starts boiling, take it off the fire and then add any of the aforementioned pulses that you like; for each *qadaḥ*, take one and a half *ghumras* [of water]. When the seeds are cooked, add the other flavourings while stirring well as this will prevent the food from burning.

TWO

Bread Making

IN ORDER TO MAKE the best bread, you need fresh, smooth white flour. Knead it vigorously and add water in small measures until the result is neither dry, nor resembles broth. The fire should be kept low and steady so that the dough does not burn. Take it out when it [still has the texture of] dough. If the fire is too weak, the bread comes out [too] thin.[26] After you take it out of the oven, leave it to rest for an hour to allow for all the moisture and steam to evaporate. It will be tasty.

1. Recipe for bread that tastes wonderful[27]

Take one *qadaḥ* of flour, four *ūqiyas* of starch[28] and ten *ūqiyas* of sugar. Knead it all together with milk and then gently bake it. Never add any water to it.

---

26 The Arabic has *mamṣūṣan* ('thin, skinny') *lāẓiyan*; the meaning of the latter is unclear in this context since it means 'burning, ablaze'. *Kanz* lists a slightly more plausible variant *lāṭiyan* (295, note No. 312), from the verb *laṭa'a/ laṭiya* ('to be low, flat'); Dozy 1877–81: II, 530.

27 cf. *Kanz*, 265 (Appendix, No. 1).

28 *nashā*. According to Ibn Jazla (fol. 228r.–v.), it is made by thoroughly washing good-quality wheat grains in water until the husks are shed and they are smooth. They should be beaten well until everything is mixed with the water and a yoghurt-like consistency is obtained. Then, it is strained several times until a consistency like *shīrāz* (thick yoghurt made with rennet and drained) has been obtained, after which it is put in bags and left in the shade until it dries. He also recommended blending almond and wheat starch, two parts of the latter and one part of

2. Another bread[29]

Take good flour and for each *raṭl* add one third of a *raṭl* of sesame oil, an *ūqiya* of sesame seeds, and a handful of pistachio and almond kernels. Then, knead [into a dough]. Once it has risen, bake it in the oven in the shape of round flat loaves, with a thickness of two fingers. When they are ready, take them out of the oven and eat with sweetmeats.

3. Recipe for salty loaves[30]

Take the required quantity of flour and knead with sesame oil – for each *raṭl* of dough, one quarter of a *raṭl* of sesame oil – and add enough salt for its flavour to be evident in the dish. After the dough has risen knead it into [round flat] loaves, like in the previous recipe, but a little thinner. When the loaves have turned ginger, take them out [of the oven]. This dish is made when one is fed up with sweetmeats. They are eaten in between sweets.

4. Recipe[31]

If dates are stuffed in a *kaʿk*, knead [the dough] with sesame oil and remove the stones before putting the dates inside it. Alternatively, you can also stuff the biscuit with sugar and ground almonds, one third of each, kneaded with rose water.[32] Gather the edges of the dough and tightly fold, as you do when making *kubbā* or *khushkān*.[33]

---

the former.

29 cf. *Kanz*, 265 (Appendix, No. 2, *khubz al-abāzīr*, 'bread with spices'). Also see *Waṣf*, 431.

30 cf. *Kanz*, 11 (No. 1, '*aqrāṣ mamlūḥa*'); *Waṣf*, 172–3 ('*aqrāṣ mumallaḥa*').

31 This recipe is heavily corrupted in the manuscript, and has been supplemented with the information in *Kanz* (265, Appendix, No. 3) and *Wuṣla* (No. 7.86), where it is called *Urnīn*. There is also a recipe by this name (but with very different instructions) in *Waṣf* (426) and al-Baghdādī (1964: 79–80/trans., 102–3).

32 *mā' al-ward*; It was a staple ingredient in cooking, and can be found in a large number of recipes. It was also used to scent dishes just before serving them. The best variety was that distilled from the damask rose. Because of its much-appreciated fragrance, rose water was also used extensively in cosmetics, for instance, as a deodorant. Ibn al-Bayṭār 1992: IV, 490–2; Ibn Jazla, fol., 206r.; Lev & Amar 2008: 264–6; *EI*[2], s.v. (F. Sanagustin).

33 The form *kubbā* is a misspelling for *kubba* ('ball'). *Khushkān* were also known as *khushkanān* or *khushkānaj* (< Persian 'dry in body') and denoted stuffed pastries which were often made on the occasion of religious festivals, or as food for travellers. Al-Warrāq 1987: 271–3; al-Baghdādī 1964: 79 (trans., 102); Nasrallah [al-Warrāq 2007]: 43; Steingass 1892: 462; Mielck 1913: 78.

5. Recipe for biscuits *(kaʿk)* that the honourable judge used to make, and would offer to dignitaries[34]

Take white finely milled sieved flour,[35] pistachios and sugar – one part of each. Finely pound the pistachios and sugar and mix in with the dough. Knead with chicken fat and sheep's tail fat[36] after having rubbed it with mastic, cinnamon, a little bit of musk[37] and camphor,[38] and lime juice. Shape into loaves and then take a copper dish, coated inside and out with sesame oil, and arrange them into it. Place the dish in the oven, over a low fire until it has turned golden, and [then] use.

34 *Kanz*, 266 (Appendix, No. 4). This ring-shaped biscuit was known as an Egyptian speciality and could be either savoury or sweet. For other recipes, see al-Tujībī 2012: 63; *Andalusian*, fols, 66v.–67r.; *Wuṣla*, Nos. 7.97–9 (the translator stating that it was 'twice-cooked bread', ring-shaped and, thus, similar to a bagel). Also see Mielck 1913: 71–3; al-Dabbābī 2017: 100–2; Corriente 1997: 463.

35 *daqīq ʿalāma* (lit. 'flour of the mark'): see Lewicka 2011: 115, note No. 185.

36 *alya*. It is obtained from the tails of a specific breed of sheep already attested in the fourth millennium BCE; in fact, most of the sheep across the Middle East are of the fat-tailed variety. The fat in the tail, rather than that in other parts of the animal's body, was preferred because it is softer, and melts more quickly. It is primarily associated with meat dishes, but was also sometimes used in the preparation of sweets. Recipes often call for the tail fat to be rendered first. It is most associated with the Near-Eastern manuals, but its popularity decreased over the centuries in favour of oils, such as sesame oil. It was not used in Maghribi cuisine, where olive oil reigned supreme. Today, it is rarely used as a frying fat in the Middle East, but is still a frequent ingredient in Central Asian cuisines. Lewicka 2011: 322; Tilsley-Benham 1986; Perry 1995; Davidson 1999: s.v. 'fat-tailed sheep'.

37 *misk* (cf. Greek *móskhos*, Middle Persian *mushk*). In cooking, musk was used as an aromatic, predominantly in sweets and breads, though it is also found in other dishes, as well as beverages, such as wine (al-Warrāq 1987: 309/trans., 470). Musk was also believed to disinfect food (Ibn Sīnā). The other principal usage was in perfumes (deodorants, breath-sweeteners). In literature, the smell of musk is often associated with the beloved. Arab scholars believed that the best musk came from a species of gazelle indigenous to China and Tibet. Its reputation as a powerful aphrodisiac was based on the fact that it is produced by a gland in the male musk deer to attract the female during the mating season. King 2017; Ibn Sīnā 1999: I, 553 (trans., 437); Lev & Amar 2008: 215–17; *EI*², s.v. 'misk' (A. Dietrich).

38 *kāfūr* (< Middle Persian *kāpūr)*. Mostly used in the form of oil extracted from the camphor tree, it was highly prized as an aromatic in pre-Islamic Persia, where it was also employed as an embalming agent. According to the Qur'ān (76:5), 'the Righteous will drink of a cup of wine mixed with camphor'. In cooking, it was used in a number of savouries as well as sweets, and often in conjunction with musk. It was – and still is – used extensively in perfumes, though Ibn Sīnā warned that regular use makes the hair grey, while it is also an anaphrodisiac. Ibn Sīnā 1999: I, 514–5 (trans., 379); *EI*², s.v. 'kāfūr' (A. Dietrich); *Encyclopedia Iranica*, s.v. 'camphor' (Hūšang Aʿlam), IV:7, pp. 743–747; Donkin 1999.

6. Another recipe[39]

Take fine flour, mixed with clarified butter or sesame oil, and musk, camphor[40] and rose water. Roll out with a thin stick. Fry with sesame oil. Put a bit of musk and rose water in rose-water syrup[41] and drizzle on the plate. Sprinkle coarsely ground pistachios on top of each layer.

7. Recipe for a sugary biscuit[42]

Take one *raṭl* of flour and eight *ūqiyas* of sugar. Finely grind the sugar and mix it with the flour, together with two *ūqiyas* of sesame oil. Add four *ūqiyas* of water and vigorously knead together, shaping it into a cake or loaves. Bake, and place on a copper dish. It will taste great.

8. Recipe for a date-paste-filled biscuit[43]

For each *raṭl* of flour, [take] half a *raṭl* of sesame oil and eight *ūqiyas* of date paste,[44] together with rose water, saffron, *aṭrāf al-ṭīb*, pepper and ginger.

9. Recipe for *maltūt*[45]

Take finely milled flour, sesame oil, shampoo ginger, and mastic. Knead the flour with sesame oil first and then knead it with water. Pound the shampoo ginger with mastic and a little bit of moistened tree wormwood. Add to the flour and shape into rings.

---

39 cf. *Kanz*, 11 (No. 2).

40 This ingredient is omitted from *Kanz*.

41 *jullāb* (Persian *gul*, 'rose' and *āb*, 'water'), mainly used as a sweetener as well as in beverages. It was thought to be useful against hangovers, to dampen the heat of the stomach and suppress fevers and thirst. Ibn Buṭlān 1990: 111–2 (trans., 224–5); Ibn Jazla, fol. 54v.

42 cf. *Kanz*, 11–12 (No. 4).

43 cf. *Kanz*, 12 (No. 5).

44 Though strictly referring to a type of dates, *'ajwa* here denotes the paste made from such dates (usually in palm leaves or skin). *Kanz* simply has 'paste' (*ma'jūn*). See Lane 1863–74: IV, 1969.

45 The participle of the verb *latta*, 'to pound; mix with water (flour); to knead'; Wehr 1993: 1006. cf. *Kanz*, 12 (No. 6).

THREE

On Drinking Water[46]

SCHOLARS HAVE SAID that those wishing to safeguard their health should drink water on an empty stomach, and not at the table (i.e. during dinner), nor after eating, until the upper parts of the stomach have dried and then only in a quantity [required] to quench the thirst. It should not be drunk in large amounts until the upper part of the stomach has dried, the food has descended from it and the one who drinks has been sated. Date juice should not be drunk at the table, except by children. Caution should be exercised as regards water and ice by those with weak nerves, and whoever has a cold stomach and liver. Generally speaking, it should not be drunk by individuals with delayed digestion as it weakens the spirit and makes them sluggish.

Those who have a lot of flesh, a sanguine complexion and strong lust should not be afraid of it and can drink water or date juice whenever they like at the table since it will cause them only little harm.

Drinking water on an empty stomach is only beneficial for someone who has a severe inflammation and fever, and yearns to drink a lot of cold water in one gulp. When it is drunk in multiple gulps, they should be of the same quantity. This is sound practice and safeguards a person's bodily strength. This is how you should do things, Allah willing!

On the Characteristics of Water Chilled in the Air[47]

Know that water preserves the body's innate moistness, tenderizes nutriments and processes them. It suppresses heat, so drinking water is good for those with a hot temperament. The best type of water is that which is most beneficial, the lightest in weight, the quickest to absorb heat and cold, and the freshest in taste, i.e. which closely resembles sweetness in flavour. Know

---

46 This entire chapter is for the most part borrowed from *Kanz* (12–13) but can also be found in al-Warrāq 1987: 294–6 (trans., 450–3). Also see al-Rāzī 1881: 11.

47 In *Kanz*, this makes up Chapter 4 (p. 13). It has been retained as part of the third chapter here since it is marked as a section in *Zahr*.

that water that tastes or smells bad is very harmful and does not satisfy thirst. [Water] can also be used in medicines and treatments.

Salty water initially loosens the bowels but then tightens them. If you become addicted to it, it causes putrefaction, enlarges the spleen, and corrupts the temperament as it generates fevers.

Water chilled by snow greatly cools the liver. Only those with a hot temperament should drink it on an empty stomach. When it is drunk after food, it strengthens the stomach, increases lust, and sates hunger somewhat. Water that is extremely cold and not pleasant [in taste] inflates the belly. It does not slake the thirst, decreases lust, slackens the body, and has no benefit.

Cooked water and lukewarm water cause flatulence and have no benefits, except in [medical] treatment.

If one takes a draught of hot water on an empty stomach, it washes food residues from it, and perhaps loosens the bowels. However, excess use constricts the stomach.

FOUR

On Dishes

KNOW THAT AMONG SOUR DISHES there are those that are sweetened and those that remain sour. The former may be sweetened with sugar, honey or *dibs*.[48] All [sweet-and-sour] dishes should, therefore, be in one chapter. They include [the following]:

48 cf. Persian *dibs, dibis, dabs*, 'black'. It is extracted from pressed dates without cooking. The best kind was thought to come from Basra, and made from the juice of fresh Persian dates; Ibn Jazla, fol. 89r.; Lewicka 2011: 307; Steingass 1894: 502.

10. Vinegar stew (*sikbāj*)[49]

It is prepared by cutting up fatty meat into medium-sized pieces and placing them in a cooking pot, with enough water to cover them, as well as a little bit of salt, agarwood and cassia. When it is boiling, remove the scum and add dried coriander. Take white onions, Syrian leek and carrots (if they are in season) and aubergine, and peel all of them. Cut the aubergines crosswise and boil them in another pot in salty water. Then let them dry and leave them in the pot on top of the meat. Throw on spices and temper the saltiness. When it is nearly done, take vinegar and *dibs*, or honey, to taste, mixing it so that it is in between sourness and sweetness. Add it to the pot and leave to boil for a while. Thicken with a little bit of starch or rice. Then take shelled almonds cut in half, a handful of jujubes, dried dates and raisins, and throw all of them on the surface of the pot. Put the lid on, [and leave everything to cook] for a while. Then, reduce the heat and rub the sides of the pot with a clean cloth and sprinkle cold water[50] on top. When it simmers down, remove [from the fire].

11. A pleasant dish[51]

Cut up meat in medium-sized pieces, place them in a pot and cover entirely with water. Throw in a thin linen cloth in which coriander, ginger, pepper and finely pounded agarwood are bound. Take pieces of cassia and mastic, and cut onions crosswise into small triangles. Add all of them after the water with salt has boiled and it has dried out. Take out the cloth and soak in stale or fresh verjuice[52] squeezed by hand without boiling [the grapes], or

49 cf. *Kanz*, 14 (No. 7). This was known as the king of dishes, with recipes being found in all cookery manuals: *Wuṣla*, No. 6.109; al-Baghdādī 1964: 13 (trans., 30–1); *Waṣf*, 328–9, 371, 389, 446; *Andalusian* (fols. 21r., 34r.); al-Warrāq 1987: 132 (trans., 253–5); *Taṣānīf al-aṭʿima*, fol. 72r.–v. According to Perry, 'it was served cold as a tart, jellied dish' (*Wuṣla*, 297). In al-Tujībī's treatise (2012: 156) it is known as *mukhallal* ('pickled in vinegar'). Ibn Buṭlān (1990: 92–3/trans., 177) recommended beef for *sikbāj*, cold and strained 'which is called *hulām*, and should be eaten by those who suffer from a hot liver, jaundice and other such ailments'. A modern descendant of the dish can be found not in the Arab world, but in Spain as *escabeche*, which is fish (or meat) marinated and cooked in vinegar. The Latin American speciality *ceviche* shares the same etymon, but not the preparation as it involves raw fish marinated in a seasoned citrus fruit base. See Plouvier 2013; Clément 2015: Corriente 1997: 256; *idem* 2008: 254.

50 *Kanz* has the more logical 'rose water'.

51 In *Kanz* (p. 14, No. 8), this dish is called '*Ibrāhīmiyya*', after Ibrāhīm Ibn al-Mahdī (779–839), the famous gourmet half-brother of Hārūn al-Rashīd, and short-lived caliph (817–9). Several of the cookery books contain *Ibrāhīmiyya* dishes: al-Warrāq 1987: 152–4 (trans., 274–6); al-Baghdādī 1964: 14 (trans., 31); al-Tujībī 2012: 167; *Andalusian*, fol. 10r.

52 The juice (*māʾ*) of sour grapes (*ḥiṣrim*); it was used in both cooking and medicine. According

[use] filtered vinegar. Then, strain and thicken with finely pounded sweet almonds. Pour verjuice on top and sweeten with a bit of sugar so that the dish is not too sour. Leave on the fire until it simmers down and rub the sides of the pot with a clean cloth. Then sprinkle a bit of rose water on top and remove [from the fire].

12. *Jurjāniyya*[53]

Cut up fatty meat into medium-sized pieces and cover them with water, [seasoned] with a bit of salt. Dice some onions. When [the meat] is boiling, throw the onions on top, together with dried coriander, pepper, ginger and finely pounded cassia. If you like, you can also add shelled walnuts after removing the wood inside of them and cutting them into medium-sized pieces. Then stir [everything]. Once the ingredients are done, add equal parts of pomegranate seeds and finely pounded black raisins, and macerate them well in water. Strain through a fine-mesh sieve, and add to the pot together with a small quantity of vinegar. Thicken with finely pounded sweet almonds. When it comes to the boil and is nearly done, sweeten with a bit of sugar to taste, and throw in a handful of jujubes. Sprinkle rose water [on top] and put the lid [on the pot] until it simmers down on the fire.

13. Pomegranate stew (*rummāniyya*) thickened with pistachios[54]

Cut up meat and throw it into the pot. Add water and bring to the boil. Remove the scum and throw in small meatballs the size of hazelnuts.[55] Let the water reduce until little is left. The dish is done when nothing but delicate foam remains. Take sour pomegranate juice, sweeten it with almonds thickened with sugar and throw it in. Add mint leaves. Pound pistachio

---

to Ibn Jazla (fol. 72r.), it is beneficial for those with inflamed and bilious temperaments, but causes wind in the stomach and bowels.

53 *Kanz*, 15 (No. 9). The dish derives its name from the city of Jurjān, the present-day Gorgan, capital of the Iranian province of Golestan. For other recipes, see: al-Warrāq 1987: 72–3; *Wuṣla*, No. 5.70; al-Baghdādī 1964: 14–5 (trans., 31–2); *Waṣf*, 306, 359; *Taṣānīf al-aṭʿima*, fol. 77r.; Marín 1992: 108.

54 cf. *Kanz*, 15 (No. 10); *Waṣf*, 307. For other *rummāniyya* recipes, see al-Baghdādī 1964: 18–9 (trans., 36); *Waṣf*, 315; al-Warrāq 1987: 156 (trans., 279) *Taṣānīf al-aṭʿima*, fol. 94v. According to Ibn Jazla (fol. 108v.), the best is made with sweet pomegranate seeds and it is useful against haemorrhages and for weak bowels.

55 There are several recipes requiring meatballs the size of hazelnuts, which survived in the modern Spanish word *albóndigas* (from the Arabic *al-bunduq*), 'meatballs' (though usually larger sized).

kernels and thicken the juice with them. Colour with a bit of saffron and *aṭrāf al-ṭīb*. Sprinkle rose water and saffron on top and remove [from the fire].

14. Sour stew (*ḥummāḍiyya*)[56]

Cut up fatty meat and place it in a pot. Cover it with slightly salted water and bring to the boil. Throw in spices such as dried coriander, pepper, ginger and finely pounded cloves, tied together in a clean linen cloth. Cut sticks of cassia into [the pot]. When [the spices in the] cloth have released their flavours, take large citrons, without their seeds, and thoroughly squeeze out the juice by hand. Then, mix with the same quantity of verjuice, and pour it into the pot. Leave to boil for a while. Finely pound enough sweet skinned almonds to suit the dish, mix them with water and add to the pot. Sweeten with sugar or, if you wish, rose-water syrup, and leave the pot on the fire for a while until it simmers down. Sprinkle rose water on top and remove [from the fire].

15. Another *ḥummāḍiyya*[57]

This is a dish of caliphs. Joint a chicken and take the meat of its thighs, remove the skin and finely pound with a cleaver. Do the same with the chicken breasts. Wash, and then throw the remainder of the chicken, its oil and fat into the pot. Cut up onions and sprinkle on water mixed with coriander, ginger, pounded roasted cumin, a stick of cassia, and a good amount of sweet almond oil. Stew everything well. Then add one *dirham* of salt and stir continuously. Throw in citron leaves. Take the pulp of a citron, devoid of its skin and seeds. Sprinkle rose water on top. Remove the parcel [of citron leaves], throw the pounded meat of the thighs and the breasts into the pot, and stew. When the flavours of the spices have been released, add mint and wild thyme. When the pot comes to a boil, add a bit of white sweet lemon and chopped onions. When they are cooked, pound a good number of sweet almonds and thicken rose water with them. Then take out the vegetables and add citron juice. When the boiling has died down, temper the sourness with rose-water syrup and coarsely ground *ṭabarzad* sugar.[58] Add almonds,

[56] cf. *Kanz*, 15–16 (No. 11). Ibn Jazla (fols. 74v.–75r.; cf. Ibn Buṭlān 1990: 94–5/trans., 190–1) states that the best citron to use is the one grown in Susa and advises it as a cure for hangovers. For other dishes by this name, see al-Baghdādī 1964: 15 (trans., 32); *Waṣf*, 307–8.

[57] cf. *Kanz*, 16 (No. 12).

[58] High-quality white translucent sugar. Ibn Jazla (fols. 123v.–124r.) explained how this was made: 'crush sugar and throw it in a pot, for each 100 *raṭls* of sugar take ten *raṭls* of milk, and

scented with rose water infused with pure camphor. When it simmers down, remove [from the fire]. This is food for caliphs.[59]

The phrase 'it quietens down and is taken up' (*yahda' wa yurfa'*) constitutes one of the basics of cooking – understand it, and do not ignore it; rather, heed it, as it is the most beneficial to know for cooking meat with these spices. However, it is even more beneficial if one of these is added without wheat.

16. *Zīrbāj*[60]

Cut up meat into small pieces, place in the pot and cover with water. Add pieces of cassia, peeled chickpeas, and a bit of salt. When the water has come to a boil, remove the scum. Add sesame oil and the same quantity of wine vinegar, a quarter of the weight of the vinegar in sugar, and finely pounded peeled almonds soaked in rose water. Add the meat and then ground dried coriander, pepper and ground mastic. For colouring, add saffron. Then put peeled and split almonds on top of the dish and sprinkle a little bit of rose water on them. Rub the sides [of the pot] and leave on the fire until [the dish] simmers down. If you like, you can make it with chicken, in which case take a scalded chicken, and wash and joint it. When the pot is bubbling, throw it in with the meat and cook. If you like the sweetness to be prominent, add some sugar or honey, Allah the Almighty willing.[61]

---

enough water to immerse everything. Boil and remove the scum. Then ladle it into a glazed jar and let it cool down. Let it dry out for a day and a night, and then return to the pot. Boil until it gains the required consistency so that when you pour it in a copper jar, it makes a sizzling sound. Then remove from the fire and place in green-glazed tubs.' See *EI*[2], s.v. 'sukkar' (D. Waines); Nasrallah [al-Warrāq 2007]: 601–602; Ouerfelli 2008: 314 *et passim*; Sato 2015: 47–8, 99.

59 The recipe in *Kanz* ends here.

60 cf. *Kanz*, 17 (No. 14). *Zahr* contains no fewer than six variations (Nos. 36, 49, 125, 237, 286) of this highly popular dish, which plays a central role in one of the *1001 Nights* tales (the so-called 'Reeve's tale'). It is typified by a combination of sour (vinegar) and sweet (sugar, honey), with almonds also being a stock ingredient. The word is of Persian origin and is composed of *zīr* ('beneath; anything dressed under meat when roasting [as rice]') and *bāj* ('stew') (Steingass 1892: 633), though Nasrallah ([al-Warrāq 2007]: 274) also suggests *zir* (gold) and *zīra* (cumin) as possible etyma. For recipes in other cookbooks, see: al-Warrāq 1987: 152–4 (trans., 274–7); al-Baghdādī 1964: 16 (trans., 33); *Wuṣla*, Nos. 5.49, 6.104–5; *Kanz*, Nos. 40, 52, 206, 212, 226; *Andalusian*, fol. 7v; al-Tujībī 2012: 155 (*zīrbājiyya*); *Taṣānīf al-aṭ'ima*, fol. 72v.

61 The religious invocation is missing from the *Kanz* recipe.

17. Pistachio stew (*fustuqiyya*)[62]

Cut up meat and cover with water. Skim off the fat and bring to a boil.[63] When the meat is done, add dainty meatballs, pounded *aṭrāf al-ṭīb*, as well as cassia, mastic, salt, sesame oil and (dried) mint. When everything is cooked and only very little of the broth remains, remove the meat and fry it in oil and spices. Return the broth to it, thicken with pounded pistachios, and stew. Improve the flavour with lemon juice. Sprinkle a little rose water [on top], and rub the sides of the pot [with it]. When the pot simmers down, remove from the fire, Allah the Almighty willing.

18. Rhubarb stew (*rībāsiyya*)[64]

This is meat rubbed [and] stewed with spices. Throw on some chopped onions and then rhubarb juice. Add a bit of sweet almond preserve and crumble a bunch of dried mint on top. Leave on a low fire before removing.

19. Barberry stew (*amīr bārisiyya*)[65]

This is like *summāqiyya*,[66] except that instead of sumac you use barberries. There are people who sweeten it with a bit of sugar.

---

[62] cf. *Kanz*, 17 (No. 15). This dish should not be confused with the *harīsa fustuqiyya* (pistachio porridge), which tended to be made with chicken and rose-water syrup (and honey), and bread crumbs. Also note that, despite the name, not every *fustuqiyya* contained pistachios; in the present text, it can be made with hazelnuts (No. 47), whereas in al-Tujībī's and the Andalusian manuals it is made with beans, with the name of the dish referring to the similarity in appearance between pistachios and the beans. *Waṣf*, 427, 459; *Kanz*, 112 (No. 291); *Wuṣla*, Nos. 7.8, 7.75; al-Tujībī 2012: 120; *Andalusian*, fols. 47r., 47v., 69v., 75v. (a pistachio candy by the same name, made with sugar, almond oil, pistachios, musk and cloves).

[63] This instruction is incomplete and/or erroneous, since the skimming of the fat (scum) can only be done after the meat has been boiled, which would imply that it is boiled a first time before skimming, and then some more afterwards. Alternatively, there may have been a reversal, and it should read 'bring to a boil and then remove the fat.'

[64] cf. *Kanz*, 18 (No. 16). For other recipes, see: al-Baghdādī 1964: 19 (trans., 36); *Waṣf*, 312; *Taṣānīf al-aṭʿima*, fol. 94v.

[65] cf. *Kanz*, 18 (No. 17). The name of this dish also appears as *anbarbārisiyya*; Ibn Jazla, fol. 27r.

[66] In the early Arabic culinary tradition, it was a highly popular dish but in *Zahr*, there is only one (No. 41), though it is not named as such. For other recipes see: al-Baghdādī 1964: 19–20 (trans., 37); *Waṣf*, 312, 327; al-Warrāq 1987: 173 (trans., 299–300); *Taṣānīf al-aṭʿima*, fol. 94v.–95r. According to Ibn Jazla (fols. 126v.–127r.) and Ibn Buṭlān (1990: 92–3/trans., 188–9) the best kind is made with fresh red sumac.

20. Sour orange stew (*nāranjiyya*)[67]

Cut up fatty meat into medium-sized pieces and leave in the pot until it boils. Once it starts boiling, remove its scum and throw in the necessary amount of salt. Cut up [onions and leeks][68] into small pieces and throw in the pot. Add salt and the aforementioned spices, bunches of mint and, for those who want meatballs, pound lean meat and make as many meatballs as you like. Add them to the pot and then take sour oranges,[69] peel them and remove the white flesh. Halve them and squeeze the juice through a colander or sieve. The one that has pressed them should not be the one who peels them. Take safflower seeds that have been picked over and washed, and soak them in hot water for a while. Pound them finely in a stone mortar, or, if it is not available, in a copper mortar, devoid of rust. Extract the juice by hand, strain and put in the pot. Crumble bunches of dried mint on top and rub the sides with a cloth cut up in the usual way. Leave for a while and then remove [from the fire].

21. (Another *nāranjiyya*)[70]

There are people who use another recipe with pounded chicken breasts and meat. For each chicken breast, use one *ūqiya* of meat and add pistachios. Take as many pistachios as needed, and throw them on the pounded meat. Add galangal, ginger, rose-water syrup, sour oranges, pistachios, mint and rose water. Those who have the acumen to increase flavours have infinite perspicacity and intelligence.

---

67 cf. *Kanz*, 19 (No. 19); al-Baghdādī 1964: 22, 37 (trans., 40, 56); *Waṣf*, 218–9. The dish appears not to have travelled westward as no recipes of it are found in either the anonymous Andalusian treatise or al-Tujībī's.

68 These have been added from al-Baghdādī's recipe since neither *Zahr* nor *Kanz* specifies what needs to be cut up.

69 *nāranj*. The fruit is believed to be native to China and was unknown in the classical world. It was imported into Europe by the Arabs, whereas sweet oranges do not appear until the end of the Middle Ages. In mediaeval Arab cooking, the sour orange tended to be used in stews. Ibn al-Bayṭār reports that it has very green leaves and white blossoms, while the flesh of the fruit is as sour as citron. Ibn al-Bayṭār 1992: IV, 470–1; Dalby 2003: 88.

70 This recipe was wrongly merged with the preceding one, but is clearly a variant; cf. *Kanz*, 19 (No. 20).

22. *Kishk*[71]

For each *raṭl* and a half of meat take one *raṭl* of *kishk*, one *ūqiya* and a half of garlic, six onion bulbs, two *dirhams* of caraway seeds and the same amount of pepper, four sticks of cinnamon, and four lemons. Boil the meat with an onion and a bit of pepper. When the meat is done, pound the garlic with olive oil and salt, put it in [with the meat] and stir. Then cut the onions in equal parts and [also] add. Add enough spices, caraway seeds, mint and cinnamon to season [the dish]. Then, squeeze the juice out of the lemons, and leave for a while until it simmers down and [everything] is done. Then remove.

23. *Makhfiyya*[72]

There are several ways in which this is made and we will mention one of them.[73] Cut up fatty meat into small pieces and melt sheep's tail fat. Throw the meat into it, together with salt and dried coriander. Remove the fat and cover [everything] with water, and bring to a boil. Remove the scum and add fresh coriander leaves, grated sticks of cassia, a handful of crushed peeled chickpeas, and two or three peeled cut onions. Finely pound the required quantity of lean meat with salt and spices. Take boiled eggs, remove the yolks and put them in each meatball [made with the lean meat]. Add to the pot and when they are boiled, return the tail fat to [the pot]. Sprinkle finely ground cassia on and remove [from the fire]. It is extremely delicious.[74]

The aim of food is to be aromatic and hearty. If you like, you can sweeten all of these, based on the science of medicine. So, know this and act accordingly.

24. *Yāqūtiyya* ('emerald' stew)[75]

Stew the meat in the usual fashion and flavour with olive oil, cassia, mastic, etc. Then cut up a gourd into bulbs and add it [to the pot]. When it is almost cooked, add red mulberry[76] juice and sweeten with bee honey, sugar or rose-water syrup and cook through. Crumble bunches of mint on top, and serve after it has simmered down over a moderate fire.

---

71 See recipe No. 69.

72 cf. *Kanz*, 20 (No. 22). The name of the dish translates as 'hidden'.

73 This sentence is missing from *Kanz*.

74 The *Kanz* recipe ends here.

75 Derived from *yāqūt*, 'emerald', in reference to the mint on top of the dish. Cf. *Kanz*, 20–1 (No. 23).

76 *tūt*; this is actually the 'black' mulberry (*Morus nigra*).

25. Sour meatballs (*mudaqqaqa*)[77]

Slice up lean meat, pound it finely and then add salt and the usual spices, as well as a bit of chopped onions. Make as many meatballs as you need and boil them in water with a moderate quantity of salt. When they are ready, and the water has dried up, take the melted sheep's tail fat and remove [any undissolved] fat. Add the meatballs to the oil, together with the onion pieces. Those who like sourness can sprinkle on citron juice, vinegar, verjuice or lemon juice – or a mixture of both. If you like, you can colour it with saffron added to the required amount of vinegar or lemon juice. Sprinkle the usual spices on. If you wish you can also crumble bunches of mint on. Leave and remove [from the fire]. [Make sure to] remove the veins from the pounded meat because they are thick.

26. Fresh date and meat stew (*ruṭabiyya*)[78]

Chop lean meat into small pieces, throw them in a pot and boil until done. Then remove the broth and fry [the meat] in fresh sheep's tail fat, with a moderate amount of salt and spices. When it is almost done, layer yellow dates on top [and] with a large needle replace [the stones] with peeled almonds.[79] Make date-shaped oblong meatballs out of the pounded lean meat and stuff the almonds inside of them. Sprinkle rose water on top of the pot and colour with a bit of saffron. [When] it simmers down on the fire, remove.

27. (Date stew (*tamriyya*))[80]

In the absence of fresh dates, the dish can be made in the same way with dried dates.

---

77 *mudaqqaq* means 'pounded'. cf. *Kanz*, 21 (No. 24); *Waṣf*, 347. There are a number of other recipes in the text (Nos. 28, 85, 130), while the finished meatballs are also sometimes required in other dishes (Nos. 75, 300, 304, 305). According to Ibn Buṭlān (1990: 96–7/trans., 194–5), the best *mudaqqaqāt* are those made from yearlings, while Ibn Jazla (fol. 208 r.) advised making them with camphor. They were considered beneficial for those who have indulged in excess sexual or physical activity, or are grappling with sadness or fear.

78 cf. *Kanz*, 22 (No. 28). The name derives from *ruṭab*, 'fresh dates', as opposed to '*tamr*' (dried dates).

79 The text is corrupted but can be corrected with *Kanz* (22, No. 28) as follows: '... layer as many dates on top as are required. Then, leave on the fire for a while, and remove. The dish can also be made by removing the stones from the dates with a needle and replacing them [i.e. the stones] with peeled almonds.'

80 This is listed as a separate recipe, in keeping with *Kanz*, 23 (No. 29). Also see recipe No. 233 below.

28. Plain meat balls[81]

Cut up fatty meat into small pieces, put them in a pot and cover with water. Then take lean meat and pound it finely. Add enough salt and spices, as well as a handful of coarsely crushed peeled chickpeas and a handful of washed rice. Then, make as many meatballs out of it as you like.[82] When it is ready and done, add the required amount of salt and spices, and reduce the water. Add the required quantity of oil and sprinkle [ground] cassia on top. Let it simmer down on a moderate fire, and then remove.

29. A type of *māwardiyya* (rose-water stew)[83]

Cut the meat into small oblong pieces and sweat it. Then cover with water [and boil]. Remove the scum. When the meat is done, and the water has reduced, throw in sugar or honey, as required, as well as a handful of coarsely ground peeled almonds. Add saffron for colour, and rose water. Stir continually until it thickens and leave on the fire until it simmers down. Then ladle up, and layer on top of stuffed fried *sanbūsak*,[84] with almonds and sugar. Sprinkle a bit of camphor on top and then it is ready. This used to be called *fālūdhajiyya*.

30. (Another) recipe[85]

There are some cooks who take the previous day's roasted meat, and turn as much as they need into some sour meat, or something else. Chop the meat into small pieces and fry in sesame oil. When it is done and the oil has dissolved, add the appropriate spices. Those who like it sour should sprinkle vinegar or lemon [juice] on top, though you can also put egg yolks on top. Sprinkle a bit of cassia on, leave over a moderate fire, and then remove.

---

81 cf. *Kanz*, 23 (No. 30); al-Baghdādī 1964: 46–47 (trans., 65); *Waṣf*, 353; *Taṣānīf al-aṭʿima*, fol. 67r.

82 The result is quite similar to the Italian *arancini*, and it is not unlikely that there is a connection between the two since the dish originated in Sicily at a time when it was still ruled by the Arabs.

83 cf. *Kanz*, 24 (No. 33), where it appears as *fālūdhajiyya*, which, as the author of *Zahr* explains at the end of the recipe, was its former name. It is also very similar to al-Baghdādī's *fālūdhajiyya* (1964: 48). Also see *Waṣf*, 354; *Taṣānīf al-aṭʿima*, fol. 77r. It should not, however, be confused with *fālūdhaj*, which is a type of sweet pudding (a descendant of which can still be found in the modern Middle East); al-Warrāq 1987: 242ff. (trans., 382–7); *Wuṣla*, Nos. 7.66–7; al-Baghdādī 1964: 76–7 (trans., 100); *Taṣānīf al-aṭʿima*, fol. 83v.; Ibn Buṭlān 1990: 98–9 (trans., 198–9).

84 See recipe No. 81.

85 This is called *qaliyyat al-shawī* in *Kanz* (25, No. 35); it does not include the prefatory remark about 'some cooks'.

31. *Maṣlūqa*[86]

Take a new clay, or tinned copper pot, and boil water and the same quantity of meat or chicken. Throw in mastic and cinnamon. Some people extract the juice from blanched almonds and add it just before removing the pot from the fire. Sprinkle a bit of rose water on top and add stems of fresh coriander.

32. Wheat stew (*qamḥiyya*)[87]

Clean the wheat by washing and throw it into a pot after having boiled it well. When you see that the kernels are splitting, strain, remove, and pour on fresh water. Then throw in meat but only add salt when [the pot] is removed [from the fire]. Whenever the broth decreases, add more cold water. Add dill, mastic and cinnamon and, if you have it, crushed cumin, when ladling up. Protect [the pot] from smoke.

33. *Shīshbarak*[88]

There are those who fry it. If it is made with yoghurt, take dough and stretch it like *tuṭmāj*.[89] Take the top of an oil cruet and cover it with a sheet cut in a round shape. Then, stuff as we have mentioned [elsewhere]. Bring water to the boil. When it starts boiling, throw in the *shīshbarak* and leave enough room between them [so they do not stick together]. When they are done, remove them [from the pot] and add yoghurt or pomegranate seeds. Stuff [the dough] like you would a *sanbūsak*.

---

86 Lit. 'boiled' – cf. *Kanz*, 25 (No. 36).

87 Kanz, 267 (Appendix, No. 8). Despite the fact that other cookery books do not have *qamḥiyya* dishes, it must have been popular since the author of *Wuṣla* states that 'it is too well known to describe (*lā yudhkar li-shuhratihi wa ma'rifatihi*)' (No. 6.98).

88 The recipe in *Kanz* (*al-shīrak* [?] *al-maqlī*) is slightly more extensive, particularly in the beginning: 'Take dough that is well kneaded and turn into sweet, sour and plain *mukaffan* and *sanbūsak*. Then fry.' (25, No. 37) For *mukaffan* recipes, see: *Wuṣla*, Nos. 7.68–9 (with recipe No. 71.4 referring to *shishbarak qālib*, i.e. a mould used for a sweetmeat); *Waṣf*, 389; *Kanz*, 99 (No. 254); Ibn Mubarrad 1937: 374 (trans., 473). Perry (*Wuṣla*, 297) states that *shushbarak* (sic) is 'a ravioli-like stuffed pasta resembling the Italian cappelletti, made by folding a circle of paste over a meat filling and then folding the "arms" over each other.' The dish is still popular in the contemporary Middle East, with variants in Central Asia, such as the Azeri *dushbara* dumpling soup.

89 See recipe No. 75 below.

34. Boiled chicken recipe[90]

Slaughter the chicken and scald it [immediately] afterwards. Remove any dirt and wash with water, salt and olive oil. Heat water until it starts to seethe and throw in the jointed chicken. Skim off the scum and add a handful of coarsely chopped chickpeas, the white of an onion, a sprig of dill, cinnamon, mastic and sesame oil. Take the yolk of an egg dissolved in a bit of the broth and throw it into the pot. Increase the fire until it is done. Then, leave to simmer down before removing [from the fire]. It is delicious.

35. Various types of chicken stuffing[91]

[There is the one] with seasonings, spices, [olive] oil, tahini, hazelnuts, almonds, and then there are those stuffed with sweet ingredients [, such as] sugar, pistachios and rose water. However, there must be olive oil and tahini, regardless of whether the stuffing is sweet, savoury, or anything else. Take the stuffing you like, try it and then add what is missing. Find what gives you pleasure, benefit from it, and stick to it.

36. Chicken *zīrbāj*[92]

Boil the chicken with water, salt, mastic and cassia. Then, cut the chicken at the joints, in half, or leave it whole. Stew with fresh sesame oil, dried coriander, mastic and cassia. Then, make a broth after stewing it with sugar, saffron, *atrāf al-ṭīb*, and sweet almond preserve. Finally, add a sprig of fresh mint.

37. Chicken *ḥāmidiyya*[93]

Boil [chicken] in sumac juice, pomegranate seed juice, or verjuice and lemon juice together, as usual.

---

90 cf. *Kanz*, 26 (No. 38).

91 This recipe appears to be very corrupted, as compared with the version in *Kanz*, where it is called 'special (*khāṣṣ*) stuffed chicken': 'Take a chicken and [cook it] until it is half done. Coat with saffron and fry in sesame oil. Add chopped parsley, toasted hazelnuts and dried coriander, and mix with pounded spices, olive oil and tahini. Pound the spices in a mortar and add the other ingredients afterwards. Knead with lemon juice, olive oil and tahini. Stuff the chicken with the mixture. You may also add sumac. Take some of the stuffing, add a bit of the chicken broth to it, and cook everything in it' (267, Appendix, No. 9).

92 cf. *Kanz*, 26 (No. 40); *Waṣf*, 357.

93 cf. *Kanz*, 27 (No. 41).

38. Recipe for chicken *jawādhib*[94]

Joint the chicken and boil after covering it with water. Throw in mastic, cassia and sesame oil. When the chicken is cooked, take it [out of the pot] and remove the oil.[95] Take rice and wash it. Mix what remains of the broth with milk and throw in the rice. Then, add the oil in which the chicken has been fried. When the sauce is cooked, put the chicken on top. Then, let all ingredients infuse for a while, and remove [from the fire].

39. Pistachio dish (*fustuqiyya*)[96]

If you want to thicken *fustuqiyya*, or another [similar] dish, with rose-water syrup[97] and if you do so in a brass pot with whatever you have chosen [by way of meat], you should add one and a half or two *ūqiyas* of starch, and an egg-white. Then, stir as this is what thickens [the sauce]. Leave the cooked chicken or [the meat] you have chosen in [the pot], and remove [from the fire].

There are those who tire and fatigue a plump chicken, and feed it vinegar and rose water before slaughtering it. Then, they grill it over a low fire and baste it with [its juices]. It comes out with the utmost tenderness and tastiness.

40. Recipe with cherries (*qarāṣiyā*)[98]

Take a superior-quality chicken and boil it with a stick of galangal and cassia until it is nearly done. Then, take ripe cherries, boil [them] and sieve. Take half of what is not strained and put in the pot with sugar and bee honey. Thicken

---

94 The plural of *jūdhāb.* Other versions of the recipe can be found in *Kanz* (27, No. 44) and *Waṣf* (358–9). The word goes back to the Persian *jūzāb,* 'a dish of sugar, rice, and meat' (Steingass 1892: 376). This recipe is, however, different from the *jūdhābs* in older culinary manuals, where it usually denoted a drip pudding; Arberry [Rodinson et al.: 2001]: 33–4; al-Baghdādī 1964: 71–3; *Waṣf,* pp. 358, 411–3; Ibn Mubarrad 1937: 371 (trans., 471); Perry, in Rodinson et al. 2006: 219–21; *Kanz*, pp. 55, 112–13 (Nos. 132, 293–4); *Wuṣla*, Nos. 7.38–43; *Taṣānīf al-aṭ ima*, fols. 86v.–87v. (six recipes). Ibn Jazla (fols. 62r.–69r.) has recipes for seven *jūdhābs* (banana, melon, *qaṭā'if,* bread, poppy, almonds, dried and fresh dates). In the anonymous Andalusian manual, one recipe (fols. 62v.–63r.) is similar to the modern Moroccan *bastilla* and is said to be good for colds and for invigorating coitus. Also see Ibn Buṭlān (1990: 96–8; trans., 196–7).

95 Both *Zahr* and *Kanz* are defective as they have the incomplete 'when it is done, boil and take its oil.' The instructions in *Waṣf* reveal that the chicken is boiled and then fried in sesame oil, whereas saffron-coloured rice is added to the dish later on as well.

96 This is an adaptation of part of a recipe in *Kanz* (28, No. 45), called *dajjāja fustuqiyya* ('pistachio chicken').

97 The mss has the clearly erroneous *jullāb khall* ('rose-water syrup vinegar').

98 cf. Kanz, 29 (No. 50).

the remainder with [ground] almonds and pour into the pot. Scent with rose water, camphor and musk. Wait for it to simmer down and then serve.

41. Sumac stew (*summāqiyya*) with taro[99]

The sumac is pounded, whether it has been soaked in hot water or not, and when the meat is done it is added. The taro[100] is put in with the meat after it has parboiled. This is how to proceed if you make *summāqiyya* with taro. If you like, you can include cloves of garlic, or something like that, as well as any condiments you like. You can also add chard if you wish.

42. Chicken *khayṭiyya*[101]

When the chicken is done, remove the breasts and shred them into hair-like strands. Then boil pistachios, pound them and strain through a sieve. Put [the almonds in a pot] and toss in white sugar. Then, add the shredded and [previously] washed meat, and boil until [the broth] has thickened. Baste the meat with pistachio oil and then spread it out on plates.

43. White *khayṭiyya*[102]

If you like, you can make a white *khayṭiyya* by using almond milk and moistening it with almond oil. Then it is ready to eat.

44. Marble stew (*rukhāmiyya*)[103]

After the meat has cooked, [add] two *ūqiyas* of rice for each *raṭl* of milk to a small quantity of the juices in which the meat has been cooked previously. Eat with honey, rose-water syrup or sugar.

---

99 Though presented as part of the previous recipe, this is clearly a new dish, as shown in *Kanz* (31, No. 56), from which the title of the dish has also been taken. The beginning of the dish in *Kanz* runs as follows: 'Cook the meat in a pot, and when it is half-done, add the taro, and let it cook until it is done.'

100 *qulqās*; originally hailing from East Asia, it is thought to be one of the oldest domesticated food plants. In mediaeval Arab cooking, its use increased after the thirteenth century as al-Warrāq (1987: 123/trans., 238) only gives one recipe (a shrimp samosa) calling for taro, and al-Baghdādī has none. It is not found in the culinary treatises of the Islamic West. Today, taro is used in the cuisines of Asia (particularly the purple variety), the Caribbean (where it is referred to as *eddo*) and, especially, the Pacific Islands (where it is also known as *poi*). Ibn Sīnā 1999: I, 654; Ibn Jazla, fol. 179v; Grimaldi Ilaria 2018.

101 cf. *Kanz*, 31–2 (No. 57), where it appears under the clearly erroneous name of *ghayṭiyya*. The name is derived from *khayṭ*, 'thread', in reference to the 'threads' of chicken after shredding.

102 cf. *Kanz*, 32 (No. 58).

103 This is an abridgement of a recipe in *Kanz* (268, Appendix, No. 13), where the full

45. Another *khayṭiyya*[104]

The *khayṭiyya* is similar to [the preceding recipe] and is made by taking lean meat. The best is that from a hogget.[105] Cut it up and boil until it is done. Once it is thoroughly cooked, drain the water and remove [the meat]. Shred the meat into hair-like fibres and wash with water until both the meat and the water in which it is washed are white. Place milk on the fire, wash the rice and throw it in. Pound some more rice and strain. Sprinkle it on, little by little, [all the while] stirring the meat. For each *raṭl* of meat take four *ūqiyas* of rice, three *raṭls* of milk, two *raṭls* of water and two *ūqiyas* of pounded rice. When it is ready, eat it with rose-water syrup.

46. Jew's mallow recipe (*mulūkhiyya*)[106]

Wash and cut the meat. Tenderize and fry it, and then pour water over it. Let the Jew's mallow wilt in the sun and chop it up finely and thinly. It is best if you do not chop it up before it has wilted. Put the mallow in a pot with water. Pound coriander and caraway [seeds], hot spices, salt and garlic. Pound everything [together] and dissolve in the water. When it is done, leave the pot to simmer down and then eat.

47. Pistachio stew (*fustuqiyya*) and hazelnut stew (*bunduqiyya*)[107]

For each *raṭl* of rose-water syrup take half a *raṭl* of either pistachios or hazelnuts – this is the measure for two chickens. Hull the hazelnuts or pistachios, pound them and strain through a sieve. Put in a brass pot and stir with the rose-water syrup, together with one and a half to two *ūqiyas* of starch and egg-whites. Smother the chickens with it. Add as much musk and rose water

---

instructions can be found: 'Boil the meat until it is tender. If there is a lot of water, remove some of it; conversely, if there is only a little bit, pour on some milk. Take the rice, wash it, and throw it in, together with mastic and cassia, as well as milk, one *raṭl* or two *ūqiyas* of it. When it is ready, put it in a jar. Eat with honey, sugar or rose-water syrup. It is extremely tasty.' The dish derives its name from the fact that its colour is similar to marble (*rukhām*). Also see recipes Nos. 50 and 234 below.

104 This is part of the preceding recipe in the mss, but a separate one in *Kanz* (269, Appendix, No. 14).

105 The translation is based on the term in *Kanz*, '*thanī*', as the *Zahr* mss has the unidentifiable '*zamāmīn*'. The preference for young animals over older ones was posited by physicians as well, starting with Hippocrates (II, 547), who said that 'lamb is lighter than sheep (…) because they have less blood and are more moist.' This view was later echoed by Galen, al-Rāzī, Ibn Sīnā and Maimonides; Bos 1997: 89 (note No. 32).

106 *Kanz*, 269 (Appendix, No 15).

107 This is a highly abridged version of two separate recipes in *Kanz* (22–3, Nos. 60–1).

as you deem fit. Do the same thing in the *jullābiyya* (rose-water syrup stew); all of these dishes closely resemble one another.

48. Lemon stew (*laymūniyya*)[108]

For two chickens, take one *raṭl* of rose-water syrup and one quarter of a *raṭl* of almonds. Put the syrup on the fire in a brass pot and heat it up. If you like, you can make it with sugar dissolved in rose-water syrup until it thickens. Then, blanch the almonds and remove the skins. Strain them through a sieve [to a consistency] similar to refined semolina[109] after pounding them into a mortar. Then place them in the pot on top of the rose-water syrup, and stir. Afterwards throw in one and a half *ūqiyas* of starch extracted from seed and grain kernels, egg whites and two sprigs of mint and stir. Two chickens will have been prepared in the way described above. When the [syrup] has attained the required consistency, put [the chickens] in the pot with the syrup. Then transfer them to bowls and turn the pot upside down. Add musk and rose water to taste. Leave for a while until thickened. It is extremely good.

49. *Zīrbāj*[110]

The same goes for the *zīrbāj* – for two chickens [use] one *raṭl* of rose-water syrup and half a *raṭl* of almonds. Proceed as before, but also add four *ūqiyas* of good wine vinegar insofar as it is available, and stir. Also add one *dirham* of southern[111] saffron, egg-whites and two sprigs of mint that is not off. Then

---

[108] cf. *Kanz*, 269 (Appendix, No. 16).

[109] *samīdh*; ultimately derived from the Akkadian *samīdu*, which denoted 'fine flour', the Arabic word is also related to the Greek *semídalis*, the etymon of the Latin *simila*, which, in turn, resulted in the English 'semolina'. It is also the etymon of the Egyptian Colloquial Arabic *samīṭ* (rings of bread sprinkled with sesame seeds, similar to pretzels). According to al-Isrā'īlī, *samīdh* is bran-free germ with starch (*yabqā jawharuhu wa lubābuhu*). It is the purest flour and more nourishing and easily digestible than bran flour. Ibn Khalṣūn stated that it was similar to *madhūn* (low-bran wheat flour) and that it is used in three ways: to make bread, couscous, or boiled in water, in which case you should sprinkle on fresh water, wait an hour while stirring throughout before kneading it into dough and then cooking it. When it is boiled, it should be eaten with honey. When it is used for couscous, it should be made with fatty meat. According to Ibn Jazla (fol. 78v.), it was best with *isfīdhbāj* and salted *ṭabāhaja*. Nasrallah defined it as 'purest and finest flour used, high in starch content, low in gluten, and free of bran', while Müller suggests 'durum wheat flour'. Mielck 1913: 75–6; Ibn Khalṣūn 1996: 156 (trans., 81); Nasrallah [al-Warrāq 2007]: 573; Dozy 1877–81: I, 469; al-Isrā'īlī 1992: 190; *EI²*, s.v. 'khubz'; Müller [al-Samarqandī 2017]: 30 (trans., 31), 42 (trans., 43), 278 (trans., 279).

[110] This is a highly abridged version of the recipe in *Kanz* (36, No. 63), which also calls for double the amount of saffron.

[111] *janūbī*; it is not clear what is meant here.

add it with the chicken as described earlier. This is a summary of the recipe as an intelligent person derives more from a few words than from many.

50. Marble stew (*rukhāmiyya*)[112]

For each *qadaḥ* of rice, [take] three *raṭls* of milk, safflower, ginger, one stick of cinnamon and a quarter of a *dirham* of mastic. Put half of these in a pot with one and a half *raṭls* of milk and the same quantity of water. Put in the stick of cinnamon, the ginger and the mastic. When the water and milk are boiling, wash rice and put it in a soapstone pot. Then add [the remaining] one *raṭl* and a half of milk little by little, heating it over a moderate fire while stirring it. The fire should be low while you are slowly stirring. The best thing would be to use coal. When it has cooked, let it simmer down for a while, and remove. The smoke should not linger. If something is smoking while you are cooking, take a bunch of sulphur [sticks] and cut off the ends. Bind them together and toss into the pot; this will capture all of the smoke. Or throw in a hollow pierced hazelnut; this will also absorb the smoke. When you ladle it onto the plates, add sesame oil and dust the plates with sugar. This is extremely good.

51. Tamarind stew (*tamr hindiyya*)[113]

Boil chickens well, dry them [and fry] with sesame oil. Stuff the insides of each chicken with almonds and sugar, one *ūqiya* of each. [First] pound [the almonds and sugar] in a mortar with some camphor and rose water, and then stuff the mixture inside the chickens. Take the dissolved rose-water syrup and put it in a brass pot. For each hundred *dirhams* of the syrup, add one *ūqiya* of tamarind soaked in hot or cold water. Add the syrup to the pot and cover the chickens with it. Wait for it to simmer down.

52. *Khayṭiyya*[114]

Take two *qadaḥs* of oasis rice and wash it in water until it is clean, and its water remains. Take six Egyptian *raṭls* of water and boil on the fire with mastic pellets and a piece of cinnamon. Add the rice [and boil] until it has

---

[112] cf. *Kanz*, 34 (No. 64). Also see recipes Nos. 44 and 234 here. For similar *rukhāmiyya* recipes, see: al-Baghdādī 1964: 28 (trans., 46); *Waṣf*, 331–2, 342; *Wuṣla*, No. 6.91; Ibn Jazla, fol. 107r.; *Taṣānīf al-aṭ'ima*, fol. 77r.

[113] cf. *Kanz*, 270 (Appendix, No. 17).

[114] cf. *Kanz*, 270 (Appendix, No. 18).

absorbed [the liquid]. Then gradually pour in six *raṭls* of milk until the milk has been absorbed. Add two *raṭls* of the boiled plucked meat. Beat well until all the ingredients have been mixed together. Remove from the fire. Add rose-water syrup or bee honey and then use.

53. *Ma'mūniyya*[115]

For each *raṭl* of milk take two *ūqiyas* of pounded rice. Boil enough rose-water syrup to sweeten it. Sheep's tail fat will have been rendered previously. Alternate adding melted sheep's tail fat and syrup until the former releases its oil.

54. Breadcrumb stew (*lubābiyya*)[116]

Take a chicken cut into small pieces and meat. Boil, and fry in sesame oil. Take breadcrumbs and poppy seeds, rub them, sift, and then toast them until golden. Put the chicken or meat stock in a pot, add the poppy seeds and breadcrumbs, and then moisten with rose-water syrup. Leave until it is cooked. Mix in sheep's tail fat, followed by the meat and the chicken. Add saffron, musk and rose water as well as peeled whole pistachios.

55. *Ma'mūniyya* with chicken[117]

Take two *qadaḥs* of oasis rice, and wash it thoroughly so as to remove the salt. Then dry it in the sun and pound finely. Strain it in a fine-mesh sieve, and then take two *raṭls* of sugar and eight Egyptian *raṭls* of milk. Mix everything together, and then take the breasts of two chickens. Boil them very well until they are done and shred into hair-like fibres. Wash them thoroughly with water after boiling. Let the meat dry and mix with the milk, and sugar. Put on a fire and stir continuously until its consistency is that of *'aṣīda*.[118]

---

[115] cf. *Kanz*, 37 (No. 71). Named after its alleged originator, the famous Abbasid caliph al-Ma'mūn (813–33), during whose reign many of the Greek scientific works were translated into Arabic. The extant recipes reveal that it was made either with meat or without. See Rodinson, in *idem* et al. 2001: 183–97; *Waṣf*, 316, 425; *Wuṣla*, Nos. 7.5–7.

[116] cf. *Kanz*, 270 (Appendix, No. 19; '*labaniyya*').

[117] cf. *Kanz*, 271 (Appendix, No. 22).

[118] A kind of gruel, which, according to Lane, was 'heat-flour moistened and stirred about with clarified butter, and cooked' (1863–74: III, 2060). This is one of the oldest native Arabian dishes and is attested in a number of hadiths. According to the Egyptian historian Ibn Taghrī Birdī (1411–1470), it was known in his day as *ma'mūniyya*. It is unclear when this semantic merger occurred; Ibn Mubārak Shāh was a contemporary of Ibn Taghrī Birdī and yet considered them distinct dishes, as shown by the reference to *'aṣīda* in this recipe. In al-Warrāq's treatise, it appears as a sweet as well, cooked with dates. It is still eaten today in a number of countries all over the Arab world, often in the guise of an 'island' of cooked

Remove from the fire, and flavour with musk and camphor, and then moisten the dish with sesame oil.

56. Rice pudding (*aruzz bi 'l-laban*)[119]

For each *raṭl* and a half of rice, take ten *raṭls* of milk.

57. Recipe for Jew's mallow (*mulūkhiyya*)[120]

You need meat, fat and Jew's mallow. If you want to, you can add chicken or young pigeons, together with garlic and pepper. Boil the meat, and then strain [the liquid]. Pound garlic, pepper, caraway and fried onions. Add these to the meat [which has been pounded] and shape into meatballs. Return the broth to the meat in the pot. Chop up the Jew's mallow and when the broth is boiling, throw on the mallow. Cook [everything] until it is done, and serve.

58. Milk stew (*labaniyya*)[121]

You need to [cook] milk and meat together. Only add the onions after a good hour, and then also throw in mastic, cinnamon, as well as a bit of mint and leeks. When the meat is done and the milk has not yet thickened, add a piece of date spadix, or a bit of rice or starch until it thickens. Allow it to simmer and then serve.

59. Recipe for yellow rice[122]

First boil[123] the honey, and then wash the rice and add it to it. Add a little water and sesame oil to the honey – for each *raṭl* of honey, use a third of a

---

wheat flour dough in butter or honey, or, as in Egypt, a thick gruel made with flour and butter. The date *ʿaṣīda*, too, has survived. See al-Warrāq 1987: 18 (trans., 97–8); al-Baghdādī 1964: 83 (trans., 106); *Waṣf*, 473; Marín 1998: 163; Lewicka 2011: 67, 68 ('pudding of pounded rice boiled in milk, boiled pounded chicken, syrup, and tail fat'), 148–9 ('rural-style preparation made of flour, rice and sesame oil, covered with honey or syrup and sprinkled with nuts'); al-Dabbābī 2017: 60–3; Hinds & Badawi 1987: 581.

[119] The full recipe can be found in *Kanz*, 271–2 (Appendix, No. 23). Also see *Waṣf*, 367; *Wuṣla*, No. 7.110; al-Shirbīnī 2013: 349–50; Ibn Sūdūn 1998: 72.

[120] cf. *Kanz*, 40 (No. 84).

[121] cf. *Kanz*, 41 (No. 87), which is more detailed.

[122] This is an abridged version of the recipe in *Kanz* (273, Appendix, No. 27). The beginning, which is omitted here, contains crucial instructions: 'You need rice, honey, saffron, pistachios, and *aṭrāf ṭīb*. For each *qadaḥ* of rice, use three *raṭls* of honey, and a little water. Put the honey into the pot until it starts boiling. Wash the rice three times and dye with saffron. Put it on the honey in the pot, and when it is done, add a little bit of pistachios and almonds to it. Serve.'

[123] The mss. has the nonsensical 'wash' (*yughsal*).

qadaḥ of rice. Colour the rice in the pot with saffron. When it is done, throw in pistachios and almonds.

60. Cumin stew (*kammūniyya*)[124]

You need meat, turnips, chickpeas, pepper, garlic and fresh coriander. Boil the meat and add the garlic, coriander and pepper. Return the broth to the meat. Cut up the turnip and add it to the pot.

61. Fried *Būrāniyya*[125]

You need meat, fried aubergine, pepper, dried coriander, mint, and onions. Boil the meat and onion bulbs, [remove the broth] and then fry [them] with pepper, coriander and mint. Return the broth [to the pot]. Fry the aubergine and then add the meat and the seasonings to it.

62. *Narjisiyya*[126]

You need meat, rice, carrots, pepper, a bit of Syrian cheese, cumin, fresh coriander, chickpeas and onions. Boil the meat, fry the coriander and pepper and make a broth with it. Wash the carrots after having cut them up and

---

124 cf. *Kanz*, 43 (No. 94).

125 cf. *Kanz*, 43 (No. 93). *Zahr* contains more *Būrāniyyas* (Nos. 136, 274), as do a number of other culinary treatises which include dishes variously called *Būrān* or *Būrāniyya*: *Waṣf*, 347; al-Warrāq 1987: 115–6 (trans., 227, chap 45); *Wuṣla*, Nos. 627–9; al-Baghdādī 1964: 38–9 (*Būrān*), 40 (trans., 58, 59); *Andalusian*, fols. 47r.–v., 48v.–49r, 51v.–52r; Ibn Mubarrad 1937: 372 (trans., 471). Though aubergine was a necessary ingredient, one author also has a 'gourd *Būrāniyya*' (al-Baghdādī 1964: 43–4/trans., 62). The dish has survived in the present-day Spanish ratatouille-style dish *alboronía*. Nasrallah (2010) points out that both *Būrāniyya* and *maghmūma* (see recipe below No. 72) are ancestors to moussaka (cf. Egyptian *misaqqaʿa*). They share a number of things: firstly, the aubergine as its core ingredient, secondly, a minced meat, and, thirdly, the layering of the ingredients in a shallow pan. Also see Marín 1981; van Gelder 2000: 63; Perry, 'Būrān: eleven hundred years in the history of a dish', in Rodinson et al. 2001: 239–250.

126 cf. *Kanz*, 43 (No. 95). Also see below, Nos. 256 and 307. The dish derives its name from the fact that recipes by this name usually involved adding egg yolks at the end of the cooking process thought to resemble floating narcissus flowers (*narjis*). The anonymous *Andalusian* cookbook (fol. 50v.) instructs adding eggs that have been beaten with saffron and then cutting the resultant omelette into the shape of a narcissus flower. According to Ibn Jazla (fol. 228r.), the dish has aphrodisiacal properties as well as being beneficial for those engaged in strenuous exercise (cf. Ibn Buṭlān 1990: 94–5/trans., 190–1). His recipe includes pistachios and almonds as decoration for the eggs. For other recipes, also see al-Baghdādī 1964: 42 (trans., 60–1); *Waṣf*, 349; *Wuṣla*, Nos. 6.59–61; al-Warrāq 1987: 180–3 (trans., 306, 309–10); *Taṣānīf al-aṭʿima*, fol. 67v.

then throw them in the pot. When they are cooked, add the rice, the cumin [and the cheese]. If you like, you can also make it without cheese or cumin.

63. Okra stew[127]
Boil the meat, then fry the onion. Cut it up into thin pieces with pepper, fresh coriander and garlic. Return the broth to it with the okra and throw in the pot. Extract [and add] the juice of one lime so that it doesn't become stringy. Remove from the fire and ladle up. Know [that this is the way to do it].

64. Recipe for a dish with broad beans (*fūliyya*)[128]
It is made with meat, which is boiled and [then taken out and] fried, with its broth returned [afterwards]. Add it to the beans and place an egg on top when they are done. Serve. Most dishes refer to one another since they are made in a similar style. Know this.

65. Recipe for cowpeas[129]
Ditto.

66. Recipe for *farīkiyya*[130]
You need meat, green wheat, pepper, cheese and cumin. Boil the meat and add the hulled and crushed wheat. When it is done, add milk, cheese, cumin, a little bit of dill, mastic and cinnamon. Remove from the fire.

67. *Harīsa* (meat pottage)[131]
You need beef, mastic, cinnamon, cheese and cumin. Boil meat and hulled wheat together with the mastic, cinnamon and dill. Heat until the meat is

---

127 cf. *Kanz*, 273 (Appendix, No. 29), where the beginning of the recipe is found: 'You need meat or young pigeons, as well as okra, pepper and coriander.'

128 The recipe in *Kanz* (273, Appendix, No. 30) is much more elaborate.

129 The recipe in *Kanz* (44, No. 96) includes the following instructions: 'You need meat, cowpeas, garlic, black pepper, fresh coriander, and gourd. Boil the meat, and fry with the spices until it is done. Pour on the broth and then the cowpeas.'

130 cf. *Kanz*, 44–5 (No. 99). The dish takes its name from *farīk*, which is derived from the verb *faraka*, 'to rub [grain so that the integument becomes stripped off from the kernel]'; Lane 1863–74: VI, 2388; Corriente 1997: 397 (*farīk*, 'green, unripe (barley or garlic)'). For other recipes, see al-Baghdādī 1964: 31 (trans., 49–50); *Waṣf*, 335.

131 cf. *Kanz*, 274 (Appendix, No. 31). The name of the dish is derived from the verb *harasa*, 'to beat, crush, shred' (e.g. *laḥm mahrūs*, 'minced meat'). It is made with wheat or rice; Dozy 1877–81: II, 754; Corriente 1997: 549; Brisville 2017. The popularity of this dish, which was

done. Beat [all the ingredients] until they are mixed together. Remove from the fire and ladle up.

68. Recipe for a wheat stew (*qamḥiyya*)[132]

You need meat, hulled wheat, mastic, cinnamon, dill and cumin. Boil the meat and the wheat together if you make it with beef. If [you make it with] lamb, boil the wheat berries first until they split, and then throw in the lamb [and cook] until it is done. Add mastic, cinnamon, dill and cumin. If you like, you can [also] add milk. Increase the fire until it is done, and then remove.

69. Recipe for *kishk* (dried yoghurt)[133]

You need meat, young pigeons or pullet, or innards, as well as *kishk*, lemon, sour grapes or *kabbād* citrus, [134] pepper, garlic, chickpeas, onions and

---

commonly prepared and sold at markets, was such that its ingredients were carefully monitored by the market inspector; see e.g. al-Muḥtasib 2003: 232; al-Shayzarī n.d.: 223 (trans., 60–61). Recipes for this dish can be found in nearly all cookery books and many dietary manuals: e.g. al-Warrāq 1987: 123–4, 138–9 (trans., 85, 238, 256–8) [5 in total]; al-Baghdādī 1964: 52 (trans., 72); *Waṣf*, 366–7; *Wuṣla*, Nos. 7.8, 7.10. 7.75; *Andalusian*, fols. 60v.–61v. [6 in total]; al-Tujībī 2012: 94, 148–9; Ibn Zuhr 1992: 75, 111 (trans., 98, 129); al-Isrā'ilī 1992: 206; Ibn al-Jazzār 1999: I, 46; al-Dabbābī 2017: 49–52. It was also very popular in Persia, as evidenced by the number of recipes in a Safavid cookbook (Afshār 1981: 268–9): *harīsa-ye berenj* (with rice), *harīsa-ye ghāz* (with goose), *harīsa-ye jow* (with barley), *harīsa-ye shīr-berenj* (with rice and milk), *harīsa-ye shīr-o-bar[r]a* (with milk and lamb), *harīsa-ye baṭṭ* (with duck), *harisa-ye kolang* (with crane), *harīsa-ye gandom* (with wheat), *harīsa-ye morgh* (with chicken), and *harisa-ye maghz-e pesta* (with pistachio). Ibn Jazla stated that 'wheat (*ḥinṭa*) *harīsa* greatly increases sexual potency' (fols. 235v.–236r.; cf. Ibn Buṭlān 1990: 92–3/trans., 188–9). According to Ibn Khalṣūn (1996: 80/trans., 104) *harīsa* 'made with fat is highly nutritional, but difficult to digest. The best type is with good lamb, and it should be eaten after exerting oneself and one is genuinely hungry (*'alā jū' ṣādiq*)'. Ibn Sīnā warned that the wheat variety can cause worms (1999: I, 482–3).

132 cf. *Kanz*, 45 (No. 100).

133 cf. *Kanz*, 45–6 (No. 102). The term (also *kashk*), like the condiment, itself, may go back to the Babylonian flavour enhancer *kisimmu*. The Arab *kishk* mostly involved crushed grain mixed with yoghurt and then dried in the sun. When needed, it was crushed, dissolved in liquid, and added to the pot. According to al-Rāzī, the best *kishk* is that with pure wheat, celery, mint, rue, rice, verjuice, fresh coriander, and citron. Medically, it was thought to be beneficial to those suffering from fevers or a hot temperament. Ibn Jazla, fols. 187v.–188r.; al-Rāzī 2000: 3278; F. Aubaile-Sallenave, 'Al-Kishk: the past and present of a complex culinary practice', in Zubaida & Tapper 2000: 105–39; Lewicka 2011: 229–30. For recipes in other cookery manuals, see: al-Warrāq 1987: 102–3, 165 (*kishkiyyāt*, i.e. *kishk*-based stews), 289 (trans., 208–10, 291–2, 443); *Waṣf*, 322–3; *Wuṣla* 22, Nos. 6.101–2, 7.35 (where it is a sweetmeat, made with rose-water syrup).

134 *Zahr* is one of only three (with *Kanz* and *Wuṣla*) cookery books to have a recipe with *kabbād* (or *kubbād*). The fruit has been identified as 'trifoliate (or hardy) orange', *Poncirus*

aubergine, or onions and chard, or onions and the white [parts] of turnips, and mint. Boil the meat and the chickpeas, [and then] roast. Pour out the broth. Add the aubergine or something else [and cook] until it is done. Dissolve the *kishk* and let it steep a little in the meat broth. Then, add it and bring [everything] to a boil. Add the pepper, garlic, mint and lemon. If you use sour grapes, boil them and strain through a flour sieve and then add the juice [to the dish]. Remove [from the fire] and serve.

70. Recipe for sour grape stew (*ḥiṣrimiyya*)[135]
You need meat, safflower seeds, mastic, cinnamon, mint, sour grapes and aubergine. Finely pound the safflower. Take the sour grapes and put them in the pot, without water. Stew them. Add to the safflower and mix both. Pour liquid from the pot on.[136] Strain [the grapes] through a flour sieve, [and add] mint. If the sour grapes are not done [when using] this recipe, boil them [some more].

71. Recipe for *khayṭiyya*[137]
You need milk, bee honey, ground rice and scalded chicken breasts. Shred the breasts into hair-like fibres. Put the rice in milk and bring to a boil. Toss in the shredded chicken breasts and beat until they become stringy. Remove from the fire. Add bee honey to the [serving] plates, not the pot.

72. Recipe for *bahaṭṭa*[138]
You need milk, ground rice and white sugar. Cook the rice in the milk until it is done. Add the sugar after pounding it, and make sure to stir continuously

---

trifoliate (Rodinson, in Rodinson et al. 2001: 144; Lewicka 2011: 267, 278), whereas Perry (*Wuṣla*) suggests it is the pomelo. The word is still in use in Syro-Lebanese dialects, where it denotes 'citron'. See Chapot 1963.

135 cf. *Kanz*, 46 (No. 103). For other recipes, see al-Baghdādī: 17–8 (trans., 35); al-Warrāq 1987: 163 (trans., 289–90); *Waṣf*, 313–4, 321; *Andalusian*, fol. 33v.; *Wuṣla*, Nos. 6.70–4; Ibn Mubarrad 1937: 372 (trans., 471); *Taṣānīf al-aṭʿima*, fol. 74r. According to Ibn Jazla (fol. 72r) and Ibn Buṭlān (1990: 94–5/trans., 190–1) the dish suppresses yellow bile, burdens the stomach and is harmful those with a weak disposition. Any nefarious effects can be remedied by almond conserve. Ibn Jazla recommends eating raisins and honey after it, whereas Ibn Buṭlān warns about its astringent and constipating properties.

136 This instruction is defective in both *Kanz* and *Zahr* and there is clearly a stage missing. A comparison with recipes in other cookery books reveals that this must refer to the broth of the meat that has been boiled.

137 cf. *Kanz*, 46 (No. 104).

138 cf. *Kanz*, 46 (No. 105); *Waṣf*, 335, 367, 447; Nasrallah [al-Warrāq 2007]: 110 (it does not

until it is done. Remove from the fire. If you like it to be yellow then add saffron with the sugar after the rice is done.

73. Recipe for *hayṭaliyya*[139]

Take finely crushed hulled wheat and milk. Put the wheat in an earthenware bowl, crush and add water. Then, strain with a flour sieve into a vessel. Repeat this two or three times. Strain and put a lid on until the following morning. Drain the water that has turned yellow, and the starch will remain. Cook [the starch] in milk in a pot. Add mastic, tree wormwood and shampoo ginger root and let the mixture thicken over a gentle fire until it is done. Ladle onto plates and drizzle honey on top.

74. Recipe for strained lentils[140]

You need hulled lentils, vinegar, honey, saffron, jujubes, blanched almonds and raisins. Boil the lentils until they are done. Strain through a flour sieve. Clean the honey and put it in the pot with the lentils until it is cooked. Stir continuously. Then, add vinegar with small quantities of jujubes and raisins, the required amount of pepper, as well as some blanched and saffron-dyed almonds. Arrange some jujubes and raisins on top of the bowls for decoration, and serve.

75. Recipe for *tuṭmāj*[141]

You need sour milk, meat, garlic, pepper and fresh coriander. Shape some meat into meatballs. Add a bit of pepper, dried coriander, some fresh coriander

---

appear in the 1987 Arabic edition of al-Warrāq's text). See Ibn al-Ḥashshā' 1941: 14–15. Also see recipe No. 245.

139 cf. *Kanz*, 47 (No. 107).

140 cf. *Kanz*, 274 (Appendix, No. 32).

141 cf. *Kanz*, 47 (No. 109). This is essentially a tagliatelle-type noodle dish even though its main ingredient, *tuṭmāj*, is not mentioned in the recipe itself. Nasrallah ([al-Warrāq 2007]: 574) defined it as 'stiff unfermented dough to be flattened thin, cut into strips, and spread outside to dry out in the air for half a day. The strips are then cut into two-finger long pieces, cooked in a small amount of water, and served with fried meat.' Perry suggested that this 'traditional pasta of the Turkish nomads' was cut into squares, rather than into thin strips like the Persian *rishtā*. Its shape explains why recipes often say to roll out *tuṭmāj* when producing a sheet of dough to be stuffed' (*Wuṣla*, xxxii–xxxiii; for uses in recipes, see Nos. 7.13, 7.3, 7.33). According to Maimonides, 'dough cooked like noodles and vermicelli' was called *tuṭmāj* by the Persians (Bar Shela et al. 1964: 18). However, he advised against eating it because, like most wheat dishes, it has poor nutritional value. The origins of *tuṭmāj* lie on the eastern confines of the Turkish lands, and the eleventh-century lexicographer al-Kāshgharī already reported

and grilled onions. Cut up some [of the remaining] meat into lean slices and then boil it. Boil [the meatballs] and then cook with the broth, together with pepper, fresh coriander and garlic. Fry the meat slices separately and then put them in hot water. Put the dough [i.e. the *tuṭmāj*] in sour yoghurt and then place both the slices and meatballs on top.

76. Rice pilaf (*aruzz mufalfal*)[142]

You need meat and a lot of fat, rice, mastic, cinnamon and chickpeas. Boil the meat, knead it and add a little bit of broth. Add the rice after washing it, and parboil. Remove from the fire. Leave [the pot] for a good hour on the floor and ladle up.

77. Recipe for sweetened rice[143]

You need rice, fatty meat or chicken, fat, bee honey, *aṭrāf al-ṭīb*, mastic, cinnamon and saffron. If you like, you can use only meat and no chicken. Boil the meat or the chicken, and then roast with fat or sesame oil. Add enough honey so that the liquid gains the consistency of honey. Once the pot has come to a boil, add rice which has been washed and rubbed with saffron. Then add mastic, cinnamon and *aṭrāf al-ṭīb*, and drizzle on some fat.

---

that it was a well-known food among them (1914: 376–7/trans., I, 340), adding that a skewer is used for the 'arrangement' of *tuṭmāj* (1914: 277/trans., I, 263) and that it was eaten with gravy (362/327) or, more commonly, with yoghurt. In the fourteenth-century Chinese dietary manual by Hu Szu-Hui, it appears as *tutum ash* and involves noodles stuffed with roasted mutton, after which onions, garlic cream (or yoghurt) and basil are added. According to Isin, the origin of the word is the Turkish *tutmak* ('to knead dough') and *aš* ('soup, stew'). It has survived today in a number of forms, including the Armenian yoghurt soup (*tutmaj*). See *Waṣf*, 430; Doerfer 1963–75: II, 457–9; Buell & Anderson 2016: 115, 298–9 (No. 40), 579, 625–6; Isin 2018: 16–7.

142 cf. *Kanz*, 274 (Appendix, No. 33). The word *mufalfal* literally means 'peppered', presumably in reference to the appearance of the grains of rice. There is another recipe further down (No. 266). Both al-Baghdādī (1964: 28) and *Wuṣla* (No. 6.92) have a dish by the same name, but the instructions vary considerably.

143 cf. *Kanz*, 48 (No. 110).

78. Recipe for *Umm Nārayn*[144] (bread pudding)
This requires stale white bread,[145] milk, mastic, cinnamon, butter, shampoo ginger and tree wormwood. Put the milk in the pot with the seasonings, and bring to a boil. Remove the crust [until you are left with the] breadpith and crumble it very finely. Add to the pot [and cook] until the pudding is done. Add a small amount of butter[146] and when it has been absorbed, put a bit more on top [of the dish].

79. Quince stew (*safarjaliyya*)[147]
Most of the dishes that have not been mentioned, such as *safarjaliyya*, *tuffāḥiyya* (apple stew),[148] and others, are made in the way that we have described. It is easy for you to try them and you will find them tasty.[149]

The basic thing in all of these is that the meat is boiled and roasted as we have described in the [above] dishes, and that broth is added. Cut the quince or whatever else you are using, clean out the core and then cut up like turnips. Put it in a pot with the meat and the broth. Heat until everything is done. Dissolve saffron in vinegar or anything else you choose to use that serves the same purpose, and add some starch dissolved in a bit of broth. Add this [to the pot]. Strive to do that and become proficient by experimenting with things that have not been mentioned and increase your skills in this way.

80. Recipe for a rose-water stew (*māwardiyya*)[150]
This requires meat, rose water, lemons, onions, pepper, mastic and cinnamon. Boil the meat. Add some onion bulbs that have been cut up, and cook until

144 cf. *Kanz*, 48 (No. 111). The name, which literally translates as 'the mother of two fires', refers to the fact that it is cooked thoroughly, from top to bottom. The expression was also used as a sales pitch by *qadāme* (see recipe No. 144) sellers in Damascus to tell customers that their chickpeas were roasted from all sides; Denker 2015: 85.

145 *Kanz* adds *'alāma*, i.e. made from white finely milled sieved flour.

146 *Kanz* adds that it should be done 'while it is on the fire (*wa huwa 'alā 'l-nār*).'

147 For other *safarjaliyya* recipes, see: al-Baghdādī 1964: 36–7 (trans., 55); *Waṣf*, 344; *Taṣānīf al-aṭ'ima*, fol. 94v.

148 For recipes of this dish, see: *Kanz*, 57 (No. 138); Ibn Mubarrad 1937: 372 (trans., 471); al-Baghdādī 1964: 17 (trans., 34–5); *Waṣf*, 311, 352; *Taṣānīf al-aṭ'ima*, fol. 94v. It was thought to cause coughs and joint pain, and reduce sexual potency; Ibn Jazla fol. 49r.–v.; Ibn Buṭlān 1990: 94–5 (trans., 192–3).

149 This is a personal comment by Ibn Mubārak Shāh (or the copyist) on the recipe in *Kanz* (48–9, No. 113), which is more elaborate.

150 cf. *Kanz*, 49 (No. 114).

it is done. Pound the pepper and add it [to the pot]. Squeeze the juice of the lemons [and add it]. Leave the rose buds whole, without pounding, and add them to the broth so that it obtains the requisite consistency.

81. Samosa (*sanbūsak*)[151]

It requires thin sheets of *kunāfa*[152] and sweetmeat, as well as coarsely pounded hazelnuts. Toast the sugar and the hazelnuts. Knead with sugar dissolved in water,[153] or honey. Cut the sheets, stuff them and seal with a bit of dough. You must sprinkle some rose water on the sugar. Fry in sesame oil, and after arranging them on plates, sprinkle on sugar, hazelnuts and rose water.

82. Sour samosas (*sanbūsak ḥāmiḍ*)[154]

As for the sour variety, this requires herbs, sesame oil, vinegar, pepper, hazelnuts or almonds, and *kunāfa* sheets. Finely pound all the meat together and shape like a disc to suit the size of a flatbread,[155] or smaller, depending on the quantity of the meat. Then, boil and turn over in the pan. Skim the froth until it is cooked. Take out and pound finely. Remove the veins of the meat and hang the pot to cool down. Add sesame oil and fry the pounded meat in it until it is browned. Pour the vinegar into the pan and chop the vegetables in it, turning them over until they wilt. Blanch the almonds and pound coarsely. Add them to the pot. Pound the pepper and add it. Keep the pot on the boil until all of the vinegar has dried out. Cut up the *kunāfa*

---

151 cf. *Kanz*, 49 (No. 115). The word goes back to the Persian *sambōsag*, which Perry ([al-Baghdādī 2005]: 78, note No. 2) traces to the Pahlavi *se*, 'three' and *ambos*, 'bread'. It also appears as *sanbūsaj* or *sanbūsaka* (e.g. recipe No. 87). They could be both savoury and sweet. According to Ibn Jazla (fol. 129r.) and Ibn Buṭlān (1990: 96–7; trans., 194–5), the best type of samosa is that soured with fruit juice. It was considered highly nutritional, and particularly beneficial for people engaged in strenuous exercise. For other recipes, see: al-Baghdādī 1964: 58 (trans., 78); *Waṣf*, 379, 382; *Andalusian*, fols, 14v, 15r, 36r, 49r, 68v; al-Tujībī 2012: 251; *Wuṣla*, Nos. 6.2-5, 7.1; al-Warrāq 1987: 89–90, 123 (trans., 190–1, 237); Ibn Jazla, fol. 129r.; al-Dabbābī 2017: 124–5.

152 According to Perry, *kunāfa* was a 'paper-thin pancake made on a special polished griddle' (*Waṣf*, 418). Also see recipe No. 183, below.

153 *qaṭr*, which Dozy (1877-81: II, 364) defines as 'sugar dissolved in water and boiled until it has gained a consistency so that it can be used instead of honey in the preparation of certain sweets.'

154 cf. *Kanz*, 49–50 (No. 116). cf. *Taṣānīf al-aṭʿima*, fol. 64v.; *Waṣf*, 386.

155 *raghīf* (pl. *arghifa*); derived fom the verb *raghafa* ('to compress dough'), this type of bread (originally a cake of between half an an inch and an inch in thickness) is still popular in many Middle Eastern countries. Lane 1863–74: II, 1113; Mielck 1913: 69–70.

sheets to a width of four fingers and remove the seasonings from the fire. Let it cool down. Take the required amount of filling, put it in a sheet and fold. Then, seal with a bit of dough. Fry in sesame oil. Cut up the fresh herbs, put them on platters and add the samosas to it. Sprinkle a bit of jasmine, or something else, on top, and serve.

83. Recipe for *laḥm taqliyya*[156]

It requires meat, onions, pepper, cinnamon, dried coriander and some good raisins. Boil the meat with mastic and cinnamon. Use good oil to roast the pepper and coriander. Pour broth onto it. Chop up the onions and add. Boil everything until it is done. Squeeze lemons into it.

84. Recipe for kebabs (*sharā'iḥ*)[157]

It requires meat, fat and sesame oil, or only sheep's tail fat, mastic and cinnamon. Slice the meat and boil with mastic and cinnamon. Strain off [the broth] and fry [the meat] in the sesame oil. If you are using tail fat, boil it with the meat, then pound it and use it to fry [the meat].

85. Recipe for fried *mudaqqaqa*[158]

It requires meat, pepper, fresh coriander, dried coriander, a bit of good olive oil or sesame oil and a bit of onion. Pound the meat and mix with one grilled onion bulb. Pound all of the seasonings. Hang a pot over the fire. Put a little water in it until it boils. Add the pounded meat, parboil, and remove. Then add the sesame oil to the pot over the fire and fry the meat after having boiled it. Afterwards pound some dried coriander and sprinkle it on the plates.

86. Recipe for couscous (*kuskusū*)[159]

This requires meat, sheep's tail fat, pepper, a bit of good-quality olive oil, mastic, cinnamon, dried coriander and chicken. Boil the chicken, meat and

---

156 cf. *Kanz*, 52 (No. 124).

157 cf. *Kanz*, 274 (Appendix, No. 34). The Arabic is the plural of *sharīḥa* and simply means 'slices'. Also see recipe No. 293.

158 cf. *Kanz*, 53 (No. 125).

159 cf. *Kanz*, 52 (No. 123, '*kishk*'); *Wuṣla* (6.131, *kuskusū al-maghāriba*, 'Moroccan couscous'). Couscous (< *kaskasa*, 'to grind, crush') is one of the earliest dishes to have migrated from North Africa to the East, and other recipes can be found in *Waṣf*, 344–5; *Wuṣla*, No. 6.130 (*K. sha'īriyya*); al-Tujībī 2012: 87–90 (five recipes). Perry (*Wuṣla*, 286) points out that *kuskusū* 'could mean either the steamed granules characteristic of North African cuisine or a small soup noodle.' Interestingly enough, the recipes in *Wuṣla* only required flour (*daqīq*), while

tail fat with mastic, cinnamon and the olive oil. Twist dough [into granules] like [you do] for *mufattala.*[160] Put [the ingredients] in a pot with a perforated bottom and add the granules [i.e. couscous]. Put [another pot] on top of the one in which the meat has been placed. Pound the tail fat and melt it down with an onion bulb. Add the couscous to it and fold into the fat. Brown the meat with an onion bulb, pepper and dried coriander, and layer everything on the couscous. Make a sour meat-filled *sanbūsak,* and put it on top. Let it simmer down and serve.

87. Recipe for samosas (*sanbūsaka*)[161]

Take pounded meat and fry in a pot. Then sweat it, together with a piece of cinnamon, a bit of mastic and a sliced onion. When the meat has released its juices, fry it in sesame oil in order to remove any other impurities. Then throw on the juice of toasted sumac [berries]. Let it cook until the water has evaporated. Cut in some lemon and mint. Leave the aromatic spices in. Fry with fresh sesame oil. Before frying, dye with saffron dissolved in rose water.

88. Recipe for Jew's mallow (*mulūkhiyya*)[162]

Boil meat and when it is tender, fry and add fresh coriander, crushed salt and garlic, pepper, dried coriander, roasted and grilled onions, caraway [seeds], almond kernels, hazelnuts and pistachios. When [the pot] is boiling, throw it all in after finely pounding everything. Boil thoroughly, and then sprinkle on Jew's mallow, but do not put a lid on the pot. When it is cooked, sprinkle a bit of rose water on top. Return to the fire. Add sheep's tail fat which has been melted with mastic, cassia and good olive oil, or sesame oil. Sprinkle cassia on top. Add aubergine fried in sheep's tail fat to make [the dish] even better.

---

al-Tujībī's generally refer to semolina (87–9). According to Bolens (1990: 61–7), couscous was already being prepared by Berbers as early as 238 to 149 BCE, whereas Perry (1990) dates its origins to the transition between the Zirid and Almohad dynasties, between the eleventh and thirteenth centuries. See *EI*², s.v. 'kuskusū' (C. Pellat); Rosenberger, 'Diversité des manières de consommer les céréales dans le Maghreb précolonial', in Marín & Waines 1994: 327–34; Marceau Gast, 'Une hypothèse sur l'origine historique et du couscous', in Franconie et al. 2010: 67–82; al-Dabbābī 2017: 70–86.

160 The meaning of *mufattal,* 'braided', is not really helpful, nor is Dozy's definition of *mufattala* as 'pasta made with the finest flour' (1877–81: II, 240). The answer is provided by the *Wuṣla* couscous recipes, which call for dough to be twisted like barley grains (*yufattal mithl al-sha'īr*).

161 Most of this recipe is included with another for a lamb dish (*kharūf mamzūj*) in *Kanz* (53, No. 126).

162 cf. *Kanz*, 56 (No. 134).

Tip: You should avoid blue-eyed quail and not eat it since it causes testicular illness. This has been tested.

89. Chicken recipe[163]
Roast [a chicken], and pour on walnut or almond oil with a little bit of salt and saffron. The best kind of chicken to use is one that has been tired out, fattened up and then fed vinegar and rose water before slaughter. Scald it in the usual fashion. Use a bit of sesame oil, salt and saffron and then roast the chicken over a moderate fire. Baste it so that it becomes extremely succulent and good.

90. Sparrows[164]
The best are those that are fried after they have been cut in half across the back. Clean and then fry them with olive oil and a little bit of salt. Sprinkle spices on top once they are plated up.

Instructions for making a glass pot[165]
This is like making bottles or goblets. The secret in making this lies in the thickness of the glass. It is like making a pot, except that the glassmaker places a punty at the bottom when it [the glass] is moist, and then raises it upwards three-thirds of the height of the bottle so as to create an inner cylinder, but without perforating the top [of the bottle]. When you make it in this way, you can cook any dish in it after you put it on a coal fire, or even the strongest fires. However, when you cook in it, there are conditions. Firstly, the water cannot be lower than halfway up the stem, otherwise it will break. Secondly, it should not be put over a strong fire suddenly, or moved suddenly from heat to cold, since that would also break the glass. Instead, put it over a moderate fire and allow it to grow gradually underneath. Do not add cold water afterwards, but [put] all that is required at the outset.

---

163 cf. *Kanz*, 58 (No. 139, '*dajāja karandāj*').

164 cf. *Kanz*, 60 (No. 147), which is slightly more expansive, whereas it has two more recipes for sparrows, one (No. 149) an extremely elaborate one 'made in al-Andalus and the Maghrib.'

165 cf. *Kanz*, 61–2 (No. 149), where the pot is linked to a dish for cooking sparrows in it. The inclusion here is somewhat random as the author does not refer to any particular recipe.

FIVE

On Making *Murrī*[166]

91. Recipe for steeped *murrī*[167]

Take two *rub*ʿ*s*[168] of good fresh barley flour and knead it into dough without salt but with its bran. Shape it into small moulds like those for sugar, and use your fingers to push a hole into the centre of each one. Put them on a board on which bran has been spread in the shade, and leave for twenty days. Then, turn them upside down and leave for another twenty nights. Afterwards, remove the bran and dust, and coarsely pound [the dough] to the size of broad beans. Add one *rub*ʿ of barley flour with its bran. Then, take four *mudds* of salt, and place everything in an olive jar that does not leak. Add enough water and store the jar in a place where it is in the sunlight throughout the day. Stir with a stick made from the wood of the wild fig tree[169] at least four times a day – more if possible – for a period of eight days. Then, take one *rub*ʿ of wheat flour, and knead it into a dough with its bran, but without salt, and shape into flatbreads which are put in the oven until they are done, and thrown into the jar while hot after having been cut into bite-sized pieces. Cover the jar [and leave for] three days, then put your hand in what is left, break it up and stir with the wild fig-tree stick four times a day – or more if possible – for eight days. Afterwards, take one *rub*ʿ of wheat flour and knead into dough with one *mudd* of salt. Shape [the dough] into thick cake loaves and leave overnight in the oven, or cook over a fire, until they become firm.[170] Don't let the heat get too high so that the loaves don't get burnt. [Remove from the heat,] pound them and then place in the jar. Stir [the mixture] with the stick for a period of two months. Do not neglect

166 In *Kanz*, the title includes 'and the storage of verjuice and lemon juice', which better reflects the contents of the chapter.

167 *murrī naqī*ʿ; cf. *Kanz*, 63–4 (No. 150).

168 In *Kanz*, the amount is eight *qadaḥs*.

169 *dhukkār*; Dozy 1877–81: I, 487 (*caprificus*).

170 The text is heavily corrupted here and was supplemented with information from the recipe in *Kanz*.

to do this and do not let someone who is ritually unclean[171] come near it. Once the two months are over, you will see that the *murrī* has risen to the surface of the water. Take a basket, and fill it with the jar's contents. Hang the basket and place a large bowl underneath it. Leave for one day and one night.[172] Take the contents of the bowl and place it in a green-glazed jar. Take what is left over in the basket and leave to one side. Do likewise with what remains in the olive jar. Then add the first batch to the second, and add the dregs of the second to those of the first. Decant to the olive jar and add a sufficient amount of water. Stir for a period of twenty days and then do what you did the first time around, i.e. hanging and straining the mixture, and then add it to the first batch. Place the bowl in the sun for three days. Then remove, and use.

92. A recipe for Moroccan barley *murrī*[173]

Take the leaves of citrons,[174] limes, peaches, and lemon balm,[175] and immerse them in sweetened water in bowls and leave in the sun for four days. Take barley, sift it and pick it over. Then roast it and finely ground. Mix it with one quarter of its amount in pulverized salt, and knead well. Shape into thin unleavened bread loaves (*faṭā'ir*) and bake them through, until no moisture is left inside of them. Let everything cool down and then add the loaves to the bowls, and submerge in water. Leave out in the hot sun for two weeks and then macerate, sieve and cook well. Make sure you will have mixed in two *qadaḥs* of ground, sieved and roasted caraway seeds. Then remove. It is extremely good.

93. A recipe for making verjuice[176]

Take sour grapes, sprinkle salt on them and trample them with your feet. Then, squeeze and strain their juice and put it in flagons. Leave the lids off until [the juice] starts to ferment, scum forms on the surface and sediment appears at the bottom. Strain into other flagons and also leave these open until what remains of the scum rises to the surface. Once the boiling dies down,

---

171 The Arabic *najis* is applied to a variety of things, such as wine, pigs, or dead animals, as well as people who are in a state of impurity, such as a woman on her period.

172 The last two sentences are missing from the text and have been taken from *Kanz*.

173 cf. *Kanz*, 64–5 (No. 151).

174 *Kanz* adds 'and sour oranges' (*nāranj*).

175 *rayḥān utrunjī* (*Mellissa officinalis*) also known as *rayḥān turunjānī* (Corriente 1997: 221).

176 cf. *Kanz*, 65 (No. 152).

fill the other flagons with them. Add purified olive oil,[177] bunches of mint, and leave in the sun until the clay has dried.[178] Then store and use [at need].

94. Another recipe[179]

Take sour grapes, clean them, and then extract their juice with a press and pound them in a wooden bowl until nothing remains of the skins.[180] Then transfer to a new pot and leave at night to settle. Remove the contents and place them in a pot over a high fire. Let it boil until half of it has evaporated and its colour remains carnelian red, at which point add a piece of cassia, and stir with large bunches of mint for several hours. Each time a bunch becomes spoilt, replace it with another one. Remove [the pot from the fire], leave until it has settled, and then strain. When it has cooled down and the scum settled, remove the juice and fill glass containers with it. Seal it with a small amount of sesame oil. If there is a gap in the containers, their contents will go off. The liquid will remain good for years without having to be replaced.

95. Recipe for mint vinegar[181]

This is well known.

96. Recipe for sour orange juice[182]

There are recipes for sun-dried sour oranges, and those that have not been dried in the sun.[183] Pick the oranges when they are fully ripened. Remove the peel around the middle and throw it away. Cut the oranges in half but do not use the same knife as the one used for peeling so that it does not become bitter. The person cutting the oranges should not be the same one who peels them.[184] Use a sieve or strainer to remove seeds from the juice

---

177 The Arabic *zayt maghsūl* literally means 'washed olive oil', and refers to the washing with hot water towards the end of the pressing process. See al-Kindi 1948: 32 (No. 3), 141.

178 The clay is used to seal the containers, as explained in the recipe that follows in *Kanz* (p. 66, No. 153), but omitted in *Zahr*.

179 cf. *Kanz*, 65–6 (No. 154).

180 The text omits 'its skins' (*qishrihi*), which is found in *Kanz*.

181 For the full recipe, see *Kanz*, 66 (No. 157), and 321 (note No. 2131).

182 cf. *Kanz*, 67 (No. 160).

183 This opening sentence is missing from *Kanz*.

184 The same instruction is found in al-Baghdādī (1964: 22–3/trans., 40) and *Kanz*. However, in the latter the bitterness is attributed to the person, rather than the knife, with the recommendation to peel the orange and then hand it to someone for cutting and extraction of the juice.

and then transfer it to glass bottles. Seal them with olive oil and use when needed. If you want to use some of it, open the bottle and pour as much as you like in the palm of your hand. The oil will rise to the top of the bottle. Open your palm and take what is needed. Then put the bottle back and refill it with sour orange juice, if you have it, or olive oil. If the bottle is not full, the liquid will go bad,[185] and you should throw it out.

97. Recipe for lemon juice[186]

(Crush good-quality sugar and place it underneath an oiled lemon-juice press. Squeeze the lemons into it, and then pour through a strainer or sieve. Throw away any pips and) transfer [the juice] to flagons. Seal with almond oil or sesame oil, and when you want to use it, mop up the oil with cotton from the top of the container, and use the juice to make syrups, *aqsimāʾ*[187] as well as most other beverages, except salty ones, for which the juice is not suitable.

98. Recipe for mint *murrī*[188]

Take two parts of barley flour and one part of salt. Pulverize the salt, mix it in with the flour and knead the mixture into a *faṭīr* loaf. Leave [to bake] in an oven overnight and remove in the morning. The loaves should be burnt on the outside and inside; if not, place them back in the oven until they are burnt. [After removing them], break up [the bread] into dainty pieces,[189] and submerge in water. Add a handful of thyme, mint, two stalks of fennel, crushed pine nuts and citron peels and leaves. Return [everything] to the oven and leave overnight. Remove, then strain, and throw in enough good honey to break the saltiness. Transfer to clean containers and pour good olive oil on it in order to preserve it. It is wonderful.

---

185 The Arabic has two verbs *qaṭṭana* and *talafa*, both of which mean 'to be spoilt' (food). The former verb does not have diacritics in the manuscript and was amended with the help of *Kanz* (321, note No. 2150).

186 cf. *Kanz*, 67–8 (No. 161). The first part of the recipe (enclosed in brackets) is missing from the manuscript and was augmented with the text from *Kanz*.

187 A sweetened digestive drink, often with raisins, though other ingredients (but never pomegranate juice) were also included. Its popularity appears to have been limited geographically and chronologically, with only one recipe each in *Waṣf* (440) and *Wuṣla* (No. 2.14 = *Kanz*, No. 401), but ten in *Kanz* (Nos. 401, 402, 404, 405, 416, 417, 420, 423, 424, 432). Also see Lewicka 2011: 471–3.

188 cf. *Kanz*, 68–9 (No. 164).

189 According to the recipe in *Kanz*, the pieces should be the size of broad beans.

99. Another recipe for a perfumed *murrī*[190]

Take two *kaylas* of wheat flour and add half a *kayla* of salt. Knead [the dough] into flatbreads, and leave [to bake] in the oven overnight. If they are burnt, that is good; if not, continue baking until they are. Then, break the loaves into small pieces and place in a pot together with a handful of thyme, bay leaves, sour orange[191] leaves, mint, basil, and two handfuls of fennel.[192] Immerse everything in water and also leave overnight[193] after macerating. Remove [from the oven] in the morning and strain. If you wish, you can add the two liquids. Alternatively, you may wish to leave each one separate from the other. If you dissolve a bit of starch in it, it will loosen the consistency [of the liquid].[194] If you add honey[195] to it, it will also be good.[196]

SIX

On Making Omelettes and Other Things[197]

100. An omelette recipe[198]

Take meat [pound] and boil it. Once it is cooked, pound it for a second time and fry in oil. Chop parsley[199] and put it on top of the meat in a bowl. Break eggs on [the mixture and add] hot spices, fresh and dried coriander,

190 cf. *Kanz*, 69 (No. 165).

191 The *Kanz* recipe has 'citron' (*utrujj*).

192 The text adds 'one handful of each', which is unclear in this context. Logically – but not syntactically – it may refer to the quantity to be used of bay leaves, mint and basil, even though this is specified earlier in the sentence.

193 *Kanz* specifies that it should be placed in the oven but omits the soaking in water.

194 The aim of adding starch is taken from *Kanz* since it was omitted from the text.

195 *Kanz* adds that the honey should be 'slightly burnt.'

196 The recipe in *Kanz* ends with 'and know this.'

197 The title of this chapter is slightly different in *Kanz*: 'Chapter regarding eggs used to make omelettes, and other (things).'

198 cf. *Kanz*, 69–70 (No. 166).

199 *maqdūnis*; *Kanz* has the more usual *baqdūnis*.

pounded bread, and cinnamon, and fry in an earthenware pan with olive oil and sesame oil. Make sure the frying pan is round, with high sides and a long handle, like a ladle. Put on a low coal fire, and pour into it a few *jumjumas* of sesame oil. Wait until it heats up and then add eggs and the spices. For each omelette, use five eggs and some spices, as well as fried meat. Put everything in a frying pan and leave until the contents dry out. Turn over every now and again[200] until it is cooked through.

101. Sour omelette[201]

Make the omelette as mentioned above or, if you wish, with salty lemon cut into pieces. Fry the omelette, and when it is close to being cooked,[202] add vinegar and lemon juice with a spoon, after having perforated[203] it with a knife. Then wait a little while until [the vinegar and juice] have been absorbed. Then add vinegar and lemon juice [again] and continue to do so six or seven times. Be patient and it will become a sour omelette, Allah the Almighty willing.

102. Preserved omelette[204]

Take eggs and boil them. Then, remove the shells and pierce them with a needle. Place them in a jar, and add a bit of salt, as well as honey and vinegar, making sure the vinegar is the dominant [flavour].

103. Pickled omelette[205]

Boil eggs and when they are cooked, take them out, peel them and pierce them with the tip of a thin knife[206] or needle. Soak them in salty water for a couple of days, and then wash them with fresh water until the taste of salt has been removed and only a little of it is left. Put enough wine vinegar in a clean pot to immerse the eggs. Take cassia, ginger, cumin, dried coriander, whole cloves, and put everything in vinegar and rue, citron leaves, celery[207]

---

200 The Arabic has *kull sāʿa*, 'every hour'.

201 cf. *Kanz*, 70 (No. 168).

202 This passage was entirely taken from *Kanz*.

203 The author uses the colloquial Egyptian Arabic verb *bakhkhasha*.

204 cf. *Kanz*, 71 (No. 173).

205 cf. *Kanz*, 72 (No. 174).

206 The text has the nonsensical 'tip of the needle of the knife.'

207 *karafs*, which could also denote parsley (to which it is related), with al-Tujībī, for instance, referring to the latter as 'celery known as *maqdūnis*' (2012: 202). The varieties used were very different from their modern counterparts in that they were more bitter and pungent, similar

and mint, as well as honey or sugar so that it is sweetened.[208] If you want it to be sour, then do not add the sweet ingredients. Put on a fire and boil until the spices are cooked through. Leave the pot on the fire and throw in the boiled eggs while everything is boiling. Leave in the pot and then remove to eat with meat or whatever you like.[209] If you want the dish to be yellow, then add saffron; if, on the other hand you want it to be red in colour, add safflower. If you don't want to cook the spices, put them in a green [glazed] or glass jar, and then add vinegar and seasonings according to your taste and then colour it in the way that you like, as explained. It stays good for days after removing it from the fire and is truly very tasty.[210]

104. Recipe for an omelette without eggs that everyone will think is made with eggs[211]

Boil and pound chickpeas until they are smooth. Boil some onions and pound them in with the chickpeas. Pour on a bit of olive oil and *murrī* and add some salt and spices – coriander, caraway and pepper – together with gum Arabic. Fry in a pot until everything is done. Whoever eats this will believe it is an omelette made from eggs.

105. Omelette recipe[212]

You need eggs, green herbs, whole onions, sesame oil or seed[213] oil and pepper. Chop up the onions into fine pieces and add a little water and good olive

---

to smallage. Celery was already used in Roman times as a starter and flavouring. In Arab cuisine, both the seeds and leaves (but not the stems) were used as an ingredient in cooking. In some cases, it may have referred to Chinese (water) celery (*Oenanthe javanica*). Arabic scholars identified a number of varieties, the principal ones being mountain, wild and cultivated celery. Just like Hippocrates before them, Islamic physicians referred to the aphrodisiacal qualities of celery, as a result of which its use was allegedly prohibited for wetnurses since their state of sexual excitation could spoil their milk. Ibn Sīnā 1999: I, 528–30 (trans., 386–8); Ibn Jazla, fol. 185r.–v.; al-Isrā'īlī 1992: 365; Ibn Buṭlān 1992: 80–1 (trans 164–5); Ibn al-Bayṭār 1992: IV, 310–4; al-Rāzī 2000: 3279–82; Lev & Amar 2008: 136–8; Dalby 2003: 77.

208 The Arabic *muzz* means 'sour' but this of course does not make sense here and was thus rendered as 'sweetened'.

209 *Kanz* states that it is eaten with 'cold *sikbāj* meat added with rose water.'

210 The last two sentences are not found in *Kanz* and can, therefore, be assumed to be an addition by Ibn Mubārak Shāh.

211 cf. *Kanz*, 71 (No. 171).

212 cf. *Kanz*, 73 (No. 177).

213 The mss has the nonsensical *badan* ('[human] body') and was corrected to *bizr* (seeds), which is the form that appears in *Kanz*. However, it is not clear what kind of seeds are meant here, and thus it may be a scribal error, or an ellipsis of a substance that was well known.

oil or sesame oil [and cook] until they are done. Chop the green herbs into it and [leave] until they have dried up. Then remove from the fire, pound pepper and add it. Break eggs into it, beat them with a stick and fry in an earthenware pan over a fire, with sesame oil. After it has been heated, add the herbs to the eggs until done on one side. Then, turn over and repeat. Once [both sides are] done, transfer to a plate. If one side is done and you want to cook the other, add sesame oil to the pan if there is not enough left anymore. Proceed in the same way that we have set forth.[214]

106. 'Buried' omelette recipe[215]

You need meat, eggs, onions, green herbs, pepper, mastic and cinnamon. Boil the meat and then fry it after drying. Chop up the onions and transfer them to a separate container. Hang an earthenware pot over a fire and put the chopped onions in there, with some salted water and bring to the boil. Add a little sesame oil and bring to the boil [again]. Then, add the green herbs [and cook] until they are dried up. Pound pepper and add the meat to it. Break the eggs over it and beat them. Hang the pot over a fire and add sesame oil. When it heats up, add the herbs to the meat [and cook] until everything is done.

107. Recipe for making *maṣūṣ* eggs[216]

Pour sesame oil in an earthenware pan, strip celery leaves from the stalks and add [what remains]. Then, cook everything. Add cassia, mastic, coriander and caraway, and then pour on a sufficient quantity of vinegar. Colour with a little saffron, and moderate the taste with salt. Break eggs over it and then put a lid on the pot. When they have stiffened, remove [from the fire]. It is tasty.

108. Recipe for mustard eggs[217]

Boil [eggs], pierce them with a thin needle and season with a little salt and ground cumin. Plate up and leave from early morning until midday. Then,

---

214 The final sentence is missing from *Kanz*.

215 cf. *Kanz*, 74 (No. 179).

216 cf. al-Baghdādī 1964: 59 (trans., 80); *Kanz*, 74 (No. 180). The recipe can also be translated as '*à la maṣūṣ*', which is a vinegar poultry stew (also *maṣūṣiyya*). Perry ([al-Baghdādī 2005]: 41, note No. 1) links it to the verb *maṣṣa* ('to suck'), in reference to the fact that it was made with sucking kid. For other recipes, see al-Warrāq 2007: 123 (trans., 238), 286–7 (trans., 440–1), 612; *Wuṣla*, Nos. 5.22–4, 6.108.

217 cf. *Kanz*, 74 (No. 181), which does not include the instruction to leave overnight.

take [the eggs] and colour them with saffron. Add wine vinegar, mustard seeds, mint and *aṭrāf al-ṭīb*. Leave overnight and eat.

109. Recipe for a delicious omelette[218]

Take one *raṭl* of milk, vinegar, and smoothly boiled chickpeas. Mix everything together and sieve. Then, take fifteen eggs, beat them well and add three sour lemons, cumin, hazelnuts, walnuts, pepper and parsley. Boil one *ūqiya* and a half of sesame oil, and add to it one chopped up onion and one *ūqiya* of olives. Cook over a fire. It will turn into a nice omelette.

110. Recipe for an omelette with few provisions[219]

Take one *rubʿ* of *mujawhar*[220] chickpeas and pound them finely. Then beat [the mixture] into milk and break five eggs into it. Beat them until everything is mixed together, and then fry with clarified butter. The result is delicious.[221]

111. Omelette for increasing sexual potency[222]

Take four onions and cook them in the oven until they are done. Peel and pound them very finely. Also take half a *raṭl* of meat that has already been boiled and [after removing the broth] fry it until it is done. Pound the meat and add it to the cooked onions with what remains of the broth. Break twenty chicken egg yolks into [the pot] and beat everything. Then, add the aforementioned spices to bring out their flavours, as well as a little salt. Fry in sesame oil or clarified butter and add to the pounded onions and meat, as described.[223]

---

218 cf. *Kanz*, 75 (No. 183).

219 cf. *Kanz*, 75 (No. 184).

220 This word literally means 'covered with jewels', but in this context it refers to chickpeas that have been toasted until they have turned bright yellow; Dozy 1877–81: I, 237. They are also called for in a *Wuṣla* recipe (No. 7.57).

221 This is an addition by the author as it is not found in the *Kanz* recipe, which is identical apart from this.

222 cf. *Kanz*, 75–6 (No. 185), whose title is somewhat more expansive: 'Recipe for a tasty omelette that is eaten to increase sexual potency and strengthen it.' *Kanz* contains another two aphrodisiac omelettes (Nos. 187–8).

223 The last part of the recipe is slightly different in *Kanz*: 'it is preferable to use skink (*saqanqūr*) salt. Fry in sesame oil or clarified butter. If it is carrot season, add them and fry as mentioned.'

112. Recipe for an omelette deemed delicious[224]

[Take][225] some meat, fat and sumac, and pound in a mortar, together with spices. Also squeeze in lemon juice, add mint and mix with eggs. Fry on a moderate fire. This is considered delicious.

113. Recipe for a sour *muba'thara*[226]

Boil the meat and tear it up. Then transfer [to a container] and douse with a little lemon and wine vinegar. Cook until half done. Break the eggs and add spices. Then, bring sesame oil to a boil over a fire and when it starts boiling, throw the meat in the eggs and beat everything together well. Then, transfer to an earthenware pan and thoroughly mix everything in the way that you like it.

114. Recipe for *muba'thara* and omelette spices[227]

Take some ginger, galangal, rolled cinnamon, saffron strands, pepper, cumin, and good thyme – of each, one part; one part of rosebuds and one eighth of a part of good spikenard.[228] Pound all the spices smoothly and set aside until needed. If you add them to omelettes, first use a bit of fresh pounded Syrian cheese, which has been fried and beaten with the omelette. Throw in the spices after it has cooked.

115. Recipe for a *mu'tamidiyya* omelette with cheese[229]

Take two chicken breasts and slice them thinly. Take one *raṭl* of meat and slice it in the same way. Wash and put in a pot over a fire and pour on one

224 cf. *Kanz*, 77 (No. 190).

225 This is included in *Kanz*.

226 cf. *Kanz*, 77 (No. 191).

227 cf. *Kanz*, 79 (No. 198). The word *muba'thara* means 'scattered' and refers to a dish with eggs cracked over other ingredients and spreading among them. Lane 1863–74: I, 223.

228 *sunbul*; the root of several fragrant Indian perennial plants of the Valerian family, it was already used in Roman and Byzantine cuisine. Bitter in flavour and musky in odour, it was one of the basic aromatic spices in the Muslim world, and was used in perfumes, breath sweeteners and the like, as well as in dishes and beverages. Dalby 2003: 229–30; Ibn Sīnā 1999: I, 575, 602–3; Ibn al-Bayṭār 1992: III, 48–51 (trans., II, 295–6); Lev & Amar 2008: 289–93; Nasrallah [al-Warrāq 2007]: 673; Lewicka 2011: 146.

229 cf. *Kanz*, 80–81 (No. 202). The dish may get its name from the Abbasid caliph al-Mu'tamid ['alā Allāh] (870–892), whom Nasrallah ([al-Warrāq 2007]: 18) mentions had a cookbook written for him, citing the anonymous author of *Anwā'* (53) as proof. However, the reference in the latter work – and in its source text, *Andalusian* (fol. 22v.) – is more likely to be to al-Mu'tamid Ibn al-'Abbād (d. 1095), the last ruler of Seville. Furthermore, the text states that

raṭl of good olive olive and two *dirhams* of salt. Boil until nearly done. Then, slice one quarter of a *raṭl* of cheese, and throw it into the pot with the meat. Season with two *dirhams* of dried coriander, and one *dirham* each of pepper and cassia. Add ten pitted olives. Then break twenty eggs into a large green-glazed bowl and pour on one *ūqiya* of *murrī*. Finally, cut some rue in it, remove [from the fire] and serve.

---

the ruler, himself, composed a cookbook, not that one was written for him.

SEVEN

On Counterfeit Dishes[230]

IF YOU MAKE THEM WITH ONIONS, fry them first in sesame oil or fat:[231]

116. Purslane counterfeit dish, which includes one made with pomegranate seeds.
117. Spinach counterfeit dish, which includes one made with pomegranate seeds. All include sugar and mastic. The rose water [used] also includes aromatics.
118. Counterfeit dish of gourd, for those suffering from a fever.
119. *Zīrbāj* counterfeit dish, for those suffering from yellow bile.
120. Counterfeit dish with gourd and verjuice, sugar, and one *ūqiya* of the usual seasonings. Pound the gourd after boiling it. This is [good] for those suffering from yellow bile fever.
121. Counterfeit dish of pomegranate seeds, [good for] those suffering from nausea. It is thickened with sugar.
122. Counterfeit dish with pomegranate seeds, against diarrhoea.[232]

Each of the counterfeit dishes has its own specific herbs and spices, and other things, such as almonds and rose water. If you wish to thicken [the dishes], add bread crumbs. It tastes good.

123. Mung bean counterfeit dish against coughs[233]
This is made with good olive oil and peeled and ground mung beans. Sometimes, this dish is added with roasted pomegranate seeds, which are boiled after being pounded.

---

230 *muzawwarāt*; see Introduction. In *Kanz* the title is 'Regarding counterfeit vegetable dishes that are nutritional for sick people.'

231 The following recipes (117–123) are very loosely inspired by similarly named – but much more extensive – recipes in *Kanz* (82–4, Nos. 205–10).

232 The Arabic *jarayān al-jawf* literally translates as 'running of the insides'.

233 The mung bean counterfeit recipe in *Kanz* (83, No. 208) is entirely different and also omits any reference to its use in treating coughs.

124. *Zīrbāj* recipe[234]

[The temperament of this dish is] quite balanced. It is beneficial for individuals with a bilious temperament, inflamed livers, or weak stomachs. It is [also] useful against jaundice and blockages in the liver and spleen, and for people suffering from dropsy or tertiary fevers. Take a few onions, chop them up in the required quantity, throw into a clean pot and place it on over a gentle fire. Add almond oil or fresh sesame oil or good olive oil, depending on the temperaments. Once the onions start to sweat, add a little bit of ground coriander, a little mint, and what is required in terms of spikenard, mastic and cinnamon. Then, add clean vinegar mixed with the required amount of water. Sweeten with sugar and thicken the liquid with smoothly ground peeled almonds. Colour with saffron and rose water. There is no harm in making it with a bit of starch either. [Then,] remove [from the fire].

125. Recipe with pomegranate seeds[235]

It is cold and dry and beneficial for those suffering from fevers [caused by excess] yellow bile, or inflamed livers. It quenches the thirst and suppresses yellow bile. It suppresses nausea and is suitable for the bodies of sick people, depending on which herbs are added. Take a little pounded coriander and fry it in almond oil, sesame oil or olive oil. Then, also fry a little spikenard in it and pour over the required quantity of pomegranate juice mixed with water. Alternatively, you can use pomegranate seeds boiled in water, pounded, macerated and strained, as much as you like. They are more astringent when they are pounded than if they are boiled, and also generate more wind. When the pot is boiling, sweeten with sugar, and thicken with pounded almonds perfumed with rose water. If it needs to be astringent, then toast the almonds before pounding them. Conversely, if you don't want it to be astringent, add stalks of spinach, chard and purslane. Remove [from the fire].

---

234 cf. *Kanz*, 88 (No. 226).

235 cf. *Kanz*, 88–9 (Nos. 226–7).

EIGHT

Fish[236]

126. Recipe to make tahini fish[237]

Wash the fish, season with flour, and fry in sesame oil, which should be boiling. If you want it with tahini, [then] pound pepper with *aṭrāf al-ṭīb* and also add onions. Put over a fire and melt the tahini with vinegar and saffron and also boil over the fire.[238] When it is cooked, transfer the fish to it (*sc.* the sauce).

127. If you like it with coriander (*kuzbariyya*)[239]

Take onions and slice them very finely. Pound fresh coriander and garlic and put them in an earthenware pan. Pound pepper and add it. Stir until everything is done. Make sure there is enough broth to pour over the fish.

128. If you like it with raisins[240]

(You need fresh fish, raisins, wine vinegar, *aṭrāf al-ṭīb*, saffron, pepper, almonds, and sesame oil. Wash the fish, and fry it after dusting it with a bit of flour, and then leave to cool.)[241] Boil the vinegar and throw in the raisins, ground pepper, and *aṭrāf al-ṭīb*. Blanch the almonds and smear them with saffron. Finally, pour [everything] on the fish. Know that fried fish is also used in many other dishes, such as *sikbāj* (vinegar stew), *laymūniyya* (lemon stew),[242] *summāqiyya* (sumac stew), *ṭabāhaja* (fried meat slices),[243] *kuzbariyya* (coriander stew), and others.[244]

---

236 The title of the chapter in *Kanz* is more detailed: 'Chapter on making all kinds of fish dishes.'

237 The title of the recipe has been taken from *Kanz* (89, No. 228).

238 The recipe in *Kanz* states that the tahini should be added to 'the seasonings' (*ḥawā'ij*) rather than 'over a fire', and then brought to a boil.

239 *Kanz,* 89 (No. 229), from which the title has been taken as it is omitted from the manuscript.

240 cf. *Kanz*, 90 (No. 230), where the title is *zabībiyya* ('raisin dish').

241 The beginning is missing from the manuscript and has been taken from *Kanz*.

242 In *Kanz*, there is a fish *laymūniyya* (No. 231) following this recipe.

243 See recipes Nos. 250–1, 255 below.

244 The final sentence is missing from *Kanz*.

129. *Mudaqqaqa*[245]

(You need fresh fish, pepper, sesame oil, dried coriander, a little bit of good oil and one onion. Wash the fish and remove the bones. Finely pound it in a mortar, then crush pepper and dried coriander and add them to the fish, along with a bit of good olive oil.)[246] Pound everything together and shape into ring[s] and discs.[247] Hang the pot over a fire and wait until it heats up and then add the pounded fish. When it is cooked, remove and place an earthenware pan over a fire. Pour in sesame oil and fry the fish in it. Transfer to platters and then pound some pepper, dried coriander and salt. Sprinkle all of them on top, and serve.

130. Recipe for *maḥshī* fish[248]

Take fresh fish, wash it and leave it to dry for an hour. Then, take vinegar, caraway, garlic and coriander, and coat the fish with them. Leave for an hour and then roll [the fish] in flour and fry it in a pan with sesame oil. Take caraway, almonds, and fried onion with garlic and pepper, and dissolve everything in vinegar. When the fish is fried, put it in [the onion and vinegar sauce].[249]

131. Another recipe like it[250]

Take fish, wash it, and coat it with coriander and caraway. Leave aside for a little while. Add flour to it and fry in a pan with olive oil or sesame oil. Take sumac and all of the *maḥshī* fish dressing ingredients, and mix with lemon juice. Make sure that it includes salted lemons. Boil a little water in a pot and then add the mixture to it. It should contain a little garlic, too. Bring to a boil two or three times over a fire. Arrange the [previously fried] fish in a bowl and pour on the *maḥshī* sauce. The base of the sauce consists of

---

245 cf. *Kanz*, 90 (No. 232), where the title is *al-samak al-mudaqqaqa* ('fish *mudaqqaqa*').

246 Most of this section is missing from the manuscript and has been taken from *Kanz*. The clearly defective passage in *Zahr* reads as follows: 'without frying, remove its bones, and pound after having added ground pepper, dried coriander and a little bit of good olive oil.'

247 Interestingly enough, unlike *Kanz* the manuscript omits *mudaqqaqa*, even though it is the name of the dish.

248 cf. *Kanz*, 90–1 (No. 233).

249 The second half of the manuscript is somewhat different in *Kanz*, where the instructions are as follows: 'Pound pepper and *aṭrāf al-ṭīb*, and add to the onion, folding it in. Dissolve tahini in vinegar with saffron, add it to the seasonings, and bring to a boil. When it is cooked, transfer the fish to it.'

250 cf. *Kanz*, 91 (No. 234, 'recipe for another *maḥshī* fish').

carrots, sumac, coriander, thyme, a little garlic, pepper, chopped up salted lemons, and celery.

132. Recipe for fish *mashwī*[251]

Take pepper, cinnamon, caraway, ginger, sumac, dried coriander, thyme, and a little cumin, and pound everything together with a little mint, and strain. Peel and finely pound garlic in a mortar, together with a rock of salt and good olive oil. Add enough of the herbs and spices to form a dough-like paste. Once the paste has been kneaded, add pounded walnuts. Then, take lemon, tahini and good olive oil in the required quantity. Mix everything together and knead with aromatic spices. Take the fish and thoroughly coat the sides of the fish with the paste. Place thick sticks or a thin wooden board at the bottom of an earthenware pan so that it [the fish] does not stick. Then put into the oven, and when the top is cooked, take it out and leave to cool for an hour. Turn the fish over with the help of the wooden board and return to the oven [for further baking] until it is ready.

133. Recipe for fried fish[252]

Take fresh fish, remove its scales and bones. Then cut it open and remove the insides. Wash it very thoroughly and sprinkle with salt. Leave for a good hour, put in a basket and fold it over. Put a tile both underneath and on top of the basket, and leave until all the water has come out [of the fish]. Afterwards, cut it into small pieces and dust with good flour. Place the earthenware pan over a fire and add enough sesame oil or good olive oil, as you wish, for the fish to float in it. Fry very well until there is no moisture left. Then, take grape vinegar, toasted coriander, caraway, *aṭrāf al-ṭīb* and saffron, and stir [everything].[253] Transfer the fried fish in it, making sure it is immersed. Put into vitreous jars or a narrow-mouthed jar smeared with pitch. Pour the vinegar on top and leave until such time as you wish to eat it. It remains unspoiled for days, and some people even travel with it to faraway places without it going off.

---

[251] cf. *Kanz*, 92 (No. 236).

[252] cf. *Kanz*, 93 (No. 237).

[253] *Kanz* adds 'this mixture' (*hādhā 'l-mizāj*).

134. Fish with sumac[254]

There are many ways to make fish with sumac, tahini, dates and raisins. Wash the fish with hot olive oil, then with water. It is said that doing it this way removes the odour. Or, wash it with hot olive oil after washing it with salt. There are those who use both at the same time. Others use salt before and after, and then wash it with water afterwards. Still others fry [the fish] without seasoning it with flour, or who sprinkle it [with flour] after washing so as to drain all the moisture, and then they fry it without flour.

135. Recipe for 'buried' (*madfūn*) mullet (*būrī*)[255]

Take some onions, bake them, chop them up into small pieces and wash in salted water. Fry in good olive oil and then put to one side. Then take saffron, *aṭrāf al-ṭīb*, hazelnuts, ginger, rue, green herbs, and raisins. Put [everything] in wine vinegar, boil, and pour onto the fried fish. Let the fish rest overnight and then eat. It is extremely tasty.

136. *Ṣaḥnāt* (fish paste)[256]

There are many varieties, but we will not mention all of them. The ones that we will mention increase the appetite, strengthen the stomach and loosen the phlegm. Take as many small fish as you like and put them in undiluted wine or lemon juice in order to soften them, and then sieve. Add pounded almonds or walnuts, sumac, good olive oil, good herbs and spices, aromatics, saffron, rose water, as well as salted lemon. If you like, you can add a bit of garlic as well, which makes it fragrant.

137. Fake *ṣaḥnāt*, without fish[257]

(Take)[258] raisins and pound [them], together with good olive oil – eleven *dirhams* of each – and enough vinegar, lemons, cinnamon, mastic, pepper, caraway and *aṭrāf al-ṭīb* to adjust the flavour [of the dish].

---

[254] cf. *Kanz*, 93–94 (No. 238), from which the title has also been taken. However, rather than this survey of cooking sumac fish dishes, *Kanz* comprises one full recipe.

[255] cf. *Kanz*, 99 (No. 254).

[256] It also appears as *ṣaḥnā(t)* or *ṣaḥnā'*; cf. *Kanz*, 275 (Appendix, No. 37). Also see *Wuṣla*, Nos. 8.54, 8.64–5.

[257] cf. *Kanz*, 100 (No. 257).

[258] This is missing from the mss but is found in *Kanz*.

138. Fake *ṣaḥnāt* which is useful for those with excess yellow bile and which revives the stomach[259]

Take sumac, pound with salt and remove the husks [from the berries]. Soak in water and then squeeze [the juice through] a cloth until the essence is extracted. Leave a little of the sumac unsoaked [and add] chopped parsley and rue in equal parts. Rub a bit of salt [into them] so that they wilt and fold into finely ground walnuts which have been toasted until they are swimming in their oil.[260] Pour lime juice and rue juice on the spices with a little bit of ground sumac. Do not use a lot, or it will turn black. Mix everything together well and add ground garlic and dried thyme. Use a lot of both since this is what will bring out the [distinctive] flavour. [Also add] dried coriander and ground caraway (both toasted), pepper, ginger, *aṭrāf al-ṭīb*, salt, and good olive oil. Mix everything in. The consistency should be such that you can put the [paste] on a piece of bread. Cut salted lemon into it. Whenever the quantity of walnuts and tahini is increased, the colour changes. When you ladle it up, add quality olive oil. It will only taste good if you use a lot of olive oil. If you like, you can use hazelnuts instead of walnuts [as this is more beneficial] for melancholic temperaments. If you wish, you can also sprinkle pistachios on top.

139. Recipe for a pure and royal Alexandrian *ṣaḥna* which is made in the present day[261]

The best type [of fish] to use is the *ṣīr*.[262] [Put] ten *raṭls* [of it] in a tub and leave for two or three days, until it has softened. Then, thoroughly knead by hand, and add three-quarters of a *qadaḥ* of salt, and four *qadaḥs* of ground coriander. Mix [everything] with salt, or pound it in [with the other ingredients]. Add one *raṭl* and a quarter of both pepper and clove, one *qadaḥ* and a quarter of Syrian coriander, one quarter of a *qadaḥ* of thyme, seven *ūqiyas* of pounded garlic, three *ūqiyas* of caraway, half a *raṭl* of cinnamon, and half

---

259 cf. *Kanz*, 101 (No. 259); *Wuṣla*, No. 8.54.

260 The Arabic literally reads as 'playing in their oil (*yal'ab fī duhnihi*)'.

261 cf. *Kanz*, 102 (No. 262), where the title also adds that the dish was made 'for kings and leaders (*li 'l-mulūk wa 'l-ru'asā'*)'. *Wuṣla* has two variants of the 'Alexandrian' *ṣaḥna* dish, which are, however, much more compressed: 'Put [the fish] in olive oil, fresh lemon juice, hot spices, and garlic, and it is ready to use' (No. 8.64); 'Add the following to the *ṣaḥna*: sumac, *aṭrāf al-ṭīb*, tahini, finely ground walnuts, and hot spices' (No. 8.65).

262 The word denoted a number of small Nile fish, such as tilapia (*bulṭī*), which were salted and brined. Both *ṣīr* and *ṣaḥna* were a staple in the diet of the common Cairene at the time; Lewicka 2011: 219–23. For more recipes with *ṣīr*, see *Kanz*, 95 (Nos. 242–5), 101 (No. 260).

an *ūqiya* each of ginger, pepper, and pepperwood; half an *ūqiya* of galangal; one *raṭl* and a half of good olive oil; one quarter of an *ūqiya* each of dried mint and dried rue; and one *dirham* of celery [leaves]. Heighten [the taste] with one *qīrāṭ* of musk, dissolved in rose water. Mix everything together well. Transfer to glass jars and add enough olive oil on top in order to cover everything. Whenever the level of olive oil goes down, replenish it.

140. Recipe for another *ṣaḥna*[263]

Take one *qadaḥ* of dried coriander, one *qadaḥ* of caraway, one quarter of a *qadaḥ* of thyme, one quarter of a *qadaḥ* of pennyroyal,[264] one *raṭl* of sumac husks, one *ūqiya* of rolled cinnamon, one *ūqiya* of mastic, a bit of spikenard, and one quarter of an *ūqiya* each of betel leaves, cardamom and cloves. Pound (everything together well)[265] and then put in a sufficient amount of salt. Pound everything together well[266] and then put to one side. [Then,] chop and pound mint, rue and celery. Take five *raṭls* of almond kernels and tart wine vinegar. Leave for a day and a night, or two days, and then macerate well. Add to the pounded spices and then add good olive oil and tahini, after which it is ready for use.

141. Recipe for *kunāfa*[267]

Cut the *kunāfa*[268] and throw into a brass pan with four *ūqiyas* of sesame oil. Also add one *raṭl* of coarsely ground sugar, and stir it in until it is fully dissolved in the sesame oil.[269] Add four *ūqiyas* of bee honey, and stir. Then add four *ūqiyas* of hazelnuts.

---

[263] cf. *Kanz*, 103 (No. 264).

[264] The Arabic text has the clearly erroneous *qulayya*, instead of *fulayya*, which is also the form in *Kanz*.

[265] The defective text was corrected with *Kanz*.

[266] The addition of this instruction here, rather than earlier on in the recipe, is clearly a mistake by the copyist.

[267] This is a compressed version of a recipe found in *Kanz* (111–2, No. 290) and *Wuṣla* (No. 7.24), where it is called *Akhmīmiyya*, i.e. from the Upper-Egyptian town of Akhmim. Unlike in *Kanz*, there is no chapter break for the sweet recipes that follow. However, the recipe has been kept here, rather than moving it to the next chapter where it would precede the preface.

[268] The reference is somewhat misleading as it actually refers to previously prepared *kunāfa* sheets.

[269] The Arabic 'which is a sign that it is fried' has been omitted for the sake of readability.

NINE

Sweets[270]

THE AMOUNT OF FAT one needs with flour [to make sweets] is well known. For instance, [in some cases] it is when flour and fat start sticking together when pressed by hand. [In others,] it is when the fat is released. These are all well known [among cooks].

142. Recipe for a Persian sweet[271]

For each *raṭl* (of flour)[272] take one *raṭl* of sheep's tail fat or sesame oil. (Thoroughly toast the flour)[273] until it changes colour, and pour on the fat or oil. Then take two *raṭls* of bee honey for each *raṭl* of flour, and add one *dirham* of saffron and rose water. Heat up the honey and put to one side on a live-coal fire so that it remains hot. Toast the flour over a low fire until it turns amber.[274] You can check if it is ready by taking a bit of the flour and mixing it with the honey; if it splashes,[275] then it is done. Remove the embers from underneath [the pot], pour the honey in and fold it in until everything is mixed. Remove [the pot] from the fire and cover with a lid. [Before serving], sprinkle on pistachios and coarsely ground sugar.

---

270 In *Kanz* (103), the chapter is called 'On Types of Sweets'. It omits the prefatory comments here, which are an addition by Ibn Mubārak Shāh.

271 cf. *Kanz*, 115 (No. 303); *Wuṣla*, No. 7.72 (which has more extensive final instructions). The Arabic *ʿajamiyya* is derived from *ʿajam*, which means 'foreign' (as in non-Arabic speaker) but was traditionally used for Persians (though in Andalusi Arabic it referred to the Romance language). The recipe is similar to those for *khabīṣ* (see No. 147). The dish has survived in modern Egypt, and denotes 'a filling of clarified butter, honey and sesame used in pastries etc.' (Hinds & Badawi 1987: 564).

272 This was missing from the mss and has been added from *Kanz*.

273 This was added from *Kanz*.

274 *aṣfar*, 'yellow'.

275 The author uses the Egyptian colloquial *ṭashṭasha* (Hinds & Badawi 1987: 539–40).

143. Recipe for Turkish *qāwūt*[276]

Take sieved wheat and wash it. Then, boil[277] and leave to dry overnight. Take it to the *qaḍāma* (roasted and salted chickpeas)[278] maker, [and have] him toast [the flour] in the way of *qaḍāma*, over a gentle fire. Grind the wheat to a medium-coarse flour. For each *raṭl* of flour, take four *ūqiyas* of clarified butter and sesame oil, and four *ūqiyas* of bee honey. Dissolve the clarified butter with sesame oil, and rub the flour with the mixture. Afterwards, dissolve the honey with saffron and use it to cover the rubbed flour, together with peeled pistachios, almonds and hazelnuts – one *ūqiya* of each – as well as one *ūqiya* of poppy seeds and one of rose water. Mix everything together in a clean knapsack.

144. Recipe for peasant *qāwūt*[279]

Take one *raṭl* of flour thoroughly toasted in one quarter of an *ūqiya* of clarified butter. Fold in one quarter of a *raṭl* of saffron-dyed honey, one *ūqiya* of rose water, one *ūqiya* of hazelnuts, one *ūqiya* of poppy seeds, and three *ūqiyas* of coarsely ground sugar. Do not remove until it has cooled down. Put in boxes or on trays.

145. Recipe for a gourd dish (*qarʿiyya*)[280]

Take a green sweet gourd, remove the outer peel and continue to pare until the white core becomes visible.[281] For each *raṭl* of peeled gourd, [take] nine *ūqiyas* of sugar and half a *raṭl* of honey. Put the gourd in a copper pot, together with one half each of the honey and rose-water syrup. Place over a gentle fire and fold over with a wooden pestle. If it becomes dry, add [some more of the liquid] bit by bit, until it obtains [the consistency of] date paste. Then sprinkle on two *ūqiyas* of pistachios and finely ground musk-scented sugar. Add

---

276 cf. *Kanz*, 116 (No. 304). *Wuṣla* also has a *qāwūt* dish (No. 7.94) but it is quite different from the one here, not least in the fact that it does not give any measures for the ingredients.

277 *Kanz* specifies that it should be a quarter boiled (*yuṣlaq rubʿ silqihā*).

278 For centuries, this has been a Damascene speciality: Grehan 2007: 108. Toasted chickpeas are also a popular snack today in Turkey, where it is known as *leblebi* (not to be confused with the homonymous Tunisian chickpea soup).

279 cf. *Kanz*, 117 (No. 307).

280 cf. *Kanz*, 118 (No. 312).

281 The Arabic text has the nonsensical 'until the white [core] does not become visible'. As a result, the text has been amended in line with a variation in *Kanz* (394, note No. 4098).

rose water and remove [from the fire]. If the *qar'iyya* is of the *suyūr*[282] type, immediately put it on a slab to cool down when you remove it [from the fire].

146. Recipe for a gourd dish (*qar'iyya*), which has moistening and dissolving properties[283]

Take poppy seeds, pound them and milk them by means of water and a cloth. Take the extract and pour it over sugar and dissolve it without [using] eggs. Take a green sweet gourd, peel it and then remove the white core and pare, as usual. Then, take almonds; peel, ground and milk them. Take the extract and dissolve starch in it; for each *raṭl* of sugar, take one *ūqiya* and a half of starch. Take the pared gourd and boil it with three *ūqiyas* of honey. Remove [from the fire] and throw in half of the rose-water syrup. Then, add the starch, stir and mix in sesame oil. Pour in [the remaining rose-water syrup] bit by bit, followed by the boiled gourd. Stir and when it is ready, remove [from the fire].

147. Recipe for a cold *khabīṣ*[284]

Take one *raṭl* and a half of pounded peeled almonds, strained through a fine-mesh sieve. Then take two *raṭls* and a half of ground *ṭabarzad* sugar. Strain and sieve approximately one quarter of a *raṭl* of sugar. Mix the almonds in with the sugar and pour over one quarter of a *raṭl* of almond oil, one quarter of a *raṭl* of rose water, and one *dāniq* of cassia. Mix everything together, and knead vigorously until it becomes like a *khabīṣ*. Then, spread out on a marble slab, sprinkle sugar on top, and serve.

148. Recipe for a sweet called *kāhīn*[285]

Take egg-whites – for each one, two *dirhams* of starch. Finely crush the starch and beat with the egg-whites, mixing everything well. (Throw into

---

[282] A full recipe for this kind of dish – named after the fact that the gourd is in strips (*suyūr*) – is found in *Kanz* (118–9, No. 313), from which the last instruction is also taken.

[283] cf. *Kanz*, 119 (No. 314).

[284] cf. *Kanz*, 121 (No. 319). This was a very popular pudding, with a large number of recipes across the cookery books: al-Baghdādī 1964: 72, 73–4 (trans., 93, 95–7; a total of seven recipes); *Waṣf*, 412–15; *Andalusian*, fol. 27r.–v.; *Taṣānīf al-aṭ'ima*, fols. 81v.–82r. 83v., 84r., 86v. (nine recipes). Ibn Buṭlān (1990: 98–9/trans., 198–9) and Ibn Jazla (fol. 80r.–v.) considered it very nutritional, but slow to digest, and recommend making it with wheat flour, honey, oil or another fat.

[285] cf. *Kanz*, 121 (No. 320).

an earthenware pan and fry [after having shaped them into] discs),[286] and then put in the rose-water syrup. This is delicious and tasty.

149. Recipe for a *jamāliya*[287]

Take some butter and throw into a brass pot [and fry] until it dissolves. Then add pitted *ʿajwa* dates[288] [and continue frying] until they have dissolved and blended with the butter. Afterwards, throw in crumbs from bread made with white finely milled sieved flour and stir as if it were a pudding (*ḥalāwa*). Sprinkle pounded sugar and pistachios on top, stir and remove from the fire. It is tasty.

150. Recipe to make the best Cairene sweet (*Qāhiriyya*)[289]

Take one *raṭl* of sugar, one quarter of a *raṭl* of almonds, and one quarter of a *raṭl* of finely milled sieved flour. Finely pound the sugar in a mortar and sieve the flour until it becomes like semolina. Take blanched almonds, peel and pound them in the mortar as well, and sieve. Repeat the pounding and sieving of the rough [almonds]. Then mix everything together and knead with a quantity of four *ūqiyas* of sesame oil. Afterwards, mix with water and knead until it (*sc.* the consistency) resembles *kaʿk* dough. Then, shape the dough into *Qāhiriyya* rings, which are like *kaʿk* ones.[290] Then, sprinkle flour on a wooden board and place the rings on it. Leave them exposed to the air. If you have made them in the afternoon, leave them to dry until the second day in the morning. In the morning, take a bowl [and fill it with] one *raṭl* and a half of good yeast and beat it vigorously with your hand, as you do

---

286 The section enclosed in round brackets was missing from the mss., and has been taken from *Kanz*.

287 cf. *Kanz*, 121 (No. 321).

288 This variety of dates from Medina was called *umm al-tamr* ('the mother of all dates'), and it is said that the Prophet recommended eating seven of them every day in the morning in order to ward off the effects of poison and other ills. Mcauliffe 2001–6: I, 495.

289 cf. *Kanz*, 122 (No. 322). According to Perry ('"A thousand and one fritters": the food of the *Arabian Nights*', in Rodinson et al. 2001: 493), the *Qāhiriyya* was a *ṣābūniyya* (see note to Recipe No. 157), dipped in batter and fried.

290 See above, recipe No. 5.

for *zulābiyya*[291] dough. Then put in two egg whites[292] and beat everything together until you get a *zulābiyya* dough. At this point add musk, rose water and camphor, as much as you like, and knead it in with the sugar. Then, put the bowl in your right hand and put an earthenware pan on the fire. Put a lot of sesame oil in it until the rings float in it. Boil the sesame oil and put some good honey in a bowl in your left hand. Take the rings that have dried, one by one, with an iron skewer and cover them with the leavened dough that is in the bowl and transfer them to the pan. Proceed in the same way with all of them until all [the rings] are done. Then transfer them one by one to the bowl with the honey. Boil all of them in the honey and then put in bowls. Sprinkle musk and rose water on top, as much as is necessary. Also pound pistachios and sprinkle them on top. This is the recipe for a *Qāhiriyya*, and Allah knows best.[293] There are those who boil the honey, remove the scum,[294] and then roll it into *kunāfa* sheets with sesame oil in a pan, turning them over in the honey when it simmers down. Then they serve it.

151. Stale bread[295]

This is included with the sweet *harīsas* and other things like it.

291 (also *zalābiyya*). These are fried fritters in various shapes (fingers, rings), sometimes added with honey and almonds, or with milk and clarified butter poured on. It was made in a special good-quality copper pan (*Kanz*, 141, No. 377) and often sold at markets by dedicated *zulābiyya* makers, known as *zulbāniyyūn*. It is still very popular today and found all over the Middle East as well as South Asia (e.g. Bangladesh), and comes in the shape of the American crullers, funnel cake or doughnuts, all of which tend to be soaked in syrup. It is a popular treat for different religious communities and, depending on the region, is made during Ramadan, Christmas and Hanaka (Yemen). Al-Warrāq devoted an entire chapter (No. 100) to recipes (1987: 267–70/trans., 413–7). Also see *Andalusian*, fol. 69v.; *Wuṣla*, No. 7.11, 7.74; *Taṣānīf al-aṭʿima*, fol. 84r.–v.; Lewicka 2011: 309 *et passim*. Medicinally, al-Ghassānī (2000: 150) stated that *zulābiyya* were lighter than other sweets like *lawzīnaj* (marzipan) and *qatāʾif* (see recipe No. 321) and easily digestible. According to al-Rāzī (2000: 3018), the sweet generates thick humours, whereas Ibn Jazla warned about it causing moistness in the lungs and blockages in the liver. The latter (fol. 114v.) also included a recipe for *zulābiyya* stuffed with almonds and sugar (cf. *Wuṣla*, 7.74).

292 *Kanz* also requires two *dirhams* of natron.

293 The recipe in *Kanz* ends here.

294 The author uses the dialectal *rīm*, rather than the classical Arabic *raghwa*; Hinds & Badawi 1986: 361.

295 The Arabic *bāyit* (stale) is commonly associated with the Egyptian dialect.

152. Recipe for a type of Persian confection[296]

[Take] finely milled sieved flour, bee honey, sesame oil, saffron, musk and rose water. Toast the flour until it turns brown, but not burnt. Put the honey in an earthenware pan and bring to a boil, [gradually] adding the flour to it. Stir and pour in the sesame oil, musk and rose water. Sprinkle in the sesame oil little by little until everything is done. Transfer to platters and add a bit of musk and rose water.

153. Recipe for a cooked *kunāfa*[297]

For each *raṭl* of *kunāfa* take half a *raṭl* of sesame oil. Mix together in a brass pot and heat it over a fire until it is boiling. Take one *raṭl* of *kunāfa*, cut it up like noodles,[298] throw in sesame oil, and bring to a boil. Add half a *raṭl* of ground white sugar and stir until it has been dissolved. Add one *raṭl* of honey and stir until the oil rises. [Continue] stirring until it looks right. Make sure you have some blanched almonds or pistachios and colour them with saffron. Fold them into the *kunāfa* and stir well. Add musk and rose water while it is on the fire. Then, ladle up and transfer [to a container]. It will remain for a year without going bad.

154. Recipe for a date (*ʿajwa*) confection[299]

Render sheep's tail fat, and remove the clarified fat. Take dates, remove the stones and add them to the tail fat. Cook everything over a fire until it becomes like a confection. Blanch almonds and dye them with saffron. Also add a little bit of poppy seeds. Stir until it looks ready and remove [from the fire]. Spread on plates and add pistachios, white sugar, musk, and rose water.

155. Recipe for a confection made from chate melon[300]

Peel and sun-dry [the melon] until it dries out, turns brown, and [the pulp] sticks together. Then take rose-water syrup and put it over a fire. Remove

---

296 cf. *Kanz*, 124 (No. 327). The result may be likened to the Iranian *sōhān* (a saffron brittle candy), albeit without the pistachios, which, however, are required for the similar 'Persian sweet' (No. 142).

297 cf. *Kanz*, 126–127 (No. 333).

298 *rishta*; see note to Recipe No. 75.

299 cf. *Kanz*, 127 (No. 334).

300 cf. *Kanz*, 127–28 (No. 336). In contemporary Egypt, *biṭṭīkh ʿabdalī* (or ʿAbdallāwī) denotes a hairy cucumber melon (*Cucumis melo var. chate*). It takes its name from a Governor of Egypt, ʿAbd Allāh Ibn Ṭāhir, who is credited with importing the fruit from Khorasan in 825

the foam and add the melon to it. Stir[301] with a paddle in a delicate brass pan until it becomes like *musayyar*.[302] Add pistachios and transfer to a slab. Spread out in discs in the way of *ʿaqīd* (brittle candy),[303] and cut into triangles. Put them in a box, alternating sugar and triangles. Flavour with rose water and musk before placing in the box. This is good, tasty and beneficial for illnesses caused by [imbalances in] black bile.

156. Recipe for a confection made with *malban* [304]

Take *malban* and fry in fresh sesame oil. Add ground sugar and if it becomes like a *ṣābūniyya*,[305] leave [aside] and eat it [when you like].[306]

157. Recipe for a confection made with *ʿajwa* dates[307]

Thoroughly render sheep's tail fat in a brass pot with a little bit of sesame oil, and transfer to a jar. Take bee honey[308] and add it to the cauldron. Then remove the stones from good quality *ʿajwa* dates and pound them finely in a mortar with a little Syrian rose water. Then, throw in some honey after boiling it with egg-white and skimming the froth. Boil until such time as it gains in consistency and then add saffron-dyed blanched almonds. Stir

---

CE; Lewicka 2011: 245 (note No. 361); Watson 1983: 89; Hinds & Badawi 1986: 563. Also see note on *ʿajjūr* below.

301 The Arabic text is clearly corrupted as it refers to the contents being 'dried with the stirrer'.

302 This refers to a recipe in *Kanz* (108, No. 280) for a 'gourd *musayyar*', which is a sliced gourd cooked with starch and rose-water syrup into a thick porridge or paste. Its name is somewhat mysterious since the word literally means 'controlled, directed.'

303 See recipes Nos. 162–4.

304 A jelly-like sweet made from molasses thickened with starch. It is more commonly known in English as 'Turkish delight', contemporary variations of which are known as *malban* in Egypt and Lebanon. Elsewhere, it is referred to as *ḥulqūm* ('throat') or *rāḥat al-ḥulqūm* ('relief of the throat'), from which the Turkish *lokum* was derived. It is said to have been an Ottoman invention.

305 This was a sweet consisting of dough made with sugar, sesame oil, rose-water syrup, honey and starch. It probably gets its name from the texture which is similar to that of soap, and was sometimes shaped into bars, according to Perry (*Wuṣla*, 294). It was also used in other sweets as a filling (*Wuṣla*, Nos. 7.13–5) or topping (No. 7.52). For *ṣābūniyya* recipes, see al-Baghdādī 1964: 75 (trans., 99); *Waṣf*, 417, 456; *Wuṣla*, Nos. 7.58, 7.60; *Kanz*, 115 (No. 302); *Taṣānīf al-aṭʿima*, fol. 81r. According to the Egyptian author Ibn al-Ukhuwwa (d. 1338), 'for every ten *raṭls* of sugar, it should contain two *raṭls* of cornstarch, two *raṭls* of unripe dates and a good-quality aromatic' (1937: 114).

306 The recipe in *Kanz* adds that it is 'extremely tasty' (*fa-innahu ladhīdh ilā ghāya*).

307 cf. *Kanz*, 128 (No. 338, 'Recipe for another confection').

308 *Kanz* also adds rose-water syrup.

everything with the paddle and sprinkle on the rendered sheep's tail fat until the oil splits. Remove [from the fire] and add aromatics, as well as some poppy seeds, almonds, and musk-infused rose water. When you ladle it onto plates, put some toasted hazelnuts on top, together with pistachios and coarsely ground white sugar, before eating. Those who are poor can make it with sugar molasses[309] or sugar cane honey [*sc.* syrup].

158. Recipe for honeyed fresh dates[310]

Take fresh dates that have [just] been harvested, and spread them outside in the shade for two days. Then, remove their stones from underneath by means of a needle and replace each with a peeled almond.[311] For each ten *raṭls* [of dates] take one *raṭl* of bee honey with vinegar and one *ūqiya* of rose water, and put over a fire. When it is boiling, remove the froth, and colour with half a *dirham* of saffron before throwing in the dates. When [the pot] is boiling [again] slightly stir and let the honey be absorbed. Then remove from the fire and spread on a heath tray. When the heat has died down, sprinkle some finely ground sugar on top. Those who like to enhance its hotness[312] can also add musk, spikenard and a bit of aromatics. Those who wish to enhance its coldness should add camphor and poppy seeds. Transfer to glass jars and only use in cold weather, or in the date season.

159. Fresh dates with almonds[313]

This is made by drying [fresh dates] in the sun for a little while, and then removing the stones and filling them with almonds. Then, layer them in a large glass jar. Pour on some bee honey with the foam skimmed off. You should monitor it every week so as to make sure that the dates have not released any liquid, which sours the dish.

---

309 *quṭāra*; Diem 1994: 175.

310 cf. *Kanz*, 129 (No. 340); *Waṣf*, 432; *Wuṣla*, No. 7.87.

311 *Kanz* adds that they should be 'sweet almonds of superior quality'.

312 This does not refer to the temperature of the dish, but to its potential humoral properties.

313 cf. *Kanz*, 129 (No. 341, 'Recipe for a fresh date preserve'), which is more expansive.

160. Dried dates with almonds[314]

These [are made by] boiling vinegar and honey together.[315] Skim the foam [from the liquid] and add the dried dates. Immediately [after boiling] transfer them to a wide-mouthed jar after colouring them with saffron and adding musk, rose water and camphor. It should not be too hot; rather, you should leave the container open so that it can fully cool down, and it will have a good consistency. It is extremely delicious.

161. Another confection with dried dates[316]

Remove the stones from the dates and then put them in a brass pot. Add some water and boil until they are done. Strain through a fine-mesh sieve and then return to the pot. Heat over a fire until [the liquid] thickens. If you want to use it to make a confection then add bee honey, clarified butter and ground toasted hazelnuts. Stir and remove [from the fire]. Flavour with musk, rose water. Then add saffron-dyed blanched almonds. This is extremely good, Allah willing!

162. Oxymel (*sakanjabīn*) *ʿaqīd* (brittle candy)[317]

This is one of the finest sweets to have with wine for those with hot temperaments. The recipe is as follows: thicken rose-water syrup and for each *raṭl* add three *ūqiyas* of thick clear pure sour vinegar.[318] Do not remove [from the fire] until it becomes solid enough to be broken. Then, spread out on marble after rubbing it with oil, and then eat.

---

[314] cf. *Kanz*, 129–30 (No. 342).

[315] The recipe in *Kanz* provides additional prior instructions: 'Wash dried Iraqi dates in hot water, take out their stones and replace them with pistachios or blanched almonds.'

[316] cf. *Kanz*, 130 (No. 344, 'Recipe for a date confection').

[317] cf. *Kanz*, 132 (No. 348, 'Recipe for a date confection'). This is part of a chapter (No. 11) devoted to 'stomachics (*juwārishnāt*), electuaries (*maʿājin*) and beverages (*ashriba*) which are served before and after meals'. Oxymel is a medicinal drink consisting of vinegar and honey as a base, often with other ingredients. It was sometimes used as an expectorant, but al-Kindī also included it as an ointment to cure baldness. The Arabic word (also *sikanjabīn*) is a borrowing from the Persian *sikangubīn* (also *sakanjabīn*, *siganjabīn*, *sirkangubīn*; from *sik/sirkā* 'vinegar' and *ang/jubīn*, 'honey'). It became a regular item in European medicine for many centuries and was used to administer medicinal ingredients that tasted badly. See Levey & al-Khaledy 1967: 108, 172; *Kanz*, Nos. 363–364; Colin & Renaud 1934: 173 (No. 400); Marín & Waines 1995.

[318] Nasrallah [al-Warrāq 2007]: 577.

163. Another similar recipe[319]

Peel a citron, cut it into triangles, and fry in sesame oil. Then, take it out. Boil honey and rose-water syrup, and remove the froth. Add the fried citron to it and leave until it thickens up and has absorbed the rose-water syrup. Put some *aṭrāf al-ṭīb* on it, together with saffron, ground Khmer agarwood, musk, and rose water. Then, remove [from the fire] and arrange on plates. Sprinkle on sugar, and serve.

164. Recipe for tamarind *ʿaqīd*[320]

Take one *ūqiya* of tamarind and soak in water. Extract the juice and put it in a pot over a low fire, that is to say, an ember fire. Stir until it acquires the consistency of *ʿaqīd*, i.e. it can be broken up. Then, transfer to a mortar rubbed with almond oil.

165. Verjuice syrup with mint[321]

Take rose-water syrup after dissolving and purifying it. Extract the juice from sour grapes – four *ūqiyas* for each *raṭl* [of syrup]. Then, take a bunch of fresh mint and stir the rose-water syrup with it while it is on the fire. If you like you can throw it into the pot until its flavour is released. Remove [from the fire] and strain into a container.

TEN

On Beverages Like *Fuqqāʿ* and *Sūbiyya*

319 cf. *Kanz*, 134 (No. 356, 'Recipe for making [a] citron confection').

320 cf. *Kanz*, 138 (No. 371).

321 cf. *Kanz*, 137 (No. 365).

166. Recipe for making special *fuqqā*ʿ[322]
Dissolve half a *raṭl* of sugar in five *raṭls* of water. Add one *ūqiya* of pomegranate seeds and three *ūqiyas* of hot bread. Macerate everything well, and squeeze [the juice of] one lime into it. Then strain and add one *dirham* of spices, most of it nutmeg, and a piece of musk.[323] Fill jars [with the liquid] and put them in cold water for a day.[324]

167. A type of *fuqqā*ʿ that is easy to use and cheap[325]
Soak bread from early morning until the evening and then strain off the liquid. Add one *ūqiya* of pomegranate seeds for each *raṭl* of water, or lemon juice, and one and a half *ūqiyas* of sugar, *aṭrāf al-ṭīb*, pepper, and rue. Put in jars, arrange and transfer.

168. Recipe for another *fuqqā*ʿ[326]
Macerate flatbread in water from morning until noon, and then strain. Soak pomegranate seeds, or lemon juice, in [the strained liquid], [and leave] until the afternoon prayer. Then, add sugar and rue, and season with a bit of musk. Put in jars and close the tops. Leave them upside down in a large bowl, and sprinkle water on top. It can be drunk the next morning.

169. Recipe for a *sūbiya* made from rice, which is useful against dyspepsia, indigestion and sweetens the breath[327]
Take rice and boil it well. Push it through a sieve and then take ʿ*ajwa* dates and soak them in four times the volume of water. Leave them overnight,

---

322 cf. *Kanz*, 147 (No. 392).

323 There were *fuqqā*ʿ-specific spices, which are mentioned in *Kanz* (No. 412): cardamom, black pepper, betel leaves and spikenard. Interestingly enough, none of the recipes here contains these ingredients. Ibn al-Bayṭār (1992: III, 225–6/trans., III, 38–9) reports that it was usually made with barley, spikenard, cloves, rue and celery, but this engenders bad humours and constipation, even if it is useful against leprosy. All *fuqqā*ʿ should be drunk on an empty stomach, before the meal, never afterwards, because it corrupts food. According to al-Rāzī (1881: 20), *fuqqā*ʿ was useful against stomach inflammations and extreme thirst caused by a hangover. For recipes in other cookery books see: al-Warrāq 1987: 297–301 (trans., 453–9); *Waṣf*, 440. It also occurs as an ingredient in some recipes (*Wuṣla*, Nos. 2.1, 2.4–5).

324 According to the recipe in *Kanz*, it should be left 'a day and a night, until it is done, and then drunk.'

325 cf. *Kanz*, 155 (No. 413).

326 cf. *Kanz*, 155 (No. 414).

327 cf. *Kanz*, 160 (No. 429). Another recipe in *Kanz* (No. 430) recommends serving *sūbiyya* with ice to enhance the flavour.

boil them, and then strain. Dissolve strained rice into it. This thickens the liquid. Then, throw in all of the *aṭrāf al-ṭīb* and orange peels, followed by ginger, dried rue, and mint. Ferment [all of it] in a jar, and then drink. It is highly beneficial and tasty.

170. Another one[328]

Take one *qadaḥ* of high-quality finely milled sieved flour and thicken it to the consistency of *ʿaṣīda*, without salt. Remove from the fire and let it cool down in a large bowl. Then heat up some water and beat the *ʿaṣīda* into a bowl until the consistency becomes like that of *sawīq* (grain gruel).[329] Then take a sufficient quantity of *aṭrāf al-ṭīb*, which consists of spikenard, betel (leaves), clove sticks,[330] cardamom, nutmeg, mace, pepper, ginger and rose buds. Pound everything and throw it into what you have made. For each *raṭl* of flour, take two *ūqiyas* of *aṭrāf al-ṭīb*, and pound together with two *ūqiyas* of mint. Take a bunch of rue, pound half of it and leave the other half whole. Add all of it to the *sūbiya*. Also pour in two and a half *raṭls* of bee honey, or good sugar molasses, and transfer to a clean jar, and dissolve half a *dirham* of saffron in it. Then, put everything in a big jar that does not leak. Use [at need].[331]

171. Macerated apricots[332]

Squeeze on sour pomegranate juice and sweeten with sugar and water, added with rose water and Egyptian lotus water, and other beneficial things

---

328 cf. *Kanz*, 162 (No. 434).

329 This pre-Islamic drink was particularly enjoyed as a refreshment for travellers, as evidenced in al-Warrāq's cookbook (1987: 37–8/trans., 118–9). Physicians, however, were less favourable towards it since it was said to be lacking in nutrition, though Ibn Sīnā said it was beneficial for chest and lung afflictions (1999: I, 604). According to Ibn Zuhr (1992: 11/trans., 47), it suppresses bilious humours and is particularly good for people suffering from fevers. Al-Rāzī (1887: 10) stated that *sawīq* made from barley is colder than that of wheat and generates more wind; however, both are bloating because they slow down digestion Also see Lewicka 2011: 68, note No. 5; Nasrallah [al-Warrāq 2007]: 126–7, 555; Waines 2010: 83–4; al-Isrā'īlī 1992: 220; Dozy 1877–81: I, 706.

330 This does not refer to cloves proper, but to *qirfat al-qaranful* ('clove bark'), a thick bark which looks like cinnamon, but tastes like cloves. According to Ibn Jazla (fol. 170v.), it is the bark of the clove tree mixed with agarwood strips, sweeter than clove, but not as sweet as cassia.

331 The *Kanz* recipe states that it should be left overnight before using and ends with: 'Know this and rely on it.'

332 cf. *Kanz*, 162 (No. 435), where it is actually the title of a new chapter (No. 13), containing various apricot preserves (six in total), with the first one being 'almond apricots' (*mishmish lawzī*). The recipe is also more expansive. Today, the Arabic *naqūʿ* (from the verb *naqaʿ*, 'to

172. Medicine for nausea[333]

Take raisins, pomegranate seeds and tamarind, and remove the seeds.[334] Pound everything in a mortar, together with mint, pepper and cinnamon. Add wine vinegar and saffron. If you want it to be special, leave out the wine vinegar, and then put over a fire.[335] As it is boiling, stir with the root of sweet basil, and flavour with agarwood, ambergris,[336] musk, and rose water. Remove [from the fire] after it is parboiled, and transfer to a jar, and use at the required time.

Tip: If you don't want to pound mustard seeds, or think it is too difficult, add cotton, and then they can be pounded easily and quickly, Allah willing.[337]

---

soak') still denotes dried apricots (Wehr 1976: 1165).

333 cf. *Kanz*, 165 (No. 441). In *Kanz*, this recipe is put in a new chapter (No. 14), 'On recipes for making nausea medicines' (*fī ṣifat ʿamal adwiyat al-qaraf*), which contains a total of 26 compounds to counteract nausea.

334 One has to assume that this only applies to the raisins and tamarind, as it is only the seeds of the pomegranates that are used in the recipe.

335 This instruction does not appear in *Kanz*.

336 *ʿanbar*; also known as grey ambergris, it is the secretion of the sperm whale's gall bladder. It is grey and becomes black over time. Also known as amber, it should not be confused with yellow amber, which is fossilized tree resin. Ambergris was mainly used in perfumes and medicines. One of the earliest references to the importation of ambergris occurs in the ninth-century travel book *Akhbār al-Sīn wa 'l-Hind* ('News from China and the Hind') where people of an island called Lanjabālūs in the Sea of Harkand (Bay of Bengal) traded ambergris for iron with Arab merchants (Mackintosh-Smith & Montgomery 2014: 5–6). According to Ibn al-Bayṭār (1992: III, 183–4 (trans., II, 469–71)), adding ambergris to wine has an immediate intoxicating effect. Also see Ibn Sīnā 1999: I: 613–14 (trans., 331); Ibn Māsawayh 1937: 11–12; Lev & Amar 2008: 331–3; *EI*², s.v. 'ʿanbar' (J. Ruska/M. Plessner).

337 This addendum is missing from *Kanz*, where it appears in a recipe for mustard (173, No. 468), which specifies that it is a 'piece (*qitʿa*)' of cotton.

ELEVEN

[On Making Mustard][338]

173. Mustard recipe[339]

Take mustard [seeds] and sieve them with a *ḥuwwārā*[340] sieve and knead in a kneading bowl. The dough should be dry and then softened little by little. Add hot water and take your time to knead [the dough] very well with the palm of your hand until foam like soap forms on top. Throw on a bit of rock salt and a little vinegar. Then, pour on cold water while putting your hand into the bowl, and gently swirl your fingers around the inside, as the water is poured inside. Made sure that it is very cold. Then take [the dough] out, and leave for an hour. Foam and bubbles will rise. Gradually sprinkle on water until the bubbles die down. Then, take handfuls of water from the top and put it in a jar until it resembles hailstones when you take it out. If you like, put in sugar, raisins or honey.[341] Alternatively, just leave it alone. This is one type [of mustard recipe]. Some people make it with almond paste, rock salt and vinegar. There are many other types which I have left out because they are labour intensive or expensive to make. I have collected them only for the handmaidens in my house, adapted to our meagre income.

---

338 The recipe follows on from the preceding ones without a break. However, it is given its own chapter here, analogous to *Kanz,* where the recipe below is the last in a chapter (No. 15), entitled 'On making mild, hot and pungent mustard' (*fī 'amal al-khardal al-laṭīf wa 'l-ḥārr wa 'l-ḥirrīf*).

339 cf. *Kanz*, 179 (No. 484).

340 It was considered the finest white bread flour and a Syrian speciality according to the tenth-century traveller al-Muqaddasī (1877: 151, 164). Also see Mielck 1913: 38–9, 75–6 (on *ḥuwwārā* bread). Ibn Jazla (fol. 78v.) described *ḥuwwārā* bread as being in between *samīdh* and *khushkār* (coarsely milled unsifted wheat flour). According to Nasrallah ([al-Warrāq 2007]: 203, 561, 807), it is 'fine bran-free wheat flour made from red wheat. In comparison with *samīdh,* it is higher in gluten and lower in starch content, which makes it more suitable for making breads chewy in texture.' The Persian borrowing *khushkār* (*khushk*, 'dry' and *ārd,* 'flour meal') also means 'fried egg' in the language. Steingass 1892: 462; Mielck, ibid.: 78; Dozy 1877–81: I, 373; Serrano et al. 2006: 298.

341 The recipe in *Kanz* ends here.

TWELVE

[Sauces][342]

174. Recipe for a sauce[343]

There are many types of them, and we have simplified and summarised them. Take blanched walnut kernels and mash them in a mortar with lemon juice, until [its consistency] resembles unguent. Add ground ginger and nutmeg and also pound them well in the mortar, until you obtain an unguent-like consistency. If it is made for the common man, add as much sugar as you like. [Conversely,] if it's made for a Turk, then add garlic steeped in olive oil.

175. Sauce which cools inflammation of the stomach[344]

It strengthens the stomach and aids digestion, strengthens the bowels, suppresses viscous phlegm in the stomach, purifies the blood and heats it. It soothes [the blood] when it is boiling, refines its coarseness, suppresses the creation of black bile, sweetens the breath, and improves the complexion.

Take half a *raṭl* of lemon balm, one *raṭl* of parsley leaves without the stems, (pound each of them)[345] separately, and sprinkle on good-quality olive oil, as well as a little bit of salt.[346]

176. Sauce recipe[347]

Take as much mustard (seeds) as you like and pour on enough water to cover them. Leave overnight and then remove the water. Wash [the seeds] three times and then pound half of them, straining off the froth until it is all gone,

[342] The chapter break and title have been introduced by analogy with *Kanz* (Chap. No. 16).

[343] This is a highly abridged version of the third recipe of the chapter in *Kanz* (180, No. 488).

[344] cf. *Kanz*, 182 (No. 492).

[345] The mss is clearly defective here and the missing information was added from *Kanz*.

[346] The recipe in *Kanz* has the following: 'Pound them separately in a stone mortar with a wooden pestle, and then weigh them. Mix together and add enough salt so as to make its flavour become apparent.'

[347] cf. *Kanz*, 178–9 (No. 483), where it is said to be 'for both sedentary people and travellers' (*li 'l-haḍar wa 'l-safar*). It appears in the section on mustards (Chap. 15), rather than sauces (Chap. 16).

and throw in a bit of salt. Dry the other half until it is completely dry and no moisture remains. Then, add to the froth that you have removed [from the other half], and knead together, until you are left with a ball. Dry it and when it is dry, remove. If you like, you can eat it after adding vinegar, sugar, or pounded almonds. This makes it whiter in colour, and sweeter.

177. Another sauce recipe[348]

[Take] sumac, dried coriander, caraway, toasted hazelnuts, pepper, rolled cinnamon, thyme, good quality olive oil, tahini, parsley, garlic, lemon, rose-buds,[349] and *aṭrāf al-ṭīb*. Pound everything together and soak in olive oil, tahini, and lemon. Leave to ferment, and eat.[350] There are those who make it with jujubes, and others, with many other things, each to fit his financial status. Allah grants success!

THIRTEEN

On Dairy Dishes[351]

SOME PEOPLE MAKE *KĀMAKH* from rotten bread and milk. Then flat loaves are added and left in the sun for several days with olive oil. I don't like this and I will not [therefore] mention the relevant recipe. Instead, I will mention [the following].[352]

348 cf. *Kanz*, 182 (No. 493).

349 *Kanz* adds the following ingredients: 'long pepper, ginger, cassia, mint, and a little bit of rue.'

350 The recipe in *Kanz* ends here.

351 The title of the chapter (No. 17) in *Kanz* is much broader: 'About how to make dairy dishes, *kawāmikh*, *jājaq*, and those with caper, thyme, *bīrāf*, etc.'

352 This is a personal comment by the author/copyist and is absent from *Kanz*.

178. A recipe for wheat *kāmakh*[353]

It is [made] by taking one *rub'* of good quality wheat from a young crop and picking it over. Then, boil slightly and remove [from the pot]. Spread the wheat out and when it is dry, place it in a brass pan and fry thoroughly. Afterwards, grind it coarsely and separate the flour from the coarse grounds,[354] and knead the former vigorously. Fashion [the dough] like meatballs and leave them out in the sun to dry until they become like elixir.[355] Then take the coarsely ground wheat, which you have set aside, and place it in a jar with a narrow mouth but wide body. Pour in just enough milk to immerse everything, and then add three fig twigs. Leave in a wide-mouthed clay jar after covering the top with some parchment.[356] Then, pour on olive oil and a little ground milk [and leave for] three days and serve. Then [add some more] olive oil, which makes it much more delicious.

179. A recipe for making colostrum[357]

Colostrum provides good nourishment. It is moist and favoured by people. It is highly nutritious for those with bilious temperaments and those

[353] cf. *Kanz*, 185–86 (No. 501), where the recipe has a slightly different title (*kāmakh ladhīdh*, 'delicious *kāmakh*'). The word goes back to the Middle Persian *kāmag* (early New Persian *kāma*, 'gruel, soup'; *kāmakh*, 'sourish kind of tonic for creating an appetite and promoting digestion'); Steingass 1892: 1009. It denoted condiments made from fermented rotted grains or, in some cases, milk (the so-called *kāmakh rijāl* or *baghdādī*, a kind of semi-solid cheese). Recipes for variants can be found in other Eastern cookery books as well; *Wuṣla*, No. 8.66 (*kāmakh al-rijāl*); al-Baghdādī 1964: 68 (*kāmakh al-rijāl*, trans., 89); al-Warrāq 1987: 62–3, 97–103 (trans., 152–3, 202–5); *Kanz*, 285–7 (Nos. 500–6). Al-Warrāq also used *mā' kāmakh* ('*kāmakh juice*') as a synonym for *murrī*. *Kāmakh* was served as a dip for bread, or in-between courses as a palate cleanser. Ibn Khalṣūn (1996: 163; trans., 92) explained *kawāmikh* as various types of olives, capers, citron preserve, mixed condiments, aubergine, and *ṣināb* (mustard raisin condiment).

[354] *dashīsh*, a variant of *jashīsh* (both *jashsha* and *dashsha* meaning 'to grind, crush'), which denoted (and still does) a kind of porridge made of crushed wheat, for which there are several recipes in the Maghribi manuals: al-Tujībī 2012: 61–2 (three recipes); *Andalusian*, fol. 61v. (two recipes). Also see al-Isrā'ilī 1992: 208, 218; al-Dabbābī 2017: 41–45.

[355] *Kanz* adds that 'this is called *qamna* in the vernacular.' The word 'elixir' (*al-iksīr*) originally referred to a medicinal powder but is best known as the alchemists' powder aiding the transformation of substances into precious metals. It was said to penetrate like yeast (*khamīra*) through dough. In *Waṣf* (408–9, 443), it denotes a decoction. *EI²*, s.v. 'al-iksīr' (M. Ullmann); Dozy 1877–81: II, 466.

[356] The *Kanz* recipe contains a number of other instructions, including that it should be left for ten days, adding that in the end 'it tastes like *fuqqā'* and has the colour of saffron.'

[357] cf. *Kanz*, 189 (No. 512). According to Ibn Jazla (fol. 193v.), it is beneficial for those with hot livers, but is slow to digest and causes flatulence, hiccups and kidney stones. His recipe is a lot

whose yellow bile is burnt. It soothes the character and many people eat it with dates. Others eat it by itself. Recipe for making it: take one part[358] of milk and one of lamb colostrum, taken when the animal is three days old. Mix everything together, put in a soapstone or earthenware pot, and place over a low fire, or on hot embers for one night. When morning comes, you will find that it is hot and the surface is golden. Serve. Whenever you find that the milk has gone down, add some more, as this will make it better and sweeter. Some people make it with one *rub*ʿ of colostrum and three of milk, and this comes out very nicely. If you increase the quantity of colostrum, the milk will go off and become hard as a stone, and lose all of its flavour.[359] This is not good. There were farmhands on one of my farms who made this for me and brought it to me. I did not think that it tasted nice, until I directed them to mix it with milk.

180. Another recipe[360]

Take colostrum – for each *raṭl*, four egg whites – and beat well in an earthenware pot and put over a gentle fire until it thickens. Add one egg yolk and it will be wonderful.

181. Another recipe[361]

Take a clean earthenware pot and place it over a fire. Pour [colostrum] milk[362] into it, as much as you like. Then, take milk, one quarter of the quantity of colostrum, and put it to one side. Heat the pot over a gentle fire and when it begins to foam and the colostrum obtains a head of froth, take a little bit of the yoghurt[363] with your hand and sprinkle on [the colostrum]. Leave until it foams, and continue gently sprinkling on [yoghurt] with your hand until the yoghurt is gone. When it is all in, remove the embers from underneath

---

shorter: 'soak one *raṭl* of colostrum in ten *raṭls* of milk and boil in an earthenware pot over a low fire. Afterwards leave until it becomes cold.' Also see Ibn al-Bayṭār 1992: IV, 373–4 (trans., III, 227–8); al-Samarqandī 2017: 110, 116.

358 The *Kanz* recipe requires two parts.

359 The recipe in *Kanz* ends here. What follows is a personal comment by Ibn Mubārak Shāh.

360 cf. *Kanz*, 189 (No. 513).

361 cf. *Kanz*, 189–90 (No. 514).

362 The recipe is clearly corrupted since it states *laban ḥalīb* (milk), but later on this is referred to as *libaʾ*.

363 Failing the omission of part of the recipe (in both *Kanz* and *Zahr*), it would appear that the 'milk' mentioned in the beginning of the recipe is to be corrected to 'yoghurt'.

the pot, and allow it to settle until it cools down. Then remove everything and eat with honey, sugar or dates.

182. A recipe for *qanbarīs* (dried yoghurt)[364]

Take new pots, pour in tart vinegar, and place over a fire until it starts boiling. [When it does,] remove from the fire and pour in milk. Set [the pots] aside and do not touch them. In the morning open them up,[365] and you will find that [the milk] has coagulated[366] into *qanbarīs*.[367] Milk has harmful properties, but these are outweighed by its benefits; it is tasty and there are people who do not enjoy their food unless there is cheese on the table.

183. A recipe for *bīrāf* (clotted cream)[368]

The name refers to the skimming with a shell of the cream that is on the surface of milk when it has been left outdoors overnight.[369] The [containers with the cream] are covered with cages or a sieve so that nothing evaporates. When the cream appears early in the morning, skim what is on the surface and move it to a cool place to remove what may have come up, if you wish.[370]

364 cf. *Kanz*, 190 (No. 515). Nasrallah ([al-Warrāq 2007]: 93, 589) translates *qanbarīs* as 'yoghurt cheese' or 'sourish soft cheese'. According to Perry (*Wuṣla*, 287), it was 'sun-dried and used in the same ways as thickened yogurt. [and] ... may have entered commerce as round balls similar to the Central Asian *qurut,* but in recipes it is always used in powdered form.' Whilst recipe No. 240 supports this statement, this one is closer to something like a cottage cheese.

365 This presumes, of course, that lids have to be put on the pots before storing them, even though neither the mss, nor *Kanz* mentions this.

366 *tajiduhā jāmida*; the recipe in *Kanz* has 'dried' (*yābisa*).

367 The recipe in *Kanz* ends here. The comments about milk that follow actually appear under a separate entry in *Kanz* (187, No. 506) entitled 'Recipes for making *jājaq*, capers and *birāf*, and other similar things.'

368 cf. *Kanz*, 187–88 (No. 507), of which the recipe here is a highly abridged version. Also see Nasrallah [al-Warrāq 2007]: 585.

369 This prefatory statement is absent from the *Kanz* recipe.

370 The mss is clearly corrupted here, but can fortunately be supplemented by *Kanz*, whose full recipe merits inclusion here: 'Take containers resembling wide frying pans. Then, bring the milk, and strain it into the vessels while it is lukewarm. This should be done in the evening after the sheep have left the pastures. Leave the pans outdoors, exposed to dew, and cover them with cages. The next day before sunrise remove what is on the surface with a long shell and put everything you skim off in another clean earthenware vessel. Continue doing this until nothing remains on the surface. Then, cover [the pans] and leave. If you are afraid that they will be exposed to the sun, move them to a cool place. During the daytime, take whatever rises to the surface, and serve. Many people elect to eat *bīrāf* by itself, and it is the finest food. Another group prefer to have it with honey, while still others grind *ṭabarzad* sugar and mix it in before eating it. Aḥmad al-Tīfāshī said: "As for me, I choose to eat it with rose-water syrup, as I think

Those who wish can eat *bīrāf* with rose-water syrup, honey or sugar, or by itself, in which case doctors take[371] a quince-based oxymel drink afterwards, or suck on a quince or two pears.

184. A recipe for *jājaq*[372]

It is made from pepper cress[373] and is beneficial to the back and invigorates coitus. It is wonderful.[374]

185. *Jājaq* with wild mustard[375]

The recipe is that one takes wild mustard and washes it clean. Finely chop it up and put in a clean porcelain bowl. Throw on thirty *dirhams* of crushed rock salt and rub it in well by hand. Take five *raṭls* of sour yoghurt, five bunches of wild mustard, or more. For each handful, take one *raṭl* and hang the yoghurt in a clean bag so that [the moisture] that is inside comes out. Remove [the yoghurt] and mix it in a jar together with the chopped up mustard. Stir until they are mixed,[376] and then add ten *dirhams* of chopped mint. Add good olive oil and cook with it; Allah knows best!

186. Seasoning *ḥālūm* cheese[377]

Boil milk with salt and Syrian thyme until one third of it has evaporated. Remove from the fire, and let it cool. In a silk cloth,[378] add a little bit of

---

this is the best. I described it to a group of my friends and they liked it; rose-water syrup not only makes it nicer but also has benefits and removes harmful effects. Those who are afraid of eating *bīrāf* by itself because of the effects on the stomach, should after eating it take a quince-based oxymel drink, or suck on a quince or a pear and a fig. I have seen people eating *bīrāf* with *zulābiyya*. I ate it that way and found it to be nice."'

371 The choice of verb is somewhat odd here as it implies that it is only doctors that do this. It is more likely that doctors recommend that it should be followed by oxymel and quince or pears.

372 cf. *Kanz*, 190–1 (No. 518), where there is a full recipe. This is another Turkish dish (a salad of chopped cucumber dressed with curds and garlic), which has survived – both in name and form – in the present-day Armenian *jajik* (a spinach and cucumber dip), Turkish *cacık* (a cucumber and herb yoghurt) and Greek tzatziki.

373 *ḥashīshat al-sulṭān;* according to Freytag (1830: I, 479), it was the Egyptian Arabic word for *kharfaq*, a type of *ḥurf* (cress, wild rue).

374 This also ends the recipe in *Kanz*.

375 cf. *Kanz*, 191 (No. 519).

376 The recipe in *Kanz* concludes with 'and put in the *jājaq* spices mentioned at the beginning.'

377 cf. *Kanz*, 192 (No. 521).

378 *Kanz* has the rather enigmatic *jarīr* ('lime'), which must be a scribal error as it would not make any sense here. It also recommends adding it with the cheese.

ground soapwort with cheese in the jar, together with a bit of (sour) orange, *kabbād* citrus, citron, lemon, and fresh thyme. Put one layer of cheese, one layer of fresh (orange) leaves[379] and thyme until the jar is filled up. Then, add the boiled milk until it fills up the jar, and seal [the top] with a bit of good quality olive oil, and store. Transfer to a container when needed.

187. Recipe for making yoghurt during winter[380]

Pound and strain dried sour grapes which have been soaked in hot water. Pour on as much milk as you like. It will acidulate and turn into curds,[381] Allah willing.[382]

188. Recipe for making yoghurt (*laban yāghurt*)[383]

Boil cow's or buffalo milk and remove [from the fire] (after it is boiling so that it can)[384] cool down. If it is an Egyptian *qinṭār*, take one *raṭl* of tart[385] yoghurt, which is the fermenting agent. Take half an *ūqiya* of rennet beaten in water and mix it in an earthenware bowl, and then decant to jars. If it is made early in the morning, it is good [to use] in the evening, and if you make it in the evening, it will be good the next morning.

189. Recipe for *qanbarīs*[386]

It is eaten with aubergine, or anything else you like that requires yoghurt. The recipe is [as follows]: Take milk and boil it until it starts bubbling. Then take a new pot and leave it to cool for an hour. Then take *laban yāghurt* – for each ten *raṭls* of milk, take half a *raṭl* of *laban yāghurt*, and stir with a ladle. Cover the pot and leave in a warm place. Put a little bit of straw underneath and leave overnight, and it will become like a disc. Put [the yoghurt] in a

---

379 *qulūb*, 'tender tips of herb sprigs'; Nasrallah [al-Warrāq 2007]: 668.

380 cf. *Kanz*, 193 (No. 527).

381 *rā'ib*; Nasrallah [al-Warrāq 2007]: 590 ('yoghurt without rennet').

382 The religious invocation is missing from *Kanz*.

383 cf. *Kanz*, 194 (No. 528). The word *yāghurt* is a borrowing from Turkish (*yūghūrt*), the first element of which (*yūgh*) denotes 'curd'; see e.g. Redhouse 1884: 202. According to Nasrallah ([al-Warrāq 2007]: 587), *laban yāghart* is 'yogurt made with cow's milk and rennet,' which is clearly contradicted by the present recipe.

384 The manuscript is defective here as it reads 'remove if after it has cooled down'. The text has been corrected using the *Kanz* recipe.

385 The Arabic word *maqṭū'* literally means 'cut'.

386 cf. *Kanz*, 194–5 (No. 531), which does not have the opening sentence, a variant of which appears at the end.

bag, and strain, after which it will become *qanbarīs*. Remove it from the bag, add salt, and serve when you need to. Afterwards transfer to a clean container [for storage].[387]

190. Recipe to make thyme[388]
(Take thyme) [and] clean its leaves. Wash and rub with salt and squeeze [the juice out. Then add][389] good quality olive oil on top; for each ten *raṭls* [of thyme], take one *raṭl* of olive oil. Place in an oiled wide-mouthed clay jar and seal. Add ground salt and if you want to season it, [add] pounded peeled garlic, a little bit of salt and good-quality oil until it becomes like ointment. Add pounded walnuts and eat; it is extremely tasty.

FOURTEEN

On Pickles[390]

191. Recipe to make turnip pickles with yeast[391]
Take turnips, peel them and cut into pieces. Boil them one time in a pot, and then place them in containers of your choice. Dissolve yeast with salt in water and pour it on so that [the turnips] are immersed. Take mustard, ground it and extract the juice through a cloth (the way you would from purslane

387 The *Kanz* recipe continues, and recommends serving the yoghurt with 'mace, *bāzār*, cucumber, aubergine, or anything else you want. It will be extremely tasty.' The ingredient *bāzār* is a variant of *abzār*, 'spices'; Dozy 1877–81: I, 81; Lane 1863–74: I, 199.

388 cf. *Kanz*, 195 (No. 533).

389 The mss is defective here as it reads 'squeeze good quality olive oil on it', rather than the more logical 'rub with salt, squeeze, and add (...)', which is the instruction in *Kanz*.

390 The title of the chapter (No. 18) in *Kanz* is: 'On all types of pickles made with turnips and onions, the pickling of all types of fruit and vegetables, and the salting of lemon, *kabbād*, etc.' This is also a lengthy chapter (No. 8) in *Wuṣla* (196ff.).

391 cf. *Kanz*, 195–6 (No. 534); *Wuṣla*, No. 8.12.

seeds).[392] Pour it on top and cover the top [of the pot]. Do not touch it. The amount of yeast and mustard should be the same as that of the turnips.

192. Another turnip [pickles] recipe to be eaten after one day[393]
This is when you peel and parboil turnips, after which you take them out and leave them to drain the liquid. Then put them in a pot with vinegar. If you want them to be red, dye them first with safflower before putting them in the pot.[394]

193. Another turnip [pickles] recipe made to last the entire year[395]
Take [turnips], peel them, (and cut them into large thick chunks). (Sprinkle on salt and leave overnight) in jars until the water has drained from them and they have wilted. Afterwards, remove the turnips [and put them in another vessel to which you] add vinegar, mustard and seasonings. This is the way all turnip [pickles] are made.

194. Recipe to make mustard for [the pickling of] turnips and other vegetables[396]
Take the white ones (of the mustard seeds) and pound with a little bit of salt so that they do not become bitter. Take the turnips [or any other vegetables you are using]. If hazelnuts are added to pickles, [make sure] they are toasted and left to cool. Remove their skins so they are white. Pound finely. Do the same with walnuts and mix with mustard. Use with any pickles of your choosing, turnips or others.

392 This part was missing from the mss, and was added from *Kanz*.

393 cf. *Kanz*, 196 (No. 536).

394 The ending of the recipe is slightly different in *Kanz*: '[and] colour as mentioned above.' This refers to an earlier recipe (No. 534, another turnip pickle recipe), which states the following: 'if you want [the turnips] to be red, dye them with safflower. You can also add mustard if you like.' The preceding recipe (No. 535) in *Kanz* recommends the use of saffron if the colour yellow is preferred.

395 cf. *Kanz*, 196 (No. 537); *Wuṣla*, No. 8.1.

396 cf. *Kanz*, 196 (No. 538); *Wuṣla*, No. 8.1.

195. Turnip (pickles) which last for one month[397]

Cut up the turnips, as mentioned already, and boil water in a brass pot until it starts to bubble. Throw in the turnips and remove the pot (from the fire).[398] Put [the turnips] in a strainer and squeeze by hand until their liquid has been drained. Sprinkle on mustard and seasonings, as mentioned.[399] If you like it sweetened, add wine vinegar sweetened with honey or sugar – as mentioned already for the pickles that can be kept for one year – together with *aṭrāf al-ṭīb*. The vinegar should immerse the turnips. Then add mint, rue, tender tips of herb sprigs,[400] and, if you like, sugar. Some people also sprinkle on *aṭrāf al-ṭīb* and hulled sesame seeds.

196. Recipe for Greek turnip (pickles)[401]

Take as many small and large turnips as you like and cut off their stems, leaving only the leaf nodule about one finger in size, without either the stems or the leaves. Peel and make long and wide cuts into them.[402] Sprinkle on salt and water, and leave for two days and two nights. Then remove from the water and salt, fill the cuts with mustard and salt, and smother in wine vinegar before storing. It will keep for a whole year.

197. Another turnip (pickles) recipe[403]

Cut turnips into small pieces and dye with saffron. When the dye begins to take, throw on wine vinegar sweetened with honey, sugar or *dibs*, as well as mint, (rue) leaves,[404] mustard (seeds) and *aṭrāf al-ṭīb*.[405] There are those who crush safflower in a bit of vinegar before dying. Add sweetened vinegar and seasonings if you want it to be red.

---

397 cf. *Kanz*, 197 (No. 539); *Wuṣla*, No. 8.2.

398 This is taken from *Kanz* as it was omitted from *Zahr*.

399 This is where the recipes in *Kanz* and *Wuṣla* end. The remainder of the recipe is actually taken from another one in *Kanz* (No. 541), which is, aptly, entitled 'Another recipe for sweetened white turnip [pickles]'.

400 *waraq qulūb*, Nasrallah [al-Warrāq 2007]: 668.

401 cf. *Kanz*, 197–98 (No. 542); *Wuṣla*, No. 8.5.

402 The *Kanz* recipe specifies that it should be scored in seven or eight places.

403 cf. *Kanz*, 198 (No. 544); *Wuṣla*, No. 8.6. In both of these, the recipe refers to 'yellow turnip [pickles]' (*lift aṣfar*).

404 The manuscript omits 'rue', which is included in the *Kanz* recipe.

405 The *Kanz* recipe ends here.

198. Another turnip (pickles) recipe, known as *maḥshī*[406]
Take turnips and [let them] wilt, as we have mentioned, and sprinkle on mustard seeds. Take black raisins, pound them finely, and strain several times with wine vinegar until nothing of the raisins remains and [the mixture] has become viscous. If it is bitter, sweeten it, and then add mint, rue, *aṭrāf al-ṭīb*, sesame seeds, and toasted hemp seeds.[407] Pour [the liquid] over the turnips so that they are immersed.

199. Persian turnip (pickles) recipe[408]
Take turnips and cut its leaves from the middle and throw away the long stems which do not have leaves so that about three fingers remain in length.[409] Then split the bulbs [into] four equal parts, but do not detach them from another, and leave the stems as they are at the shoulder of the root. Then boil water and throw them in. Remove the pot from the fire and strain the water. Sprinkle on salt and mustard while it is still hot, and leave until it cools down. Take vinegar and add a good amount of pounded toasted hazelnuts, as we have already mentioned. Also add good olive oil, pounded toasted dried coriander, caraway seeds, *aṭrāf al-ṭīb*, pounded garlic, hulled sesame, and hemp seeds. Wrap it all in the turnip leaves, transfer to a container and add a lot more olive oil. Those who want to keep [the pickles] for one year[410] should not put the turnips in boiling water; conversely, those who want to eat the pickles quickly should leave them to stew on the fire, as we have mentioned. Those who want to sweeten the dish with sugar or honey can do so. You can also add pieces of peeled toasted almonds, but take care when adding pounded walnuts since they will turn the vinegar and hazelnuts green. This the best (in terms of taste).[411]

---

406 cf. *Kanz*, 198 (No. 545), *ṣifat lift maḥshī*; the use of the word *maḥshī* here does not denote any stuffing as it does in modern Arabic culinary terminology, but rather a sauce. The recipe is also found in *Wuṣla* (No. 8.7), where it is called *muqirra*.

407 *shahdhānaq* is a corruption of the *shahdhānaj*, a borrowing from Persian. It was more commonly known as (*bizr*) *qinnab*. In cooking, hemp seeds were usually crushed and/or toasted, and are predominantly found in desserts or spice mixes. See Ibn al-Bayṭār 1992: III, 94, IV, 290–1; Ibn Jazla, fols. 139v., 181r.; Nasrallah [al-Warrāq 2007]: 671–2; Steingass 1892: 769

408 cf. *Kanz*, 198–99 (No. 546); *Wuṣla*, No. 8.8.

409 The recipe in *Kanz* is slightly different here: 'Pick out the leaves together with what remains of the stems, and cut them three fingers in length. As for the small bulbs, leave them alone. Strip away the dry and yellow leaves, too, and split the heads...'

410 In *Kanz*, these two instructions are reversed.

411 This was added from *Kanz*, as the *Zahr* mss only has *ajwad* ('the best'). However, this, too,

200. Recipe for turnip [pickles] with pomegranate seeds[412]

Pound pomegranate seeds and strain with wine vinegar several times, so that nothing remains of the seeds. Add honey or sugar and put on a fire. Let it thicken well, and then add mint, rue, *aṭrāf al-ṭīb*, pepper, ginger, poppy seeds, sesame seeds, hemp seeds and toasted walnut pieces. When the mixture thickens, take garlic, pare it [and cut it up into pieces] with a knife. Throw the garlic into sesame oil until it turns golden, and then add pieces of turnip after they have been peeled and cut into small pieces. Let them wilt, as we have mentioned. Boil in a pot as much as you want, and add pomegranate seeds. Boil them well. This is exquisite.[413]

201. Recipe for easy-to-use Persian turnip [pickles][414]

You need turnips, dried coriander, caraway, and a sufficient amount of ground mustard seeds. Boil the turnip and add a sufficient quantity of the coriander, caraway and mustard.

202. Another turnip [pickles] recipe[415]

Peel and cut up [turnips], each piece the size of broad beans,[416] and then put them in water for two days. Afterwards, remove and squeeze well. Add wine vinegar, bee honey, *aṭrāf al-ṭīb*, mint and seasoning. Transfer [when needed].

203. Another turnip [pickles] recipe with yeast[417]

Take barley flour and knead it with yeast, hot water and a bit of salt. Leave until it becomes very sour. When it reaches (the required level of) sourness, parboil and remove the water.[418] Completely dissolve yeast in it and return

---

is incomplete, as shown by the recipe in *Wuṣla* (No. 8.08), which has 'and hazelnuts are better in terms of flavour, and do not alter [the colour of] the vinegar.'

412 cf. *Kanz*, 199 (No. 547); *Wuṣla*, No. 8.13.

413 The recipe in *Kanz* adds: 'As for dying turnips, if you want it yellow, use saffron after cutting [the turnips]. If you want it blue, then [use] indigo, and if you want it red, mallow. If you want it white, leave it alone.'

414 cf. *Kanz*, 199 (No. 548).

415 cf. *Kanz*, 200 (No. 549).

416 'broad beans' (*fūl*) was missing, and added from *Kanz*.

417 cf. *Kanz*, 200 (No. 550: 'white turnip pickles recipe with yeast').

418 The recipe in *Kanz* deviates considerably here and adds: 'When it reaches [the required degree of] sourness, strain it in hot water in which turnips have been boiled. Transfer, and put aside. Add liquid and repeatedly strain until it is thin, and then drink. Throw in the turnips which have been peeled and cut after (parboiling…).'

to the turnips. Sprinkle on mustard and leave until it cools down, and then transfer to the broth with the yeast. Add a lot of mint and rue, as well as sour orange leaves and *aṭrāf al-ṭīb*. Pound the yeast which is in it [and leave] in a warm place. Take [what you need], and eat.

204. Another turnip [pickles] recipe, which is very tasty[419]

Peel half a *qinṭār* of turnips, throw them in a pot and immerse in water.[420] Heat up the pot until the water is very warm, but without it boiling. Then, remove [from the fire], and throw in cold water so that it cools down. Put in a cask. Take two *raṭls* and a half of wheat dough yeast and dissolve it in the cold water in which you have returned the turnips. Add to the turnips until they are covered. If they are not fully immersed, add more of the cold water in which they were washed. Take one eighth of a *qadaḥ* of mustard seeds and 'milk' them with water until all of their contents have been extracted, and add the liquid [to the turnips]. Mix by hand until everything is mixed together and what was on top is now at the bottom. Leave until it reaches the right flavour and then use.

205. Another turnip [pickles] recipe[421]

Peel and cut up [the turnips] and cook them in salted water [until] they still have some strength. Take white bee honey, *ṭabarzad* sugar or ground mustard and put it in any kind of wide-mouthed clay jar that you like, with any colour you like. Tightly seal [the vessels] so that the colour clings to the turnips.

206. Another turnip [pickles] recipe[422]

Peel the turnips and cut into small and big pieces. Bring to the boil twice, so that they are still hard when they are removed. Season with mustard and salt, place in a wooden bowl, and chop rue into it. Take sour yeast which is five days old and dissolve into hot water. Leave until it settles and strain the water on the turnips. Leave for four days, and use.

---

419 cf. *Kanz*, 200 (No. 551).

420 *Kanz* adds that 'water should be added several times until [the turnips] are immersed.'

421 The recipe in *Kanz*, 200–1 (No. 552) is considerably more detailed.

422 cf. *Kanz*, 201 (No. 553).

207. Persian turnip [pickles] recipe[423]

Take the turnip shoulders and parboil. Then, put in [a mixture of] vinegar, mustard, tahini, hazelnuts, walnut kernels, dried coriander and good quality oil, and sprinkle on caraway seeds.

208. Another turnip [pickles] recipe[424]

Take turnips, boil them [in water], and then drain. Rub the turnips thoroughly (with mustard and cardamom)[425] so that they become infused [with the spices]. Then add sugar, wine vinegar, cardamom and saffron strands. Let the mixture ferment for three days and when it turns golden yellow it can be eaten.

209. Another turnip [pickles] recipe[426]

Cut up white turnips lengthwise and in round shapes, and soak in water and salt for three days. Then, wash them and soak in fresh water for two days. Afterwards take four *raṭls* of yeast dissolved in water until [the mixture] becomes very thin. Leave until it settles, and remove the clear part [of the liquid]. Take the turnips out of the water and throw them in a wide-mouthed clay jar, together with the clear yeast water, three *ūqiyas* of ground mustard washed with natron, rue, mint, and a small amount of rosebuds. Leave for five days and put in some fresh rue and mint. Put in fresh yeast as well, and stir with sugar or honey. Whenever you want to eat it, stir the jar. It is extremely tasty.

210. Recipe for lime-soaked (*mulakkas*) olives[427]

Take olives free from bruises or defects and wash big jars to put them in. Then, take lime that has been slaked, and leave overnight. Take lye and pound very well, and sieve. For each *mudd* of olives, put one *mudd* of lye. [Note that] the weight of one Damascene *mudd* is [equivalent to] ten Egyptian *raṭls*.[428] Then, take enough water to cover the olives and pour into a copper

---

423 cf. *Kanz*, 201 (No. 555).

424 cf. *Kanz*, 201–2 (No. 556).

425 This was omitted from the mss, and added from *Kanz*.

426 cf. *Kanz*, 201–2 (No. 556). The numbering of the *Kanz* edition is incorrect here, but for referencing purposes this has not been corrected.

427 cf. *Kanz*, 202 (No. 557).

428 This passage is somewhat problematic in the Arabic. Firstly, it has the nonsensical 'and an *ūqiya* and the weight of the Damascene *mudd* . . .' Secondly, the latter weight was about 2.84 kg,

pot, together with the lime and lye. Boil the water until it is reduced by one third. Remove [the pot] from the fire, pour [the contents] in an earthenware vessel and leave overnight. It will become clear and have the colour of sesame oil. Pour the clear water onto the olives, [making sure] they are immersed. On top of the olives put whatever green leaves [are available] to weigh them down.[429] Leave in the jars for three days. Then take the olives out and split them open; if their stones have turned black, they will taste sweet. Transfer the olives to a *quffa*, or any other type of basket.[430] Wash them with water until they are [fully] clean. Immediately take them out so that they do not turn black, and put them in fresh water, without salt, for three days, after which you add water that has a good amount of salt in it. Take some of the olives out and eat; they will be good.

211. Another recipe for lime-soaked olives[431]

Take good green olives with oil in them, and free from bruises or marks. Put them in a jar for two days, with enough water to cover them. Then remove from the water and replace it with the same quantity of water and lime – for each *mudd* of olives, take two Damascene *ūqiyas* of lime. Leave them in the lime until they are ready to eat, and then take them out and wash them. Leave in salted water until such time as you need to use them.[432]

212. Another similar recipe[433]

Take green olives from which the oil has been extracted,[434] and which are free from marks and bruises,[435] and are firm. Put them in a jar and pour on salt and water. Leave for one week. Then sieve the ashes and add them so that

---

which would make it closer to five Egyptian *raṭls* (450 g). Hinz 1955: 46.

429 The recipe in *Kanz* adds that this is done 'so that the olives do not rise to the top and turn black.'

430 In *Kanz*, it is a 'vessel' (*'āniya*).

431 cf. *Kanz*, 202 (No. 559). *Kanz* does not have a No. 558, presumably to make up for the incorrect numbering of what should have been recipes 556 and 557 (see above).

432 *Kanz* has '(leave in salted water) and eat.'

433 cf. *Kanz*, 202 (No. 561). Actually, this is not similar to the preceding recipe at all, but rather to the one in *Kanz* (No. 560), 'olives in ashes' (*zaytūn murammad*), where the ashes are kneaded with lime until 'they become like *'aṣīda*'.

434 This specification is omitted from *Kanz*.

435 *Kanz* only mentions 'marks' (*khadash*), not bruises (*ḍarbāt*).

they stick to the olives like mud. Leave for a month or more. If you'd like to eat some, take what you need from the jar.[436] Wash before eating.

213. Olives that you can eat[437]

Remove their stones and pound enough garlic for its flavour to manifest itself. Add as much as you like of sesame oil, almonds, walnuts, sesame seeds, ground sifted sumac, thyme and mint. There are those who change the water so that it becomes sweeter, and extract the juice thoroughly. All of this is done after removal of the stones. Then take toasted caraway seeds and coriander, as much as is required, as well as *aṭrāf al-ṭīb*, hazelnuts, tahini and tart wine vinegar. Put everything in a jar for three days and add on good olive oil, after which it is ready for use.

214. This is a type of seasoned (*mutabbal*) [olives][438]

There are those who add sumac to the seasoning, while others add sesame oil. The more seasonings you use, the better it is, except for sumac, which should be used sparingly, and its sprigs toasted.

215. As for making onion (pickles)[439]

The water and salt need to be replaced, and this should be repeated with the water. Then you do what you like. In most cases, the tart variety does not require sesame oil.

216. Recipe for pickling radishes in vinegar, which helps digest food and is very good[440]

Take large radishes, cut them into fingers, and put them in a wide-mouthed bottle. Pour on enough good-quality wine vinegar to cover them. Add asafoetida,[441] nigella and a bit of pounded chickpeas, pounded mustard paste

---

436 This instruction is omitted from *Kanz*.

437 cf. *Kanz*, 204 (No. 564: 'Recipe for tasty olives'), which is, however, very different.

438 *Kanz* contains three *mutabbal* olive recipes (Nos. 565–567) but none corresponds to the one used here, with the exception of the reference to the use of the ingredients, which is found in No. 566 but without the toasting instruction.

439 The recipe is clearly defective but no better version has been located. *Wuṣla* has three pickled onion recipes (Nos. 4.87–9), the first of which might have inspired the one here. However, there is an overlap in only the first sentence, with the remainder being different.

440 cf. *Kanz*, 210 (No. 584).

441 *anjudān*, the gum resin of the root or stem of a perennial plant whose origins lie in India. It was introduced into the Western Mediterranean by Alexander the Great and gets its name

from which the bitterness has been extracted, pounded thyme, and salt. Let the asafoetida [flavour] prevail, but pound it before eating. It aids digestion.

217. Recipe for making *kabbād* [pickles][442]

Slice up *kabbād* and [then] take salt, toasted caraway seeds, rue, good-quality olive oil, whole ginger pieces, pieces of cinnamon, and whole clove sticks. Put the *kabbād*, citrus, salt, toasted caraway seeds, and good olive oil in a container and seal with good-quality olive oil. Cover with a cloth until you need to use the mixture. It will be done in three days' time. The mixture requires attention and monitoring. If there is no longer enough water, top it up with good-quality olive oil, and transfer to a smaller container. It is truly wonderful.

218. Recipe for [pickling] citron pulp[443]

Take citron pulp, remove its strands (i.e. the vesicles),[444] and add sugar, pistachio kernels and toasted hazelnuts. Take rose jam which has been cooked beforehand for this purpose, and add it [to the mixture] together with saffron, musk and rose water. Put over a fire and increase the amount of rose water so that [the liquid] thickens and obtains the consistency of rose-water syrup. Fumigate a wide-mouthed clay jar with agarwood and ambergris, and then put the pulp in. Cover it very well so that the vapours cannot escape. This is the height of goodness.

---

from its offensive odour prior to cooking. Ibn al-Bayṭār reported that *anjudān* referred to the leaf, *ḥiltīt* to the gum and *maḥrūth* to the root. Al-Ghāfiqī distinguished between Greek asafoetida, and *sarakhsī*, 'which is good for eating and comes in white and black'. In cooking, only the white-leaf variety was used; the black variety is foetid and restricted to medicines. It is generally found in condiments, sauces and dips (e.g. al-Warrāq, *Waṣf*). In the Muslim West, it is rarer, with one only usage in the anonymous Andalusian treatise, as a flavouring in a *ṭabāhaja* named after the plant (*anjudāniyya*). Today, asafoetida (also known as 'hing') is commonly used in curry dishes. Ibn al-Bayṭār 1992: I, 48–9, 80–2 (trans., I, 83–4, 141–5); al-Ghāfiqī 2014: 55a; *Andalusian*, fol. 41v.; *Waṣf*, 404; Nasrallah [al-Warrāq 2007]: 644–5; Lev & Amar 2008: 339–40; Dalby 2000: 110–12; *idem* 2003: 29.

442 cf. *Kanz*, 210–11 (No. 585).

443 cf. *Kanz*, 211 (No. 586).

444 *sha'īruhu*.

219. Recipe for pickling cucumber in vinegar[445]

Take October cucumbers, especially the small ones, and soak them in salted water for two days and nights. Then, take them out of the salted water and put them in a large glass jar. Pour on wine vinegar, and add the tender ends of celery, mint and rue. Make sure there is more rue than celery in it. Leave for a few days before use.[446]

220. Recipe for capers in vinegar[447]

Take salted capers and rinse them with water so that nothing of the salt remains. Soak in vinegar sweetened with sugar or honey and add a bit of pounded garlic, dried coriander, as well as good-quality olive oil.

221. Another recipe with sumac[448]

Take salted capers and soak them until all the salt has been removed. Take vinegar and lemon juice, and use a cloth to strain the [juice of] pounded sumac into it. Add the capers and sprinkle a bit of finely pounded sumac on top, together with dried coriander, caraway seeds, and dried thyme. Cut some salted lemon into it, in small pieces. Finally, pour some good-quality olive oil on top.

222. A recipe for cured garlic[449]

Take as much [garlic] as you like and put its bulbs in a container smeared with pitch. Pour in enough water to immerse the garlic. Add a handful of salt and a handful of barley. Seal the top with clay and leave until [the garlic] has turned sour and becomes tasty. This is also how Syrian leeks and pungent small yellow onions are prepared.

223. A recipe for salted lemon[450]

Take salted lemons, cut them into small pieces and put them in a jar. Squeeze the juice of lime and sour oranges into it. Add good quality olive oil, *aṭrāf*

---

445 *Kanz*, 214 (No. 596); *Wuṣla*, No. 8.41.

446 *Wuṣla* adds that 'it is quite good and will last for up to a year.'

447 *Kanz*, 215 (No. 601: 'Recipe for capers'); *Wuṣla*, No. 8.30. The word *qubbār* is a variant of *kabar*. Corriente 1997: 411.

448 *Wuṣla*, No. 8.31.

449 *Kanz*, 215–16 (No. 602).

450 *Kanz*, 218 (No. 604); *Wuṣla*, No. 8.20. In *Kanz*, this recipe and the three that follow it appear after the 'Benefits and Properties' section (see below).

al-ṭīb, dried pounded and toasted coriander, chopped parsley, mint and rue. This is the best and tastiest [recipe] there is.[451] There are people who pour on vinegar sweetened with bee honey and good olive oil.

224. [Another] recipe[452]

When the lemons have been salted, add a fistful of rue, a bit of bee honey, good olive oil and saffron to each jar [in which you have placed lemons]. Use lemons harvested in the [Coptic] months of Tobi (*ṭūba*) and Meshir (*amshīr*).[453] This will make it delicious.

225. Lemon recipe[454]

Make cuts into the lemons and fill them with salt. Cram them [in a container][455] for two days and then squeeze out [more] juice, and take out the pips. Place a ginger root, stick of mint, and rue in each lemon. Return it to its container, add saffron and bee honey, and then seal with olive oil.

226. [Another] Recipe[456]

Score lemons crosswise and fill the cuts with salt. Layer the lemons on a platter and weigh them down with stones. Cover and leave for three days. Then take them out, put in a large glass jar and take the liquid. Dye it with saffron and take out the pips. If you want[457] [more] lemon juice, add some. Then tightly pack everything in a jar, making sure [the lemons] are immersed. Seal with good quality olive oil, put a lid on top, and store.

---

451 The recipe ends here in *Kanz* and *Wuṣla*.

452 Though a separate recipe here, it is the final section of another recipe in *Kanz* (217, No. 607), entitled *kabs al-laymūn* ('packing lemons'), which is also found in *Wuṣla* (No. 8.23), where the paragraph (the *Zahr* recipe) is missing.

453 These are, respectively, the fifth and sixth months in the Coptic calendar, with Tobe running from December 27 to January 25 and Meshir between January 26 and February 24.

454 *Kanz*, 218 (No. 608).

455 The manuscript has the incongruous 'breaking them after (two days),' whereas *Kanz* has the more logical *tukbasuhu* ('pressed', as in a container).

456 *Kanz*, 218 (No. 609).

457 The author uses the Egyptian colloquial verb *ʿāza* here.

Description of the Benefits and Properties[458]

Milk:[459] hot and dry.

Ṣaḥnāt: hot and dry. It induces thirst, spoils the blood and causes prurigo.

Caper *kāmakh*: hot and cold, harmful to the stomach, thirst inducing, and exhausts the body.

Garlic *kāmakh*: good for those with phlegmatic temperaments or fever fits. It also dissolves [kidney/gall]-stones.

Marjoram *kāmakh*: good against wind. It cools the stomach and relieves pains in the head caused by colds and phlegm.

All of the *kāmakhs* acquire the demulcent properties from vinegar.[460]

Capers preserved in vinegar are less hot than those preserved in salt. They are good against blockages in the liver and spleen.

Onions preserved in vinegar do not heat or cool, nor do they induce thirst. They stimulate lust.[461]

Cucumbers and snake melons preserved in vinegar: both of these have extreme cooling properties, but nevertheless are demulcent.

All salted *kāmakhs* and pickles preserved in vinegar are harmful to those with coarse throats. The salted ones, in particular, are bad for those suffering

458 This rather incongruous interpolated list is a condensed version of the one found in *Kanz* (216, No. 603), which is also found in al-Warrāq's Chapter 24 (1987: 59–60/trans., 26, 152–3). However, as already mentioned, this information can be traced back to al-Rāzī's *al-Kitāb al-Manṣūrī fi 'l-ṭibb.*

459 *laban*, which denotes both 'milk' and 'yoghurt'. This should be corrected to '*binn*', a type of condiment; al-Warrāq 1987: 1987: 59 (trans., 152–3). *Kanz* adds that 'it induces thirst, but purifies the stomach from phlegm, and is useful against bad breath (*bakhar*).'

460 The scribe presumably skipped a line here, as it is vinegar-preserved pickles (*mukhallalāt*) that obtain this property from vinegar according to *Kanz*: 'all *kāmakhs* correspond to whatever they are made from, and acquire the characteristics of salt and mould (...). All types of vinegar-preserved pickles acquire the demulcent properties from vinegar.'

461 The Arabic word *shahwa* can also mean 'appetite', which would, of course, be a possible translation in the context.

from itch, prurigo and all illnesses resulting from inflammation of the blood.

Olives preserved in water[462] are hot and dry, and loosen the belly if served before the meal. The dish strengthens the 'mouth'[463] of the stomach. As for olives, they are highly heating.

FIFTEEN

On Storing Fruits and Keeping Them When They Are Out of Season[464]

227.

It is said that [grapes can be preserved] when sumac juice is cooked down to a third, and then left to cool in a glass or earthenware jar to which the grapes are added. The top of the pot is then sealed with gypsum. If you take them out afterwards you will find that they taste fresh and smell as if they had just been picked, whereas the water [in which they were kept] will become like good vinegar afterwards.[465]

462 The legibility of the mss is quite impaired in this entry, due to foxing, and was supplemented with the text in *Kanz*. The *Zahr* scribe omitted the *Kanz* entry on pickled turnips that precedes the one on olives, and the one on pickled *usthurghāz* (appearing as *ushturgār*), i.e. asafoetida root.

463 This can refer to both the so-called gastroesophageal junction and the oesophagus.

464 This corresponds to chapter 23 in *Kanz*, whose chapters 19 (on cold dishes), 20 (on spices, toothpicks, various types of wood, and soaps), 21 (on incense, perfumes, and the such), and 22 (on perfumed powders) are skipped entirely.

465 This is adapted from the *Kanz* recipe No. 719 (251), parts of which are also reiterated later on (254). The rather obscure statement that it will be 'good vinegar' can be elucidated by the text in *Kanz*, which refers to the curative qualities of vinegar (*wa yakūn shifā'*). Although they appear by way of introduction in the mss, they are counted as separate recipes here.

228.

As for quince, it should be rolled in fig leaves, coated with clay and then dried in the sun. Afterwards, hang them there. The same applies to apples.[466] There are other medicines with other properties, but we have abridged them, and will not mention them [in full].

229. Rose recipe[467]

Take a new bowl and fill it with clay.[468] Place it in a tub already filled with water, and leave it floating on the surface.[469] Do not add more water. Then, take Iraqi rosebuds and 'plant' them in this clay. Leave for two days [and nights] and put a lid on the tub. On the third day, remove the lid and you will find the roses in their original state – the red is still red, the green is still green.[470] You [can also] take the whole dried rosebuds and soak them in rose water for three days, and they will open.

230.[471]

Or, take whole rosebuds, put them in Persian reeds, and line them up one after another. Seal the top of [each] reed with wax, tie a string around one end of the reed, and place them in the water storage tank of the bath-house in the steam of the water, for a day and a night. Take them out and you will find the [rosebuds] fresh [again].

231.[472]

If you want to store fruit, grains, seeds[473] and flour [do so] in cool clean places, far from kitchens, smoke, and bad odours. Do not store them with pomegranate seeds.

---

466 This is actually the final part of a recipe in *Kanz* (252, No. 720).

467 *Kanz*, 252 (No. 721: 'Recipe for roses when they are out of season').

468 The Arabic has *ṭīn al-qamḥ*, which would translate as 'wheat clay'.

469 The *Kanz* recipe adds that it should be left for 'an hour'.

470 *Kanz* states 'you will find roses that look as fresh as when you picked them.'

471 *Kanz*, 252 (No. 722). This recipe is added to the preceding one in the mss.

472 This is part of the recipe in both *Kanz* and *Zahr*; however, as it is essentially a new recipe, it has been allocated its own entry.

473 *Kanz* adds *qaḍāmā* ('roasted and salted chickpeas') to the list.

232. Recipe for storing grapes[474]

It is said that if you burn fig leaves and the wood [from the branches] and scatter the ashes on bunches of grapes, they will stay [good] for a long time. If you plunge [grapes] in dill juice,[475] they will stay good for one year. They will also stay fresh if you beat them with the clippings of ebony wood or cedar, or vine ashes mixed with water, like you hit marshmallow plants, and dunk the bunches in it, before taking them out and spreading or hanging them in a room in a clean place of average temperature.[476]

If you take good winter grapes with thick skins after they have ripened, they have a pronounced sweetness in the second half of the month of November,[477] or at the end [of it], depending on whether the soil produces [them] early[478] or late. Make sure [the grapes] are cut with a sharp iron, when the sun has risen and the dew has dried in the morning. You should aim to do it when the moon is waning. Remove the seeds that are not ripe[479] or rotten, and spread them out in jars until the cask is filled with layer after layer of grapes alternating with figs, away from the air. Seal the mouths [of the jar] with clay. Put the jars in a place where the sun does not come, and the grapes will stay succulent for a whole year.

Bunches (of grapes) may also be immersed in water with salt, and then spread out on [a layer of] hay from lupine beans, broad beans or barley, whichever is available. Make sure you put them in a cold place (that is not in the sun) or heated by fire, and they can keep for a long time. If you put the bunches [of grapes] in an earthenware jar, seal the top tightly with leather and bury it in the soil; [the grapes] will [still] be good whenever you want to take them out. They will remain good to eat if you put the jar in water up to its neck and cut the stalks and leaves of the bunches and dip the spot where you've cut in dissolved (*sc.* liquid) tar and hang up the bunches at a distance from one another.

---

474 This recipe is only half of the one in *Kanz*, 253 (No. 723). A more extensive version of the recipe can be found in *'Ilm al-malāḥa fī 'ilm al-filāḥa* ('The science of elegance in the science of agriculture') by 'Abd al-Ghanī al-Nābulusī (1641–1731); 1882: 246–50.

475 *Kanz* adds that they should be hung.

476 The mss omits the following sentence in *Kanz*: 'If you make a jar from cow droppings with a little bit of white clay, making sure that it will not crack, put the bunches of grapes inside and cover the top with clay, and place it in a clean cool place, it will remain good until *Nayrūz* (the Coptic New Year).

477 *nuwanbar*; in *Kanz*, the word appears as *nuwanbarā*.

478 Instead of *tabkīr* (referring to something happening ahead of time), the recipe in *Kanz* has the nonsensical *takbir*, which denotes an 'enlargement (of the soil)'.

479 *Kanz* has 'bad' (*ghayr ṣaḥīḥ*), rather than 'not ripe' (*ghayr naḍīj*).

SIXTEEN

[Dishes]

233. *Tamriyya* (date stew)

Take meat, cut it up into small pieces, and wash in hot water. Then, [boil and] tenderize it and fry thoroughly. Take good pressed dates and cut them in half. Throw away the stones. Take almonds, boil them in water to remove the peels, and toast them. Put the almonds inside the dates in place of the stones. Then, mix some rose water with a bit of water and one *ūqiya* of sesame oil, and put into a pot. Add the dates, and stir gently.[480] When it is done, eat it.

234. *Rukhāmiyya* ('marble' stew)[481]

Boil the meat until it is done. If a lot of liquid remains, remove some of it. If there is only a little left of the liquid, add some milk to it. Take rice, mastic and cassia and, together with the milk, add them to the meat; for each *raṭl* of milk (take two *ūqiyas* of)[482] rice. When it is ready, transfer it to a container, and eat with honey, sugar, or sweetened rose-water syrup.[483] Cut up the meat into small pieces and wash with hot water. Boil it until done, and then fry. When it has been fried well, add honey, dissolved sugar or *dibs*. Pound and strain the rice, and throw in peeled almonds or walnut kernels. Then, pound hot spices and season the dish with them.

235. *Khayṭiyya*[484]

Take good lean meat,[485] cut it up and boil until it is done. When it is thoroughly tenderized, drain off the liquid. Then remove the meat strand by strand and wash with water until both the meat and the water used for washing are colourless. Put the milk over a fire, wash the rice and add it. Then pound

---

480 The instruction in *Kanz* is to allow the liquid to dry a little (*yunshaf qalīl*).

481 cf. *Kanz*, 268 (Appendix, No. 13).

482 The proportion of rice is only mentioned in *Kanz*, which, however, omits the word 'rice'.

483 The recipe in *Kanz* ends here.

484 cf. *Kanz*, 269 (Appendix, No. 14: *hinṭiyya*, 'wheat stew').

485 *Kanz* adds that 'the best meat is that of a hogget.'

some more rice, strain it, and sprinkle a bit on. Then, stir.[486] Take one *raṭl* of meat for four *ūqiyas* of rice, three or two *raṭls* of milk, one *raṭl* of water, and two *ūqiyas* of pounded rice. When it is ready, serve with rose-water syrup.

236. *Zīrbāj*

Wash the meat, tenderize it, and fry. Put a little bit of water on it and two *thulths* of *dibs* and one *thulth* of vinegar. Pound rice, strain, dissolve in water and add it to the meat. When the rice is done, add almonds and jujubes. Pound hot spices and add them, too. Keep stirring the rice so that it does not stick. Use enough vinegar to temper the taste [of the dish]. Then let it settle.

237. *Kammūniyya*

Wash the meat and add a bit of water to it. When it is boiling well, add a little salt and when it is done, add cheese and onion. Pound caraway seeds, [dried] coriander and hot spices, and add them. Chop up mint, fresh coriander, herbs, celery, and parsley, and put them in a jar, to which spices are added. Crack eggs into the mixture, beat them, and pour them in a pot. Do not touch it until it comes to a boil. Then dissolve saffron and pour it into the pot. Add the cheese with vegetables, if some are left over, or without, together with peeled almonds and jujubes, and put everything in the pot. Leave until it has finished cooking.

238. *Sikbāj*

Wash the meat and [boil it to] tenderize it. Fry with a little water. Cut up carrots, turnips, aubergine, onions and leeks, and put everything on the meat. When everything has been brought to a boil three times, add two *thulths* of vinegar and *dibs*, and one *thulth* of vinegar. Dissolve saffron in it, and season with hot spices, garlic and cumin. Then it is ready for use.

239. *Mulūkhiyya*

Take meat after washing it, and [boil it to] tenderize it. Then, fry and add water to it. Let the Jew's mallow wilt in the sun and chop it up very finely. You can chop it up without wilting it first, but it is better to do so afterwards. Put the Jew's mallow in a pot with water. Pound coriander, caraway seeds,

---

486 *Kanz* states that it should be sprinkled on 'bit by bit' (*qalīl qalīl*). The *Zahr* manuscript is corrupted here as the instruction to beat the mixture is repeated, and should also be done 'a little'. As a result, the text has been slightly amended in line with *Kanz*.

hot spices, salt, and garlic, and then dissolve in water. Put the meat in it, and when it is done cooking, the dish is ready to be eaten.

240. *Qanbarīsiyya*[487]

Wash the meat with hot water, and drain off the water. Then, dissolve *qanbarīs*, and put it in a pot. When it is boiling, add the meat, together with cassia and a bit of salt, and then use.[488]

241. *Tabbāla*[489]

Wash the meat, put it in a pot and [pour on enough water] to cover it. When it comes to a boil, [add] rice to it and boil two or three times. Put in chard, and when it is done, add *iṭriyya*.[490] If you like, you can break [some] eggs over

---

487 cf. *Kanz*, 271 (Appendix, No. 21).

488 The recipe in *Kanz* also recommends adding mastic, while it does not restrict the amount of salt.

489 There are a number of similarities with *Wuṣla*, No. 6.129, which, however, requires chickpeas and *rishtā* (see note below), and also suggests topping the dish with 'kebabs, *sanbūsak*, fried hard-boiled eggs, fried chicken, an egg cake, a sweetmeat, or the like.' This type of dish, which is best described as 'meat upon meat', is rather unusual and does not appear in many treatises, *Wuṣla* being the exception in that it contains three (Nos. 5.16, 5.21, 6.129).

490 The word is derived from the Greek *ítrion* (itself a borrowing from Aramaic), which denoted a kind of cake, possibly including sesame. Galen (Wilkins 2013: 33 ff.) distinguished between two types of *itria*, i.e. *ryēmata* and *lágana*, the latter of which is the etymon of *lasagne* and was unleavened bread or a pancake. Later on, *itriya* referred to a wheat-flour pasta usually used in sweets, like the Roman *libum* (a small cake). The Arabic *iṭriyya* is somewhat of a mystery item as it is both an ingredient and the name of dishes that contain it. It appears in a number of culinary manuals, but only al-Tujībī actually gave instructions, which are as follows: 'vigorously knead semolina or flour and water into a stiff dough and stretch it out on a table or an elongated board. String the dough with both hands as thinly as you can. Then dry in the sun, and bake.' Ibn Jazla (from Ibn Sīnā) states that it was made with 'stiff pancake (*faṭīr*) dough, made into strings and then put into water and cooked with meat or other things.' According to al-Rāzī, it was made from thick wheat flour. References to the use of 'handfuls' of *iṭriyya* leave little doubt that it was dried pasta. Perry ([al-Baghdādī] 2005: 48, note 2) calls it 'a small soup noodle' and equates it with the Italian *orza*. Al-Tujībī's comment that he gives the recipe for *iṭriyya* 'in case it is not available' indicates that it was usually purchased ready made at the market. The fresh variety was known as *rishta* (or *rishtā*), which was a borrowing from the Persian meaning 'thread', and is described by al-Baghdādī as 'dough kneaded and stretched out thinly, and cut into strips four finger-widths long' (1964: 30/trans., 48), though Ibn Sīnā said that in his region it was the name for *iṭriyya*. Nasrallah ([al-Warrāq 2007]: 562) defines it as 'dried thin strings of noodles made with stiff unfermented dough.' According to Ibn Khalṣūn (1996: 156/trans., 82), the best *iṭriyya* are thinly rolled and made with semolina, and they are cooked with meat confit (*awdāk*) and eaten with hot spices. Corriente suggested that both *aṭriya* and *tharīd* go back to the same Latin word *adtrita* ('waste') because the latter was made with pieces of crushed stale bread. The word travelled to the Christian West very early

it. When everything has cooked, pound [and add] cheese, coriander, caraway seeds, mastic, and cassia for seasoning. Then it is ready for use.

242. Raisins and vinegar

Wash the meat, put it in a pot and pour on enough water to immerse it. Then pound half a *raṭl* of raisins and extract [their juices] with three *ūqiyas* of vinegar. Strain and then pound them again until all their essences have been extracted. When there is no vinegar left, strain with water in order to temper the flavour. Then, cut chard, turnip, onions, and aubergine and put everything into the pot. When the vegetables are done, pound hot spices with cumin and garlic, and dissolve in a bowl with the cooking broth. Add them to the pot, and stir the vegetables until everything is [thoroughly] mixed. Afterwards, let it simmer down and then use.

243. Spinach stew (*iṣfānakhiyya*)[491]

When the meat has been tenderized [after boiling], put three *ūqiyas* of rice and half a *raṭl* of meat [in a pot]. Take a bunch of spinach, pick it over, wash, and put it in the pot. Stir a little so that it does not break up. If there is a lot of spinach, boil it first, and strain. Then put it on the rice and make sure that it is neither sticky nor [too] firm. Also add mastic rubbed between the palms, and chopped cassia. When it has finished cooking, eat it.

---

and there is a mention of *ale/atria* as early as the fourteenth century both in the anonymous Catalan cookbook *Libre de sent soví* and a medical treatise by Arnau de Vilanova, as a type of macaroni boiled in almond milk. Vilanova (1947: 135, 137) adds that it was the common people's name for the '*fideus*', another borrowing from Arabic (*fidawsh*), which denoted fresh pasta in Andalusian cookery books (e.g. *Andalusian*, fol. 58r.), and is the direct ancestor of the modern Spanish *fideos* and the Italian *fedelini*. The Arabic *iṭriyya* has survived in the Egyptian *treyya*, as well as in European dishes, such as the southern Italian *ciceri e tria* (chickpeas and tagliatelle) and the Portuguese *aletria* (sweet angel-hair pasta). In some dialects (e.g. Tunisia), *iṭriyya* denotes the generic 'pasta'. See *Andalusian*, fol. 58v.; al-Baghdādī 1964: 29 (trans., 48); al-Tujībī 2012: 91 (No. 8); Ibn Mubarrad 1937: 273 (trans., 471); al-Warrāq 1987: 151 (trans., 308); *Waṣf*, 333, 337; *Taṣānīf al-aṭʿima*, fol. 81r.; Nasrallah [al-Warrāq 2007]: 561–2; Ibn Buṭlān 1990: 78–9 (trans., 158–9); al-Samarqandī 2016: 357–8; Ibn Sīnā 1999: I, 380 (trans., 65); Ibn Jazla, fols. 22v.–23r.; al-Rāzī 2000: 3018; Zaouila 2009: 116; Laurioux 1995: 203; Corriente 1997: 20, 208; Rosenberger 1989: 87ff.; Dalby 2003: 251; Serventi & Sabban 2002: 16ff.; Perry 1981; Oubahli 2006–08.

491 There are not that many spinach stews in the cookery treatises, and they differ considerably from one another, as shown by the recipes in *Wuṣla* (Nos. 6.48-51) or al-Baghdādī (1964: 27/ trans., 45), but often also contain garlic and chickpeas. Also see Ibn Jazla, fols. 16v-17r.; *Taṣānīf al-aṭʿima*, fols. 66r., 77v.

244. Milk stew (*labaniyya*)[492]

Take meat, wash it, and transfer to a bowl. Put milk [and water] in a pot; one third of water and two-thirds of milk. Continue to stir with a ladle until it comes to a boil and then add three or four onions. When the milk and meat are done, pound a few cumin seeds and garlic, and add them to the pot. Throw in mastic and whole cassia [sticks]. Leave to simmer until it is ready,[493] and then serve.

245. *Muhallabiyya*[494]

Take meat, cut it in dainty pieces, and add a little bit of water [and boil]. When it is parboiled, fry it, and then add half a *raṭl* of water. Wash rice, dye it with saffron, and add it to the pot. When [the rice] is done, pour on *dibs* or honey and [cook until] the honey or *dibs* have been absorbed. When it is finished, serve.

246. *Qaliya* with carrots

Tenderize the meat [by boiling it] and then fry. Remove any liquid that remains after frying, and transfer it to a bowl. Add chopped up carrots and onions to the meat and cook off the liquid. When everything is done, pound spices, coriander, caraway seeds into it, along with a bit of salt and let them be absorbed. When it is ready, serve.

247. Truffles

Soak truffles [in water] and scrape off all the soil and dirt. Fry meat and add a little bit of water on it. Boil the truffles. When they are done, drain

---

492 cf. *Kanz*, 37–8 (No. 74).

493 The recipe in *Kanz* ends here.

494 The name of the dish, which was also commonly known as *bahaṭṭa* (see recipe No. 72), goes back to al-Muhallab Ibn Abī Sufra, late seventh-century governor of Khorasan (al-Baghdādī, trans., 50, Note 1; *Wuṣla*, 291). The anonymous Andalusian cookbook narrates the story of a Persian cook whose residence was next to Muhallab Ibn Abī Sufra's and who prepared a dish to prove his culinary prowess. The resultant output met with the ruler's approval and so he called it *muhallabiyya* (*Andalusian*, fol. 59r.; *Anwāʿ*, 153–4). Similarly named recipes are found in a number of cookery books: *Waṣf*, 335, 361; al-Baghdādī 1964: 31 (trans., 50); *Wuṣla*, No. 6.89; al-Warrāq 1987: 139 (trans., 258 [*harīsa kānūniyya*], 279, 404, 407, 408). Al-Warrāq describes it as a *harīsa* with chicken breasts, rice, milk, and sugar; Nasrallah ([al-Warrāq 2007]: 534. Ibn Jazla (fol. 223v.) and Ibn Buṭlān (1990: 94–5/trans., 192–3) stated that the best variety of *muhallabiyya* is that cooked in chicken fat. It was thought to purify the mind and make dreams pleasurable. The *muhallabiyya* is probably the precursor to the European *blancmange*, which, unlike the modern sweet, was a rice pudding with meat.

off the water and put the truffles on the fried meat. Cook off the liquid, and season with coriander, caraway seeds and hot spices. The dish should contain carrots, truffles and fresh coriander.

248. *Maḍīra* (sour milk stew)[495]

Fry onions and when they are done, put in milk and water, in equal quantities. When they are cooked, add chard, onions (or leeks), and carrots. When the vegetables are done, season with garlic, cumin and a little bit of salt. If the dish is made with meat, add it when boiling the milk or whatever else you are using. Once the vegetables are cooked and the seasonings added, then it is ready to eat.

249. *Ṭabāhaja*[496] with broad beans

Pound meat with onions, hot spices, coriander and caraway seeds, and then shape into flat discs. Add a little water and boil until it is done. Fry, and then

495 The dish takes its name from the key ingredient, sour milk (*maḍīr*). Legend has it that it was created by the founder of the Umayyad dynasty, Muʿāwiya (d. 680). According to the tenth-century poet Kushājim, it is the 'most delicious, wondrous and strangest dish of humankind' (al-Warrāq 1987: 175). The anonymous Andalusian treatise (fol. 22r.) associates it with Egyptian cuisine as 'the people of Tanis in Egypt cook fresh fish as they cook their meat, such as *maḍīra*.' Al-Tujībī, who has two recipes with this name, also classes it as an 'Eastern' dish (2012: 89). In Muslim Spain it denoted a dish of meat and yoghurt (Corriente 1997: 504). According to Ibn Jazla, 'the best kind is of medium acidity and added with salted lemon, while the taste can be sweetened by eating honey after it and by cooking it together with hot spices such as cassia, pepper and galangal (fols. 215r. –216v.). The dish was immortalised in literature in the eponymously titled story (*maqāma*) by al-Hamadhānī (d. 1008). Al-Rāzī 1881: 29; *Waṣf*, 327–8; al-Baghdādī 1964: 20–1 (trans., 41–2); al-Warrāq 1987: 174–5 (trans., 300–2); *Taṣānīf al-aṭʿima*, fol. 75v.; Malti-Douglas 1985. For literary references to *maḍīra*, see van Gelder 2000: 48–51.

496 This dish of fried slices of meat was very popular, as evidenced by its occurrence in a number of culinary treatises. Al-Warrāq devoted a whole chapter (No. 86) with ten recipes to the dish. He traced it back to the Sasanid king Bahrām whose retinue shot a deer and cut part of it in thin slices, which they proceeded to cook in fat. At first the king was shocked at what he considered the spoiling of the meat by slicing but after tasting it he greatly liked it. The etymology of the name is unclear; Perry suggests it is the Persian *ṭābah* (also *tāwa*, 'skillet, frying pan'), though Nasrallah ([al-Warrāq 2007]: 354–5, Note 4) may be closer to the truth with *tabāh* ('spoilt'), in reference to the king exclaiming that his servants had spoilt the meat. In Persian, *ṭabāhja* denoted an omelette or 'soft meat' (Steingass 1894: 808). According to Ibn Sīda (2000: IV, 468), the Persian etymon meant 'fried meat'. Al-Warrāq contrasted *ṭabāhajas* with *muṭajjanāt* (braised dishes); the former contain boneless and sliced meat, and the latter jointed chickens with the bones. He added that *ṭabāhajas* differed from *maqlī* (fried) dishes in that the former contain a sauce (*ṣibāgh*) and vegetables such as eggplant, with the meat being sliced. *Maqlī* involves fried meat cut into hazelnut-sized pieces, but without vegetables. *Zahr* has another two *ṭabāhajas* (Nos. 251, 255), while *Kanz* has one (No. 83), which bears little resemblance to

throw in skinned green broad beans. When the beans are cooked, break some eggs into [the pot] and leave until everything is done. Sprinkle on the pounded spices, and serve.

250. *Ṭabāhaja* recipe

Wash the meat and pour on enough water to cover it. When it is done and there is still a lot of water left, remove it and fry the meat. Once the meat has been fried, add the water that you took out. Make sure that the broad beans have been skinned. Then, add the onions and put [everything] in a pot. Continue cooking until everything is done. Pound coriander, caraway seeds and hot spices, and then gradually add fresh coriander to ensure that the spices and herbs are all thoroughly mixed together. If you have some spices left over, sprinkle them on top, and then serve.

251. Recipe for pomegranate seeds with olive oil

Cut up the meat and wash it. Fry it without water. Then, pound pomegranate seeds with raisins – one and a half *raṭls* of raisins for each *raṭl* of pomegranate seeds. Pound each separately, strain, and add to the meat. Continue pounding and straining with water until the flavour is tempered. Cut up chard, onions, carrots, turnips, and aubergines. When the meat is half-done, throw in the aforesaid ingredients. Pound garlic and cumin, and season the dish with them. Serve.

252. *Qamḥiyya* recipe

Season the wheat. Pound, dry and wash meat, and put it in a pot together with the wheat. When everything is cooked and the wheat starch has softened, add mastic and cassia. Pound cumin and cheese, and add. Then serve.

253. *Summāqiyya* recipe

Heat water until it comes to a boil. Pound sumac berries, soak them in water and strain. Wash the meat and put it in a pot [with oil]. When it has been

---

the ones here. Ibn Jazla (fol. 147r.–v.) and Ibn Buṭlān (1990: 96–7/trans., 194–5) refer to a sour (*ḥāmiḍa*) and salty (*māliḥa*) *ṭabāhaja*. The dish was sometimes served with a fried thin flatbread or a small *sanbūsaj* on top. Interestingly enough, only the sour *ṭabāhaja* actually includes salt (half a *dirham*), whereas the salty one does not (Ibn Jazla). Steingass 1892: 278, 804; al-Warrāq 1987: 74, 219–23 (trans., 172, 354–9); *Taṣānīf al-aṭʿima*, fol. 65r.–v.; al-Baghdādī 1964: 16–7 (trans., 34); *Waṣf*, 14; al-Tujībī 2012: 119 (*ṭabāhajiyya*, where it is referred to as an 'Oriental dish'); Ibn al-Ḥashshāʾ 1941: No. 571.

fried, add the sumac juice to it, and bring to a boil. When it has boiled four or five times, throw in carrots, turnip, chard, onions, and aubergine. When everything is cooked, season with walnuts and chopped up vegetables, celery, garlic, and cumin. When it is finished [cooking], serve.

254. Recipe for a *ṭabāhaja* with snake melon[497]

Tenderize the meat [by boiling] and fry with a bit of onions. Peel small snake melons and put them in the pot with the onions, and cook them down. When it is done, season with coriander, caraway seeds, and hot spices. Make sure that the meat is fatty.

255. *Narjisiyya* recipe

Tenderize the meat [by boiling] and fry it. Add carrots, and boil [everything] two or three times. Then, wash rice, sprinkle it on and let it cook. When everything is done, pound mastic, cassia and hot spices, sprinkle them on top, and stir. If you like, you can layer eggs on top. If not, leave as is.

256. Recipe for rice pudding (*aruzz bi-laban ḥalīb*)

Wash and boil the rice and add a bit of mastic and cassia to it. For each *raṭl* of milk, take three *ūqiyas* of rice. Make sure the fire underneath is a gentle one. When it is done, put in containers to cool down. It is eaten with honey, *dibs*, or sugar.

257. Recipe for a *qaliya* with carrots and lemon juice

Tenderize the meat [by boiling], and [then] fry. When it is half fried, chop up onions and add. When everything is cooked, take lemon juice and mix it with a quantity of water that exceeds it, and put it in a pot. Boil twice, and season with coriander, caraway seeds, hot spices and salt, and then serve.

Chickens: before you slaughter them, tire them out thoroughly until they are no longer able to fly or walk because of fatigue. At this point, you can

497 *ʿajjūr* (cf. *ʿajr*, 'green, unripe'); this vegetable is used in only one recipe in Ibn Mubarrad's book (1937: 374), two in *Kanz* (Nos. 630, 631), but no fewer than eight times in *Wuṣla* (Nos. 6.35–9, 8.79–81), where it is the main ingredient in stews, or topped or stuffed with meat and vegetables. Perry (*Wuṣla*, 294) equates it with *qiththā'* and identifies it as the ridged cucumber or unripe snake melon, i.e. the Armenian cucumber or *ghootah*. In Arabic it was also known as *faqqūṣ*. Ibn al-Bayṭār 1992: IV, 226; *Wuṣla*, 294; Lewicka 2011: 245 (note No. 361); Watson 1983: 89; Hinds & Badawi 1986: 563; Dozy 1877–81: II, 96.

slaughter them and roast them. The meat will be more tender.[498]

258. [Another] recipe

Take pullets and boil them. Make sure they are completely jointed. When the meat has boiled and tenderized, pour on enough sesame oil to cover it. Fry everything and sprinkle on dried coriander. Then, put in a bowl.

259. *Laymūniyya* (lemon stew) recipe

Take chickens and boil them. When they are done, take the broth, and squeeze lime juice into it. Add sugar, sprigs of mint, cinnamon, and mastic to the chicken. Boil twice and ladle up.

260. Another kind

Take chickens and boil them. Add finely pounded peeled almonds to the broth, and strain through a fine-mesh sieve. Throw in a piece of gourd. When the mixture has thickened, add as much lime juice as you like to sour the dish. Then boil the chicken in it.

261. Another similar recipe

Instead of almonds, use safflower seeds, and cook until it has the consistency of *qanbarīsiyya*.[499]

262. Another kind

Take fatty chickens and parboil them. Peel almonds and pound them finely until they are swimming in their oil. Add the chicken broth and strain through a fine-mesh sieve. Return it to the chicken and add six or seven *dirhams* of walnuts dissolved in the chicken broth. Add sugar and thicken the mixture over a fire so that it can be drunk from a wooden bowl. When it is ready, squeeze lime juice and add it after straining. Bring it to the boil two or three times, add blanched pistachios, mint, cinnamon and mastic, and then ladle up.

---

498 This recommendation is taken from *Wuṣla* (No. 5.1.), except for the ending: '[the meat] is more tender than that of chickens that can walk'. *Kanz* (28–9, No. 48).

499 See recipe No. 240.

263. Pomegranate seeds

Pound them finely, strain and thicken with almonds. Add sugar, sprigs of mint, cinnamon and mastic. Then, [cook] over a fire to thicken. Add chicken that has been fried, and stew everything. If you want to add some gourd, do so.

264. *Bunduqiyya* (hazelnut stew) recipe

Tenderize the meat [by boiling] and fry it in sesame oil. Transfer to a vessel and then put water into a pot, together with rose water and white sugar. Boil until it becomes like rose-water syrup. Peel the hazelnuts using hot water and then pound and strain them before sprinkling them on top. Then, pour all of it over the chicken, and eat.

265. The Nubian Lady (*Sitt al-Nūba*)[500]

Take a chicken, scald it and parboil. Then, fry in sesame oil and transfer to a platter. Take almonds that have been blanched and toasted. Pound them and strain until you obtain [almond] milk. Then dissolve saffron and boil it in the almond milk with sugar until it thickens.

Take the chicken [put it in the pot] and on top place almonds, jujubes and black raisins that have been macerated in musk-infused rose water. Take blanched pistachios, split them in half, and boil with the rest. Then add toasted almond oil, and eat.

266. Rice pilaf (*aruzz mufalfal*)

Once the meat has been tenderized, soak the rice and then rinse it. Add cinnamon, mastic and a little salt. When adding the rice make sure that the meat is immersed in water – for each *raṭl* of meat, take three *ūqiyas* of rice. Add a bit of water to the top of the pot until it heats up. If you want something else, pour it on top, and then eat.

267. *Sanbūsak* recipe

Pound the meat very finely and boil it. Don't leave it alone so that it does not coagulate into a lump. When the meat has been tenderized and dried, it is fried until no liquid remains [in the pan]. Chop up the vegetables, parsley, fresh coriander and mint, and pound (dried) coriander, caraway seeds and hot spices. Mix the meat with the vegetables. Pound walnuts and almonds

---

500 There are three dishes by this name in *Kanz* (Nos. 59, 66, 137). This one appears to have been adapted from No. 59 (p. 32).

and mix them in, or sprinkle on a little lemon [juice] so that the pounded spices do not overcook. Add a little sumac for the same reason. Fry in sesame oil or sheep's tail fat.

268. Section on omelettes

They are like *sanbūsak* recipes but with the addition of eggs. Fry in olive oil and if it is an omelette without meat, chop up greens like celery, parsley, mint and fresh coriander, and pound dried coriander, caraway seeds, hot spices, cheese and walnuts and mix all of these ingredients with two eggs so that it turns into an omelette. Then fry in olive oil and eat.

269. *Mutawakkiliyya*[501]

After tenderizing and frying meat, pound coriander, caraway seeds, hot spices, a little cumin, a full handful of peeled garlic, and salt. Pound everything finely together and mix it with the fried meat. Fry everything together. Pound lupine beans and strain them through a sieve. Pound walnuts finely, and add them to the beans, making sure the mixture is smooth. Then, add the walnuts to the fried meat and spices, and bring to a boil. When it is boiling, reduce the fire and serve.

270. Recipe for a *mufarraka*[502]

Boil the offal of yearlings and when it has tenderized, parboil and chop some onion into it. Then fry and when everything is cooked, break some eggs into it and stir. When everything is done, season with coriander, caraway seeds, hot spices, and eat.

---

501 This is one of two dishes in the text (the other one being No. 305), named after and/or inspired by the Abbasid caliph al-Mutawakkil (d. 861). Similarly named dishes are also found elsewhere: two in *Kanz* (No. 89, Appendix No. 10); three in al-Warrāq (1987: 142, 156, 216/ trans., 124, 150, 479); two in *Waṣf* (340, 349); and one in *Wuṣla* (No. 6.40). The Andalusian treatises do not contain any of these recipes, though al-Tujībī (2012: 253) includes a recipe which he says is called 'the brain (*dimāgh*) of al-Mutawakkil' in a chapter on 'Oriental dishes' (*anwāʿ sharqiyya*) and is unusual in that it is a type of candy.

502 The name comes from the verb *farraka*, 'to rub'. *Waṣf* contains two recipes by this name (179–80, 391), but neither seems to have been the model for the one here.

271. Recipe

Wash the meat and then tenderize it. When it is tender, cut some onions and chard, and add them. When everything has cooked, break eggs into it and season with hot spices.

272. *Maghmūma* recipe[503]

Tenderize meat and fry it. Then put it in [a pot with enough] water to immerse it. Cut an aubergine into quarters, and put it in a pot together with onions. Cook until everything is done, and season with coriander, caraway seeds and hot spices.

273. *Būrāniyya* recipe

Tenderize the meat and fry it. When it has half-done, add onion to it. When everything is cooked, fry the aubergine and add it to the meat in the pot. Finally, season with coriander, caraway seeds, and salt.

274. *Maḥshī* recipe

Take fresh fish and remove its scales with a knife, and split it in half. Wash and rinse with water. Then take parsley, celery, mint and fresh coriander, and chop everything up thoroughly. Add lemon juice to it and one *ūqiya* of crushed sumac, and the same quantity of carrots, *qanbarīs* and tahini. Then take coriander, garlic, caraway seeds and hot spices, and pound everything together with a little bit of salt. Add them to all the other ingredients, and slather the fish with the mixture before putting it in a frying pan. Then, add some good-quality moderately hot olive oil, or half sesame oil and half olive oil. Roast it in the oven and eat.

---

503 The name of the dish literally means 'hidden', in reference to the fact that the pot is covered with a disc of bread for the final stage in the cooking process: al-Warrāq 1987: 184–6 (trans., 311–4); al-Baghdādī 1964: 20–1 (trans., 38–9); *Waṣf*, 317, 371–2, 372, 447; *Andalusian*, fol. 9v. (attributed to the caliph Ibn al-Mahdī); al-Tujībī 2012: 168; *Taṣānīf al-aṭʿima*, fol. 67v. Interestingly enough, the recipes in the anonymous Andalusian, al-Tujībī and al-Warrāq (who has five in total) are all made with onion layers alternating with meat layers (producing a potpie somewhat like a Lancashire hotpot), whereas those in *Waṣf* and al-Baghdādī add aubergine as well. The *Andalusian* is the odd one out since it uses only onion juice. The fact that the recipe here dispenses with onions may indicate the rise in popularity of the aubergine in the intervening period. According to Ibn Buṭlān (1990: 94–5/trans., 192–3), it is very nutritional, but not recommended for those with a weak stomach. Ibn Jazla's recipe includes vinegar and *murrī*, while the latter part of the process involves covering it with a semolina-flour flatbread until it is fully cooked (fols. 220v.–221r.).

275. [How to prepare] Chickens

Scald a chicken, split it open and wash [with water]. Take a pot, fill it with water [and boil the chicken] until it is half done. Then stuff it with the seasonings of this recipe. Put the chicken in a pan and pour on sesame oil instead of olive oil since olive oil cuts the bad odour of fish, whereas sesame oil improves the flavour of chickens. Then, roast in the oven and eat.

276. Using the *maḥshī* preparation with meat

Cut up the meat in dainty pieces and rinse them in hot water. Put it in a pot, immerse in water, and cook until it is done. Then, remove the water and put it in a vessel. Fry the meat thoroughly and cut onion into it. Then, return to the water you removed earlier. When it is boiling slightly, dissolve into it the *maḥshī* seasonings. Put everything into a pot [and heat] until it comes to a boil. [Reduce the heat and] let it simmer down.

Tip: If the dish gets slightly burnt, take some saltwort tied in a cloth bundle and put it in the pot, pushing it all the way to the bottom. Leave it there for an hour. This will remove the burnt flavour. If it is too salty, take the peel of a dried yellow melon and throw it into the pot, pushing it all the way to the bottom. This will eradicate the saltiness.

277. Recipe for strained lentils with vinegar and *dibs*

You need one *raṭl* of crushed winnowed lentils for each three *raṭls* of water, two *raṭls* of *dibs*, one third of a *raṭl* of vinegar, as well as jujubes and saffron, if you like.

278. Recipe for a *muhallabiyya* without meat

For each *raṭl* of rice, take four *raṭls* of water, and one *raṭl* of bee honey or two *raṭls* of *dibs*, and two *ūqiyas* of sesame oil. If you use honey, take three *dirhams* of saffron. If you use *dibs*, take one *dirham* of saffron, and the required amount of hot spices.

279. Pomegranate seeds[504]

This type is the best there is. Take pomegranate seeds and strain them after pounding and boiling them. Add sugar, mint and cinnamon and throw in a chicken that has been washed. [Then cook] until it is done, and eat.

---

504 cf. *Wuṣla*, No. 5.35.

280. Another kind[505]

Take pomegranate seeds, strain them, and sweeten with sugar. [Boil and] thicken with ground almonds, and then add hot ginger, pieces of quince and *Fatḥī* apple.[506] Cut up a boiled chicken, fry it and then add it [to the mixture].

281. *Kuzbariyya* (coriander stew)

Take a chicken, boil it, and cut it up. Then fry with onions, sesame oil, hot spices, pounded garlic and fresh coriander. When it is fried, finely crush coriander leaves. Return the broth [to the pot][507] and throw in the coriander, as you would when making a *mulūkhiyya*.

282. Another kind

Cook the chicken as described above, and then fry it with garlic, chopped up onions, sesame oil, chicken fat, and hot spices. When everything has fried, finely pound fresh coriander and put it in the broth. Then, strain through a sieve several times so as to produce a viscous liquid. Cook it with the chicken and add well-sifted rice flour. It will thicken and retain its flavour. This is one of the Western dishes.

283. Recipe for a tamarind dish for those suffering from excess yellow bile and which balances the temperament[508]

Boil the chicken and fry it. Then, mash tamarinds several times and put them in the chicken broth. Add sugar and thicken over a gentle fire, just as you do for pomegranate seeds. Finally, add mint and cinnamon.

284. Recipe for barberries, which is beneficial for diarrhoea[509]

Boil the barberries, strain them, and thicken with sugar. Add them to chicken with a little bit of mint.

---

505 cf. *Wuṣla*, No. 5.36, where the dish is called *rummān mukhaththara* ('thickened pomegranate').

506 This type of apple is also used in *Wuṣla*, No. 5.48 (a chicken quince stew). It is unclear which variety this refers to.

507 The broth would have been left to one side before frying the chicken.

508 cf. *Wuṣla*, No. 5.40, with 'spices' (*abāzīr*) being added, rather than just cinnamon.

509 cf. *Wuṣla*, No. 5.41.

285. *Zīrbāj*[510]
Boil and fry a chicken. Take the chicken broth and add sugar, vinegar and saffron, and thicken with pounded boiled and strained almond kernels, as well as a little bit of starch. Add pistachios and almonds. If you like, you can make it with vinegar and lemon juice. This will be very tasty.

286. Recipe for a parsley dish[511]
Take a chicken, boil and fry it. Then, strip parsley from the stems, pound it finely, and add vinegar. Pound everything together with the vinegar until it becomes so thin that it can be soaked up with bread. Add ginger, pepper, garlic, together with *afwāh al-ṭīb*. Put the chicken in it while it is still hot. This is very flavoursome.

287. Recipe for a delicious dish
Take a fatty chicken, and boil and fry it until it is golden and looks nice. Add eggs without the white, so that only the yolks remain. Take the chicken broth and fat and pour it over the fried chicken that has been cut up and the egg yolks. Add mastic, a little dried coriander and pepper to the broth and fat. Boil it many times to cook off the broth, and then ladle up. It is delicious.

288. Syrian mulberry dish[512]
Take mulberries, macerate and strain them. Add sugar, thicken it, and add mint and *aṭrāf al-ṭīb* before putting a fried chicken into [the mixture].

289. Dish with local ripe cherries[513]
Take cherries and boil them in a little water. Then strain and thicken over a fire. Add fried chicken to it.

Tip: If you cook fatty chickens and add half an ūqiya *of sheep's tail fat for each chicken, it will turn into chicken fat.*[514]

---

510 cf. *Wuṣla*, No. 5.49, where the last two sentences are missing as they were presumably added by the author of *Zahr*.

511 cf. *Wuṣla*, No. 5.54.

512 cf. *Wuṣla*, No. 5.71, where it is specified that it is to be made with chicken (*bi-dajāj*).

513 cf. *Wuṣla*, No. 5.72, which adds mint together with the chicken.

514 This section is missing from *Wuṣla*.

290. A kind of *sanbūsak*[515]

Take thigh and loin meat and pound it with a cleaver on a wooden board. Boil until it is done and then drain off the water. Pound in a mortar until it is smooth, and then put it in a brass pot and add sheep's tail fat on it, together with dried coriander, cassia, mastic, pepper, and roast. Add one part chopped up parsley, one part of mint, and half a part rue. Boil everything. Then add tart vinegar to it and boil until it becomes white vinegar. Then, add lemon juice to it and boil several times. Afterwards fill the *sanbūsak* sheets. This is the best way to make them.

291. Another kind[516]

Add sumac, shelled pistachios and walnuts to the [*sanbūsak*] filling.

292. Another kind[517]

Take breadcrumbs and dye them with saffron. Sift through a sieve and add pounded sugar, bee honey and sesame oil. Then, proceed as you would with an *Asyūṭiyya*.[518] When it is done, add black poppy seeds and pistachio kernels, and use this to stuff the *sanbūsak* with.

293. Kebabs[519]

Cut fillet and loins in big slices, and put them on a skewer. Rub [the meat] with sesame oil, olive oil, dried coriander, and pounded garlic. Roast on a skewer over a gentle fire.

294. Another kind, the best there is[520]

[Take] fillet meat and cut it up into pieces. Cut sheep's tail fat into matching pieces. Put both of them on a skewer, alternating sheep's tail fat with meat. Roast over a coal fire. Whenever the fat is dripping, move one end of the skewer until the fat drops [back] on the meat. Rub with rose water and

---

515 cf. *Wuṣla*, No. 6.2.

516 cf. *Wuṣla*, No. 6.3.

517 cf. *Wuṣla*, No. 6.5.

518 A type of bread pudding, consisting of baked flatbreads filled with nuts, honey, etc., somewhat similar to *jūdhāb* recipes (without the chicken). It is named after the Upper-Egyptian town of Asyut. For recipes, *Kanz*, Nos. 131, 269, 274; *Wuṣla*, No. 7.53.

519 cf. recipe No. 84; *Wuṣla*, No. 6.7.

520 cf. *Wuṣla*, No. 6.8.

sesame oil. Do this several times until it is done. Sprinkle dried coriander on top, and eat.

295.[521]

Take meat and cut it up in thick slices. Hang it on a hook at the top of the *tannūr* until it releases all the blood and juices, as you do for smoked kebabs, and then put in an earthenware jug. There are people who add apple and quince juice when they put the meat in the jug. Others put in vinegar, lemon juice, mint, and *aṭrāf al-ṭīb*.[522] Still others add verjuice, or fresh pomegranate juice with sugar. For most of the types of meat slices that are in the jug, drizzle on good-quality olive oil, rose water, mastic and cinnamon when you put the meat in. Seal the top of the jug and then put it in the brick oven. You should not add water to it.

296.[523]

Take liver and boil it.[524] Add hot spices, *aṭrāf al-ṭīb*, and make sausages [with it]. Then, grill. This is very good.

297.[525]

Take ribs, backbone and loins. Cut them up[526] and take a large pot, covered with a wide-mesh strainer[527] on which you place the meat. Fill half of the pot with water and throw in onion, chickpeas, cinnamon, mastic and rue. Boil and tightly seal the edges with clay. Then, put on a gentle fire from the evening until the morning. When you eat it, moisten breadcrumbs with *kumāj*[528] broth, and put the meat on top.[529] This is very delicious.

---

521 cf. *Wuṣla*, No. 6.9.

522 The ingredients in *Wuṣla* also include olive oil, rose buds, mastic, three sprigs of coriander and cinnamon.

523 cf. *Wuṣla*, No. 6.16.

524 The recipe in *Wuṣla* also instructs to pound it with the same amount of sheep's tail fat.

525 cf. *Wuṣla*, No. 6.18, where it is called 'the monk's roast (*shuwā al-rāhib*)'.

526 The recipe in *Wuṣla* adds that it can be 'as much as you like.'

527 'or a cage (*qafṣ*)' (*Wuṣla*).

528 < Persian *kumāj* (or *kumāch*), 'unleavened bread; bread baked in the ashes'; Steingass 1892: 1046; Dozy 1877–81: II, 487; Mielck 1913: 77. The word is still used today, particularly in Lebanon to refer to the local round flatbread, while in Egypt *kimāj* is a type of wheat bread (Hinds & Badawi 1986: 763).

529 *Wuṣla* also advises 'to make sure no steam escapes from the pot.'

298. Recipe for bone marrow[530]

Take a copper pipe, the size of a thighbone, and make sure one end of it is closed off. Take liver and boil it. Use one part of it and two parts of sheep's tail fat, and finely pound. Put [the mixture] into the copper pipes and seal the end with dough. Place it in water and boil until it is done. Then, transfer to a bowl. It will have the colour and taste of marrow.

299. *Mulūkhiyya*[531]

Take meat and cut it into small pieces. Then, pound some of it with onion and coriander, as well as cinnamon and mastic. Parboil the meat and then fry with chopped onion, garlic pounded with fresh coriander, pepper, dried coriander, caraway seeds, and salt. Add sheep's tail fat to the meat and fry until golden. Shape into meatballs, and boil. When they are almost done, add the meat broth and boil. Finely chop Jew's mallow and throw it in. It should not be too thin, nor should there be any hotness [in the taste].[532]

300. Another type[533]

There are people who add fresh or preserved lime juice and then boil it several times after frying in order to bring out the sourness. Afterwards, return and cook as usual.

301. [534]

Other people will roast six onions or so until they become like marrow when done. Use a mortar to finely pound the onions with fresh or dried coriander, garlic, and pepper. Then, add to the *mulūkhiyya* when it is done. Pour rendered sheep's tail fat on, and ladle up. When eating the *mulūkhiyya*, also dice some common mallow. In each [individual] bowl, put a bunch of [diced] common mallow and a handful of dried Jew's mallow rubbed by hand, and mix everything together.

---

530 cf. *Wuṣla*, No. 6.19.

531 cf. *Wuṣla*, No. 6.23.

532 The recipe in *Wuṣla* adds that 'it should be neither thin nor thick, while neither the salt nor the hotness should dominate.'

533 cf. *Wuṣla*, No. 6.24.

534 This recipe is a type of *mulūkhiyya* and is an adaptation from *Wuṣla*, Nos. 6.25–6.

302. Aubergine

Before frying it, you should prick it with a knife and soak in water to extract its black juices. Then, squeeze it, parboil, and squeeze [again].

303. Stuffed aubergines[535]

Take large aubergines and cut the heads (pericarps) from the stem. Scoop out the inside and remove the core but do not cut all the way down to the peel. Then, take meat, shape it into meatballs, and boil. When they are done, pound them in a mortar for a second time, until they are smooth. Put the meat in a brass pot and add dried coriander, caraway seeds, pepper, cassia, and a lot of chopped fresh coriander and parsley. Fry everything until it is golden, season with salt, and stuff the aubergines [with the mixture]. At the location of the pericarps, prick three wooden skewers through [the aubergines] and then put them in the pot. Fry in sheep's tail fat until they are golden. Put on a plate, and sprinkle on dried coriander. Remove the skewers and eat.

304. *Mutawakkiliyya* with taro[536]

Boil meat, make meatballs with it, and fry in oil. Cut up onions and fry them with the meat. Add pounded garlic, fresh and dried coriander and hot spices and [continue to] fry until [everything is] done. Then, cut up the taro and boil until froth appears, and when it does, strain off the water. Add a little salt and a drop of good-quality olive oil. Rub well and wash several times until it is no longer viscous. Afterwards, add the meat and boil over a gentle fire until it is done. Then, ladle up.

305. *Fūliyya* (broad brean stew)

It must contain fresh thyme. This is the basis and reduces the broth. Break eggs into it. The rest is well known.

306. A type of *narjisiyya*[537]

Cut meat into small pieces and make into small-sized meatballs with spices and fresh coriander. Fry in oil and pare carrots like for a *narjisiyya* and throw on the meat. Cover and do not add water to the carrots. Leave until it is done in the oil on a gentle fire. It is very nice.

---

535 cf. *Wuṣla*, No. 6.32.

536 cf. *Wuṣla*, No. 6.40.

537 cf. *Wuṣla*, No. 6.64.

307. A type of *ḥiṣrimiyya*[538]

Take sour grapes and strip [them from their stalks]. Boil them until they are cooked, strain [off the juice] and then transfer [the pot] to a fire. Boil raw meat and large meatballs [made] with crushed chickpeas and rice. [Add] chard ribs, onion, mint, gourd and aubergines cut in half, and sour apples cut in half from which the seeds and cores have been removed, as well as fresh barley. If you can't find [fresh barley] use the dried one. Thicken with bread, or pounded rice, which is better as it will turn the dish white. When it is done, pound some garlic and fresh coriander [to sprinkle on].

308. Turnip dish

Serve the meat in the usual manner, that is to say with hot spices and seasonings as you would if it was not made with turnips. When it has been fried golden without using sheep's tail fat, throw in turnip, cover until it is done and then ladle up.

309. A type of sumac dish[539]

Take sumac, pound it, winnow the fruit, remove the seeds, and soak in water what remains of the flowers. Chop up parsley, mint and rue. Sift bread crumbs and knead it with the greens until they wilt. Add the sumac flowers with spices, a lot of dried thyme and *aṭrāf al-ṭīb*; knead everything with lemon juice, tahini, a little bit of milk, pounded and toasted almond kernels, and make a stuffing out of it. Cut sour lemons into small pieces and add it as well. Then take the water [in which the the sumac has been soaked] and put it in a pot. Add the meat and meat balls, and also knead finely chopped sour lemons into balls. Boil and add the chard ribs, aubergine, gourd, pieces of quince, carrots and turnips. When everything is done, throw in chopped table leeks and garlic pounded with fresh coriander. Throw in the stuffing with crushed chickpeas in the meat broth and boil twice. Make it as sour as you like. Do not let [the sumac] boil a lot since that will turn it black, and do not add more sumac berries. If you like, you can remove them with the lemon juice and do the same with the meat broth so that the colour does not become darker. If you add a lot of hazelnuts to it, that is better than using walnuts.

538 cf. *Wuṣla*, No. 6.70.

539 cf. *Wuṣla*, No. 6.80.

310. Another type[540]

Take sumac, pound it and soak in water. Strain and put in a pot. Sweeten with sugar, and thicken with blanched pounded almonds that have been milked with sumac juice. Thicken over a fire. Take meat, boil and deep-fry in oil, together with onions. Put it in the sumac and boil until the meat becomes sour and then enhance [the taste] by adding a bit of lemon juice.

311. A dish called *maʿshūqa*[541]

Take one *raṭl* of meat without bones and cut it into small pieces. Parboil and strain off the liquid. Put it in a frying pan with two-thirds of a *raṭl* of sheep's tail fat cut up into small pieces, just like the meat, and add it to the meat. Put on a gentle fire and parboil, until the oil has browned. Take two *raṭls* of good dates, remove the stones and replace them with pounded pistachios and sugar kneaded with rose water and musk. Put the dates on top of the meat and the oil and put on a low fire until the dates are done. Sprinkle on hard-boiled egg yolks and whole blanched musk-infused pistachios. This is very good.[542]

312. A type of *Ma'mūniyya*[543]

Take sheep's tail fat and boil it in water until it has come apart, and then strain off the water. Afterwards, macerate and remove the fat through a sieve. Put in a bowl and then prepare rice by washing it. Pound and sieve it. Grind sugar and put it with the fat into a brass pot. Cook over a gentle fire until it is done and has thickened up. Spread onto a plate and throw on some whole pistachio kernels.

313. Another type[544]

Take rice, wash it, finely pound it and sift it through a sieve. Take good-quality milk and boil it over a fire. Add sugar until it dissolves, and then add rice and cook like a thin *ʿaṣīda*. Add a good deal of rendered sheep's tail fat, which will be absorbed in the mixture. Continue to cook over a gentle fire until the fat comes out. You will know it is done is when the oil has been released

---

540 cf. *Wuṣla*, No. 6.84.

541 cf. *Wuṣla*, No. 6.132. *Kanz* also contains a recipe by this name (No. 669), which literally means 'the beloved', but for an incense preparation, rather than an edible.

542 The sequence is slightly different in *Wuṣla*: 'Sprinkle on whole blanched [and peeled] pistachios, musk, and rose water, and remove [from the fire]. You can add hardboiled egg yolks.'

543 cf. *Wuṣla*, No. 7.5.

544 cf. *Wuṣla*, No. 7.6.

and the rice has browned. Add peeled pistachios, pomegranate seeds and dyed hard candies.[545]

314. Another kind, which is tasty and is made with chicken breasts[546]
Take fatty chickens, boil them and fry in sesame oil. Take the breasts, let them cool off, and then shred them to hair-like threads. When that is done, take rice, wash it, pound it, and strain it smoothly. For each *raṭl* of rice use two shredded chicken breasts, together with enough sugar to make it as sweet as you like. Boil milk, and melt sugar in it so that it becomes very sweet. When the sugar has been dissolved, add the shredded chicken breasts to it and boil thoroughly. Then return the rice [to the pot] and stir so that it does not stick. When it becomes like *'aṣīda*, throw in sheep's tail fat and cook over a gentle fire until it releases its oil, and has browned. Continue stirring until it becomes like something that can be stretched out on a plate. Then ladle it up and in the middle throw peeled pistachios, which will be surrounded by chicken breasts. This was made in the house of al-Malik Ashraf[547] – may Allah have mercy on his soul.

315. Pistachio *harīsa* (pottage)[548]
Take blanched pistachios,[549] dry them, and heat them over a gentle fire. Pound them finely – use one *raṭl* of pistachios for the breasts of two chickens. Boil the chicken breasts without salt, and then fry them in good-quality olive oil and sesame oil.[550] Let it cool down, and once it has, remove the bones and shred the meat, and if you have some chard leaves, wrap the meat in them so that it stays moist. Then, make a thin half-thickened rose-water syrup[551] and add the chicken to it. Stir with a thin wooden stick.[552] When the chicken breasts have browned, throw in the aforementioned pistachios first, and vigorously beat with a ladle, as you do for a *harīsa* so that [the pottage] thickens.

---

545 *aqrāṣ laymūn*; these were actually used as a stomachic (*juwārishn*). According to the recipe in *Kanz* (p. 132: No. 349), they are made by boiling down rose-water syrup and lemon juice until it becomes like candy. In *Wuṣla*, they are used only as garnish (Nos. 7.6, 7.8, 7.94).

546 cf. *Wuṣla*, No. 7.7, where it is simply stated that it is 'better than the' preceding one.

547 Ayyubid Sultan of Egypt (1262–1293).

548 cf. *Wuṣla*, No. 7.8.

549 *Wuṣla* adds that the pistachios should also be peeled and then roasted over a low fire.

550 The recipe in *Wuṣla* omits sesame oil.

551 *Wuṣla*: 'use sugar to make delicate rose-water syrup.'

552 The Arabic *nushshāba* translates as 'arrow'.

Add milk in which rose water has been dissolved; for each *raṭl* of pistachios, take one and a half *ūqiyas* of good-quality honey and also put in the fat that came out of the chickens. At the same time, add enough chopped chard to dye the dish in the colour that you like.[553] Add musk and rose water, spread [the stew] out on plates and decorate with hard candies and pounded sugar.

316. Pistachio stew (*fustuqiyya*) without chicken breasts[554]

Take pistachios, blanch and roast them, and then pound until they swim in their oil, like for a *harīsa*. Thicken the rose-water syrup and throw in the pistachios, together with starch. Cook until it thickens, and use. Dye [green] with chard leaves.

317. Salted lemon[555]

Take salted lemons, cut them into small pieces, and put them in a jar. Squeeze [the juice of] limes – or sour oranges, which are lower [in acidity] than lime – and pour in enough of it to immerse the salted lemons. Add good-quality olive oil, pounded and toasted dried coriander, chopped [fresh] parsley, as well as mint and rue. This the best and tastiest recipe there is.

318. Another type[556]

Take lemons and remove the outer peel without stripping away the soft [inner] peel. Rub with saffron and dissolved sugar. Put them in a large glass jar and throw on enough lemon juice to cover them, as well as salt. In order to prevent the lemons from going off, seal with olive oil. This is another unusual variation, but very delicious.

319. Another one[557]

Take wine vinegar, sweeten it with sugar or honey, and add fresh dates.[558] Then put the salted lemons in [the mixture].

---

553 Most of this sentence is illegible in the manuscript and was adapted from the recipe in *Wuṣla*.

554 cf. *Wuṣla*, No. 7.10.

555 cf. *Wuṣla*, No. 8.20. Salted lemons were clearly well established very early on as the author of *Wuṣla* states that the basic variety of them 'is so famous that it requires no explanation.'

556 cf. *Wuṣla*, No. 8.22.

557 cf. *Wuṣla*, No. 8.21.

558 *ruṭab*; this is a strange instruction, indeed, and should perhaps be corrected with that in *Wuṣla*, where it is 'good-quality olive oil'.

320. *Baqṣamāṭ* (biscuits)[559]

Take fine white flour and knead it with dough and clarified butter. The proportions are as follows: for each four *raṭls* of dough, use one *raṭl* of clarified butter, and then knead with milk. Add the spices and shape into discs. Cut them crosswise [into quarters] with a sharp knife, and bake, keeping [the pieces] apart as you do so. Then toast them again and rub one side with honey, eggs and rose water.

321. [Another] type[560]

Take dried dates, remove the stones, and replace them with a paste made with blanched pistachios pounded with sugar and water[561] infused with musk. Take *qaṭā'if*[562] batter, and add starch dissolved in rose water just as you do for latticed sweets.[563] Dip the dates in the batter, and fry in sesame oil.[564] Immerse [the dates] for a second time in the batter, and fry a second time. Then, throw [the dates] in rose-water syrup and layer them on a plate. Sprinkle sugar and pistachio kernels on top, and drizzle on rose water and musk.

559 cf. *Wuṣla*, No. 7.105. Ibn al-Bayṭār 1992: II, 316 (trans., II, 215) also calls it *khubz rūmī* (Byzantine bread) and says that it is synonymous with *ka'k* and, in al-Andalus, *bishmāṭ* (related to the Greek *paxamádion*). They were often eaten soaked in water; Ibn Zuhr 1992: 13 (trans., 49); Crecelius & Bakr 1996: 169; Dozy 1877–81: I, 91; Corriente 1997: 54; Ibn al-Ḥashshā' 1941: 66 (No. 616).

560 cf. *Wuṣla*, No. 7.11, which was used to supplement missing words from the manuscript due to damage.

561 The recipe in *Wuṣla* specifies that it should be rose water.

562 A kind of crêpe, which is a very popular treat in the Middle East during Ramadan; it usually comes filled with nuts (especially almonds) and slathered in syrup or honey. Al-Warrāq 1987: 274–5 (trans., 422–4); *Waṣf*, 428, 434–5; al-Baghdādī 1964: (trans., 103–4); *Taṣānīf al-aṭ'ima*, fol. 87r. According to al-Rāzī (2000: 3018), it causes thick and viscous humours, as a result of which it tightens the bowels.

563 The reference here is to *zulābiyya* (see recipe No. 150 above).

564 The manuscript omits the crucial 'and throw into thick rose-water syrup,' which is found in the *Wuṣla* recipe.

SEVENTEEN

On Making Cold Dishes[565]

322. Chard recipe[566]

Take chard and cut each leaf into small pieces, each the size of a finger. Boil and squeeze out its liquid. Add strained yoghurt and garlic.

323. Another recipe like it[567]

Boil and fry [the chard]. Take sumac soaked in water, extract [the juice] and strain through a cloth. Finely pound walnuts and pour lemon[568] juice on them. Add *aṭrāf al-ṭīb* and put it on the chard. On top, put good-quality olive oil, as well as mint and rue. If you like, you can add verjuice as well, do so.

324. Snake melon recipe[569]

Take snake melon, peel, boil and extract the juices. Fry in good-quality olive oil and sesame oil after cutting them in half. Chop on good onions and fry. Also add chopped parsley and fry until it wilts. Put everything on top of the fried snake melon and pour on tart vinegar. Bring to the boil several times and add *aṭrāf al-ṭīb*, dried coriander, sprigs of mint, and pepper. Some people put on a little garlic, while others add sugar, or pounded walnut kernels. As for [adding] pistachio kernels, this is always delicious.

---

565 *Bawārid* (plural of *bārid*, 'cold'). These tended to be cold vegetable dishes (though some are with meat and fish as well) eaten as snacks or appetizers; see al-Warrāq 1987: 69–73 (trans., 163–70), 78–82 (trans., 176–81), 106–9 (trans., 214–9). The word was borrowed by Spanish as *buared* ('dishes usually seasoned with oil and vinegar'); Corriente 2008: 236.

566 cf. *Wuṣla*, No. 8.105.

567 cf. *Wuṣla*, No. 8.107.

568 According to the recipe in *Kanz*, it should be the sumac juice that is added at this stage. As lemon juice is required immediately after, it would seem that the mss is corrupted here.

569 *Wuṣla* contains three snake melon recipes (Nos. 7.79–81), but none appears to have been the model for this one.

325. Recipe to cook gourd in milk

You need gourd, sour milk, good-quality olive oil, and a little black cumin. Cut the gourd thinly, as usual, and then boil and extract its liquid. Pound peeled garlic and beat into milk. Add a little bit of good-quality olive oil and then put the gourd into the milk. Transfer to jars and sprinkle the cumin on top.

EIGHTEEN

On Toothpicks

326.

All types of wood that are cold and dry can be used to make toothpicks, and are, in fact, more beneficial than those that are hot and dry. The best way to use toothpicks in the mouth is to first soak them in water for one or two nights so that they bend when using them, and do not break in between the teeth, requiring tweezers to remove [the splinters]. You should take willow wood, which is cold and dry, causes little harm to the teeth, and has many benefits. It is the best kind there is to clean the teeth.[570]

[570] The entire section was extracted from al-Warrāq 1987: 325 (trans., 492], with only the part on willow wood being found in *Kanz* (226–7, No. 638), which contains much more information, all of it also borrowed from al-Warrāq. As one line is only partly legible due to a restoration strip, *Kanz* was used to complete the sentence. Neither *Zahr* nor *Kanz* included al-Warrāq's reference to willow wood being particularly effective in removing bad odours (*zuhūmāt*).

NINETEEN

On Fragrances

327. Recipe for incense[571]

[Take] lemons, sour orange peel, myrtle, oryncha, sandarac, mastic, saffron strands, sandalwood, and rock candy. Pound all of them separately, and to the same weight. Knead together with Nisibin[572] rose water, shape into discs, and store.

328. A fragrance from the people of Yemen[573]

Take sugar dissolved in rose water and pour on a grater.[574] Grate camphor and a bit of raw ambergris, white sandalwood, and good agarwood. Gather everything together, mix, and use as fragrance.

329. Recipe for wonderfully fragrant water used by kings[575]

Take flowers, lotus blossom and Nisibin roses [and put them] in a jar. Distil, and then put [the water] in musk, and seal the top of the jar.[576] It is very fragrant.

330. Recipe for incense tablets (*aqrāṣ*)[577]

Take the peels of citron, sour oranges, *kabbād* citrus, and apples, together with myrtle. Finely pound everything together, sieve, and take two-thirds

---

571 cf. *Kanz*, 232 (No. 655).

572 The present-day town Nusaybin, in eastern Turkey.

573 cf. *Kanz*, 284 (Appendix, No. 66).

574 *miḥakka*; originally a stone on which money was rubbed to test its quality, or a 'scratching stick', used by soldiers on horseback to remove fleas, etc. The reference here to grating sugar and rose water may appear somewhat cryptic, but presumably the idea was to have the mixture coat the grooves and thus infuse whatever was grated subsequently. Lane 1863–74: II, 615; Dozy 1877–81: I, 309.

575 cf. *Kanz*, 284 (Appendix, No. 67).

576 *Kanz* adds that this should be done with ambergris.

577 cf. *Kanz*, 287 (Appendix, No. 74), with significant differences in terms of ingredients and quantities.

of a *dirham* of each.[578] Take Khmer (*Qamārī*) agarwood and Ceylon sandalwood,[579] two *mithqāls* of each. Also take amber ladanum, mastic and rubbed saffron strands. Put everything at the bottom of another pot, with equal parts of all aromatics. Turn the pot containing the discs on its head, and seal with clay so to prevent evaporation of the fragrance. Put the pot containing the incense on a gentle moderate fire so that it can produce smoke. When the incense gets burnt, open the pot, take it out and dry in the shade. Pulverise and add ambergris, pounded agarwood, and a little bit of musk. Use in a small bowl when you need it.

331. Recipe for pills that sweeten the breath and can also be used as incense[580]

Take two and a third *dirhams* of agarwood, two *dāniqs* of clove, one *qīrāṭ* of saffron, one quarter of a *dirham* of walnuts, one *qīrāṭ* and a half of musk, two *dāniqs* of sugar, and also dissolve one *dāniq* of gum tragacanth in Nisibin rose water. Shape [the resulting paste] into pills the size of chickpeas and dry them in the shade.[581] Put them in your mouth in the morning and before you go to sleep. If you want to use it as incense, do so.

332. Recipe for pills to sweeten the breath[582]

They strengthen the teeth and [help] digest food after eating. Place a pill in the mouth before sleeping and the sweet fragrance will linger. They can also be used as incense. If you want, you can crush the pills like *dharīra* (fragrant powder) and perfume yourself with it when it is dry. If the pills are

578 The Arabic has the unnecessarily convoluted 'one half and one sixth of a *dirham*.'

579 *ṣandal*; unlike agarwood, it was only used in perfumes, incense, etc. It was thought to come from China. Ibn Sīnā (1999: 1, 637–8/trans., 300–1) identified three varieties: yellow, red, and whitish yellow.

580 cf. *Wuṣla*, No. 10.35.

581 The recipe in *Wuṣla* ends here.

582 *Kanz*, 234 (No. 661); there are some overlaps with a recipe in *Wuṣla* (No. 10.36), which is, however, much shorter.

pulverized[583] in ben oil[584] you can rub it on yourself like *ghāliya*.[585] If you dissolve the pills in rose water, they are good for wiping your body. Take seven *dirhams* of Indian agarwood, three *dirhams* of cubeb, four *dirhams* of cloves, four *dirhams* of mace, five *dirhams* of white Kufan cyprus and of sandalwood, three *dirhams* of black cardamom, half an *ūqiya* of musk pastilles,[586] one *mithqāl* of musk, and half a *mithqāl* of camphor. Crush all of these and knead with Persian rose water, but that of Nisibin is the best. Make pills from it similar in size to chickpeas, or slightly bigger. Dry in the shade and use when having your meals. Swirl them around in the mouth until they dissolve, and swallow the liquid. Do the same thing when going to sleep.

COMPLETED – PRAISE BE TO ALLAH, prayers to our Lord Muḥammad, and peace be upon him – by the humble servant of Allah the Almighty, Muḥammad ʿAbd Allāh al-ʿUmarī, may Allah forgive him and his parents and all Muslims.

583 The text has the nonsensical *ṣaḥantuhu*, which has been corrected to *saḥaqtahu*, which is the variant in the Dār al-Kutub manuscript of *Kanz* (399, note No. 7722).

584 Oil pressed from the seeds of the *Moringa oleifera* tree. It was predominantly used in scents. Medically, it is useful against chapped skin caused by winter cold. When amber and musk are dissolved in the oil, it is beneficial for the brain, and also unblocks ears. Ibn Jazla, fol. 98r.–v.; Ibn al-Bayṭār 1992: II, 398 (trans., II, 119–20).

585 A perfume containing a wide variety of ingredients, especially musk and amber. Medically, it was said to soften the hard swellings, whereas its fragrance is beneficial for epileptics and coma patients. When blended with wine it enhances intoxication. It is particularly useful for women because it acts as an emmenagogue and also purifies the uterus with a view to pregnancy. Ibn al-Bayṭār 1992: III, 202 (trans., III, 6–7); Ibn Sīnā 1999: I, 727 (trans., 338); Ibn Jazla, fol. 159r.–v.; al-Kindī 1948: 50–9.

586 *sukk al-misk*. According to Ibn Sīnā (1999: I, 587), the real *sukk* came from China and contains embelic myrobalan (*amlaj*), but due to the scarcity of this ingredient, it was also made from gall-nut (*afṣ*) and unripe dates (*balaḥ*). Ibn Jazla fol. 125r.; Colin & Renaud 1934: 379; Nasrallah [al-Warrāq] 2010: 776–7.

REFERENCES

I. MANUSCRIPTS

Anonymous: MS G.S. Colin arabe 7009 BNF, Paris. [= *Andalusian*]
Anonymous: *Kitāb Waṣf al-aṭʿima al-muʿtāda*, Cairo, Dār al-Kutub, Ṣināʿa 51; Ṣināʿa 52; English translation, Charles Perry, 'The Description of Familiar Foods', in M. Rodinson et al., 2001, pp. 273–466.
Anonymous: *Taṣānīf al-aṭʿima*: Wellcome, WMS Arabic 57.
al-Baghdādī, *Kitāb al-Ṭabīkh*, Istanbul, Ayasofia 3710.
Ibn Baklārīsh: *Kitāb al-Mustaʿīnī* (*Kitāb al-adwiya al-mufrada*), Arcadia Library (London), mss ARCS007.
Ibn Jazla: *Minhāj al-bayān fīmā yastaʿmiluhu al-insān*, British Library, Or.7499.
al-Rāzī, Abū Bakr: *Dafʿ maḍārr al-aghdhiya*, Yale University, Beinecke Rare Book and Manuscript Library, Landberg MSS 473.

II. PRINTED MATERIALS

Arabic and Persian

Afshār, Irfan (ed.) (1360/1981): *Āshpazī-e dawra-ye safavī. Matn-e do resāla az ān dawra*, Tehran.
Anonymous (2017): *al-Wuṣla ilā al-ḥabīb fī waṣf al-ṭayyibāt wa 'l-ṭīb*, Charles Perry (ed./English translation), *Scents and Flavors: A Syrian Cookbook*, New York: New York University Press. [= *Wuṣla*]
Anonymous (2010): *Anwāʿ al-ṣaydala fī alwān al-aṭʿima*, ʿAbd al-Ghanī Abū 'l-ʿAzm (ed.), Rabat: Muʾassasat al-Ghanī li 'l-Nashr. [= *Anwāʿ*].
al-Anṭākī, Dawūd (1952): *Tadhkirat ūlī 'l-ābāb wa 'l-jāmiʿ li 'l-ʿajab al-ʿujāb*, 2 vols, Cairo.
Anwāʿ: *see* Anonymous 2010.
al-Baghdādī, Muḥammad Ibn al-Ḥasan Ibn Muḥammad Ibn Karīm al-Kātib (1964): *Kitāb al ṭabīkh*, ed. Fakhrī al-Bārūdī, Damascus: Dār al-Kitāb

al-Jadīd; English translation Charles Perry: *A Baghdad Cookery Book*, Totnes: Prospect Books (2005).

al-Baghdādī, Ismā'īl Bāshā (1951): *Hadiyat al-'ārifīn, asmā' al-mu'allifīn wa-āthār al-muṣannifīn*, Beirut: Dār Iḥyā' al-Turāth al-'Arabī.

Ben Mrād, Ibrāhīm (1985): *al-Muṣṭalaḥ al-a'jamī fī kutub al-ṭibb wa 'l-ṣaydala al-'Arabiyya*, Beirut: Dār al-Gharb al-Islāmī.

al-Ghāfiqī (2014): *Kitāb al-adwiya al-mufrada*, Faith Wallis, Jamil Ragep, Pamela Miller & Adam Gacek (eds), *The Herbal of al-Ghāfiqī: A Facsimile Edition with Critical Essays*, Montreal: McGill-Queen's University Press.

al-Ghassānī, Ibn Rasūl (2000): *al-Mu'tamad fī 'l-adwiya al-mufrada*, Muḥammad 'Umar al-Dimyāṭī (ed.), Beirut: Dār al-Kutub al-'Ilmiyya.

al-Ghazzī, Taqī 'l-Dīn (1983): *al-Ṭabaqāt al-sunniyya fī tarājim al-Ḥanafiyya*, 4 vols, Riyad: Dār al-Rāfi'ī.

Ḥājjī Khalīfa (n.d.): *Kashf al-ẓunūn 'an asāmī al-kutub wa'l-funūn*, 2 vols., Beirut: Dār 'Iḥyā al-Turāth al-'Arabī.

Ibn al-'Awwām (1866): *Kitāb al-Filāḥa, Le Livre de l'Agriculture,* 2 vols, French translation J.J. Clément-Mullet, Paris: Librairie A. Franck.

Ibn al-Bayṭār, Abū Muḥammad (1992): *al-Jāmi' li-mufradāt al-adwiya wa 'l-aghdhiya*, Beirut: Dār al-Kutub al-'Ilmiyya; French translation, Lucien Leclerq, 'Traité des simples par Ibn el-Beïthar', *Notices et extraits des manuscrits de la Bibliothèque nationale et autres bibliothèques*, 23:1 (1877), 25:1 (1881), 26:1 (1883), Paris: Imprimerie Nationale.

Ibn Buṭlān (1990): *Taqwīm al-ṣiḥḥa. Le Taqwim al-Sihha (Tacuini Sanitatis) d'Ibn Butlan: un traité médical du XIe siècle,* Hosam Elkhadem (ed./French translation), Louvain: Peeters.

Ibn Buṭlān (1968): *Maqāla fī tadbīr al-amrāḍ al-'āriḍa li 'l-ruhbān al-sākinīn fī 'l-dayr wa min bu'd 'an al-madīna*, Samira Yousef Jadon (ed.), *The Arab Physician ibn Butlan's (d. 1066) Medical Manual for the Use of Monks and Country People*, unpublished PhD dissertation, UCLA.

Ibn al-Ḥashshā' (1941): *Mufīd al-'ulūm wa mubīd al-humūm*, G. S. Colin & H. Renaud (eds), *Ibn al-Ḥaššā. Glossaire sur le Mans'uri, de Razès, Xe siècle*, Rabat: Impr. Économique.

Ibn al-Jazzār, A. (1999): *Zād al-musāfir wa-qūt al-ḥāḍir*, 2 vols, Muḥammad al-Suwaysī, al-Rāḍī al-Jāzī, Jum'a Shaykha and Fārūq al-'Asalī (eds), Tunis: Bayt al-Ḥikma.

Ibn Khalṣūn (1996): *Kitāb al-Aghdhiya,* Suzanne Gigandet (ed./French translation), *Kitāb al-Aġḏiya (Le livre des aliments),* Damascus: Presses de l'Ifpo.

Ibn Khurradādhbih (1889): *Kitāb al-masālik wa 'l-mamālik*, Michael Johan de Goeje (ed.), Leiden: Brill.

Ibn Māsawayh (1937): *Kitāb jawāhir al-ṭīb al-mufrada*, Paul Sbath (ed.), 'Traité sur les substances simples aromatiques par Yahanna Ben Massawaïh', *Bulletin de l'Institut d'Égypte* 19, pp. 5–27.

Ibn Mibrad: *see* Ibn Mubarrad.

Ibn Mubarrad (1937): '*Kitāb al-ṭibākha*', Ḥabīb al-Zayyāt (ed.), *al-Mashriq*, 35, pp. 370–6.

Ibn Munqidh, Usāma (2003): *Kitāb al-iʿtibār*, ʿAbd al-Karīm Ushtar (ed.), Beirut: al-Maktab al-Islāmī; English translation Philip Hitti, *An Arab-Syrian Gentleman and Warrior in the Period of the Crusades: Memoirs of Usama Ibn-Munqidh*, New York: Columbia University Press (1929).

Ibn al-Nadīm (1871–72): *Kitāb al-fihrist*, 2 vols, Gustav Flügel (ed.), Leipzig: F. C. W. Vogel; English translation, Bayard Dodge, *The Fihrist of al-Nadim*, 2 vols, New York: Columbia University Press (1970).

Ibn Sharīfa, M. (1982): 'Ḥawla Ibn Razīn mu'allif Kitāb al-Ṭabīkh', *Majallat Kulliyat al-Ādāb wa 'l-ʿUlūm al-Insāniyya bi Ribāṭ*, 8, pp. 95–118.

Ibn Sīda, Abū 'l-Ḥasan (2000): *al-Muḥkam wa 'l-muḥīṭ al-aʿẓam*, 11 vols, ed. ʿAbd al-Ḥamīd al-Hindāwī, Beirut: Dār al-Kutub al-ʿIlmiyya.

Ibn Sīnā (1999): *al-Qānūn fī 'l-ṭibb*, 3 vols, ed. Muḥammad Amīn al-Ḍannāwī, Beirut: Dār al-Kutub al-ʿIlmiyya; English translation, *Canon of Medicine Book II: Materia Medica*, New Delhi: Hamdard University (1998).

Ibn Sūdūn al-Bashbughāwī (1998): *Nuzhat an-nufūs wa-muḍḥik al-ʿabūs*, Arnoud Vrolijk (ed.), *Bringing a Laugh to a Scowling Face: A Study and Critical Edition of the Nuzhat al-Nufūs wa-Muḍḥik al-ʿAbūs by ʿAlī Ibn Sūdūn al-Bašbuġāwī (Cairo 810/1407–Damascus 868/1464)*. Leiden: Research School CNWS, School of Asian, African, and Amerindian Studies.

Ibn al-Ukhuwwa, Muhammad (1937): *Maʿālim al-qurba fī aḥkām al-ḥisba*, Reuben Levy (ed./trans.), Cambridge: Cambridge University Press.

Ibn Waḥshiyya (1993–98): *al-Filāḥa al-Nabaṭiyya*, 3 vols, Toufic Fahd (ed.), Damascus: Institut Français de Damas.

Ibn Zuhr, Abū al-ʿAlā' Ibn ʿAbd al-Malik (1992): *Kitāb al-aghdhiya. Tratado de los alimentos*, Expiración García Sánchez (ed.), Madrid: Consejo superior de investigaciones científicas, Instituto de cooperación con el mundo árabe.

al-Isrā'ilī, Isḥāq Sulaymān (1992): *Kitāb al-aghdhiya wa 'l-adwiya*, ed.

Muḥammad al-Ṣabāḥ, Beirut: Mu'assasat ʿIzz al-Dīn li ʾl-Ṭibāʿa wa ʾl-Nashr.

Kaḥḥāla, ʿUmar Riḍā (1992): *Muʿjam al-muʾallifīn. Tarājim muṣannifīn al-kutub al-ʿArabiyya*, 4 vols, Beirut: Dār al-Iḥyāʾ al-Turāth al-ʿArabī.

al-Kāshgharī, Maḥmūd (1333/1914): *Dīwān lughāt al-Turk*, Istanbul: Imperial Press; English translation, Robert Dankoff & James Kelly, *Mahmūd al-Kāšgarī: Compendium of the Turkic Dialects (Dīwān Luγāt at-Turk), Parts I–III*, Duxbury, Mass.: Sources of Oriental Languages and Literatures (1982, 1984, 1985).

al-Kindī (1948): *Kīmiyāʾ al-ʿiṭr wa ʾl-taṣʿīdāt*, Karl Garbers (ed./German translation), *Buch über die Chemie des Parfums und die Distillationen. Ein Beitrag zur Geschichte des arabischen Parfumchemie und Drogenkunde aus dem 9. Jahrhundert*, Leipzig.

al-Masʿūdī, ʿAlī Ibn Ḥusayn (1861–77): *Murūj al-dhahab wa maʿādin al-jawhar*, Barbier de Meynard & Pavet de Courteille (eds/trans.), 9 vols, Paris: Imprimerie Nationale.

Miranda, Ambrosio Huici (1961–62): 'Kitāb al-ṭabīkh fi ʾl-Maghrib wa ʾl-Andalus fī ʿaṣr al-Muwaḥḥidīn, li-mu'allif majhūl (Un libro anónimo de la Cocina hispano-magribí, de la época almohade)', *Revista del Instituto de estudios islámicos*, IX/X, pp. 15–256.

al-Muḥtasib, Muḥammad Bassām (2003): *Nihāyat al-rutba fī ṭalab al-ḥisba*, M. Ismāʿīl & A. al-Mazīdī (eds), Beirut: Dār al-Kutub al-ʿIlmiyya.

al-Muqaddasī, Shams al-Dīn Abū ʿAbd Allāh (1877): *Aḥsan al-taqāsīm fī maʿrifat al-aqālīm*, M. J. de Goeje (ed.), Leiden: Brill.

al-Nābulusī, ʿAbd al-Ghanī Ibn Ismāʿīl (1882): *Kitāb ʿalam al-milāḥa fī ʿilm al-filāḥa*, Damascus: n.p.

al-Qazwīnī, Zakariyyāʾ Ibn Muḥammad (1849): *ʿAjāʾib al-makhlūqāt wa āthār al-bilād*, Ferdinand Wüstenfeld (ed.), *Zakarija Ben Muhammed Ben Mahmud el-Cazwini's Kosmographie. Erster Theil. ʿAjāʾib al-makhlūqāt. Die Wunder der Schöpfung. Aus den Handschriften der Bibliotheken zu Berlin, Gotha, Dresden und Hamburg*, Göttingen: Dieterischen Buchhandlung.

al-Rāzī, Abū Bakr Muḥammad Ibn Zakariyyāʾ (2000): *al-Ḥāwī fī ʾl-tibb*, 8 vols, Beirut: Dār al-Kutub al-ʿIlmiyya.

al-Rāzī, A. (1987): *al-Manṣūrī fī ʾl-ṭibb*, Ḥasan al-Bakrī al-Ṣiddīqī (ed.), Kuwait: al-Munaẓẓama al-ʿArabiyya li ʾl-Tarbiya wa ʾl-Thaqāfa wa ʾl-ʿUlūm.

al-Rāzī, A. (1305/1881): *Manāfiʿ al-aghdhiya wa dafʿ maḍārrihā*, Cairo: al-Maṭbaʿa al-Khayriyya.

Saʿd al-Dīn, Kāẓim (1984): 'Kitāb al-tabīkh', *Majallat al-Turāth al-Shaʿbī*, 9-10, pp. 207–24.
al-Sakhāwī, Muḥammad (1992), *al-Ḍawʾ al-lāmiʿ fī aʿyān al-qarn al-tāsiʿ*, 12 vols. Beirut: Dār al-Jīl.
al-Samarqandī (2017): *Kitāb al-aghdhiyya wa 'l-ashriba*, Juliane Müller (ed./German translation), *Nahrungsmittel in der arabischen Medizin. Das Kitāb al-Aġḏiya wa-l-ašriba des Naǧīb ad-Dīn as-Samarqandī*, Leiden: Brill.
al-Shayzarī, ʿAbd al-Raḥmān (n.d.): *Kitāb nihāyat al-rutba fī ṭalab al-ḥisba*, Muḥammad Ḥasan Muḥammad Ḥasan Ismāʿīl & Aḥmad Farīd al-Mizyudī (eds), Beirut: Dār al-Kutub al-ʿIlmiyya; English translation, Ronald Buckley, *The Book of the Islamic Market Inspector*, Oxford: Oxford University Press (1999).
al-Shirbīnī, Yūsuf (2004): *Kitāb hazz al-quḥūf bi-sharḥ qaṣīd Abī Shādūf*, Humphrey T. Davies (ed.), Leuven: Peeters.
al-Thaʿālibī, ʿAbd al-Malik Ibn Muḥammad (1900): *Ghurar akhbār mulūk Fars wa siyarihim*, Hermann Zotenberg (ed./French translation), Paris: Imprimerie nationale.
al-Tujībī, Ibn Razīn (2012): *Fuḍālat al-khiwān fī ṭayyibāt al-ṭaʿām wa 'l-alwān*, M. I. ᶜA. Ibn Shaqrūn (ed.), Beirut: Dār al-Gharb al-Islāmī.
al-Warrāq, Abū Muḥammad al-Muẓaffar Ibn Naṣr Ibn Sayyār (1987): *Kitāb al-ṭabīkh*, Kaj Öhrnberg & Sahban Mroueh (eds), Helsinki, Finnish Oriental Society; English translation Nawal Nasrallah, *Annals of the Caliphs' Kitchens: Ibn Sayyâr al-Warrâq's Tenth-century Baghdadi Cookbook*, Leiden: Brill (2007).
Waṣf: see 'Manuscripts', Anynomous*: Kitāb Waṣf al-aṭʿima al-muʿtāda*.
Wuṣla: see Anonymous 2017.
al-Ziriklī, Khayr al-Dīn (1954–59): *al-Aʿlām: qāmus tarājim li-ashhur al-rijāl wa-al-nisāʾ min al-ʿArab wa 'l-mustaʿribīn wa-al-mustashriqīn*, 10 vols, Cairo.

European Languages

Achaya, K. T. (2012): *The Story of Our Food*, Himayatnagar: Universities Press.
Achaya, K.T. (1994): *Indian Food: A Historical Companion*, Bombay: Oxford University Press.
Agius, Dionisius A. (2008): *Classic Ships of Islam: From Mesopotamia to the Indian Ocean*, Leiden: Brill.
André, Jacques (1961): *L'Alimentation et la cuisine à Rome*, Paris: C.

Klincksieck.

Arberry, Arthur (1939): 'A Baghdad Cookery Book', *Islamic Culture*, 13, pp. 21–47, 184–214.

Ashtor, E. (1970): 'The Diet of Salaried Classes in the Mediaeval Near East', *Journal of Asian History*, 4:1, pp. 1–24.

Ashtor, E. (1968): 'Essai sur l'alimentation des diverses classes sociales dans l'Orient médiéval', *Annales ESC*, 5, pp. 1017–53.

Aubaile-Sallenave, F. (1992): 'Zanbo'a, un citrus mysterieux chez les arabes medievaux d'Al-Andalus', in Expiración Garcia Sánchez (ed.), *Ciencias de la naturaleza en Al-Andalus*, Granada: CSIC-I.C.M.A., pp. 111–33.

Balossi Restelli, Francesca & Lucia Mori (2014): 'Bread, Baking Moulds and Related Cooking Techniques in the Ancient Near East', *Food & History*, 12:3, pp. 39–56.

Bar-Sela, Ariel, Hebbel E. Hoff & Elias Faris (1964): 'Moses Maimonides: Two Treatises on the Regimen of Health', *Transactions of the American Philosophical Society*. 54:4, pp. 3–50.

Bearman, P. J., et al. (1960–2005), *Encyclopædia of Islam*, 2nd edition., 12 vols., Leiden: E. J. Brill.

Beck, Lily (2017): *Dioscorides of Anazarbus de Materia Medica*, Hildesheim: Olms-Weidmann.

Bolens-Halimi, Lucie (1991): 'Le garum en al-Andalus, un feu trouvé au fond des mers', *Gerión*, No. Extra 3 (*Ejemplar dedicado a: Alimenta: Estudios en Homenaje al Dr. Michel Ponsich*), pp. 355–71.

Bolens, Lucie (1990): *La cuisine andalouse, un art de vivre. XIe–XIIIe siècle*, Paris: Albin Michel.

Bos, Gerrit (1997): *Ibn al-Jazzār on Sexual Diseases and their Treatment: A Critical Edition of Zād al-musāfir wa qūt al-ḥāḍir, Provisions for the Traveller and Nourishment for the Sedentary, Book 6*, London/New York: Kegan Paul International.

Bottéro, Jean (2004): *The Oldest Cuisine in the World: Cooking in Mesopotamia*, Teresa Lavender Fagan (trans.), Chicago: University of Chicago Press.

Bottéro, J. (1995): *Mesopotamian Culinary Texts*, English translation, Jerrold Cooper. Winona Lake, IN: Eisenbrauns.

Bottéro, J. (1987): 'The Culinary Tablets at Yale (trans., J. M. Sasson)', *Journal of the American Oriental Society*, 107:1, pp. 11–19.

Braudel, Fernand (1974): *Capitalism and Material Life, 1400–1800*, London: Collins.

Brisville, M. (2017): 'Plats sûrs et plats sains dans l'Occident musulman médiéval. La harīsa comme contre-exemple?', in Bruno Laurioux (ed.), *L'acquisition des aliments: de la nature à la table au Moyen Âge,* Paris: CTHS, pp. 107–18.

Brockelmann, Carl (1937–49): *Geschichte der arabischen Literatur,* 2 vols, 3 supplementary vols, Leiden: Brill.

Buell, Paul D. & Eugene N. Anderson (2016): *A Soup for the Qan: Chinese Dietary Medicine of the Mongol Era as Seen in Hu Sihui's Yinshan Zhengyao,* Abingdon: Routledge.

Chapot, H. (1963): 'Le cedrat Kabbad et deux autres variétés du cédrat du Moyen-Orient', *Al Awamia,* 8 July, pp. 39–61.

Chipman, Leigh (2009): *The World of Pharmacy and Pharmacists in Mamlūk Cairo,* Leiden/Boston: Brill.

Clément, François (2015): 'Escabèche, merguez, rousquilles et autres recettes: des plaisirs de bouche partagés', in Catherine Richarté, Roland-Pierre Gayraud & Jean-Marie Poisson (eds), *Héritages arabo-islamiques dans l'Europe méditerranéenne,* Paris: INRAP, pp. 377–96.

Conrad, Lawrence I., et al. (1995): *The Western Medical Tradition, 800 BC to AD 1800,* Cambridge: Cambridge University Press.

Corcoran, Thomas H. (1963): 'Roman Fish Sauces', *The Classical Journal,* 58: 5, pp. 204–10.

Corriente, Federico (1997): *A Dictionary of Andalusi Arabic,* Leiden: Brill.

Crecelius, Daniel & Abd al-Wahhab Bakr (1996): *Al-Damurdashi's Chronicle of Egypt, 1688–1755: Al-Durra al-Musana fi Akhbār al-Kinana,* Leiden: Brill.

Curtis, Robert Irvin (1978): *The production and commerce of fish sauce in the Western Roman Empire: a social and economic study,* unpublished PhD diss., University of Maryland.

Dalby, Andrew (2003): *Food in the Ancient World from A to Z,* London: Routledge.

Dalby, A. (2000): *Dangerous Tastes: The History of Spices,* London: British Museum Press.

Dalby, A. (1996): *Siren Feasts: A History of Food and Gastronomy in Greece,* New York: Routledge.

Davidson, Alan (1999): *The Oxford Companion to Food,* Oxford: Oxford University Press.

Denker, Joel S. (2015): *The Carrot Purple and Other Curious Stories of the Food We Eat,* Lanham: Rowman & Littlefield.

de Vilanova, Arnau (1947): *Obres catalanes*, Vol. 2, *Escrits medics*, Barcelona: Barcino.

Diem, Werner (1994): *A Dictionary of the Arabic Material of S.D. Goitein's A Mediterranean Society*, Wiesbaden: Harrassowitz.

Dietrich, Albert (1988): *Dioscurides Triumphans. Ein anonymer arabischer Kommentar (Ende 12. Jahr. n. Chr.) zur Materia medica*, 2 vols, Göttingen: Vandenhoeck & Ruprecht.

Doerfer Gerhard (1963–75): *Türkische und mongolische Elemente in Neupersischen*, Wiesbaden: Otto Harrassowitz.

Dols, Michael W. (1979): 'The Second Plague Pandemic and its Recurrences in the Middle East: 1347–1894', *Journal of the Economic and Social History of the Orient*, 22:2, pp. 162–89.

Donkin, R. A. (1999): *Dragon's Brain Perfume: An Historical Geography of Camphor*, Leiden: Brill.

Dozy, Pieter Reinhart (1877–81): *Supplément aux dictionnaires arabes*, 2 vols, Leiden: Brill.

EI[2]: *see* Bearman, P. J., et al. (1960–2005).

Franconie, Hélène, Monique Chastanet, François Sigaut (eds.) (2010): *Couscous, boulgour et polenta. Transformer et consommer les céréales dans le monde,* Paris: Karthala.

Gasper, Giles E. M., Faith Wallis et al. (2014): *Zinziber – Sauces from Poitou. Twelfth-Century Culinary Recipes from Sidney Sussex College, Cambridge, MS 51*, London: Prospect Books.

Grant, Mark (2000): *Galen on Food and Diet*. London: Routledge.

Graziani, Joseph Salvatore (1980): *Arabic Medicine in the Eleventh Century as Represented in the Works of Ibn Jazlah*, Karachi: Hamdard Foundation.

Greco, Gina L. & Christine M. Rose (2009): *The Good Wife's Guide (Le Ménagier de Paris): A Mediaeval Household Book*. Ithaca: Cornell University Press.

Grehan, James (2007): *Everyday Life & Consumer Culture in 18th-Century Damascus*, Seattle: University of Washington Press.

Grewe, Rudolf (1992): 'Hispano-Arabic Cuisine in the Twelfth Century', in Carole Lambert (ed.), *Du manuscrit à la table. Essai sur la cuisine au Moyen Âge et répertoire des manuscrits médiévaux contenant des recettes culinaires*, Montreal: Les Presses de l'Université de Montreal/Paris: Champion-Slatkine, pp. 141–8.

Grimaldi Ilaria, Maria, et al. (2018): 'Literary evidence for taro in the ancient

Mediterranean: a chronology of names and uses in a multilingual world', *PLOS ONE*, 13:6, pp. 1–23.

Grocock, Christopher W. & Sally Grainger (2006): *Apicius: A Critical Edition with an Introduction and English Translation*, London: Prospect Books.

Guichard, Pierre (2008): 'Alimentation et cuisine en al-Andalus', in J. Leclant, A. Vauchez & M. Sartre (eds), *Pratiques et discours alimentaires en Méditerranée de l'Antiquité à la Renaissance*, Paris: De Boccard et Académie des Inscriptions et Belles Lettres, pp. 337–57.

Guillaumond, Cathérine (2017): *Cuisine et dietetique dans l'occident arabe médiéval d'après un traité anonyme du* XIIIe *siècle. Étude et traduction française*, Paris: L'Harmattan.

Heine, Peter (1989): 'Kochen im Exil. Zur Geschichte der arabischen Küche', *Zeitschrift der deutschen morgenländischen Gesellschaft*, 139, pp. 318–327.

Heine, P. (1982): *Weinstudien: Untersuchungen zu Anbau, Produktion und Konsum des Weins im arabisch-islamischen Mittelalter*, Wiesbaden: O. Harrassowitz.

Hernández López, Adday (2013): 'La compraventa de vino entre musulmanes y cristianos ḏimmiés a través de textos jurídicos mālikíes del Occidente islámico mediaeval', in Maribel Fierro & John Tolan (eds), *The Legal Status of Dimmī-s in the Islamic West (second/eighth–ninth/fifteenth centuries)*, Turnhout: Brepols, pp. 243–74.

Hinz, Walther (1955): *Islamische Masse und Gewichte*, Leiden: E. J. Brill.

Isin, Priscilla Mary (2018): *Bountiful Empire: A History of Ottoman Cuisine*, London: Reaktion Books.

Jeffery, Arthur (2007): *The Foreign Vocabulary of the Qur'an*, Leiden: Brill.

Jouanna, Jacques (2012): *Greek Medicine from Hippocrates to Galen: Selected Papers*, P. van der Eijk (ed.), Leiden: Brill.

Kennedy, Philip F. (1997): *The Wine Song in Classical Arabic Poetry: Abū Nuwās and the Literary Tradition*. Oxford: Oxford University Press.

King, Anya (2017): *Scent from the Garden of Paradise: Musk and the Mediaeval Islamic World*, Leiden: Brill.

Kircher, H. G. (1967): *Die 'einfachen Heilmittel' aus dem 'Handbuch der Chirurgie' des Ibn al-Quff*, Bonn: Rheinischen Friedrich-Wilhelms-Universität.

Kueny, Kathryn (2001): *The Rhetoric of Sobriety: Wine in Early Islam*, Albany: State University of New York Press.

Lane, W. E. (1863–74): *Arabic–English Lexicon Derived from the Best and the Most Copious Eastern Sources; Comprising a Very Large Number of Words and Significations Omitted in the KáMoos, With Supplements to its Abridged and Defective Explanations, Ample Grammatical And Critical Comments, And Examples in Prose and Verse*, 5 vols, London (vols 6–8 ed. Stanley Lane Poole, London, 1877–93).

Laufer, Berthold (1919): *Sino-Iranica. Chinese Contributions to the History of Civilization in Ancient Iran: With Special Reference to the History of Cultivated Plants and Products*, Chicago: Field Museum of Natural History.

Laurioux, B. (2005): *Une histoire culinaire du Moyen Âge*, Paris: Champion.

Laurioux, B. (1995): 'Des lasagnes romaines aux vermicelles arabes: quelques réflexions sur les pâtes alimentaires au Moyen Âge', in Elisabeth Mornet (ed.), *Hommes et campagnes médiévales: L'homme et son espace. Etudes offertes à Robert Fossier*, Paris, Publications de la Sorbonne, pp. 199–215.

Lev, Efraim & Zohar Amar (2007): *Practical Materia Medica of the Mediaeval Eastern Mediterranean According to the Cairo Genizah*, Leiden: Brill.

Levanoni, Amalia (2005): 'Food and Cooking During The Mamluk Era: Social and Political Implications', *Mamluk Studies Review*, 9:2, pp. 201–22.

Levey, M. & Noury al-Khaledy (1967): *The Medical Formulary of Al-Samarqandī and the Relation of Early Arabic Simples to those Found in the Indigenous Medicine of The Near East and India*, Philadelphia: University of Pennsylvania Press.

Lewicka, Paulina B. (2011): *Food and Foodways Of Mediaeval Cairenes: Aspects of Life in an Islamic Metropolis of the Eastern Mediterranean*, Leiden: Brill.

MacKenzie, Donald (1986): *Concise Pahlavi Dictionary*, Oxford University Press.

Mackintosh-Smith, Tim & James E. Montgomery (eds/trans.) (2014): *Two Arabic Travel Books: Accounts of China and India*, New York/London: New York University Press.

Marín, M. (1998): 'The Perfumed Kitchen: Arab Cookbooks from the Islamic East', *Parfums d'Orient, Res Orientales*, 11, pp. 159–166.

Marín, M. (1997): 'Cuisine d'Orient, cuisine d'Occident', *Médiévales*, 33, pp. 9–21.

Marín, M. (1992): 'Sobre alimentación y sociedad (el texto arábe de la 'La Guerra deleitosa').' *Al-Qantara*, 13:1, pp. 83–122.

Marín, M. (1981): 'Sobre Būrān y *būrāniyya*', *Al-Qantara*, 2, pp, 193–207.

Marín, Manuela & David Waines (1995): 'Ibn Sīnā on "Sakanjabīn",' *Bulletin D'études Orientales*, 47, pp. 81–97.

Marín, M. & D. Waines (eds) (1994): *La alimentación en las culturas islámicas,* Madrid: Agencia Española de Cooperación Internacional.

Marín, M. & David Waines (1989): 'The Balanced Way: Food for Pleasure and Health in Mediaeval Islam.' *Manuscripts of the Middle East,* 4, pp. 123–32.

McAuliffe, Jane Dammen (2001–06): *Encyclopaedia of the Quran,* 6 vols., Leiden: Brill.

Metz, Adam (1902): *Ein bagdader Sittenbild von Muhammad ibn Ahmad Abulmutahhar Alazdi,* Baghdad/Heidelberg: Winter.

Mielck, Reinhard (1913): *Terminologie und Technologie der Müller und Bäcker im islamischen Mittelalter,* Glückstadt/ Hamburg: J.J. Augustin.

Nasrallah, Nawal (2010): 'In the Beginning There Was No *musakka*', *Food, Culture & Society,* 13:4, pp. 595–606.

Newman, Daniel L. (2014): *The Sultan's Sex Potions: Arab Aphrodisiacs in the Middle Ages,* London: Saqi Books.

Oubahli, M. (2006–8): 'Une histoire de pâte en méditerranée occidentale. Des pâtes arabo-berbères et de leur diffusion en Europe latine au Moyen-Âge', *Horizons Maghrébins – Le droit à la mémoire,* 55, pp. 48–72; 59, pp. 14–29.

Ouerfelli, Mohamed (2008): *Le sucre. Production, commercialisation et usages dans la Méditerranée médiévale,* Leiden/Boston: Brill.

Paavilainen, H. M. (2009): *Medieval Pharmacotherapy – Continuity and Change. Case Studies from Ibn Sīnā and some of his Late Medieval Commentators,* Leiden: Brill.

Parejko, Ken (2003): 'Pliny the Elder's Silphium: First Recorded Species Extinction', *Conservation Biology,* 17:3, pp. 925–7.

Perry, Charles (2000): 'Mediaeval Arab Dairy Products', in Harlan Walker (ed.), *Proceedings of the Oxford Symposium of Food and Cookery, 1999. Milk: Beyond the Dairy,* Totnes: Prospect Books, pp. 275–8.

Perry, C. (1999): 'More Rotted Barley', *Petits Propos Culinaires,* 61, pp. 42–3.

Perry, C. (1998): 'Rot of Ages', *Los Angeles Times,* 1 April.

Perry, C. (1995): 'The Fate of the Tail', in Harlan Walker (ed.), *Proceedings of the Oxford Symposium on Food and Cookery 1994: Disappearing Foods. Studies in Foods and Dishes at Risk,* Totnes: Prospect Books, pp. 150–3.

Perry, C. (1990): 'Couscous and its Cousins', in Harlan Walker (ed.), *Oxford Symposium on Food and Cookery 1989. Staple Foods,* London: Prospect Books, pp. 176–8.

Perry, C. (1988): 'Mediaeval Near Eastern Rotted Condiments', Tom Jaine (ed.), *Oxford Symposium on Food and Cookery, 1987. Taste*, London: Prospect Books, pp. 169–77.

Perry, C. (1983): 'A Nuanced Apology to Rotted Barley', *Petits Propos Culinaires*, 58, pp. 22–4.

Perry, C. (1981): 'Three Mediaeval Arabic Cook Books', in Alan Davidson (ed.), *National and Regional Styles of Cookery. Oxford Symposium, 1981*, Totnes: Prospect Books, I, pp. 96–105.

Pertsch, Wilhelm (1859–1893): *Die orientalischen Handschriften der Herzoglichen Bibliothek zu Gotha*, 7 vols, Gotha: Friedr. Andr. Perthes.

Plouvier, Liliane (2013): 'Du sikbaj perso-arabe à l'escabèche méditerranéenne. Pérégrination gourmande à travers les livres de cuisine méditerranéens de l'Antiquité au Moyen Âge', *Horizons maghrébins: Le Droit à la Mémoire*, No. 69 (*Manger au Maghreb: le goût de la viande, partie III*), pp. 162–177.

Rebstock, Ulrich (2008): 'Weights and Measures in Islam', in Helaine Selin (ed.), *Encyclopaedia of the History of Science, Technology and Medicine in Non-Western Cultures*, Berlin: Springer, pp. 2255–2267.

Redhouse, James William (1884): *A Lexicon, English and Turkish: Shewing, in Turkish, the Literal, Incidental, Figurative, Colloquial, and Technical Significations of the English Terms*, Constantinople: A. H. Boyajian.

Renaud, H. & G. S. Colin (1934): *Tuḥfat al-aḥbāb: Glossaire de la matière médicale marocaine*, Paris: Paul Geuthner.

Rodinson, Maxime, A. J. Arberry & Charles Perry (eds) (2001): *Mediaeval Arab Cookery*, Totnes: Prospect Books.

Rosenberger, Bernard (2014): 'Se nourrir dans les rues et sur les chemins de l'Occident musulman (XIIe–XVIIIe siècle)', *Afriques. Débats, méthodes et terrains d'histoire*, 5.

Rosenberger, B. (2003): 'Diététique et cuisine dans l'Espagne musulmane du XIIIe siècle', in O. Redon, L. Sallman & S. Steinberg (eds), *Le désir et le goût, une autre histoire (XIIIe–XVIIIe)*, Paris: PU de Vincennes, pp. 175–180.

Rosenberger, B. (1989): 'Les pâtes dans le monde musulman', *Médiévales*, 16–17, pp. 77–98.

Salloum, Habeeb, Muna Salloum & Leila Salloum Elias (2013): *Scheherazade's Feasts: Foods of the Mediaeval Arab World*, University of Pennsylvania Press.

Salonen, A. (1964): 'Die Öfen der alten Mesopotamier', *Baghdader Mitteilungen*, III, pp. 100–24.

Sancisi-Weerdenburg, Heleen (1995): 'Persian Food: Stereotypes and Political

Identity', in John Wilkins, David Harvey & Mike Dobson (eds.), *Food in Antiquity*. Exeter: University of Exeter Press, pp. 286–302.

Sato, Tsugitaka (2015): *Sugar in the Social Life of Mediaeval Islam*, Leiden: Brill.

Sen, Colleen Taylor (2015): *Feasts and Fasts: A History of Food in India*, London: Reaktion Books.

Serrano, Ana, María Jesús Viguera et al. (2006): *Ibn Khaldun: the Mediterranean in the 14th Century: Rise and Fall of Empires*, Seville: Fundación El Legado Andalusí: Fundación José Manuel Lara.

Serventi, Silvano, & Françoise Sabban (2000): *Pasta: The History of a Universal Food*, English translation, Antony Shugaar, New York: Columbia University Press.

Steingass, Francis Joseph (1892): *A Comprehensive Persian-English Dictionary, Including the Arabic Words and Phrases to be Met with in Persian Literature*, London: Routledge & K. Paul.

Tilsley-Benham, Jill (1986): 'Sheep with Two Tails: Sheep's Tail-Fat as Cooking Medium in the Middle East', *Oxford Symposium on Food History. The Cooking Medium*. pp. 47–50.

Ullmann, Manfred (1970): *Die Medizin im Islam*, Brill: Leiden.

Unvala, J. (1921): *The Pahlavi Text 'King Husraw and His Boy,'* Paris, n.d.

Vallvé Bermejo, Joaquín (1984), 'Notas de metrología hispano-árabe. III. Pesos y monedas', *Al-Qantara*, V, pp. 147–69.

Vallvé Bermejo, Joaquín (1977): 'Notas de metrología hispano-árabe. II. Medidas de capacidad', *Al-Andalus*, 42:1, pp. 61–110.

Vallvé Bermejo, Joaquín (1976): 'Notas de metrología hispano-árabe. El codo en la España musulmana', *Al-Andalus*, 41:2, pp. 339–54.

van Gelder, Geert Jan (2000): *Of Dishes and Discourse: Classical Arabic Literary Representations of Food*, Richmond: Curzon.

van Gelder, G. (1995): 'A Muslim Encomium on Wine: The Racecourse of the Bay (*Halbat al-Kumayt*) by al-Nawagi (d. 859/1455) as a Post-Classical Arabic Work', *Arabica*, 42, pp. 222–34.

Versteegh, Kees et al. (eds) (2006–2009): *Encyclopedia of Arabic Language and Linguistics*, 5 vols, Leiden: Brill

Waines, David (2011): *Food Culture and Health in Pre-Modern Muslim Societies*, Leiden: Brill.

Waines, D. (2010): 'Cookery', in Robert Irwin (ed.), *The New Cambridge History of Islam, Volume 4: Islamic Cultures and Societies to the End of the*

Eighteenth Century, Cambridge: Cambridge University Press, pp. 751–63.
Waines, D. (ed.) (2002): *Patterns of Everyday Life*, Aldershot: Ashgate.
Waines D. (1992): 'The Culinary Culture of Al-Andalus', in S. Jayyusi (ed.), *The Legacy of Muslim Spain*. Leiden: EJ Brill, pp. 725–40.
Waines, D. (1991): 'Murrī: The Tale of a Condiment', *Al-Qantara*, 12, pp. 371–88.
Waines, D. (1989): *In a Caliph's Kitchen*, London: Riad El-Rayyes.
Waines, D. (1987): 'Bread, Cereals and Society', *Journal of Economic and Social History of the Orient*, 30, pp. 255–85.
Waines, D. & Manuela Marín (1989): 'The Balanced Way: Food for Pleasure and Health in Mediaeval Islam', *Manuscripts of the Middle East*, 4, pp. 123–32.
Waines, D. & Sami Zubaida (2016): 'Food: Muslim and Jewish Food and Foodways', in Joseph Méri (ed.), *Handbook of Muslim–Jewish Relations*, Abingdon: Routledge, pp. 475–95.
Weingarten, Susan (2005): 'Mouldy Bread and Rotten Fish: Delicacies in the Ancient World', *Food and History*, 3, pp. 61–72.
Wilkins, John (2013): *Galien: Sur les facultés des aliments*, Paris: Budé.
Wilkins, J. (2000): *The Boastful Chef: The Discourse of Food in Ancient Greek Comedy*, Oxford: Oxford University Press.
Wilkins, J. & Robin Nadeau (2015): *Companion to Food in the Ancient World*, Chichester: John Wiley & Sons.
Wilkins, J. & Shaun Hill (2006): *Food in the Ancient World*, Oxford: Oxford University Press.
Yerasimos, Stéphane & Belkis Taskeser (2001): *A la table du Grand Turc*, Paris: Actes Sud.
Yungman, L. (2017): 'Beyond Cooking: The Roles of Chefs in Mediaeval Court Kitchens of the Islamic East', *Food & History*, 15:1–2, pp. 85–114.
Zaouali, Lilia (2007): *Mediaeval Cuisine of the Islamic World: A Concise History with 174 Recipes*, Los Angeles: University of California Press
Zubaida, Sami & Richard Tapper (eds) (2000): *A Taste of Thyme: Culinary Cultures of the Middle East*, London/New York: Tauris Parke.

INDEX

Note: Page numbers followed by *n* denote footnotes.

كِتابُ زَهْرِ ٱلحَدِيقَةِ
فِي ٱلأَطْعِمَةِ ٱلأَنِيقَةِ

تأليف الإمام العالم الفاضل الكامل المفيد الفريد
العلّامة شهاب الدين أحمد ابن المرحوم
مبارك شاه الحنفي رحمه الله تعالى

<١ظ> بِسْمِ اللهِ ٱلرَّحْمٰنِ ٱلرَّحِيم

قالَ الشَّيْخُ شِهابُ الدِّين أَحْمَد اِبْن مُبارَك شَاه رَحِمَهُ الله الحَمْد لِلّٰه رَبُّ العَالَمِينَ اللّٰهُمَّ سهل بِإِتْمَامِهِ بِحَقِّ مُحَمَّد وَآلِهِ.

فوائدُ يَجِبُ عَلَى الطَّبَّاخ مَعْرِفَتَها

أَلْبَابُ ٱلْأَوَّلُ

فِيمَا يُلْزِمِ ٱلطَّبَّاخُ مَعْرِفَتَهُ

وهو أن يكون محترزًا من مماسّة القاذورات لأنّ ذلك ممّا ينفر الطبائع عن أطعمته. وأن يكون نظيفًا في ذاته ذكيًّا في طبعه مقصوص الأظفار نظيف الثياب أيضًا لأنّ ذلك أميل لقلوب الناس إليه.

وليعلم أنّ خير القدور الموجودة البرام فليختارها ثمّ الفخّار والنحاس ردئ ولابدّ من بياضه.

وليختار من الحطب ما كان جافًّا ليس له دخان ساطع لنداوته فإن طبخه يومًا ما عند رئيسه فليختار حطبًا له رائحة طيّبة وكنت أطبخ بعراجين البلح اليابسة فكان يطيب لي روائح دخانها وبعضهم يختار الملح الأندراني فإن لم يتيسر فالملح النقي البياض الذي لا يخالطه تراب ولا حجارة.

ويختار من كلّ شيء أحسنه في البقول والأبازير ويسأل عن الأحسن فيما لم يعلمه ليصير عالمًا به. وجديد الفلفل خير من قديمه والزنجبيل خيره ما لم يكن مسوسًا ويبالغ في تنقية الأبازير ولا يطحن منها إلّا ما يستعمله لئلّا تتحلّ قوته. وليغسل الأواني والقدور بالطين الحرّ والأشنان والورد اليابس ويبخر الزبادي بالمصطكاء والعود ثمّ يغرف فيها طعامه ويمسح القدور بعد غسلها بورق النارنج أو ورق الأترجّ مفروكين ويختار لدقّ اللحم هاونًا من حجر وللأبازير هاونًا

من نحاس. في الطبخ أخذ رغوة اللحم وزبده وسخه وما عساه أن يطفو عليه عند الغليان ويغسل قبل ذلك بالماء الحارّ والملح وينقيه من الغدد والعروق والأغشية وغير ذلك من الفضلات التي لا تقصد للأكل. والمشوي يخرج وفيه بقية من رطوبته والمهزول يدهن قبل شيّه.

وينبغي أن يكون الساطور والسكاكين <٢و> محدودة وسكّين البصل لا يقطّع بها غيره ويتعاهد الخوان بالخردل ويفرد لكلّ قدر مغرفة إذا كانت الألوان مختلفة وليهيئ ماء حارًّا ليزاد به في القدر أن اضطر إليه. ولا يدقّ الأبازير في هاون واحد به أثر زفر ولا العصارات.

ولا يغرف من القدور إلّا بعد سكون غليانها وحدّة نارها وفورتها وإذا تدخّنت القدر يرمى فيها بندقًا فارغًا فإنّه يلقط دخانها وكذلك إذا كان اللحم منتنًا.

وإذا سمط الكرش يذرّ عليه الجير ويجرده فإنّه يخرج وسخها ويغسل يده قبل الغرف ويبخرها من رائحة البصل. ومن أراد أن يتهرّأ اللحم فليطرح عليه بورقًا في القدر وشمعًا وقضبانًا من عروق البطّيخ او قشوره.

وفي طبخ الأشربة ويهيئ وعاء فيه ماء وخرقة بيضاء نظيفة ليمسح بها وهي مبلولة بالماء حافة الدست وجنباته كلّما رآها تغيّرت فإن ذلك يحفظه من التغيّر والحرق. وبراني الأشربة يمسح ظاهرها بالشيرج وينظف الموضع الذي يجعلها فيه من كلّ شيء حلو يقع على الأرض ليحفظها بذلك من النمل. والهريسة والأرزّية والفريكية لا يصلح جميع ذلك إلّا بالسمين من اللحم وخيره الثني من الضأن. والثوم يفتق روائح سائر الأدهان من ذوات الأمراق وذوات الحبوب والبقول ويزيد في طيبها. والفلفل يدخل في سائر الألوان الكبار والمبزّرات ويدخل في سائر الألوان أيضًا قطع الدار صيني والخولنجان. والوجه في ذلك أن يشدخ شدخًا قويًا ليخرج بذلك الرائحة والطعم ويغنى فيه القليل عن الكثير.

والصمغ العربي المسحوق ودقيق الأرزّ ودقيق الحمّص ممّا يخثّر الطعام وإذا طبخ شيء من الحبوب لا يزال يحرّك حتّى ينزل به عن النار لئلّا ينشيط ولا

يصبّ الزيت أو ما أشبهه في القدر إلّا بعد نزع الرغوة وإن كان في شيء من اللحوم المطبوخة غلظ أطرح فيه بورقًا أو قشر بطّيخ يابس مسحوق. وإذا كان في اللحم تغيّر وزفرة فيدقّ له <٢ظ> الجوز دقًا ناعمًا ويدلك به دلكًا بليغًا ويطرح معه في القدر فإنّه يذهب بالزفر والتغيّر ويطيّب بدهنه طعم اللحم ولا تغطّى القدر إلّا بعد أن ينحى اللهيب من تحتها ويبقى الجمر الليّن وإلّا تدخنت ويكون طرح الملح بعد الفراغ آخر ما يعمل فيها لا ممّا لا يحتاج إلى نضجه لا سيّما الحبوب. فإن الملح فيها أوّل الأمر يبطئ نضجها وكذلك صبّ الخلّ على كلّ ما والباقلّاء المطبوخ إن عمل منه بارده وصبّ عليه الخلّ قبل أكله بأدنى وقت صلب حتّى يرجع كحاله بتّا وإنّما صبّه عليه في ساعة أكله. وما كثر مرقه من أنواع الطبيخ فاحتيج إلى تنشيف فبالنار وما نشف فاحتيج إلى زيادة الماء فيه حارًّا على قدر ما يريده الطبّاخ إلّا ما كان من هريسة أو أرزّ أو لوبيا أو أصناف الحبوب وما يقع منها من البقول فإنّه متى زيد فيه بعد انتهائه فسد في جميع أحواله وذهب طعمه ولو كان قبل ذلك في غاية الطبيعة والجودة وهذا ممّا ينبغي للطبّاخ أن يقدّر له كفايته من الماء من أوّله حتّى لا يحتاج إلى تجديد ما عليه. والأصل في الطبخ حسن تأليف حوائج الشيء المطبوخ حتّى لا يكون بعضه غالبًا لبعض ليعتدل طعمه. والصواب في البصل المقطّع لسائر الأطعمة أن يغسل بعد تقطيعه بالماء غسلًا جيّدًا ثمّ يلقى في القدر وأن يمسح السكّين المفردة له وللثوم بالزيت الطيّب. وينبغي أن تكون سكاكين التنصيل قوية وسكاكين التشريح رقيقة حادّة ليعينه ذلك في مقاصده. وكلّ ما كان من باذنجان وقرع فالواجب أن يطرح بعد تقطيعه في ماء وملح ساعة جيّدة قبل طرحه في القدر وما كان يلقى من الباذنجان في لون أبيض مثل مضيرة أو حصرمية فالواجب أن يقشّر تجاه الأعلى ولباس أقماعه قبل طرحه في الماء والملح والواجب على الطبّاخ أن يجعل لكلّ لون مغرفة ولا يستعمل مغرفة لون في لون.

الثريد أطيبه ما كان في مرق حامض دهن <٣و> محلّى ويكون من رقاق أو

جردق أو كعك أو خبز نقي ويترك بمقدار ما يتشرّب ماؤه ويجلس وسطه بمقعّره ويصبّ فيها الدسم ما يقوم بها. وإذا احترقت الأرزّية فالق فيها سذابًا فإنّه يذهب برائحتها. وإذا احترقت اللوبيا القدسية بخّر تحتها بصوفة تذهب برائحتها.

وإذا وجدت الزهومة في سائر القدور فألق فيها جوزة أو جوزتين صحاحًا واتركها ساعة فإنّها تنشف الزهومة وعلامة ذلك أنّك تخرج الجوزة فلا تقدر أن تشمها من زفرة رائحتها وزهومتها. وإذا أردت أن يبقى اللحم طريًا في شدّة[١] النخالة إذا حميت حتّى تحمر وألقيت في قدر التقطت ملحها. وإذا أردت أن تنضج الحمّص سريعًا فتجعل في القدر شيئًا من خردل فإنّه ينضج سريعًا وإذا أردت أن يبقى اللحم طريًا إلى أيّ وقت شئت فيؤخذ لحم الأفخاذ ويخرج منه الشحم والعظم ويشرّح ويملح جيّدًا ويترك ليلة فإذا أصبحت اغسله من الماء غسلًا جيّدًا نظيفًا وتبسطه حتّى ينشّف ثمّ يطلى بالسمن ويجعل في بستوقة ويصبّ عليه من السمن غمره ويسدّ رأس البستوقة ودعه ما شئت. ثمّ أخرجه أيّ وقت أردت فإنك تجده طريًا في شدّة الحرّ بلا ملح فخذ اللحم واجعله في شوكة ودليّه في بئر ليكون قريبًا من الماء يكاد يمسه ثمّ أخرجه إذا أردت فإنك تجده طريًا. وإن أنتن اللحم أو تغيّرت رائحته وأردت طبخه فألق معه في القدر جوزات صحاح تكون قد ثقبت أسافلها حتّى تصل إلى أجوافها فإنّها تلتقط ويصير إلى أجوافها أنتن من الجيفة. وإذا فرغت بيضة بماء فيها في القدر التقطت نتن اللحم. وإذا سلق مع اللحم يسير حلبة ثمّ قلبت ذلك وجدّد له ماء آخر ذهب عنه النتن وطاب طعمه حتّى لا يعرف طري هو أو منتن.

وإذا كان اللحم متغيّر الرائحة يقطّع ويجعل في قدر ويجعل معه بندق مكسّر فإنّه تزول رائحته.

وإذا أردت سرعة نضج الطعام فتأخذ قشور البطّيخ الأخضر <٣ظ> تجفّفه وتطحنه وتحفظه عندك وفي وقت الحاجة إلى نضج الطعام بسرعة تلقى عليه

١ وإذا . . . شدة: مستدركة في الهامش.

منه يسيرًا. وإذا أردت الثوم لا يفيش تحرق رؤوس الكنافش الذي له فإنّه يقعد مهما أردت لا يفشّ ولا يتلف.

وإذا أردت أن السمك اللبيس لا يبقى فيه شوك يؤخذ الفول يدقّ ويشقّ اللبيس من كلّ جنب ويذرّ فيهم ويشوي يتهرّأ الشوك جميعه. وإذا أردت أن تصلق للوقت لوبيا أو لبسان أو كرنب أو سلق أخضر فألق في القدر يسيرًا من نطرون مع الماء وأغلي ذلك الماء إلى أن يشقّ ثمّ ألق فيه الذي تريده فإذا ألقيته في الماء المغلي فلا تغطّى القدر بغطاء لأنّك متى غطّيتها أصفر جميع ما فيها ولا تترك المصلوق يتهرّأ بل اترك به وفيه قوة فإنّه يكون أطيب.

وإذا سلقت الإسفاناخ اغسله بالماء وألقه في القدر ولا تجعل عليه شيئًا من الماء فإنّه يرخى ماءً كثيرًا إذا أصابه حر النار وكذلك الملوخية إذا جعلتها في القدر لا تغطّى القدر ولا تجعل تحت القدر نار أشعلة ولا تتركها على النار تتهرّأ. وإذا أردت طبخ ما تريد من الحبوب مثل العدس والبسلّا والجلبان والفول والحمّص فلا تأخذ ذلك مدشوشًا من السوق بل تأخذ ما أردت منها صحيحًا تدشّه عندك وتغربله به وتلقى عليه من الزعفران ما تحتاج وجفّفه فإذا أردت أن تطبخ منه شيئًا اغل الماء بقليل ملح. فإذا غلى الماء أرفع منه قليلًا وألق ما تريد من الحبوب المذكورة ويكون عياره لكلّ قدح غمرة ونصف غمرة فإذا نضج ألق فيه حوائجه وأنت تحرّكه وكثرة التحريك تمنع من التشييط.

أَلْبَابُ ٱلثَّانِي

فِي صَنْعَةِ ٱلْأَخْبَازِ

وما يحتاج إليه أطيب الخبز ما كان دقيقه بيضًا ناعمًا حديثًا معروك قويًا محكمًا وسقيه بالماء قليل قليل حتّى لا يكون مرقًا ولا يابسًا والنار تكون هادئة ليّنة لئلّا يتشيّط. فيخرج وهو عجين وإن ضعفت النار <٤و> أيضًا ضعفًا زائد أخرج ممصوصًا لاظيًا فإذا خرج من الخبيز روح ساعة حتّى يتشرّب ماؤه ويتصرّف بخاره ويطيب أكله.

١. صفة خُبْز لَذِيذ عَجِيب فِي اللِذَّة

يؤخذ قدح دقيق وأربع أواق نشا وعشر أواق سكّر. يعجن بلبن حليب ويخبز برفق ولا يعمل فيه ماء البتّة.

٢. آخر غَيْره

يؤخذ دقيق جيّد يجعل على كلّ رطل ثلث رطل شيرج وأوقية سمسم وكفّ لبّ فستق ولوز ويعجن. فإذا اختمر يخبز في الفرن أقراصًا مدوّرة سمك القرص

إصبعين فإذا نضج يخرج ويؤكل مع الحلوى.

٣. صفة أَقْراص مَمْلُوحَة

يؤخذ قدر الحاجة من الدقيق يعجن كلّ رطل بربع رطل شيرج ويعمل فيه ملحًا ظاهرًا ويخبز بعد تخميره كالذي قبله أو أرقّ منه بيسير فإذا تورّد يخرج. وهذا يعمل إذا وقفت النفس من الأشياء الحلوة فيستعمل هذا في أثناء الحلوى.

٤. (صفة)

والتمر إذا حشي به الكعك فإنّه يعجن بالشيرج بعد نزع نواه ثمّ يحشى به وإذا حشي بسكّر ولوز مدقوق أثلاثًا معجون بماء ورد ويجمع رأس العجين عليه محكّمًا إن عمله كالكبّا أو كالخشكان.

٥. صفة كَعْك كان القاضِي الفاضِل يَعْمَلُهُ ويُهادِي بِهِ الرُّؤَسَاءَ

يؤخذ دقيق علامة ناعم أبيض منخول وفستق وسكّر من كلّ واحد جزء. ويدقّ الفستق ناعمًا وكذلك السكّر ويخلط مع الدقيق ويعجان بدهن الدجاج والألية بعد أن يخلع الألية بالمصطكاء والقرفة ويسير من المسك والكافور وعصره ليمون أخضر ويعمل أقراصًا. ويؤخذ بعد ذلك طبق نحاس مبيّض يدهن باطنه وظاهره بشيرج ويرصّ فيه الكعك وتعبر به الفرن على هدوء النار إلى حيث يحمر وتستعمله.

٦. صفة أُخْرَى

يؤخذ دقيق ناعم يلتّ بالسمن أو بالشيرج والمسك والكافور والماء ورد ويمدّ بالسويك رفيعًا ويقلى بالشيرج ويوضع في الجلّاب يسير من المسك والماء ورد. ويرصّ في الصحن ويرشّ عليه الفستق المجروش راق براق.

٧. صفة كَعْك سُكَّرِيّ

يؤخذ دقيق ورطل سكّر ثمانية أواق تسحق السكّر ناعمًا وتخلط بالدقيق ومعه أوقيتين شيرج. ويضاف إليه أربعة أواق ماء ويعجن قوى ويعمل كعك وأقراصًا ويخبز ويرصّ <٤ظ> في طبق نحاس. تجئ غاية.

٨. صفة الكَعْك بِالعَجْوَة

لكلّ رطل دقيق نصف رطل شيرج وثمان أواق عجوة وماء ورد وزعفران وأطراف طيب وفلفل وزنجبيل.

٩. صفة المَلْتُوت

يؤخذ دقيق علامة وشيرج وعرق كافور ومصطكاء يعجن الدقيق بالشيرج أوّلًا ثمّ بعد ذلك يعجن بالماء ويدقّ عرق الكافور والمصطكاء وقليل شيبة تبلّ ويدقّ أيضًا وتعمل في الدقيق ويعمل حلق.

أَلْبَابُ ٱلثَّالِثُ

فِي تَدْبِيرِ ٱلْمَاءِ المَشْرُوبِ

قالت الحكماء ينبغي لمن يؤثر حفظ الصحّة أن لا يشرب الماء على الريق ولا على المائدة ولا عقيب الأكل إلى أن يجفّ أعالي البطن إلّا بقدر ما يسكن به العطش ولا يروى منه ريًا واسعًا حتّى إذا جفّ أعلى البطن وانحدر الطعام عنه استوفي شربه منه ومن الشراب ولا ينبغي أن يشرب ماء البلح على المائدة إلّا العليل وليحذر الماء والثلج من به ضعف في العصب ومن معدته وكبده باردان وبالجملة من يجد في هضمه تخلفًا وتضعف نفسه وتنبل فلا يستعمله. وأمّا من كان كثير اللحم والدم أحمر اللون قوي الشهوة فلا ينبغي أن يخاف منه ويشرب من الماء والبلح في أيّ وقت شاء على المائدة فإن ذلك قليل الضرر له. وأمّا شرب الماء على الريق فليس بصالح إلّا لمن به التهاب شديد وحمّى وليتوق الشرب الكثير من الماء البارد دفعة واحدة وليشربه في دفعات في كلّ دفعتين نفس فإنّه صالح ويحفظ على الإنسان قوة بدنه. وبهذا التدبير فليكن العمل إن شاء الله.

فصل
فِي خَاصِية الماء المُبَرَّد فِي الهَوَاء

اعلم أنّ الماء يحفظ على البدن رطوبته الأصلية ويرقّ الغذاء وينفذه ويقمع الحرارة وهو أوفق للمحرورين وأصحاب الأمزاج الحارّة من الشراب وأجود الماء أنفعه وأخفه وزنًا وأسرعه قبولًا للسخونة والبرودة وأعذبه طعمًا الذي يضرب في طعمه إلى الحلاوة. واعلم أن أشرب الماء الذي له طعم أو ريح مكروه فإنّها رديئة لا تصلح للشرب وقد يستعمل في الأدوية والعلاجات.

وأمّا الماء المالح فإنّه يطلق البطن أوّلًا ثمّ يعقله ثانيًا وإذا أدمن عليه ولد العفن ويعظم منه الطحال ويفسد المزاج ويتولّد منه الحمّايات. وأمّا الماء المبرّد <٥و> بالثلج فإنّه يبرد الكبد جدًّا فلا ينبغي أن يشرب على الريق إلّا للمحرورين. وأمّا على الطعام فإنّه يقوّي المعدة وينهض الشهوة ويجزى قليله وأمّا البارد الشديد البرد الذي لا يبلغ من برده أن يستلذّ فإنّه ينفخ البطن ولا يبلغ من كسر العطش مبلغًا ويسقط الشهوة ويرخى الجسد وليس بصالح.

وأمّا الماء المطبوخ والماء الفاتر فإنّه ينفخ ولا يصلح إلّا للعلاج.

وأمّا الحارّ إذا تجرع منه على الريق غسل المعدة من فضول الغذاء المتقدّم وربّما أطلق البطن غير أنّ السرف في استعماله يحلق المعدة.

أَلْبَابُ ٱلْرَابِعُ

فِي ٱلْأَطْعِمَةِ

اعلم أنّ الأطعمة الحوامض منها ما يحلّى ومنها ما يبقى على حموضته فالذي يحلى منها قد يحلّى بالسكّر أو العسل أو الدبس وحكم ذلك أجمع أن يكون في باب واحد فمن ذلك

١٠. السِّكْباجُ

صنعته أن يقطّع اللحم السمين أوساطًا ويجعله في القدر وعليه غمره ماء ويسير ملح وعود ودار صيني فإذا غلى تلقط زفره. ثمّ تجعل عليه كسفرة يابسة ثمّ تأخذ البصل الأبيض والكرّاث الشامي والجزر إن كان أوانه والباذنجان. ويقشّر الجميع ويشقّ الباذنجان صليبًا ويصلق في قدر آخر في ماء مالح ثمّ ينشّف من مائه ويترك في القدر فوق اللحم ويلقى عليه الأبازير ويعدّل ملحه فإذا قارب النضج يؤخذ من الخلّ والدبس أو العسل قدر الحاجة إليه ويعمل مزاجًا معتدلًا في الحموضة والحلاوة ويصبّ في القدر ويغلى ساعة ويختر بقليل نشا أو أرزّ. ثمّ يؤخذ لوز مقشر منصف وكفّ عنّاب وتمر يابس وزبيب فيجعل في رأس القدر ويغطّى ساعة ويقطّع الوقود ويمسح جوانب القدر بخرقة لطيفة ويرشّ عليه ماء

بارد. فإذا هدت على حمو النار رفعت.

١١. طَعَام ظَرِيف

يقطّع اللحم أوساطًا ويوضع في القدر ويغمر بالماء ويلقى فيه خرقة كتّان رفيعة مشدود فيها كسفرة وزنجبيل وفلفل وعود مدقوق ناعم. ثمّ يلقى عليه قطع دار صيني ومصطكاء ويقطّع بصله صليب ثلاثة صغار ويلقى فيها بعد غليه بالماء والملح وتتشيفه منه. وتخرج تلك الخرقة وتمرتها بماء الحصرم العتيق أو الطري المعتصر باليد <٥ظ> من غير سلق أو بالخلّ المقطّر. ثمّ يصفّى ويربّى باللوز الحلو المدقوق ناعمًا ويصبّ عليه ماء الحصرم. ثمّ يحلى بالسكّر الأبيض شيئًا يسيرًا ولا يكون كثير الحموضة ويترك على النار حتّى يهدأ ويمسح جوانب القدر بخرقة نظيفة. ثمّ يرشّ على رأسها يسيرًا من ماء ورد ويرفع.

١٢. صفة جُرْجانِيَّة

يقطّع اللحم السمين أوساطًا ويجعل عليه غمره ماء ويسير ملح ويقطع بصلًا قطعًا لطافًا. فإذا غلى عليه جعل البصل فوقه وكسفرة يابسة وفلفل وزنجبيل ودار صيني مدقوق ناعمًا ومن أحبّ أن يجعل فيه جوزًا مقشرًا قد أخرج خشبه من جوفه وقطع وسطًا. ثمّ يحرّك فإذا نضجت الحوائج يؤخذ حبّ رمّان وزبيب أسود نصفين مدقوقًا ناعمًا ويمرس بالماء جيّدًا ويصفّى على منخل ضيّق. ثمّ يلقى في القدر وليكن معه شيء يسير من خلّ ويربّى باللوز الحلو المقشر المدقوق ناعمًا. ثمّ يلقى في القدر فإذا غلى وقارب النضج تحلى بقليل سكّر قدر الحاجة ويلقى في رأس القدر كفّ عنب ويرش عليها قليل ماء ورد. ثمّ يغطّى حتّى يهدأ على النار.

١٣. صفة رُمَّانِيَّة مُخَثَّرَة بِفُستُق

يقطّع اللحم ويلقى في القدر ويلقى عليه ماء ويغلى ويؤخذ زفره ويرمى فيه مدقّقة صغارًا بعدد البندق وليكن ماؤه قليلًا بحيث إذا نضج لا يبقى منه غير زبدية لطيفة. ثمّ يؤخذ ماء الرمّان الحامض ويعدّل بالورد المربّى بالسكّر ويلقى عليه ويرمى عليه أوراق نعنع ويدقّ قلب الفستق ويخثّره به ويصبغ بقليل زعفران وجميع أطراف الطيب. ويرشّ عليه ماء ورد وزعفران ويرفع.

١٤. حُمّاضِيَّة

يقطّع اللحم السمين وينزل في القدر مع غمره ماء ويسير ملح. ثمّ يغلى عليه ويطرح الأبازير مثل الكزبرة اليابسة والفلفل والزنجبيل والقرنفل مدقوقًا ناعمًا مشدودين في خرقة كتّان نظيفة ويقطّع فيها قطع دار صيني. ثمّ يدقّ اللحم الأحمر بالأبازير ويكبّب ويجعل في القدر بعد أن يغلى عليه. فإذا نضجت الخرقة يؤخذ حماض الأترجّ الكبار المنقّى من حبّه فيعصر باليد عصرًا جيّدًا. ثمّ يمزج مع مثله ماء حصرم ثمّ يجعل في القدر على النار حتّى يغلى ساعة. ثمّ يؤخذ من اللوز الحلو المربّى المقشّر بالماء بعد دقّه ناعمًا بقدر ما <٦و> يحتمله الطبيخ فيصاف إلى القدر. ثمّ يحلّى بالسكّر. ومن أراد بالجلّاب ويترك القدر على النار حتّى يهدأ ساعة وترشّ على رأسها ماء ورد ويرفع.

١٥. حُمّاضِيَّة أُخرَى

وهي من أطعمة الخلفاء يقطّع الدجاج على مفاصله ويؤخذ لحم أفخاذه يدقّ بالساطور دقًّا ناعمًا دون جلوده ومعه صدر الدجاج ويغسل. ثمّ يلقى باقي الدجاج

ودهنه وشحمه في القدر ويقطّع عليه رؤوس البصل ويرشّ رشّة ماء بالأبازير وهي كزبرة وزنجبيل وكمّون محمّص مدقوق وقطعة دار صيني ومقدار صالح من دهن اللوز الحلو ويعرّق بذلك تعريقًا جيّدًا. ويلقى عليه مقدار درهم ملح ويحرّك متصلًا ويلقى عليه ورق أترجّ. ثمّ يأخذ حماض للأترجّ المنقّى من قشره وحبّه ويرشّ عليه ماء ورد ويخرج الذي في الصرّة من القدر ويلقى في القدر اللحم المدقوق من الأفخاذ والصدور ويعرّق به. فإذا أخذ طعم للأبازير ألقى عليه نعنع وصعتر رطب. فإذا غلى ألقى عليه شيء من الليمون الأبيض العذب ورؤوس يصل مقطّع فإذا نضج تدقّ مقدارًا صالحًا من اللوز الحلو ويربّى بماء الورد. ثمّ يخرج البقول ويلقى الحمّاض المعتصر المنقّى فإذا سكن الغليان تعدّل حمضها بالجلّاب والسكّر الطبرزد المدقوق جريشًا. ثمّ يلقى اللوز بعد ذلك ويعطّر بماء الورد والكافور الظاهر المؤثّر فيها ويهدأ ويرفع. وهي من أطعمة الخلفاء. قوله يهدأ ويرفع أصل من أصول الطبخ فافهمه ولا تهمله. وأفخر بل وأنفع ما يكون اللحم مع هذه الأبازير من غير أن يضاف إليه شيء ممّا هو دون الحنطة في النفع.

١٦. زِيرْباج

يقطّع اللحم صغارًا ويترك في القدر وغمره ماء وقطع دار صيني وحمّص مقشور ويسير ملح. فإذا غلى ماء تأخذ رغوته ثمّ تطرح عليه شيرج وخلّ خمر كفايته وربع وزن الخلّ سكّر ولوز مقشور مدقوق ناعمًا يداف بماء ورد ويطرح على اللحم ويلقى عليه كزبرة يابسة مسحوقة وفلفل ومصطكاء مسحوق. ثمّ يصبغ الزعفران ويجعل في رأس القدر لوز مقشّر مفروك نصفين ويرشّ عليها قليل ماء ورد ويمسح جوانبها. ويترك على النار حتّى يهدأ ومن أحبّ أن يجعل فيها الدجاج فيأخذ دجاجة <٦ظ> مسموطة فيغسلها ويقطّعها على مفاصلها. ثمّ إذا غليت القدر غلية خفيفة ألقاها مع اللحم تنضج. ومن أرادها ظاهرة الحلاوة فليزدها سكّر وقد

تجعل بدله عسلًا إن شاء الله تعالى.

١٧. فُسْتُقِيَّة

يقطّع اللحم مع غمره ماء ويؤخذ زفره ويغلى. فإذا نضج يلقى فيه كببًا لطاف مدقوقة بجميع أطراف الطيب مع دار صيني ومصطكاء وملح وشيرج ونعنع. فإذا نضج وبقي من مرقه قليل يزال المرق ويقلى اللحم بالدهن والأبازير. ثمّ يعاد ألية معرّقته ويدقّ الفستق ويخثّر به ويطبخ ويصلح طعمه بماء الليمون. ويرشّ عليه قليل ماء الورد ويمسح جوانب القدر ويهدأ ويرفع إن شاء الله تعالى.

١٨. صفة رِيباسِيَّة

هي لحم مصلوق معرّق بالأبازير ويطرح عليه قليل بصل مقطّع صغار. ثمّ يلقى عليه ماء الريباس ويضاف إليه شيء من اللوز الحلو المدقوق المربّى ويفرك في رأسها باقة نعنع يابس ويترك على نار هادئة ويرفع.

١٩. أمِيربارِسِيَّة

هي كالسمّاق إلّا أن عوض السمّاق الأميربارس ومن الناس من يحلّيها بقليل سكّر.

٢٠. صفة نارَنْجِيَّة

يقطّع اللحم السمين أوساطًا ويترك في القدر حتّى يغلى غلوة. فإذا على نزع رغوته وطرح عليه ملح قدر الحاجة ويقطّع قطعًا لطافًا ويطرح في القدر ويلقى عليه الملح

والأبازير المذكورة طاقات النعنع. ومن أراد الكبب فيدقّ اللحم الأحمر ويعمل منه ما يريد من الكبب ويضيفها إلى القدر. ثمّ يأخذ النارنج فيقشّر وينزع شحمه الأبيض ويقطّع نصفين ويعصر على مصفاة أو منخل وليكن الذي يعصره غير الذي يقشّره. ويؤخذ حبّ القرطم المنقّي المغسول الذي ينقع في الماء الحارّ ساعة يدقّ في هاون حجر ناعمًا فإن تعذر فهاون نحاس نظيف من الصدأ ويستحلب ماؤه باليد ويصفّى ويجعل في القدر ويفرك في رأسها طاقات نعنع يابس ويمسح أجنابها بالخرقة المقطّعة على جاري العادة. ويترك ساعة ويرفع.

٢١. (نارنجية أخرى)

ومنهم من يعملها على غير هذه الصفة <٧و> بصدور دجاج مدقوقة مع لحم لكلّ صدر دجاجة أوقيتين من لحم ويعمل فيه فستق. ثمّ يجلب اللوز ويؤخذ منه قدر صالح ويلقى على ذلك المدقوق ويضع فيه خولنجان وزنجبيل وجلّاب ونارنج بفستق ونعناع وماء ورد. ومن كان له فضل بحذق ركّب أطعمة لا نهاية لها بحذقه وذكائه.

٢٢. صفة الكِشْك

لكلّ رطل ونصف لحم رطل كشك وأوقية ونصف ثوم وستّ اروٴس بصل ودرهمين كراوية ومثلها فلفل وأربع عيدان قرفة صحيحة وأربع ليمونات. يغلى اللحم بفرد بصلة وقليل فلفل وإذا طاب اللحم يدقّ الثوم بالزيت والملح ويجعل عليه ويحرّكه. ثمّ يقطّع البصل صحيحًا ويجعله فيه ثمّ يرمى الأبازير والكراوية والنعنع والقرفة ثمّ تذّر عليه حتّى يطيب وتأخذ حتّى يعصر عليه الأربع ليمونات وتخليه ساعة حتّى يهدأ وينضج وينزل.

٢٣. صفة مَخْفِيَّة

وهي تعمل على أنواع ذكرنا نوعًا منها يقطّع اللحم السمين صغارًا ويسلّى الألية ويطرح اللحم في الدهن ويلقى عليه ملح وكسفرة يابسة وينحى الدهن ويغمر بالماء ويغلى ويكشط رغوته ويرمى عليه أوراق كسفرة خضراء وعيدان دار صيني منحوته وكفّ حمّص مقشور مرضوض وبصلتين ثلاثة مقشورة مقطّعة. ثمّ يدقّ من اللحم الأحمر مقدار الحاجة دقًّا ناعمًا بالملح والابازير ويؤخذ البيض المسلوق يستخرج منه الصفار ويجعل في وسط كلّ كبّة صفار بيضة ويطرح في القدر. فإذا انصلق يردّ إليه الدهن المسلّى ويرشّ عليه الدار صيني المسحوق ناعمًا ويرفع فإنّه غاية. والمقصود في الأطعمة أن تطيب وتدسم وإن شئت فتحلّى كلّ هذه المقاصد أصول في علم الطبّ فافهمه وتصرّف.

٢٤. صفة الياقُوتِيَّة

يعرّق اللحم العادة ويلقى فيه ما يطيبه كالزيت والدار صيني والمصطكاء وغير ذلك. ثمّ يقطّع اليقطين فصوصًا ويلقى فيه فإذا بدأ ينضج ألقى عليه ماء التوت الأحمر وحلّاه بعسل نحل أو سكّر أو جلّاب وأطبخه جيّدًا <٧ظ> ويفرك عليه طاقات نعنع واغرفه بعد هدوئه على نار ليّنة.

٢٥. صفة مُدَقَّقَة حامِضَة

يشرّح اللحم الأحمر ثمّ يدقّ ناعمًا ويلقى عليه الملح والأبازير المعروفة ويسير من بصل مخرّط. ثمّ تكبّب على قدر الحاجة ويصلق في الماء والملح المعتدل فإذا نضج ونشف الماء عنه تؤخذ الألية تسلّى ويرمى شحمها. ثمّ يلقى تلك الكبب في

ذلك الدهن مع قطع بصل. وأمّا حمضها فمن أراد يرشّ عليه ماء حماض أو خلًّا أو ماء حصرم أو ماء ليمون أو كليهما ممزوجين ومن أحبّ أن يصبغها بزعفران فليكن على الخلّ أو ماء ليمون حسب الحاجة ويذرّ عليها الأبازير المعروفة. ومن أحبّ فرك عليها طاقات نعنع وتترك وترفع. وإزالة العروق من لحم المدقّقة أصل كبير.

٢٦. صفة رُطَبِيَّة

يقطّع اللحم الأحمر صغارًا ويرمى في القدر ويصلق حتّى ينضج. ثمّ تزال المرقة ويقلى في الدهن الطري المسلّى ويغفل ملحه وأبازيره فإذا استحكم نضجه صفّ عليه من الرطب الأصفر بمسلّة ويجعل عوضه لوز مقشّر ويجعل فيه كببًا من اللحم الأحمر المدقوق وتهيّأ على هيئة الرطب مستطيلة. ويجعل في وسطها اللوزة ويرش على رأس القدر قليل ماء ورد ويصبغ بيسير من الزعفران. ويهدّأ على النار ويرفع.

٢٧. (التَمْرِيَّة)

وأمّا التمر فيعمل على هذا الوضع إذا عدم الرطب.

٢٨. صفة مُدَقَّقَة سَاذِجَة

يقطّع اللحم السمين صغارًا ويجعل في القدر ماء غمره ثمّ يؤخذ اللحم الأحمر يدقّ ناعمًا ويلقى فيه ما يحتمله من الملح والأبازير وكفّ حمّص مقشور مرضوض وكفّ أرزّ مغسول. ثمّ يلقى في القدر وبعمل منه كببًا على ما تختار فإذا نضج

واستحكم نضجه يلقى عليه ما يحتاج من الملح والأبازير وينقص من الماء الذي عليه ويطرح عليه من الدهن بقدر الحاجة ويذرّ على وجهه الدار صيني ناعمًا ويهدأ على النار الليّنة ساعة ويرفع. <٨و>

٢٩. صفة نَوْع مِنْ أَنْوَاعِ الماء وَرْدِيَّ

يقطّع اللحم مستطيلًا صغارًا ويعرّق ثمّ يغمر بالماء وتكشط رغوته. فإذا نضج ونشف الماء عنه يلقى عليه سكّرًا أو عسلًا حسب ما يحتاج إليه وكفّ لوز مقشور مرضوض ويصبغ بالزعفران وماء الورد ولا يزال يحرّك حتّى ينعقد ويترك على النار حتّى يهدأ. ثمّ يغرف ويصفّ على وجهه السنبوسك المحشي المقلو واللوز والسكّر ويذرّ على وجهه يسير كافور يأتي غاية. وهذه كانوا يسمّونها قديمًا فالوذجية.

٣٠. صفة

من الطبّاخين من يأخذ الشوي البائت فيدير منه محمّصة[٢] أو غيرها على قدر حذقه في الطبخ مثل أن يقطّع ذلك صغارًا ويغليه بالشيرج فإذا نضج وذاب دهنه ألقى عليه من الأبازير ما يحتمله. ومن أراد محمّصة رشّ عليه خلًّا أو ليمون ومن أراد أن يجعل على وجهها عيون البيض فعل ويرشّ عليها يسيرًا من الدار صينى. ثمّ يترك على نار هادئة ويرفع.

٣١. صفة المَصْلُوقة

يعمل في قدر فخّار جديد أو نحاس مبيّض وتعمل الماء قدر اللحم أو الدجاج ثمّ

٢ هكذا في المخطوطة والصواب (محمّضة).

يرمى المصطكاء والقرفة فبعضهم يدقّ اللوز المصلوق ناعمًا ويستحلبه ويضيفه عليها عندما يريد أن يشال عن النار. ويرشّ عليها قليل ماء ورد ويعمل فيها عروق كسفرة خضراء.

٣٢. صفة القَمْحِيَّة

يغسل القمح نظيف ثمّ ترميه في القدر بعد غليها جيّدًا. فإذا رأيت الحبّة قد انشقّت صقيه وشيله وصبّ ماء غيره. ثمّ ارم اللحم ولا ترم فيه ملح إلّا عند شيله وإذا رمت اللحم وكلّما نقصت المرقة زده ماء باردًا أو ارم الشبتّ والمصطكاء والقرفة ويكون عندك كمّون مطحون ووقت غرفها. احفظها من الدخان.

٣٣. صفة الشيِشْبَرَك

منهم من يقليه وإن كان في اللبن تأخذ العجين تمدّه مثل التطماج وتأخذ له رأس كوز تطبقه على الورق يطلع مدوّر القرص فتحشيه كما ذكرنا. وتغلى له الماء فإذا غلى الماء ترميه بحيث يكون مخلّصًا من بعضه بعض. فإذا نضج يشيله وتعمله في اللبن <٨ظ> أو الحبّ رمّان وحشوه كالسنبوسك.

٣٤. صفة الدَّجَاج المَصْلُوق

تذبح الدجاجة وتسمط عقب ذلك وتنقّي من أوساخها وتغسل بماء وملح وزيت دفعات. ثمّ تغلى الماء حتّى يحمى وترمى الدجاجة فيه مقطّعة على مفاصلها وتقطّف زفرها وتلقى عليه كفّ حمّص مجروش وبياض بصلة وعود شبتّ وقرفة ومصطكاء وشيرج. وتأخذ مخّ بيضة تذاب بشيء من مرقها وترمى في القدر وتقوّي

نارها حتّى تنضج. ثمّ تتركها حتّى تهدأ وترفع. في غاية الحسن.

٣٥. حَشْو الدَّجَاج عَلَى أنْوَاع

بالحوائج والأبازير والزيت والطحينة والبندق واللوز ومنهم من يحشيه **بالحلو** سكّر وفستق وماء ورد ولابدّ من الزيت والطحينة في الكلّ سواء كان الحشو حلوًا أو حامضًا أو غير ذلك فنوع ما شئت وجرّب وزد وانقص. فمهما وجدت اللذة والنفع فالزمهما.

٣٦. صفة دَجاج الزِّيرْباج

إذا سلق الدجاجة بالماء والملح والمصطكاء والدار صيني تقطّع على مفاصلها أو نصفين أو تترك بحالها الأوّل وتعرّق بالشيرج الطري والكسفرة اليابسة والمصطكاء والدار صيني. وتمرق بعد التعريق بالسكّر والزعفران ويلقى معهما أطراف الطيب ومربّى اللوز الحلو المقشّر ناعمًا ويطرح في القدر ويلقى فيه عود نعنع أخضر.

٣٧. صِفَة دَجَاجَةِ حامِضِيَّة

تمرق بماء سمّاقي أو حبّ رمّان أو ماء حصرم وماء ليمون مجموعين والأفاوه العادة.

٣٨. صِفة جَواذِب الدَّجَاج

تقطّع الدجاج على مفاصلها وتصلق بغمرها ماء وتلقى عليه مصطكاء ودار صيني

وشيرج فإذا نضجت تلغى ويؤخذ دهنها. ثمّ يؤخذ أرزّ فيغسل ثمّ يلقى على ما بقي من سليقها بعد أن تخلط به لبنًا حليبًا وتردّ عليه دهن الدجاجة التي قلبت فيه فإذا نضج وضعت عليه الدجاجة. ثمّ تخمّر ساعة وترفع.

٣٩. (فُسْتُقِيَّة)

وإذا أردت أن تعقد فستقية أو غيرها من الألوان بجلّاب خلّ[٣] فإذا جعلته في الدست وأردته بما أردت فلا تعقده إلّا بمقدار أوقيتين نشا أو أوقية ونصف وبياض بيضة <٩و> تحرّكه به فهذا الذي يعقده ثمّ يترك فيه الدجاج المستوي أو ما ارادت وترفعه. ومنهم من يكدّ الدجاجة السمينة ويتعبها ويسقيها خلًّا وماء ورد. ثمّ تذبح وتشوى على نار هادئة ليّنة وتدهن بذلك. فإنّها تخرج في غاية النعومة واللذّة.

٤٠. صِفة لَوْن بِقَرَاصِيا

يؤخذ دجاج فائق يسلق بعود خولنجان ودار صيني إلى أن يقارب النضج. ثمّ تؤخذ قراصيا بالغة تسلق وتترك من غربال فما نزل أخذ نصفه جعل على القدر بسكّر وعسل نحل ويربّى الباقي بلوز ويسقى به القدر ويطيّب بالماء الورد والكافور والمسك. وتهدّى وتغرف وتقدّم.

٤١. (سُمَّاقِيَّة بِالقُلْقاس)

السمّاق يدقّ وإمّا ينقع بماء سخن أو لا ينقع فإذا استوى اللحم وضع عليه عند ذلك والقلقاس يحطّ مع اللحم بعد نصف سلقه من اللحم هذا إذا عمل السمّاقية

٣ هكذا في الأصل.

بقلقاس وإذا شاء جعل الثوم صحاحًا أو غير ذلك والتوابل كيفما شاء على العادة. وإذا اشتهى عمل السلق.

٤٢. صِفَة خَيْطِيَّة الدَّجَاج

إذا نضج الدجاج خذ صدوره وانسله شعرة شعرة ثمّ يسلق الفستق ويدقّ ويصفّى من المنخل ويشال ويلقى عليه سكّر بياض. ثمّ يضاف إليه اللحم المغسول المنسّر ويغلى إلى أن يشتدّ ويلقى عليه دهن الفستق يسقى به ويبسط في الأواني.

٤٣. (خَيْطِيَّة بَيْضاء)

وإن أردت أن تكون الخيطية بيضًا فتغمر بماء اللوز وتسقى بدهن اللوز وتستعمل.

٤٤. صِفَة الرُّخامِيَّة

بعد نضج اللحم لكلّ رطل لبن حليب أوقيتين أرزّ على اليسير من ماء اللحم الذي سبق بالنضج. وتؤكل بالعسل أو الجلّاب أو السكّر.

٤٥. (خيطية أخرى)

والخيطية قريبة منها وصفتها يؤخذ اللحم الأحمر فإن كان زمامين[٤] كان أجود ويقطّع ويسلق حتّى يتهرأ. فإذا نضج جيّدًا ينشف الماء. ثمّ يشيله وينسره شعرة شعرة. ثمّ يغسل بالماء إلى أن يبيض اللحم والماء الذي غسل به ويحطّ اللبن

٤ هكذا في الأصل.

على النار ويغسل الأرزّ ويحطّ عليه. ثمّ يدقّ أرزّ آخر وينخل ويذرّ عليه قليلًا قليلًا ويحبط ويكون للرطل اللحم أربعة أواق أرزّ وثلاثة أرطال لبن ورطلين ماء وأرزّ مدقوق أوقيتين. فإذا انتهى <٩ظ> تؤكل بالجلّاب.

٤٦. صِفَة المُلُوخِيَّة

يؤخذ اللحم يغسل ويقطّع وينضج ويقلى ثمّ يحطّ الماء عليه وتذبل الملوخية في الشمس وتخرط خرطًا جيّدًا رقيقًا ولا يخرط من غير أن يذبل فإن ذلك أجود. ثمّ تحطّ الملوخية في الماء على القدر وتدقّ الكسفرة والكراوية والأبازير الحارّة والملح والثوم يدقّ الجميع ويذوب بالماء ويحطّ عليها. فإذا انتهت يهدأ القدر تؤكل.

٤٧. وَأمّا الفُسْتُقِيَّة وَالبُنْدُقِيَّة

فلكلّ رطل جلّاب نصف رطل من أحدهما وهو عيار دجاجتين يسمط البندق أو الفستق وينزل من غربال الدقيق ويديره في الدست أيّ يحرّكه مع الجلّاب مع أوقية ونصف أو أوقيتين نشا وبياض بيضة وتقلب ذلك على الدجاج فيعقد ويجعل عليهم من المسك والماء ورد على قدر همّتك. وكذلك تعمل في طعام الجلّابية وكلّ هذه الأطعمة متقاربة يستدلّ ببعضها على بعض.

٤٨. صفة اللَيْمُونِيَّة

لكلّ دجاجتين رطل حلّ جلّاب وربع رطل لوز. تجعل الحلّ على النار في الدست ويسخن. وإن شئت عملت السكّر وتحلّه جلّاب إلى أن يأخذ القوام. ثمّ يسمط

اللوز وتنزعه من قشره وتنخله من غربال مثل سميذ القمح بعد دقّه في الهاون. ثمّ تجعله في الدست على الجلّاب وتديره. ثمّ بعد ذلك تجعل عليه مقدار سبع ليمونات تعصرهم وتصفيهم من خرقة في الدست وتديره. ثمّ ترمى فيه بعده أوقية ونصف نشا قلب وبياض بيضة وعودين نعنع وتديره وتكون قد هيّأت دجاجتين على ما تقدم في الذي قبله. فإذا أخذت القوام جعلتهم في الدست مع الحلّ. ثمّ تشيلهم في الزبادي وتقلب الدست عليهم. ثم تجعل عليهم من المسك والماء ورد على قدر همّتك وتتركهم ساعة حتّى يعقدوا. فإنّه غاية.

٤٩. والزِّيرْبَاج

كذلك لكلّ دجاجتين رطل جلّاب ونصف رطل لوز يعمل كالذي قبله إلّا أنّك تجعل عليه أربع أواق خلًّا خمر طيّب غاية ما يكون منه وتديره وتجعل معه وزن درهم زعفران جنوبي وبياض بيضة وعودين نعناع لا غير. ثمّ تفعل بالدجاج كما وصف في الذي قبله وهذا <١٠و> مختصر العبارة لأنّ الحاذق يستدلّ بقليل الكلام على كثيره.

٥٠. صِفَة الرُّخامِيَّة

لكلّ قدح أرزّ ثلاثة أرطال لبن حليب وعصفر زنجبيل وعود قرفة ووزن ربع درهم مصطكاء. ثمّ تأخذ نصف ذلك اللبن وهو رطل ونصف وتجعله في القدر وتجعل معه مثله ماء وتجعل معه العود القرفة والعصفر زنجبيل والمصطكاء. فإذا غلى الماء واللبن غسلت عند ذلك الأرزّ وجعلته في البرمة. ثمّ تسقيه بذلك الرطل ونصف لبن الذي بقي قليلًا قليلًا على نار ليّنة. ثمّ تسقيه وتحرّكه وتكون نار هادئة وأنت تحرّكه قليلًا قليلًا وإن كان ذلك كلّه على الفحم فهو أجود. فإذا

طاب هدأته ساعة وتنزّله ولا يعلق الدخان. وإذا دخن لك شيء من الطبيخ خذ حزمة كبريت قطع طرفها وربطها وارمها في البرمة فهي تعلق الدخان كلّه أو ارم فيها بندقة فارغة مثقوبة فهي أيضًا تعلق الدخان. وإذا غرفت في الأصحن فليغرف بالشيرج ورشّ على وجه الصحن السكّر. فهو غاية.

٥١. صِفَةَ التَّمْرهِنْدِيَّة

يسلق الدجاج سلقًا جيّدًا وتتشفه بالشيرج وتحشى بطونها باللوز والسكّر لكلّ دجاجة أوقية لوز وأوقية سكّر يدقّوا في الهاون بيسير كافور وماء ورد وتحشى به بطون الدجاج. ويؤخذ الجلّاب المحلول يرمى به في الدست ويؤخذ لكلّ مائة درهم من الجلّاب أوقية تمر هندي يمرس بالماء الحارّ أو البارد ويلقى على الجلّاب في الدست ويغمر به الدجاج ويهدّأ.

٥٢. الخَيْطِيَّة

يؤخذ قدحين أرزّ واحي يغسل بالماء حتّى ينقّى ويبقى ماؤه ويؤخذ ستّة أرطال بالمصري يغلى على النار مع حصاة مصطكاء وقطعة قرفة صحيحة وينزل الأرزّ فيه حتّى يتشرّب. ثمّ يسقى ستة أرطال لبن حليب قليلًا قليلًا حتّى يتشرّب اللبن وتلقى عليه رطلين لحم مصلوق منسر ويضرب جيّدًا حتّى يدخل بعضه في بعض وينزل وتجعل عليه <١٠ظ> الجلّاب أو العسل النحل ويستعمل.

٥٣. صِفة المَأْمُونِيَّة

لكلّ رطل من اللبن الحليب أوقيتين أرزّ مدقوق ويغلى لها جلّاب مقدار ما يحلّى

ويكون قد سلّى ألية ويعمل. ثمّ جلّاب وثمّ ألية حتّى يقذف الدهن.

٥٤. صفة اللُبَابِيَّة

تؤخذ دجاجة تقطّع صغارًا ولحم ويصلق ويقلى بشيرج ويؤخذ اللباب والخشخاش يفرك من تحت الغربال ويحمّص حتّى يحمر. وتحطّ مرقة الدجاج في القدر أو اللحم وتحطّ عليها اللباب والخشخاش وتسقى بالجلّاب حتّى تنضج. يخلط عليها دهن ألية وعليها اللحم والدجاجة وتحطّ زعفران ومسك وماء ورد ويعمل فيها فستق صحاح مقشور.

٥٥. صفة مَأْمُونِيَّة بِدَجاجٍ

يؤخذ قدحين أرزّ واحي يغسل جيّدًا حتّى ينقّى من الملح ويجفّف في الشمس ويدقّ ناعمًا وينزل من غربال صفيق. ويؤخذ له رطلين سكّر وثمانية أرطال لبن حليب بالمصري يخلط الجميع ويؤخذ صدور دجاجتين يسلقوا جيّدًا حتّى يتهرّوا وينسرهم شعرة شعرة ويغسل بالماء جيّدًا بعد صلقه ويعصر من الماء وينشف ويخلط مع اللبن والسكّر. ويرفع الجميع على النار ويحرّك ولا يرفع اليد من تحريكه حتّى يصير في قوام العصيدة وينزل من على النار ويطيّب بالمسك والكافور ويعرّق بالشيرج.

٥٦. صفة الأَرُزِّ بِٱللَبَن

لكلّ رطل ونصف أرزّ عشرة أرطال لبن حليب.

٥٧. صفة المُلُوخِيَّة

تحتاج إلى لحم ودهن وملوخية وإن احتاج أن يعمل فيها دجاج أو فراخ حمام وثوم وفلفل يصلق اللحم ويصفّى ويدقّ الثوم والفلفل والكسفرة والكراوية وبصلة مشوية تعمل في المدقّقة مع الحوائج وتعمل المرق على اللحم في القدر وتخرط الملوخية. فإذا غلى الماء على اللحم ترمى الملوخية عليها وتغلى عليها إلى أن تنضج وتقدّم.

٥٨. صفة اللَبَنِيَّة

تحتاج فيه أن ترمى اللبن واللحم معًا ولا ترمى البصل إلّا بعد ساعة جيّدة ويضاف إليه المصطكاء والقرفة وقليل نعنع وكرّات فإذا نضج اللحم ولم ينعقد اللبن يرمى فيها قطعة من كوز طلع أو قليل أرزّ أو قليل نشا إلى أن ينعقد. ويهدأ ويغرف.

٥٩. صفة الأَرُزّ الأَصْفَر

يغلى[٥] العسل أوّلًا ثمّ يغسل الأرزّ ويلقى عليه ويعمل في العسل <١١و> قليل ماء وشيرج لكلّ رطل عسل ثلث قدح أرزّ ويصبغ الأرزّ في القدر بزعفران ويرمى فيه إذا نضج فستق ولوز.

٦٠. صفة الكَمُّونِيَّة

تحتاج إلى لحم ولفت وحمّص وفلفل وثوم وكزبرة خضراء يصلق اللحام ويقلى بالثوم

٥ في الأصل: يغسل.

والكزبرة والفلفل وتعيد على اللحم المرق ويقطّع اللفت ويضاف إليه في القدر.

٦١. صفة البُورَانِيَّة المَقْلِيَّة

تحتاج إلى لحم وباذنجان مقلى وفلفل وكزبرة يابسة ونعنع وبصل يسلق اللحم ورؤوس البصل ويحمّص مع الفلفل والكزبرة والنعنع وتضيف إليه المرق ويقلى الباذنجان ويعمل اللحم فيه والحوائج عليه.

٦٢. صفة النَّرْجِسِيَّة

تحتاج إلى لحم وأرزّ وجزر وفلفل وقليل جبن شامي وكمّون وكزبرة خضراء وحمّص وبصل يسلق اللحم ويقلى الكزبرة والفلفل ويعمل عليه المرق ويغسل الجزر بعد تقطيعه ويعمل عليه. فإذا نضج ترمى الأرزّ والكمّون ومن اختار لا يعمل جبن ولا كمّون فعل.

٦٣. صفة البَامِيَة

أيضًا يسلق اللحم ثمّ يقلى ببصلة تقطّع رقيق مع الفلفل والكزبرة الخضراء والثوم ويعاد عليه المرق والبامية وترمها في القدر واعصر عليها ليمونة خضراء لئلّا يتلعب وتنزل وتغرف فافهم.

٦٤. صفة الفُولِيَّة

تعمل بلحمها كذلك من السلق والقلى وإعادة المرق ويعمل عليه الفول ويوضع

البيض بعد نضج الفول ويغرف ويقدّم. وغالب الأطعمة يدلّ بعضها على بعضها لأنّها على أسلوب متقارب فافهم.

٦٥. صفة اللُوبِيَا

كذلك.

٦٦. صفة الفَرِيكِيَّة

تحتاج إلى لحم وفريك وفلفل وجبن وكمّون يصلق اللحم ويعمل عليه الفريك مدشوش فإذا نضج يعمل عليه اللبن والجبن والكمّون وقليل شبتّ والمصطكاء والقرفة وينزل.

٦٧. صفة الهَرِيسَة

تحتاج إلى لحم بقري ومصطكاء وقرفة وجبن وكمّون يصلق اللحم والقمح المقشور جميع مع المصطكاء والقرفة والشبتّ ويوقد عليه حتّى يتهرّأ اللحم يضربها إلى أن يتخيّط بعضها في بعض وينزل وتغرف.

٦٨. صفة القَمْحِيَّة

تحتاج إلى لحم وقمح مقشور ومصطكاء وقرفة وشبتّ وكمّون ويصلق اللحم والقمح جميع إن كان اللحم بقري وإن كان <١١ظ> ضأني يصلق القمح قبله إلى أن تتشقّق القمحة يرمى اللحم الضأني عليه حتّى ينضج يعمل عليه المصطكاء والقرفة والشبتّ

والكمّون. وإن شئت اعمل فيها لبن حليب وقوّي النار عليها حتّى تطيب. نزّلها.

٦٩. صفة الكِشْك

تحتاج إلى لحم أو فراخ حمام أو دجاج أو بطون وكشك وليمون وحصرم أو كبّاد وفلفل وثوم وحمّص وبصل وباذنجان أو بصل ومتلق أو بصل وبياض لفت ونعنع تسلق اللحم والحمّص ويحمّص. وتسكب المرق وترمى عليه الباذنجان أو غيره حتّى يستوي وتذوب الكشك ويكون منقوع بقليل مرق من مرق اللحم ويضاف إليه. ويغلى وترمى عليه الفلفل والثوم والنعنع والليمون وإن كان حصرم يسلق ويخرج من غربال الدقيق ويضاف إليه. وينزل ويقدّم.

٧٠. صفة الحِصْرِمِيَّة

تحتاج إلى لحم وقرطم ومصطكاء وقرفة ونعنع وحصرم وباذنجان وتدقّ القرطم ناعم ويؤخذ الحصرم ويعمل في قدر ناشف بلا ماء يعرّق ويستوي. ويعمل على القرطم ويخبص هو والقرطم ويسكب عليه ماء من القدر ويصفّى من غربال الدقيق والنعنع إذا لم يستو الحصرم على هذه الصفة يصلق.

٧١. صفة الخَيْطِيَّة

تحتاج إلى لبن حليب وعسل نحل وأرزّ مطحون وصدور دجاج مسموطة ينسّر الصدر أو غيره ويعمل الأرزّ في اللبن الحليب ويعمل على النار حتّى يغلى. ترمى عليه صدور الدجاج ويضرب حتّى يتخيّط وينزل تعمل عليها العسل النحل في الصحون لا في القدر.

٧٢. صفة البَهَطَّة

تحتاج إلى لبن حليب وأرزّ مطحون وسكّر بياض تعمل الأرزّ باللبن في القدر حتّى ينضج. وتعمل عليه السكّر مدقوق ويحرّك دائمًا لا تفتر عنه إلى أن يستوي وينزل وإن أرادها صفرًا عمل عليه الزعفران مع السكّر بعد نضج الأرزّ.

٧٣. صفة الهَيْطَلِيَّة

إن شاء فمن قمح مقشور مدشوش رفيع ولبن حليب تعمل القمح في ماجور فخّار ويهرس بماء ويصفّى من غربال الدقيق في وعاء ويرجع يفعل ذلك مرتين ثلاثة ويصفّى ويغطّى إلى باكر النهار ويصبح يصفّى عليه ماء أصفر يبقى النشا يعمل في اللبن الحليب في القدر وتعمل عليه المصطكاء <١٢و> والشيبة وعرق الكافور. ويعقد على النار إلى أن ينضج بالهدوء وينزل ويغرف في الصحون وتجعل عليها عسل نحل.

٧٤. صفة العَدَس المُصَفَّى

يحتاج إلى عدس مقشور وخلّ وعسل وزعفران وعناب ولوز مسموط وزبيب يسلق العدس إلى أن ينضج ويخرج من غربال الدقيق. وينظف العسل ويعمل مع العدس في القدر إلى أن ينضج ويحرّك ولا تفتر عنه. ويعمل الخلّ وقليل من العناب وقليل من الزبيب والفلفل وما يحتاج وقليل لوز مسموط يعمل فيه وقليل لوز يصبغ بزعفران وتحلّى بعضه أبيض وقليل عنّاب وزبيب. يعمل على الزبادي للزينة ويقدّم.

٧٥. صفة التُطْماج

يحتاج إلى لبن حامض ولحم وثوم وفلفل وكزبرة خضراء يعمل من اللحم مدقّقة يعمل فيها قليل فلفل وكزبرة يابسة وقليل كزبرة خضراء وبصلة مشوية. يصلق اللحم بعد أن تعمل منه شرائح أحمر يسلق الجميع ويقلى مع المرقة بالفلفل والكزبرة الخضراء والثوم إلّا الشرائح. فإنّها تقلى وحدها وتعمل في ماء حارّ وتعمل العجين في اللبن الحامض ويعمل عليه اللحم والشرائح والمدقّقة.

٧٦. الأرُزّ المُفَلْفَل

يحتاج إلى لحم ودهن كبير وأرزّ ومصطكاء وقرفة وحمّص يسلق اللحم ويعجن ويعمل عليه قليل مرق ويعمل عليه الأرزّ بعد غسله. ويغطّى بشيء وينزل من على النار ويترك ساعة واحدة جيّدة على الأرض ويغرف.

٧٧. صفة الأَرُزّ الحَلْو

يحتاج إلى ارزّ ولحم وسمن أو دجاج ودهن وعسل نحل وأطراف طيب ومصطكاء وقرفة وزعفران ومن أراد لا يعمل فيه لحم ولا دجاج فباختياره يسلق اللحم أو الدجاج ويحمّص بدهن أو شيرج ويعمل عليه العسل حتّى يغلى فيه الماء قوام العسل. فإذا غلى يدهن الأرزّ بزعفران بعد غسله ويضاف إلى القدر وترمى عليه المصطكاء والقرفة وأطراف الطيب وتسقيه الدهن.

٧٨. صفة أُمّ نارَيْن

تحتاج إلى خبز بارد أبيض ولبن حليب ومصطكاء وقرفة وزبد وعرق كافور وشيبة

تعمل اللبن في القدر بالحوائج ويغلى ويقطّع <١٢ظ> اللباب من القشر ويفرك رفيعًا. ويعمل في القدر حتّى ينضج تعمل عليه قليل زيد فإذا فرغ يعمل على وجهه قليل زبد آخر.

٧٩. (سَفَرْجَلِيّة)

وأكثر الأطعمة ممّا لم يذكر كالسفرجلية والتفاحية وغيرها اسلك فيها طريق ما ذكر فيسهل عليك التجربة وتقبل إلى اللذّة. والأصل في ذلك كلّه أن يصلق اللحم ويحمّص كما وصفنا في الأطعمة ويعمل عليه المرق ويقطّع السفرجل أو ما تحتاج إليه من غيره وينظفه من لبابه.[٦] ويقطّع كاللفت ويعمل في القدر مع اللحم والمرق ويوقد عليه حتّى يستوي يذوب الزعفران بالخلّ إن كان حذقك يؤدى إلى ذلك فيه ويعمل عليه قليل نشا يذوب بقليل مرق ويعمل فيه. وقس على هذا وتحذق بالتجربة ما لم يذكر وتوسع في ذلك.

٨٠. صفة الماوَرْدِيَّة

تحتاج إلى لحم وزرّ ورد وليمون وبصل وفلفل ومصطكاء وقرفة يصلق اللحم ويغلى ويقطّع عليه قليل بصل رؤوس حتّى يستوي يدقّ الفلفل ويعمل عليه ويعصر عليه الليمون ويترك الزرّ ورد عليه بلا دقّ ويعمل عليه المرق قوام ما يحتاج إليه.

٨١. السَّنْبُوسك

تحتاج إلى رقاق الكنافة والحلو تحتاج إلى بندق يدقّ خشن ويحمّص السكّر

٦ في الأصل: لعابه.

والبندق ويعجن بالقطر مع السكّر أو بالعسل النحل ويقطّع الورق ويحشى ويلبّس بقليل عجين. ولابد من رشّ الماء ورد على السكّر ويقلى بالشيرج ويرشّ عليه بعد رصّه في الأصحن من السكّر والبندق والماء ورد.

٨٢. (سَنْبُوسَك حامِض)

أمّا الحامض فإنّه يحتاج إلى حوائج بقل وشيرج وخلّ وفلفل وبندق أو لوز ورقاق متاع الكنافة. يدقّ اللحم الجميع ناعمًا ويقرص قرصة واحدة قدر الرغيف أو دونه على قدر اللحم ويسلق ويرجع يقلب في الطاجن ويقطف ريمه إلى أن يستوي يشال ويدقّ طريق آخر ناعم ويخرج منه العروق التي في اللحم ويعلق الطاجن على النار ويعمل فيه الشيرج ويقلى اللحم المدقوق فيه حتّى يحمر دفعه ويسكب عليه الخلّ في الطاجن. ويخرّط عليه البقل ويقلب حتّى يذبل ويسمط اللوز ويدقّ خشن ويعمل عليه ويدقّ الفلفل ويعمل عليه وما يزال يغلى عليه حتّى <١٣و> ينشف جميع الخلّ الذي يعمل عليه. يقطّع الرقاق على عرض أربع أصابع وينزل بالحوائج من على النار ويبرد. ويؤخذ منه على قدر ما يحتاج يعمل في الورقة ويلف إلى آخرها ويلبس بقليل عجين ويقلى بالشيرج ويقطّع أطراف البقل الأخضر وتعمل في الأوعية ويعمل السنبوسك عليه ويرشّ عليه قليل ياسمين أو غيره ويقدّم.

٨٣. صفة لَحْم تَفْلِيَّة

يحتاج إلى لحم وبصل وفلفل وقرفة وكزبرة يابسة وقليل زيت طيّب. ويصلق اللحم بالمصطكاء والقرفة والزيت الطيّب يحمّص بالفلفل والكزبرة وتعمل عليه المرق وتخرّط البصل عليه ويغلى عليه حتّى يستوي يعصر عليه الليمون.

٨٤. صفة اللَحْم الشَّرائح

يحتاج إلى لحم ودهن وشيرج أو دهن ألية[٧] ومصطكاء وقرفة يشرّح اللحم ويصلق بالمصطكاء والقرفة ويصفّي ويغلى بالشيرج وإن كان دهن ألية فيصلق مع اللحم ويدقّ ويقلى به.

٨٥. صفة المُدَقَّقة المَقْلِيَّة

تحتاج إلى لحم وفلفل وكزبرة خضراء وكزبرة يابسة وقليل زيت طيّب أو شيرج وقليل بصل. يدقّ اللحم وتعمل معه رأس بصلة مشوية ويدقّ معه جميع الحوائج. ويعلق الطاجن على النار ويعمل فيه قليل ماء حتّى يغلى وتعمل فيه المدقّة تسلق نصف سلقه وتشال. ثمّ يعمل الشيرج في طاجن على النار وتقلى فيه المدقّقة بعد أن تسلق وبعد أن تقلى يدقّ قليل كزبرة يابسة ويرشّ عليها في الأوعية.

٨٦. صفة الكُسْكُسُوا

تحتاج إلى لحم وألية وفلفل وقليل زيت طيّب ومصطكاء وقرفة وكزبرة يابسة ودجاج. يسلق الدجاج واللحم واللية بالمصطكاء والقرفة والزيت الطيّب ويفتل العجين مثل متاع المفتّلة ويعمل في قدر شقبة القاع يعمل فيها العجين. ويعمل على فم قدر أخرى غير التي فيها اللحم تدقّ الألية وتسلّى برأس بصلة ويعمل العجين فيها ويقلب في ألية ويحمّص اللحم برأس بصلة مع الفلفل والكزبرة اليابسة ويرصّص على العجين. ويعمل على وجهه سنبوسك حامض مع اللحم وبهدّأ ويقدّم.

٧ في الأصل: لية.

٨٧. صفة سَنْبُوسَكَة

يؤخذ من اللحم المدقوق فيلقى في القدر ويعرق ومعه قطعة قرفة وقليل مصطكاء وبصلة مشقوقة. فإذا تعرّق يقلى بالشيرج بحيث تزول زفرته. ثمّ يلقى عليه من ماء السمّاق ما يحمّصه ويصير عليه حتّى <١٣ظ> ينشف الماء. ثمّ يقطّع فيه الليمون والنعنع ويترك فيه الأفاويه العطرة ويقلى بالشيرج الطري. وقبل أن يقلى يلطّخ بزعفران يذاب بماء ورد.

٨٨. صفة المُلُوخِيَّة

يصلق اللحم فإذا نضج يقلى ويلقى عليه كزبرة خضراء وثوم وملح مدقوقين وفلفل وكزبرة يابسة وبصلة مشوية وكراوية وقلب لوز وبندق وفستق. فإذا غلى يلقى فيه سوى مدقوق ناعم ويغلى غليًا قويًا. ثمّ يذرّ فيه الملوخية ولا يغطّى القدر فإذا نضجت يرشّ عليها قليل ماء بارد ويعمل على النار ويجعل على وجهها دهن ألية مسلّى بمصطكاء ودار صيني وزيت طيّب أو شيرج. ويذرّ عليها دار صيني وإن عمل فيها باذنجان محشى مقلى بدهن ألية كان أحسن.

فائدة: ينبغي أن يجتنب من السمان الأزرق العين فلا يأكله فإنّه يولّد المرض لخاصية فيه قد جرّب ذلك.

٨٩. صفة دَجَاجة

تشوى وتسقى بدهن الجوز أو اللوز مع يسير ملح وزعفران وأحسن ما شوي أن تكدّ الدجاجة حتّى تتعب وتقف وتكون سمينة. ثمّ تذبح بعد أن تسقى خلًّا وماء ورد والسمط على العادة ويكون عندك قليل شيرج وملح وزعفران. وتشوي الدجاجة

على نار ليّنة وتدهن من ذلك. فإنّها تجيء في نهاية النعومة والطيبة.

٩٠. العَصَافِير

أحسن ما تكون مقلية تشقّ من ظهورها وينظّف ويقلى بزيت وملح قليل ثمّ يذرّ عليها الأبازير في الأصحن.

صفة قِدْر يُصْنَع مِن زُجَاج

كالذي يصنع منه القناني والأقداح فإنّ الحكمة إنّما هي في الصنعة ثخن الزجاج وذلك أن يكون على هيئة القدر سواء إلّا أنّه يضع الزجاج البولين في أسفلها وهي رطبة عندما يصنعها ويرفعه إلى جهة رأسها حتّى يكون فيها أنبوب غير مثقوب الأعلى إلى مقدار ثلثها. فإذا صنعت على هذه الصورة طبخ فيها الإنسان أيّ لون كان بعد أن تكون نار فحم ولو كانت أقوى النيران إلّا أنّ الطبخ فيها يحتاج شروط منها أنّ الماء لا ينقص عن ارتفاع الأنبوب الطالع في وسطها فمتى نقص انكسرت. ومنها أنّها لا توضع على النار القوية دفعة ولا تحطّ عنها إلى البرودة دفعة فإنّها <١٤و> إن فعل ذلك بها انكسرت. ثمّ توضع على نار ليّنة حتّى تقوّي النار عليها بالتدريج ومنها أن لا يزاد فيها ماء باردة أصلًا بل يجعل فيها جميع ما يحتاج إليه من أوّل الأمر.

أَلْبَابُ ٱلخامِسُ

باب فِي عَمَل ٱلمُرِّي

٩١. صفة المُرِّي النَّقِيع

يؤخذ ربعين دقيق شعير جديد طيّب فيعجن دون ملح بنخاله ويصنع منه قوالب صغار كقوالب السكّر ويثقب وسطها بالأصبع ويوضع على لوح ويبسط بنخاله في ظلّ ويترك عشرين يومًا. ثمّ يقلب أعاليها أسافلها ويترك عشرين ليلة. ثمّ تجرد القوالب ممّا عليها من النخال والغبار. ثمّ يدقّ جريشًا أمثال الفول ثمّ يضاف إلى الجميع ربع واحد من دقيق الشعير بنخاله. ثمّ يؤخذ أربعة أمداد ملحًا ويضاف إليها ويوضع الجميع في خابية كانت للزيت غير رشاحة ويضاف إلى ذلك كفايته من الماء وأكبس الخابية في موضع أخذه الشمس النهار كلّه. ثمّ يحرّك بعود ذكار أربع مرّات أو أكثر في اليوم إن أمكن مدّة ثمانية أيّام. ثمّ يؤخذ ربع دقيق قمح وتعجن بنخاله دون ملح ويصنع منه أرغفة ويضع في الفرن بمقدار انعقادها ويطرح في الخابية سخنة بعد أن تقطع لقمًا وتغطّى الخابية ثلاثة أيّام. ثمّ تدخل اليد بما[8] فيها من تفل فيقطّع ويحرّك الذكار المذكور أربع مرّات في كلّ يوم أو أكثر إن أمكن ثمانية أيّام. ثمّ يؤخذ ربع دقيق قمح ويعجن بمدّ ملح ويصنع منه

٨ في الأصل: لما.

خبز مسكيًّا ولا يبلغ حدّ الحرق ويدقّ ويجعل الجميع في الخابية وتحرّك بالعود مدة شهرين ولا يغفل عنه ولا يقربه نجس. فإذا انقضت الشهران[٩] رأيت ينابيع المرّي قد انبعث وارتفعت على الماء. ثمّ يؤخذ ما اجتمع القصرية ويوضع في إناء حنتم ويؤخذ ما بقي في القفة فيوضع ناحية ويصنع ممّا بقي في الخابية كما تقدّم ثمّ يضاف الأوّل إلى الثاني ويضاف التفل الآخر إلى التفل الأوّل ويصرف إلى الخابية ويطرح عليه كفايته من الماء ويحرّك مدة عشرين يومًا. ثمّ يصنع به ما صنع بالأوّل مع التعليق والتصفية ويضاف ذلك إلى الأوّل ويجعل ذلك في قصرية للشمس ثلاثة أيّام. ثمّ يرفع ويستعمل.

٩٢. صفةُ مُرَبَّى شَعِير <١٤ظ> مَغْرِبِي

يؤخذ ورق أترنج وليمون مراكبي وخوخ وريحان أترنجي تغمر هذه الأوراق بالماء الحلو في قصاري وتتركهم في الشمس أربعة أيّام. ويؤخذ شعير يغربل وينقى ويحمّص ويطحن ناعمًا ويخلط بمثل ربعه ملحًا مسحوقًا ويعجن جيّدًا. ويعمل فطائر رقاقًا ويخبز جيّدًا حتّى لا تبقى فيه رطوبة ويبرد ويعمل في قصاري ويغمر بالماء ويعمل في الشمس الحامية أسبوعين. ويمرسه ويصفّى ويطبخ طبخًا جيّدًا وتكون قد خلطت معه قدحين كراوية محمّصة مطحونة مغربلة وارفعه. فإنّه غاية.

٩٣. صفة عَمَل الحِصْرِم

يؤخذ الحصرم فنثر عليه ملحًا ويداس بالأرجل ويعصر ويصفّى ماؤه ويجعل في قرّابات وتترك مفتحة الرؤوس حتّى يغلى ويقذف وسخه ويرسب في أسفله التفل ثمّ يصفّى إلى قرابات أخر ويترك أيضًا مفتوحًا حتّى يقذف أيضًا ما بقي من الوسخ

٩ في الأصل: السهران.

فإذا سكن غليانه من هذا فتملأ به القرّابات ويجعل عليه زيت مغسول وطاقات نعنع ويترك في الشمس حتّى يجفّ طينه ويترك ويستعمل.

٩٤. صفة أُخْرَى

يؤخذ الحصارم ينفى ويعصر في المعصرة أو يدقّ في قصعة خشب حتّى لا يبقى فيه شيء. ثمّ يقلب في قدر على نار قوية ويغلى حتّى ينقص النصف ويبقى لونه أحمر على صفة العقيق فيجعل فيه عند ذلك قطع دار صيني. ويحرّك بباقات نعنع كبار ساعة بعد ساعة كلّما تلفت باقة حرّكها بباقة أخرى. ويرفع ويترك حتّى يرسب ويصفى فإذا برد وركد الوسخ يرفع الرايق ويملأ به إناء زجاج ويختمه بيسير شيرج. ومتى خلّي الإناء ناقصًا فسد وهو يقيم سنين لا يتغير.

٩٥. صفة خَلّ النَعْنَع

فذلك معروف.

٩٦. صفة ماء النّارَنْج

منهم من يشمسه ومنهم من لا يشمسه ويقطف بالنارنج <١٥و> عند انتهائه ويقشّر النارنجة من وسطها بدائرها يرمى. ثمّ تقطع نصفين بغير السكّين التي قشر بها لئلّا يحصل فيه المرارة والذي يعصرها غير الذي قشرها. ثمّ يصفّى من حبه بمنخل أو براووق ويوضع في القناني ويختم بالزيت ويرفع إلى وقت الحاجة. فإذا أردت أن تأخذ منه شيئًا تفتح رأس القنينة وتحطّ فمها على راحة كفّك ويصعد الزيت إلى قعرها وتفتح راحتك وتأخذ منها حاجتك. ثمّ تردّ القنينة إلى ما كانت

فإن كان عندك ماء نارنج أتمها أو زيت وإن خلّيتها ناقصة تقطّن وتتلف وترميه.

٩٧. صفة ماء اللَّيْمُون

يشال في القراريب ويختم بدهن اللوز أو بالشيرج فإذا أردت استعماله يلقط ذلك الدهن بقطنة من على فم الوعاء ويستعمل في الشراب والأقسماء وسائر المشروبات إلّا الملوحات لا يُعمل فيها.

٩٨. صفة مُرِّي النَعْنَع

يؤخذ دقيق الشعير جزئين ومن الملح جزء ويسحق الملح ويخلط مع الدقيق ويعجن منه خبز فطير. ثمّ يبيت في الفرن ويخرج من الغد فإن كان قد احترق ظاهره وباطنه وإلّا حميت عليه الفرن حتّى يحترق. ثمّ يؤخذ ويكسر في قدر لطيف ويغمر بالماء وتجعل فيه قبضة من الصعتر والنعناع وقضبان الرازيانج ورأس صنوبر مرضوض وقشر الأترنج وورقات منه ويدخل في الفرن ويبيت فيه ليلة ثمّ يخرج ويصفي ويلقى فيه من العسل الطيّب قدر ما يكسر به ملوحته. ثمّ يرفعه في الأوانئ النظاف ويصبّ عليه من الزيت الطيّب ليحفظه فإنّه عجيب.

٩٩. صفة مري آخَر عِطْرِي

يؤخذ من دقيق الحنطة كيلتين ويضاف إليه من الملح نصف كيل وتعجن منه أرغفة ويبيت في الفرن ويخرج من الغد. فإن احترقت فحسن وإلّا بالغ في حرقها ثمّ تكسير قطعًا صغارًا وتجعل في القدر مع قبضة صعتر وورق رند وورق نارنج ونعنع وريحان وقضبان رازيانج من كلّ قبضة يغمر الكلّ بالماء ويبيت أيضًا بعد

أن يمرس. فإذا أخرج من الغد صفّى فإن شئت أن تضيف المائين. وإن شئت <١٥ظ> تركت كلّ واحد منهما على حدته فإن حللت فيها شيئًا من النشا وإن جعل فيه من العسل جاء أيضًا حسنًا.

أَلْبَابُ ٱلسَّادِس

فِيمَا يُعْمَل مِن ٱلعُجَج وغَيْرِها

١٠٠. صفة عُجَّة

يؤخذ اللحم فيصلق فإذا طبخ يدقّ ثانيًا ويقلى بدهن ويخرط مقدونس ويجعل على اللحم والمقدونس في زبدية ويفقش عليه بيض وأبازير حارّة وكسفرة خضراء ويابسة وخبز مدقوق وقرفة. ويقلى في طاجن بزيت وشبيرج وتكون المقلى مدوّرة لها حافة عالية وساعد طويل مثل المغرفة وتجعل على نار فحم هادئة وتقلب عليه جمجمات زيت وشيرج ويصبر حتّى تحمر. ويعمل فيه البيض والحوائج لكلّ عجّة خمس بيضات ويسير من الحوائج ولحم مقلي. وتملأ المقلى وتترك حتّى تجف وتقلب كلّ ساعة حتّى تنضج.

١٠١. العُجَّة الحامِضَة

يقلب عليها خل وماء الليمون بالملعقة بعد أن تبخش بالسكّين وتصبر قليلًا إلى أن تتشرّب. ثمّ يقلب عليها من الخلّ وماء الليمون تفعل ذلك ستّ سبع مرات ويطول روحه فإنّها تبقى عجّة حامضة إن شاء الله تعالى.

١٠٢. صفة البَيْض المَكْبُوس

يؤخذ البيض فيسلق ويخرج من قشره وينقلب بمسلّة ويجعل في جرة ويجعل عليه يسير ملح ويلقى عليه عسل وخلّ ويكون الخلّ الغالب.

١٠٣. صفة بَيْض مُخَلَّل

يسلق البيض فإذا نضج أخرج وفشر ويثقب بطرف سكّين[١٠] دقيقة أو مسلّة وينقع في ماء وملح بعض يوم. ثمّ يغسل بماء عذب حتّى يخرج طعم الملح منه ويترك قليلًا. ويؤخذ خل خمر فيجعل في قدر نظيفة قدر ما يغمر البيض ويجعل فيه دار صينى وزنجبيل وكمّون وكسفرة يابسة وحباب قرنفل صحاح. يطرح جمع هذا في الخلّ وسذاب وورق أترجّ وكرفس ونعنع ويجعل فيه عسل أو سكّر حتّى يجيء مزّ طيّب. وإن لم يراد مزّ وأريد حامض فلا يجعل فيه حلاوة. ثمّ يحمل على النار ويغلى حتّى تنضج الأبازير ويترك القدر على النار ويلقى البيض المسلوق فيها على المكان وهو مغلى ويترك في القدر كما هو ويرفع ويؤكل مع اللحم أو كيفما أردت. وإن أردته أصفر فبالزعفران. وإن أردته أحمر فبالعصفر. وإن شئت لا تطبخ الأبازير فتجعل في برنية خضراء أو زجاج وتضع عليه الخلّ والحوائج على <١٦و> حسب ما تريد. وتصبغه إن أردت كما تقدم ويبقى إذا رفعته أيّامًا. وهو لذيذ طيّب.

١٠٤. صفة عُجَّة بِغَيْرِ بَيْض ولا ينكر أحد أنّها ببيض

أعمد إلى الحمّص فاصلقه ودقّه حتّى ينعم واصلق بصلًا ودقّه معه وصبّ عليه

١٠ في الأصل: مسلة سكين.

شيئًا من زيت ومرّي والق شيئًا من ملح وأبزار يابسة وهو كزبرة أو كراويا وفلفل واجعل معه شيئًا من الصمغ. ثمّ اقله في قدر حتّى ينضج فإن من أكله لا ينكر أنّه عجّة البيض.

١٠٥. صفة عُجَّة

تحتاج إلى بيض وحوائج بقل ورؤوس بصل وشيرج أو دهن بدن[١١] وفلفل يخرط البصل رقيقًا ويعمل عليه قليل ماء وقليل زيت طيّب أو شيرج حتّى ينضج يخرط عليه حوائج البقل يذبل وينزل به من على النار. يدقّ الفلفل ويعمل عليه ويفقش عليه البيض ويضرب بعود ويصلق الطاجن على النار ويعمل فيه الشيرج حتّى يسخن تعمل الحوائج بالبيض فيه حتّى يستوي الوجه الواحد يقلب إلى الوجه الثاني. فإذا نضجت يقلب في وعاء فإذا استوى الوجه الأوّل وأراد الثاني يعمل في الطاجن شيرج آخر للوجه الثاني إذا لم يكن بقي في الطاجن شيرج. ويعمل على ضروب أخر أضربنا عنها اختصارًا.

١٠٦. صفة المدفونة

تحتاج إلى لحم وبيض وبصل وحوائج بقل وفلفل ومصطكاء وقرفة يصلق اللحم ويقلى ناشفًا ويخرط البصل في وعاء وحده ويعلق طاجن على النار. ويعمل فيه البصل المخروط ويعمل عليه قليل ما ملح حتّى يصلق يعمل عليه قليل شيرج حتّى يغلى. تخرط عليه الحوائج البقل حتّى تذبل تدقّ الفلفل وتعمل عليه اللحم ويفقش عليه البيض ويضرب. ويعلق الطاجن على النار ويعمل فيه الشيرج إلى أن يسخن يعمل فيه الحوائج مع اللحم حتّى يستوي.

١١ هكذا في النص.

١٠٧. صفة عمل البَيْض مَصُوص

يطرح الشيرج في الطاجن وتنقي كرفس من عيدانه ويلقى عليه فإذا تطجّن معه. يذرّ عليه الدارصيني والمصطكاء والكزبرة والكراوية ثمّ يصبّ عليه من الخلّ حاجته ويصبغ بقليل زعفران ويعدل بالملح ويفقش فيه البيض. ويغطّى رأس القدر. فإذا جمد يرفع طيبًا.

١٠٨. صفة بَيْض مُخَرْدَل

يصلق ويقشّر وينخش بإبرة ويتبل بقليل ملح وكمّون مصحون في <١٦ظ> وعاء. يترك من بكرة إلى الظهر فيه ثمّ يشال ويصبغ بالزعفران ويعمل عليه الخلّ الخمر والخردل والنعنع وأطراف الطيب ويخمّر ليلة ويؤكل.

١٠٩. صفة عُجَّة جاءت مَلِيحة

يؤخذ رطل لبن حليب وخل وحمّص مسلوق ناعم يخلط في بعضه بعض وينزل من منخل. ثمّ تؤخذ خمسة عشر بيضة تضربها ضربًا جيّدًا وتضيف إلى ذلك ثلاث ليمونات مالحات وكمّون وبندق وجوز وفلفل ومقدونس. وتغلى أوقية ونصف شيرج وفيه بصلة مخروطة وأوقية زيتون ويغلى على النار وتصير عجّة طيّبة.

١١٠. صفة عُجَّة قَلِيلة المَؤُنة

يؤخذ ربع حمّص مجوهر تدقّه ناعمًا وتضربه في اللبن الحليب وافقش عليه خمس بيضات واضربه حتّى يختلط الجميع. ثمّ تقلبه بالسمن يجئ مليحًا.

١١١. عُجَّة الباه

تؤخذ أربع بصلات تشوى في الفرن إلى أن تنضج ويزال قشرها الخارج ويدقّ دقًا حسنًا كذلك يؤخذ نصف رطل لحم قد سلق ويقلى في مرقه قد استحكم نضجه. يدقّ اللحم ويعمل مع البصل المشوي مع ما بقي من المرق ويفقش عليه عشرين صفرة بيض دجاج ويضرب الجميع ويضاف إليه من الأبازير المقدّم ذكرها مقدار ما يظهر طعمها ويسير ملح ويقلى بشيرج أو سمن ويضاف إلى البصل المدقوق واللحم على ما وصف.

١١٢. صفة عُجَّة تُسْتَطاب

لحم أحمر وشحم وسمّاق يدقّ في المهراس مع الأبازير ويعصر عليه ليمون ونعنع ويخلط مع البيض ويقلى بنار ليّنة فإنّه ممّا يستطاب.

١١٣. صفة مُبَعْثَرة حامِضَة

يسلق اللحم وينسّر ثمّ يشال ويطفى في قليل ليمون وخلّ خمر وينضج نصف نضاجه. ثمّ تفقش البيض ويلقى عليه الأبازير ثمّ يغلى الشيرج على النار فإذا غلى ألقى اللحم في البيض وأضرب الجميع جيّدًا واقليهم في الطاجن وبعثرهم جيّدًا حتّى رضوك.

١١٤. صفة أبازِير المُبَعْثَرة والعُجَج

تأخذ من الزنجبيل والخولنجان والقرفة اللفّ والزعفران الشعر والفلفل والكمّون والصعتر الطيّب من كلّ واحد جزء وزر ورد ربع جزء وسنبل طيّب ثمن جزء.

وتدقّ الحوائج ناعمًا وتشال إلى وقت الحاجة إليها فإذا ألقيت على العجج منها تقلى معها يسير جبن شامي مدقوق تلقيه مع العجج والمبعثرات <١٧و> طريًا وتلقى الطيب بعده.

١١٥. صفة مُعْتَمَدِيَّة بِجُبْن

يؤخذ صدور فرخين فيشرّحان تشريحًا رقيقًا ويؤخذ رطل لحم ويشرّح مثل ذلك ويغسل ويصير في قدر على النار ويصبّ فيها نصف رطل زيت طيّب ووزن درهمين ملحًا ويغلى حتّى يقارب النضج. ويؤخذ من الجبن ربع رطل فيشرّح ويطرح في القدر مع اللحم ويبزّره بوزن درهمين كزبرة يابسة ودرهم فلفل ودار صيني مثله. ويطرح فيه عشر زيتونات منزوعات العجم ويفقش في غضارة عشرين بيضة ويصبّ عليها أوقية مرّي ويقطّع عليها سذاب وينزل ويقدّم.

أَلْبَابُ ٱلسَّابِعُ

بَابُ المُزَوَّرات

إذا عملت فيها بصل فاقليه أوّلًا مع الشيرج أو الدهن.

١١٦. مزوّرة الرجلة

منهم من يعملها بحبّ رمّان.

١١٧. مزوّرة الإسفاناخ

منهم من يعملها بحبّ رمّان وسكّر والمصطكاء في جميع المزوّرات تعمل والماء ورد أيضا فيها طيب.

١١٨. مزوّرة قرع

لمحموم.

١١٩. مزوّرة زيرباج

لأصحاب الصفراء.

١٢٠. مزوّرة قرع

بماء حصرم وسكّر وبقية الحوائج على العادة ومنهم من يدقّ القرع بعد أن يسلقه. لأصحاب الحمّى الصفراوية.

١٢١. مزوّرة حبّ الرمان

لأصحاب القرف ويعقده بالسكّر.

١٢٢. مزوّرة حبّ رمّان

لجريان الجوف

وفي كلّ مزوّرة ما يوافق من الأبازير والمطيّبات وغير ذلك كاللوز والماء ورد ومن أراد أن يختر بلباب الخبز فذلك حسن.

١٢٣. مُزَوَّرة الماش للسُّعال

وهي تعمل بالزيت الطيّب ويكون الماش مقشورًا مدقوقًا ومنهم من يحمّص الحبّ رمّان ثمّ يصلقه بعد الدقّ.

١٢٤. صفة زِيرْباج

قريبة من الاعتدال نافعة لأصحاب الأمزاج الصفراوية والأكباد الملتهبة والمعد الضعيفة وينفع من اليرقان والسدد في الكبد والطحال وأصحاب الاستسقاء والحمايات العتيقة. يؤخذ شيء من البصل يقطّع بقدر الحاجة ويلقى في قدر نظيفة[١٢] ويوضع على نار ليّنة ويلقى عليه من دهن اللوز أو الشيرج الطري أو الزيت الطيّب بحسب الموافقة لكلّ مزاج. فإذا تبّلت البصلة تلقى معها اليسير من الكزبرة المدقوقة واليسير من النعنع المطيّب وما يحتاج إليه <١٧ظ> من السنبل والمصطكاء والقرفة. ثمّ تلقى على الجميع من الخلّ النظيف الممزوج بما يحتمل من الماء بقدر الحاجة. ثمّ يحلّى بالسكّر ويختّر المرقة باللوز المقشّر المدقوق ناعمًا ويعطّر بالزعفران والماء ورد وإن عملت معها شيئًا من النشا فلا بأس وترفع.

١٢٥. مُزَوَّرة الحَبّ رُمّان

باردة يابسة تنفع للحمّى الصفراوية والأكباد الملتهبة وتسكن العطش وتقمع الصفراء وتسكن الغثيان وتلائم أبدان المرضى بحسب ما يلقى فيها من التوابل وهو أن يأخذ اليسير من الكزبرة المدقوقة فتقلى يدهن اللوز أو الشيرج أو الزيت. ثمّ يلقى فيه يسير نعنع وسنبل ويصبّ عليه ماء الرمّان قدر الحاجة ممزوجًا بالماء أو حبّ رمّان مسلوقًا بالماء. ويدقّ ويمرس ويصفّى على قدر ما تريد لأنّ المدقوق أكثر قبض من المسلوق وأكثر توليدًا للرياح. فإذا غليت يفتق بالسكّر ويختّر باللوز المدقوق ويعطّر بماء الورد فإن كانت القبض يحمّص اللوز قبل دقّه. وإن أردت لا تقبض جعلت فيها أضلاع الإسفاناخ والسلق والحمقاء وترفع.

---

١٢ في الأصل: لطيفة.

أَلْبَابُ ٱلثَّامِنُ

الأَسْماك

١٢٦. (صفة عَمَل السَّمَكة الطَّحِينِيَّة)

تغسل وتتبّل بالدقيق وتقلى بالشيرج التي يراد بها الغلي فإن أراده بالطحينة يدقّ فلفل وأطراف الطيب ويعمل على البصل ويقلب على النار ويذوّب الطحينة بالخلّ والزعفران. ويعمل على النار ويغلى فإذا أستوى ينزل السمك عليه.

١٢٧. وإنْ أرادَهُ كُزْبَرِيَّة

يؤخذ بصل يخرّط رقيقًا وتدقّ الكزبرة الخضراء والثوم ويعمل في الطاجن ويدقّ الفلفل ويعمل ويقلب حتّى يستوي. يعمل عليه مرق على قدر ما يختار ويعمل على السمك.

١٢٨. وإذا أرادَهُ بِزَبِيب

فيغلى الخلّ ويعمل فيه الزبيب والفلفل مدقوقًا وأطراف الطيب ويسمط اللوز

ويدهن بقليل زعفران ويرصّ على وجهها ويعمل على السمك. اعلم أنّهم يعملون من السمك المقلى سائر الألوان مثل السكباج والليمونية والسمّاقية والطباهجة والكزبرية وغير ذلك.

١٢٩. وَالمُدَقَّقَة

من غير القلي ينزع من عظمه ويدقّ بعد أن يضاف إليه الفلفل المدقوق والكزبرة اليابسة مع قليل زيت طيّب. يدقّ الجميع ويعمل منه حلق وقرص ويعلق القدر على النار ويعمل فيها حتّى يسخن يعمل السمك المدقوق. وبعد أن يستوي <١٨و> يشال ويعلق الطاجن ويعمل فيه الشيرج ويقلى فيه السمك. ويعمل في الأوعية ويدقّ قليل كزبرة يابسة وملح ويرشّ عليه ويقدّم.

١٣٠. صفة السَّمَك المَحْشِي

يؤخذ السمك الطري يغسل وينظف وينشف ساعة ويؤخذ الخلّ والكروية والثوم والكزبرة ويلطّخ ساعة بالحوائج ويرجع يعمل في الدقيق ويقلى في المقلى بالشيرج ويكون قد أخذ الكراوية والجوز وبصلة مقلية بثوم وفلفل ويذوب الكلّ بالخلّ وإذا قلى السمك يجعل فيه.

١٣١. صفة أُخْرَى مِنْهُ

تأخذ السمك تغسله وتعمل فيه الكزبرة والكراوية ويلطّخ به ويخلّي ساعة وتعمل عليه الدقيق ويقلى في المقلى بزيت أو شيرج وتأخذ السمّاق وجميع حوائج السمك المحشي ولتّه بماء الليمون ويكون فيه ليمون مالح ويغلى قليل ماء في

قدرة شيء يذوب الحشو به ويكون في الحشو قليل ثوم ويغلى على النار غلوتين ثلاثة ويصفّ السمك في الزبدية وتقلّب عليه حوائج المحشي وهو جزر وسمّاق وكزبرة وزعتر وقليل ثوم وفلفل وليمون مالح مقطّع وكرفس.

١٣٢. صفة السَّمَك المَشْوِي

يؤخذ الفلفل والقرفة والكراويا والزنجبيل والسمّاق والكزبرة اليابسة والصعتر ويسير كمّون يدقّ الجميع ومعهم قليل نعنع وينخل. ويؤخذ ثوم ويقشّر ويدقّ في الهاون ناعمًا بحصاة ملح وزيت طيّب ويضاف إليه من الحوائج بمقدار ما يعجنه. فإذا انعجن يؤخذ الجوز يدقّه ويضيفه إليهم. ويؤخذ الليمون والطحينة والزيت الطيّب مقدار الحاجة ويخلط الجميع ويعجن بذلك الأفاويه المعجونة. ويؤخذ السمك يحشى جيّدًا في جوانبه وبطنه ويعمل تحت الطاجين عيدان رقاق أو لوح خشب رقيق لئلّا يلصق. ثمّ بعد ذلك يؤدى إلى الفرن فإذا نضج الوجه الأوّل يخرج ويرد ساعة ويقلّب بتلك اللوح ويردّ إلى الفرن إلى حين بلوغ الحاجة.

١٣٣. صفة سَمَك مَقْلِي

يؤخذ السمك الطري ينظف من قشوره وشوكه ويشقّ بطنه ويخرج ما فيه ويغسل غسلًا مليحًا نظيفًا ويرشّ الملح ويخلّي فيه ساعة جيّدة ويعمل في قفّة. ثمّ تلفّ القفّة عليه ويحطّ عليها بلاطة ومن فوقها بلاطة وينقله إلى أن يخرج جميع مائه. ثمّ بعد ذلك يقطّع قطعًا لطافًا ويغبر بالدقيق الطيّب ويركب الطاجن على النار ويعمل فيه الشيرج أو زيت طيّب على ما يختار حتّى يعوم فيه السمك ويقلى <١٨ظ> قليًا جيّدًا حتّى لا يبقى فيه شيء من الماء. ثمّ يأخذ خلّ العنب والكسفرة المحمّصة والكراويا وأطراف الطيب وزعفران ويحرّك وتنزل السمك المقلو حتّى

يغمره. ويعمل في آنية مزجّجة أو قطرميز زجاج أو مطر مزفّت ويعمل الخلّ فوقه وتخلّيه إلى وقت الحاجة. فإنّه يقيم أيّامًا ما يفسد ومن الناس من يسافر به إلى الأماكن البعيدة ولا يفسد.

١٣٤. (السَّمَك بِالسُّمَّاق)

وأصناف أعمال الأسماك كثيرة بالسمّاق والطحينة والتمر والزبيب ويغسل السمك بالزيت الحارّ. ثمّ يغسل بالماء قالوا إن هذا العمل يذهب زفره وغسله بالزيت الحارّ بعد غسله بالملح. ومنهم من يغسله بهما معًا ومنهم من يغسله بالملح قبل وبعد. ثمّ يغسله بالماء بعد ذلك ومنهم من يقليه بغير دقيق يتبّله به ومنهم من ينثره بعد غسله على قفص حتّى ينشف من مائه. ثمّ يقليه من غير دقيق.

١٣٥. صفة البُورِي المُكَفَّن

يشوى ويؤخذ البصل تخرّطه صغارًا ويغسل بالماء والملح ويغلى الزيت الطيّب ويشال ناحية. ثمّ يؤخذ زعفران وأطراف طيب وقلب بندق وزنجبيل وسذاب وحوائج بقلي وزبيب. تعمل في خلّ خمري ويغلى وينزل على السمك المقلي ويخمّر ليلة ويؤكل. فإنّه غاية.

١٣٦. الصَّحْنات

أصنافها كثيرة ولم نذكرها وذكرنا منها هذه وهي تشهّي الأكل وتقوّي بالمعدة وتلطف البلغم. يؤخذ من السمك الصغار ما تختار فينزل عليه من الشراب

الصرف ومن ماء الليمون ما يميعه وينزل من منخل. ثمّ يضاف إليه اللوز المدقوق أو الجوز والسمّاق والزيت الطيّب والتوابل والأبازير الطيّبة والأفاويه العطرة والزعفران وماء الورد ويوضع فيها أيضًا ليمون مالح ومن يشاء يزيدها قليل ثوم. فإنّه يطيّبها.

١٣٧. صفة صَحْنة كَذَّابَة بِغَيْر سَمَك

زبيب وبندق وجوز وزيت طيّب من كلّ واحد عشرة دراهم خلّ وليمون وقرفة ومصطكاء وفلفل وكروايا وأطراف طيب ما يحتمل ويصلح طعمه.

١٣٨. صَحْنة كَذَّابَة نافِعة لأَصْحاب الصَّفْراء وَتُنْعِش المَعِدة

يؤخذ سمّاق يدقّ ملح وتخرج زهرته وينقع في ماء يسير ويستحلب من خرقة حتّى تخرج خاصيته ويخلّي من السمّاق <١٩و> بلا نقع شيء يسير مقدونس مخروط ونعنع وسذاب أجزاء متساوية يعزل يسير ملح حتّى يذبل. ويقلب عليه قلب جوزة محمّص مدقوق ناعمًا حتّى يلعب في دهنه بشيء جيّد وماء ليمون أخضر وماء سمّاق يقلب على الحوائج ويسير من السمّاق المدقوق ولا يكثره فإنّه يسوّده ويخلط خلطًا جيّدًا. ويجعل فيه ثوم مدقوق وصعتر يابس مدقوق ويكثر منه فهو الذي يظهر طعمه وكزبرة يابسة وكراوية مدقوقين محمّصين وفلفل وزنجبيل وأطراف طيب وملح وزيت طيّب يخلطه في جوفه ويكون قوامه بحيث يشال على اللقمة. ويقطّع في جوفها ليمون مالحًا وكلّما كثر جوزها وطحينتها ظهر لونها وعندما تغرف تجعل عليها زيت طيّب وما يطيّب إلّا بكثرة الزيت في جوفها وإن أردت تعمل عوض الجوز بندقًا لأجل الخلط السوداوي تعمل فإن أردت على وجهها فستق عملت.

١٣٩. صفة عَمْل الصَّحْنَة الإِسْكَنْدَرانِيَّة الخالِصة المُلُوكِيَّة الَّتِي تَعْمَل فِي هذا التَّارِيخ

وأجود أنواعه الصير عشرة أرطال تجعل في إجّانة وتترك حتّى تليّن وذلك ثلاثة أيّام أو يومين. ثمّ تعجن باليد عجنًا بالغًا ويضاف إليه نصف وربع قدح ملحًا وأربعة أقداح كزبرة مدقوقة تخلط مع الملح أو تدقّ معه ويضاف إليه فلفل وقرنفل رطل وربع كزبرة شامية قدح وربع صعتر ربع قدح وثوم سبع أواق مدقوقًا وكراوية ثلاث أواق وقرفة نصف رطل وزنجبيل وفلفل وحطب قرنفل من كلّ واحد أوقية وخولنجان نصف أوقية وزيت طيّب رطل ونصف نعناع مجفف وسذاب مجفف من كلّ واحد ربع أوقية ووزن درهم كرفس. وتقوّيه بقيراط مسك محلول في ماء ورد وتخلط الجميع ناعمًا ويرفع في براني زجاج ويجعل على وجهه في فم البرنية مقدار ما يغمره من الزيت الطيّب. وكلّما نقص زد عليه زيت طيّب.

١٤٠. صفة صَحْنَة أُخْرَى

<١٩ظ> يؤخذ قدح كزبرة يابسة وقدح كراوية وربع قدح صعتر وربع قدح فليّة[١٣] ورطل زهر سمّاق وأوقية قرفة لف وربع أوقية مصطكاء وقليل سنبل وتنبل وهال وقرنفل من الجميع ربع أوقية. يدقّ ويعمل في الملح قليل على قدر الكفاية يدقّ الجميع ناعمًا ويرفع. ثمّ يؤخذ قليل نعنع وسذاب وكرفس يجمع ويخرّط ويدقّ. ثمّ يؤخذ خمسة أرطال كسب لوز ويخمروا بخلّ خمر حادق ويتركوا يومًا وليلة أو يومين ثمّ يمرس مرسًا جيّدًا ثمّ يعلق بالحوائج المدقوقة. ثمّ يضاف زيت طيّب وطحينة وتستعمل.

١٣ في الأصل: قليه.

١٤١. صفة أَكْل الكُنَافَة

تقطّع الكنافة وتلقى في دست أربع أواق شيرج ويلقى فيه رطل سكّر مجروش ويحرّك معه حتّى يردّ الشيرج الذي شربه وهو علامة قليها. ثمّ يلقى عليه أربع أواق عسل نحل ويحرّك ويجعل فيه أربع أواق بندق.

أَلْبَابُ ٱلتَّاسِعُ

الحَلاوات

دهنها معلوم لأنّ الدقيق مع الدهن أخذه الكفاية معلوم.

منها أن يعصر باليد فيتماسك ومنها أن يقذف الدهن الذي شربه إلى غير ذلك كما هو معلوم عندهم.

١٤٢. صفة العَجَمِيَّة

يؤخذ لكلّ رطل رطل دهن ألية أو شيرج يحمّص حتّى يذهب ويسكب عليه الدهن. يؤخذ لكلّ رطل دقيق رطلان عسل نحل ووزن درهم زعفران وماء ورد ويسخن العسل ويحطّ ناحية وتحته نار جمري حتّى يكون سخنًا دائمًا ويحمّص الدقيق على نار هادئة ولا يزال يحمّصه حتّى يصفر وعلامة استوائه. يأخذ قليل دقيق تخلطه على العسل فإذا طشطش يكون قد انتهى فأخرج النار من تحته واسكب عليه العسل واسقه[١٤] حتّى يختلط وشيله من على النار وغطّيه بطبق وذرّ عليه الفستق والسكّر المصحون خشنًا.

---

١٤ في الأصل: سقه.

١٤٣. صفة القَاوُوت التُّركِي

تأخذ الحنطة المغربلة تصوّل ثمّ تصلق وتجفّف ليلة وتحمل إلى الذي يعمل القضامة <٢٠و> يحمّصها تحميص القضامة على نار هادئة ويطحنها دقيقًا وسطًا في غباره لكلّ رطل دقيق أربع أواق سمنًا وشيرج وأربع أواق عسل نحل. ثمّ تذوب السمن والشيرج وتفرك به الدقيق وبعده يذوب العسل بالزعفران ويغطّى الدقيق المفروك ويحطّ معه القلوبات المقشورة قلب فستق ولوز وبندق من كلّ واحد واحد أوقية خشخاش أوقية ماء ورد أوقية يخلط الجميع. ويحطّ في جراب نظيف.

١٤٤. صفهٔ قاوُوت بَلَدِي

يؤخذ رطل دقيق يحمّص بأربع أواق سمن تحميصًا جيّدًا واقلب عليه رطلًا وربع عسل نحل مصبوغًا بالزعفران وأوقية ماء ورد وأوقية قلب بندق وأوقية خشخاش وثلاث أواق سكّرًا مدقوقًا خشنًا ولا يشال حتّى يبرد. يشال إما في علب أو في أطباق.

١٤٥. صفة قَرْعِيَّة

يؤخذ القرع الحلو الأخضر ويقشّر قشره البرّاني ويجرد إلى أن لا يبان البياض لكلّ رطل قرع مجرود تسع أواق سكّرًا ونصف رطل عسلًا ويحطّ القرع في الدست ويسكب من العسل والجلّاب نصفه ويحطّ على نار ليّنة. ويقلب بمدقّة خشب فإذا نشف تزيده قليلًا قليلًا حتّى يصير مثل العجوة وتذرّ عليه أوقتين قلب فستق وسكّرًا مطحونًا ناعمًا بمسك وأعطيه الماء ورد قبل شيله. فإن كانت القرعية سيور

لا يشال حتّى يحطّ على البلاطة أو أطباق حتّى يبرد.

١٤٦. صفة قَرْعِيَّة فِيهَا تَرْطِيب وَتَحْلِيل

يؤخذ الخشخاش يدقّ ويستحلب بالماء من خرقة وخذ طيبه. اسكبه على السكّر وحلّه به بلا بيض وخذ القرع الحلو الأخضر قشره وأخرج بياضه واجرده العادة. ثمّ خذ اللوز قشره ودقّه واستحلبه وخذ طيبه واكسر به النشا لكلّ رطل سكّرًا أوقية ونصف نشا وخذ القرع المجرود واسلقه بثلاث أواق عسل. وشيله وألقى نصف <**٢٠ظ**> الجلّاب وأعطيه النشا وحرّكه وديره بالشيرج وأنت تسقيه قليلًا قليلًا وبعد ذلك القرع المسلوق وحرّكه. فإذا انتهى شيله.

١٤٧. خَبِيصة بِغَيْر نار

يؤخذ رطل ونصف لوز مقشّر يدقّ وينخل بمنخل شعر. ثمّ يؤخذ رطلان ونصف سكّر طبرزد يدقّ وينخل ويعزل من السكّر نحو ربع رطل. ثمّ يخلط اللوز مع السكّر ويصبّ عليه ربع رطل دهن لوز وربع رطل ماء ورد ووزن دانق دار صيني ويخلط جميعًا ويلت ويمرس جيّدًا حتّى يصير مثل الخبيص. ثمّ يبسط في جام وينثر عليه السكّر ويقدّم.

١٤٨. صفة حَلاوة تُسَمَّى بالكاهِين

يؤخذ بياض البيض لكلّ بياض بيضة وزن درهمين نشا يسحق النشا سحقًا ناعمًا ويضرب مع بياض البيض ويخلط خلطًا جيّدًا ويطرح في الجلّاب. يجئ نهاية في غاية الحسن والطيب.

١٤٩. صفة الجَمالِيَّة

يؤخذ الزبد يطرح في الدست إلى أن يذوب ويطرح عليه العجوة المنزوعة من النوى إلى حين تنحل وتليّن مع الزبد. ثمّ يطرح بعد ذلك الباب من الخبز العلامة الأبيض ويحرّك مثل الحلاوة. ثمّ يطرح عليه السكّر المهروس والفستق ويحرّك وينزل من على النار. فإنّه مليح.

١٥٠. صفة عمل القاهِرِيَّة الخالِصّ

يؤخذ رطل سكّر وربع رطل لوز وربع رطل دقيق علامة طيّب يدقّ السكّر في الهاون ناعمًا وينخل من غربال الدقيق حتّى يرجع مثل سميذ القمح. ثمّ يؤخذ اللوز يسمط وينزع من قشره ويدقّ أيضًا في الهاون وينخل من الغربال ويعاد الغليظ ساعة ويدقّ وينخل أيضًا الدقيق. ثمّ يخلط الجميع ويعجن بمقدار أربع أواق شيرج. ثمّ يعجن أيضًا بعده بالماء ويعرك حتّى يرجع كأنّه عجين الكعك. ثمّ يسقيه الماء ويعجن. ثمّ بعد ذلك يجعله حلقًا قاهرية مثل حلق الكعك. <**٢١و**> ثمّ يرشّ بعد ذلك الدقيق على اللوح الخشب ويجعل تلك الحلق عليه ويخلّيه في الهواء فإن كان عمله العصر يخلّيه حتّى يجفّ إلى ثاني يوم بكرة. فإذا كان بالغداة يأخذ قصريّة يجعل فيها مقدار رطل ونصف خميرة طيبّة وتضربها بيدك ضربًا جيّدًا مثلما تضرب عجين الزلّابية. ثمّ تجعل فيها بياض بيضتين بلا صفرة. ثمّ تضرب الجميع إلى أن يرجع مثل عجين الزلابية. ثمّ تجعل فيه المسك والماء ورد والكافور على قدر شهوتك تعجنه في أوّل الأمر مع السكّر. ثمّ تجعل القصرية على يمينك وتركب الطاجن على النار وتجعل فيه الشيرج الكبير حتّى تعوم فيه الحلق. ثمّ يغلى الشيرج وتأخذ أيضًا العسل الطيّب يجعل في قصرية على يسارك. ثمّ تأخذ تلك الحلق التي

قد نشفت تشيل واحدة واحدة بالسفود الحديد وتغطّيها في الخميرة التي في القصرية وتشيلها تجعلها في الطاجن تفعل أيضًا بالأخرى مثل الأولى إلى أن يطيّبوا فتشيل واحدة واحدة وتغطّيهم في تلك القصرية متاع العسل. ثمّ يغلى ويجعل في العسل إلى أن يفرغ فيجعله في الزبادي وترشّ عليه من المسك والماء ورد على قدر همّتك. ثمّ تدقّ أيضًا الفستق وترشّه عليه فهذا صفة القاهرية والله أعلم. ومنهم من يغلى العسل وينزع ريمه. ثمّ يدير الكنافة مع الشيرج في طاجن وتقلب عليه العسل. وتهدّئه وتقدّمه.

١٥١. الخُبْز البايت

يدخل في الهرائس الحلاواتية وغير ذلك من الطيّبات.

١٥٢. صفة نَوْع مِن الحَلاوة العَجَمِيَّة

دقيق علامة وعسل نحل وشيرج وزعفران ومسك وماء ورد تحمّص الدقيق إلى أن يحمر ولا يحترق وتعمل العسل في طاجن حتّى يغلى وتعمل الدقيق عليه وتعمل عليه الزعفران وتحرّك. وتسكب عليه الشيرج والمسك والماء ورد ويسقى بالشيرج قليلًا قليلًا حتّى ينضج ويعمل في الأوعية ويعمل عليه قليل مسك وماء ورد.

١٥٣. صفة الكُنافة المَطْبُوخَة

لكلّ رطل كنافة نصف رطل شيرج ويحطّ في الدست <**٢١ظ**> وتوقد عليها النار إلى أن تغلى. ويؤخذ رطل كنافة ويقطّع مثل الرشته وترمى على الشيرج ويغلى ويرمى عليه نصف رطل سكّر بياض مصحون وتحرّك حتّى ينحلّ جيّدًا. وترمى

عليه رطل عسل وتحرّك إلى أن تقذف دهنها وتحرّك جيّدًا إلى أن يطيّب. ويكون قد سمط لها لوز أو فستق وتصبغ بزعفران وتغلف به الكنافة ويحرّك جيّدًا ويعطى بالمسك والماء ورد وهي على النار وتغرف وتشال. تقعد سنة ما تتغير.

١٥٤. صفة حَلاوة مِن العَجْوَة

تؤخذ الألية تسلّى وتشال من السلّى ثمّ تؤخذ العجوة تنزع نواها وترمى على الألية وتطبخ على النار حتّى تبقى كالحلاوة ويسمط اللوز ويصبغ بالزعفران. ويعمل فيه مع قليل خشخاش ويلقى عليه وتحرّك حتّى يطيّب وينزل ويبسط في الصحون ويعمل عليه فستق وسكّر أبيض ومسك وماء ورد.

١٥٥. حَلاوة مِن البطّيخ العَبْدَلي

يقشّر ويجفّف في الشمس إلى أن يتقدّد ويحمرّ ويتلبّد في بعضه البعض. ثمّ تأخذ الجلّاب تجعله على النار وتأخذ رغوته وينزل عليه البطّيخ وتجفّفه بالإسطام في دست لطيف حتّى يبقى على صفة المسيّر وتعلقه قلب فستق. وتنزله على بلاطة وتمدّه قرصًا على هيئة العقيد وتقطعه شوابير ويعبًّا في علبة ساف سكّر وساف شوابير ويطيّب بماء ورد ممسّك قبل أن تجعله في العلبة. فإنّه طيّب لذيذ نافع للأمراض السوداوية.

١٥٦. صفة حَلاوة مِن المَلْبَن

يؤخذ الملبن يقلى بالشيرج الطري وينزل عليه السكّر المصحون فإنّه يبقى كالصابونية ويترك ويستعمل.

١٥٧. صفة حَلاوة مِن العَجْوَة

تسلّى ألية في دست بقليل شيرج سليًا جيّدًا ويشال في وعاء ويؤخذ العسل النحل يطرح في الدست. ثمّ تنزع العجوة الطيّبة من نواها وتدقّ ناعمًا في الجرن بقليل ماء ورد شامي. ثمّ يرمى على العسل بعد غليانه وقطف ريمه ببياض بيضة ويغلى عليه إلى أن يأخذ قوامًا ويرمى عليه لوز مسموط مصبوغ بالزعفران. ويحرّك الجميع بالإسطام ويسقى من دهن الألية إلى أن يقذف الدهن ينزل ويعمل عليه الأفاويه <٢٢و> عند نزوله مع قليل خشخاش ولوز وماء ورد ممسّك. فإذا غرف في الصحون تجعل على وجهه قلب بندق محمّص وقلب فستق وسكّر بياض مجروش ويؤكل. ومن كان فقيرًا يعمله بالقطارة أو بعسل القصب.

١٥٨. صفة رُطَب مُعَسَّل

يؤخذ الرطب الجني يبسط في الظلّ والهواء يومين ثمّ يخرج نواه من أسفله بمسلّة وتجعل عرض كلّ نواة لوزة مقشّرة. وتؤخذ لكلّ عشرة أرطال رطل عسل نحل بخلّ بأوقية ماء ورد ويرفع على النار. فإذا غلى ترفع رغوته ويصبغ بنصف درهم زعفران ويطرح الرطب فيه. فإذا غلى يحرّك تحريكًا خفيفًا بحيث يشرب العسل. ثمّ ينزل عن النار ويبسط في طبق خلنج[١٥] فإذا فترت حرارته يذرّ عليه سكّر مدقوق ناعمًا. فمن أراده للحرارة كان بالمسك والسنبل وشيئًا من الأفاويه. ومن أراده للتبريد طيّبه بالكافور والخشخاش ويرفع في أواني الزجاج. ولا يستعمل إلّا في برد الزمان وأيضًا زمان الرطب.

---

١٥ في الأصل: خبنج.

١٥٩. أمّا الرُّطَب المُلَوَّز

أيّ الذي جفّف في الشمس قليلًا ثمّ نزع نواه وحشي باللوز وصفّف في قطرميز ثمّ قلب عليه عسل نحل منزوع الرغوة. فإنّه ينبغي أن يتفقّد في كلّ أسبوع لئلّا يرخى ماؤه بحمضه.

١٦٠. أمّا التُّمور المُلَوَّزة

فإنّهم إذا غلوا الخلّ والعسل معًا وقطفوا الرغوة وألقوا فيه التمر وقلبوه على الفور في برنية بعد صبغه بالزعفران وتخميره بالمسك والماء ورد والكافور. فلا ينبغي أن بحرارته بل يترك مفتوحًا فم البرنية حتّى يبرد جيّدًا ويكون قد أخذ قوامًا جيّدًا. فإنّه يكون مليحًا في غاية.

١٦١. حَلاوة مِن التَّمْر أيضًا

يقلع نوى التمر ويرمى في الدست ويعمل عليه الماء ويغلى حتّى يتهرّأ ويصفّى من منخل شعر ويعاد إلى الدست وتوقد عليه النار إلى أن ينعقد. فإذا أردت عمل حلاوة بعد ذلك تعمل عليه العسل النحل والسمن والقلب[١٦] البنادق المحمّص المجروش ويحرّك ويشال ويطيّب بالمسك والماء ورد ويسمط اللوز ويصبغ بالزعفران ويعمل على وجهه. فإنّه غاية إن شاء الله تعالى.

١٦٢. صفة السَّكَنْجَبِين العَقِيد

وهو من أجود النقل على الشراب <٢٢ظ> لأصحاب الأمزاج الحارّة. وصفته أن

١٦ هكذا في الأصل.

يعقّد الجلّاب وينفى ويلقى عليه للرطل ثلاث أواق خلّ ثقيف صاف رائق ولا يزال يعقّد حتّى يتسكّر ويبسط على الرخام بعد دهنه ويستعمل.

١٦٣. ومنهم

من يقشّر الأترجّ ويقطّع شوابير ويقلى بالشيرج ثمّ يخرج ويغلى العسل والجلّاب ويقطف ريمه ويرمى فيه الأترجّ المقلي ويترك حتّى يأخذ قوامًا ويشرب الجلّاب. ويعمل عليه أطراف الطيب وزعفران وقماري مصحون ومسك وماء ورد. ويشال ويرصّ في الصحون ويرشّ السكّر ويقدّم.

١٦٤. صفة عَقِيد التَّمْر هِنْدِي

يؤخذ من التمر هندي أوقية تنقع في ماء ويستحلب حليبه ويعمل فيه قدر برام على نار هادئة أعني نار جمر ويحرّك حتّى يأخذ قوام العقيد أعنى يقصف. ويرفع في جرن مدهون دهن لوز.

١٦٥. شَراب الحِصْرِم المُنَعْنَع

تأخذ الجلّاب بعد حلّه ونقاوته وتعصر له من ماء الحصرم أربع أواق لكلّ رطل وتأخذ حزمة نعنع أخضر. تحرّك الجلّاب بها وهو على النار فإن شئت ترمها في الدست إلى أن تخرج خاصيتها وتشال وتصفّى في الإناء.

أَلْبَابُ ٱلعَاشِرُ

ٱلأَشْرِبَةُ كَٱلفُقَّاع وَٱلسُّوبِيَّة وَغَيْر ذَلِكَ

١٦٦. صفة عَمَل فُقَّاع خاصّ

يحلّ نصف رطل سكّر في خمسة أرطال ماء ويضاف إليه أوقية حبّ رمّان ويجعل فيه ثلاث أواق خبز سخن. ثمّ يمرس مرسًا جيّدًا ويعصر فيه ليمون أخضر. ثمّ يصفّى ويعمل فيه زنة درهم طيب أكثره جوزة وحبّة مسك وتملأ منه كيزان ويحطّون في ماء بارد يومًا.

١٦٧. نَوْع مِن أَنْواع الفُقَّاع قَرِيب المَأْخذ رَخِيص الثَّمَن

يبلّ الخبز من بكرة إلى العشاء ويمرس ويروّق ويصفّى ماؤه. ويلقى عليه لكلّ رطل ماء أوقية حبّ رمّان أو ماء ليمونة واحدة ونصف أوقية سكّر وأطراف طيب وفلفل وسذاب وترميه في الكيزان ويرصّ ويشال.

١٦٨. صفة فُقَّاع آخَر

ينقع رغيف خبز في ماء من بكرة إلى الظهر ثمّ يمرس ويصفّى بعد أن يروّق وينقع فيه حبّ رمّان أو ماء ليمون إلى صلاة العصر. ويجعل فيه سكّر وسذاب ويطيّب بيسير من المسك ويجعل في الكيزان. <٢٣و> ويسدّ رؤوسهم ويتركهم في قصرية على رؤوسهم ويرشّ بالماء ويشرب بالغداة.

١٦٩. صفة سُوبِيَّة مِن الأَرُزّ
نَافِع مِن التُّخْمَة وَالإمْتِلاء وَيُطَيِّب النَّفْس

يؤخذ أرزّ يصلق ناعمًا ويمرس من غربال ثمّ تؤخذ عجوة تنقع في أربعة أمثالها ماء وتبيّت وتغلى وتصفّى ويذوّب فيها الأرزّ الذي صفيته ويؤخد لها قوام. ثمّ يلقى عليها أطراف طيب كامل وقشور النارنج ويلقى الزنجبيل والسذاب اليابس والنعنع ويخمَّر في وعاء ضاري وتشرب. نافعة طيّبة.

١٧٠. أُخْرَى

يؤخذ دقيق علامة عال قدح وتعقد عصيدة بلا ملح وينزل ويبرد في قصرية ويسخن ماء ويضرب به هذه العصيدة في جفنة حتّى ترجع في قوام السويق. ثمّ تأخذ من أطراف الطيب كفايتها وهو سنبل وتتبّل وحطب وقرنفل وهال وجوزة وبسباسة وفلفل وزنجبيل وزرّ ورد يسحق ويرمى في هذا المعمول. ويكون لكلّ رطل دقيق أوقيتان من أطراف الطيب. ويسحق مع هذه الحوائج أوقيتين نعنع وباقة سذاب النصف منها مضروب مع الحوائج المذكورة والنصف الآخر يرمى مع السوبية صحيحًا ويضاف إليه رطلان ونصف عسل نحل أو قطارة طيّب.

ويعمل في وعاء نظيف ويذوب فيه نصف درهم زعفران ويعمل الجميع في جرّة غير رشاحة ويستعمل.

١٧١. نَقُوع المِشْمِش

منهم من يعصر عليه ماء رمّان حامض ويحلّى بسكّر مع ماء يضاف إليه من الماء ورد وماء نيلوفر وغير ذلك من المنافع.

١٧٢. دَوا قَرَف

يؤخذ زبيب وحبّ رمّان وتمر هندي ينزع من حبّه ويدقّ الجميع في جرن ومعه نعنع وفلفل وقرفة ويجعل معه خلّ خمر وزعفران. وإن أردته خاصّ يستخرج بخلّ خمر ويجعل على النار ويغلى ويحرّك بعرق جماجم وريحان ويطيّب بعود وعنبر ومسك وماء ورد. ينزل عليه بعد الغليان ويشال في برنية. ويستعمل وقت الحاجة.

فائدة: الخردل إذا دقّ وامتنع أو تعسر يجعل معه قطن فإنّه يدقّ بسهولة وسرعة إن شاء الله. <٢٣ظ>

(أَلْبَابُ ٱلحادِي عَشَرُ)

(في عَمَلِ الخَرْدَلِ)

١٧٣. صفة خَرْدَل

يؤخذ الخردل وينخل بمنخل حوّاري ثمّ يعجن في جفنة العجين ويكون عجنه يابسًا ويليّن بعد ذلك قليلًا قليلًا. ثمّ يرشّ عليه ماء حارّ ثمّ يدلك بالراحة دلكًا جيّدًا حتّى ترتفع له رغوة مثل الصابون ويطرح عليه قليل ملح أندراني وقليل خلّ. ثمّ يحمل عليه ماء بارد وتكون اليد في جوف الجفنة. ثمّ يدار بالأصابع حول الجفنة من داخلها قليلًا قليلًا والماء يصبّ عليه وليكن باردًا جدًّا. ثمّ يخرج ويتركه ساعة فإنّه يرغى ويرتفع له نفّاخات يرشّ عليها الماء قليلًا قليلًا حتّى يسكن. ثمّ يؤخذ فوق الماء بالراحة ويجعل في إناء حتّى يخرج مثل البرد فإن أردت تجعل فيه سكّر أو زبيبًا أو عسلًا. فأفعل أو فدعه على حاله وهذا صنف منه. وبعضهم يعمله بجوز معجون بملح أندراني بخلّ. وله أنواع كثيرة أضربنا عنها لكثرة عمالتها وغلو أثمانها لأنّ هذا التعليق ما جمعناه إلّا للجوار في البيت على حسب ضعف حالنا.

(أَلْبَابُ ٱلثَّانِي عَشَرُ)

(في عَمَلِ الصُّلُوصات)

١٧٤. صفة صَلْص

وهو كثير الأنواع ومنا إلى أسهله وأخصره. يؤخذ قلب اللوز يسمط ويهرس في الجرن بماء ليمون إلى أن يبقى كالمرهم ويترك عليه الزنجبيل المطحون وجوزة الطيب أيضًا مطحونة ويخدم في الجرن خدمة جيّدة إلى أن يبقى مثل المرهم. فإن كان هذا الصلص للعوامّ فيضاف إليه السكّر قدر ما تحبّه وإن كان للترك يضاف إليه الثوم المريب بالزيت.

١٧٥. صَلْص مُبَرِّد لإلْتِهاب المَعِدة

مقوّي لها معين على الهضم مقوّي للأحشاء مقطّع للبلغم اللزج من المعدة مطفي للدم ووهج جذبه مسكّن لغليانه مطفئ لغلظه قاطع لما يتولّد من السوداء ويطيّب النكهة ويحسن اللون. يؤخذ ريحان أترنجي نصف رطل وورق مقدونس منقّى من عيدانه رطل واحد منهم بمفرده ويقطر عليه زيت طيّب ويجعل عليه يسير ملح. <٢٤و>.

١٧٦. صفة صَلْص

تأخذ من الخردل ما أردت تلقى عليه ماءً يغمره ودعه ليلة ثمّ نحى ماءه واغسله ثلاث مرّات. ثمّ ذقّ نصفه واستخرج رغوته بمنخل حتّى لا يبقى فيه شيء من الرغوة والق عليه قليل ملح وجفّف النصف الآخر. فإذا جفّ دقّه حتّى ينشف ولا تبقى فيه نداوة ثمّ القه في الرغوة التي استخرجتها واعجنه بها حتّى تبقى كبّة. ثمّ جفّفه فإذا جفّ فارفعه فإذا أردت أن تأكل منه شيئًا الق عليه خلّ سكّر واجعل فيه جوزًا مدقوقًا فإنّه أشدّ لبياضه وأطيب عذوبة.

١٧٧. صفة صَلْص آخَر

سمّاق وكزبرة يابسة وكراوية وبندق محمّص وفلفل وقرفة لفّ وصعتر وزيت طيّب وطحينة ومقدونس وثوم وليمون وزرّ ورد وأطراف طيب. يدقّ الجميع ويحلّوا بالزيت والطحينة والليمون ويخمّر ويؤكل. ومنهم من يعمل عنّاب وغيره وأشياء كثيرة كلّ أحد على جنب غناه وفقره والله الموفّق.

أَلْبَابُ ٱلثالِثُ عَشَرُ

ما يُعْمَل مِن الأَلْبان

بعضهم يعمل كامخ من الخبز المعفّن واللبن الحليب ويضيف إلى ذلك الفطير ويدعه في الشمس أيّامًا بزيت. وهذا ممّا لم أحبّه فلم أذكر صفته ولكنّني أذكر:

١٧٨. صفة كامَخ مِن قَمْح

وهو أن يؤخذ ربع قمح طيّب زريعة فنقيه ثمّ تسلقه سلقًا خفيفًا ثمّ تخرجه من الصلق فينشره. فإذا جفّ تركه في دست فاقليه جيّدًا ثمّ بعد ذلك اطحنه جريشا فإذا طحنته فاعزل منه الدقيق ناحية والدشيش ناحية ويعجن الدقيق عجنًا شديدًا ويعمل كببًا وتتركهم في الشمس ييبسوا ويصيروا كالإكسير. ثمّ تأخذ الدشيش الذي عزلته يجعل في وعاء ضيّق الفم واسع الجوف كالمطر تجعل عليه غمره وفوقه يسير لبن حليب. ثمّ ترمى فيه ثلاثة أعواد تين ويترك بعدما غطّيت رأسه برقّ في برنية ويصبّ عليه الزيت وقليل ملح مسحوق ثلاثة أيّام ويقرب وعليه[١٧] الزيت. فإنّه أطيب ما يكون.

١٧ هكذا في الأصل.

١٧٩. صفة <٢٤ظ> عمل اللِبَأ

اللبأ غذا طيّب رطب يستحسنه الناس يغدوا غذًا صالحًا لأصحاب الصفراء والاحتراقات ويليّن الطبيعة وكثير من الناس يأكلونه بالتمر ومن الناس من يأكله واحد.

صفة عمله: يؤخذ من اللبن الحليب جزء ومن لبأ الغنم التي وضعت ولها ثلاثة أيّام جزء ويخلط الجميع ويجعل في قدر برام أو فخّار ويجعل على نار هادئة أو رماد حارّ ليلة. فإذا كان من الغد تجده قد حمى وأحمر وجهه فخذه وقربه وكلّما نقص اللبأ وزاد اللبن كان أطيب وأعذب وبعضهم يجعل الربع لبأ والثلاثة أرباع لبنًا فيجئ طيّبًا. فإذا كثر اللبأ يذهب اللبن ويصلب ويصير مثل الحجر لا لذّة له ولا هو طيّب. وكان الفلّاحون في ضيعة ليّ يصنعونه ويأتون به فما كان يطيّب لي أكله حتّى دللتهم على خلطه باللبن.

١٨٠. صفة أُخْرَى

يؤخذ لبن حليب ويخلط معه لكلّ رطل بياض أربع بيضات ويضرب به جيّدًا في قدر فخّار ويوقد تحته برفق حتّى ينعقد وليكن عليه محّ بيضة واحدة. فإنّه يجئ عجيب.

١٨١. صفة أُخْرَى

تأخذ قدرًا فخّارًا لطيفة وتضعها على النار وتصبّ فيها من اللبن الحليب ما شئت. وتأخذ قدر ربع ذلك اللبأ لبنًا حليبًا فتضعه إلى جانبك وتوقد تحت القدر نارًا ليّنة. فإذا رغت القدر باللبأ وارتفع له زبد فخذ بيدك قليلًا من ذلك اللبن الرائب

فارششه عليه. ثمّ تدعه فإذا رغا وأزبد رششت أيضًا فلا تزال تفعل ذلك وبرفق وبيدك حتّى يدخل ذلك اللبن الحليب. فإذا أدخلته في جميعه نزعت ما تحت القدر من جمر وأقررتها حتّى تبرد. ثمّ أخرجه فكلّه بعسل أو سكّر أو بتمر.

١٨٢. صفة عمل قَنْبَرِيس

خذ قدورًا جددًا فاجعل فيها خلًّا حادقًا ثمّ تضعها على النار حتّى تغلى ثمّ اعزلها عن النار. ثمّ صبّ فيها اللبن وارفعها في مكان ولا تحرّكها فإذا كان من الغد فتحتها. فإنك تجدها جامدة مثل القنبريس واللبن فيه مضارّ لكنّ منافعه أكثر وهو مع ذلك لذيذ. ومن <٢٥و> الناس من لا يطيب له الأكل إلّا أن يكون على مائدته جبن.

١٨٣. صفة البِيرَاف

وهو اسم لما يقشط بالمحّارة من على وجه اللبن الحليب المبيت تحت السماء ويغطّى بأقفاص أو غربال حتّى لا يدخله شيء. فإذا قشط باكر جمع ما على وجهه يجرّه إلى موضع بارد ليقشط ما عساه يعلو إن أراد ذلك. من شاء أكله بالجلّاب أو العسل أو السكّر أو وحده والأطبّاء يأخذون بعده شربة سكنجبين سفرجل أو يمصّ سفرجلة أو كمّثراتين.

١٨٤. الجاجَق

إن عمل من حشيشة السلطان فهو ينفع للظهر ويقوّي على الجماع وهو عجيب.

١٨٥. جاجَق اللَّبْسَان

صفته أن يؤخذ اللبسان يغسل نظيف ويقطّع صغارًا ويوضع في زبدية نظيفة ويطرح عليه ثلاثين درهم ملح أندراني مسحوق ويدلك باليد جيّدًا. ويؤخذ خمسة أرطال لبن حامض لخمس باقات لبسان وما زاد يجعل لكلّ قبضة رطل يعلق اللبن في كيس نظيف حتّى يقطر ما فيه من الماء ويبقى منه. ثمّ يخرج ويخلط في وعاء ويحطّ فيه اللبسان المقطّع ويحرّك حتّى يختلط ويحطّ فيها بقدر عشرة دراهم نعنع مفروم ثمّ مع زيت طيّب يطبخ بذلك. والله أعلم.

١٨٦. صفة تَطْيِيب الجُبْن الحالُوم

يغلى اللبن الحليب مع الملح والصعتر الشامي إلى أن ينقص الثلث وينزل من على النار ويبرد ويعمل في صرّة حرير قليل كندس مطحون مع الجبن في المطر وقلوب النارنج والكبّاد والترنج والليمون والصعتر الأخضر يُعمل راق جبن وراق قلوب وصعتر إلى أن تمتلي المطر ويقلب عليه اللبن المغلي إلى أن يمتلئ المطر وتختمه بقليل زيت طيّب. ويكبس ويشال إلى وقت الحاجة.

١٨٧. صفة تَحْمِيض اللَّبَن في الشتاء

يؤخذ الحصرم المجفّف ينقعه في ماء حارّ ثمّ دقّه وصفّيه وصبّ عليه من اللبن الحليب ما تريد. فإنّه يحمض ويصير رائبًا إن شاء الله تعالى.

١٨٨. صفة عمل اللَّبَن الياغُرْت

يغلى اللبن البقري أو الجاموسي وتشيله بعد أن يبرد فإن كان قنطار مصري يؤخذ

رطل لبن مقطوع وهو خميرة. <٢٥ظ> وتأخذ نصف أوقية منفحة مضروبة بالماء وتخلطه في الماجور وتملأ به الأوعية. إن عملته بكرة طاب عشية وإن عملته عشية طاب بكرة.

١٨٩. صفة قَنْبَرِيس

يستعمل مع ما شئت من الباذنجان وغيره ممّا يحتاج إلى اللبن. **وصفته** أن يؤخذ اللبن الحليب يغلى حتّى يفور. ثمّ بعمل في قدر جديد وتخلّي حتّى يبرد ساعة وتأخذ له من اللبن الياغرت لكلّ عشرة أرطال نصف رطل لبن ياغرت ويحرّك بالمغرفة. ويغطّى ويحطّ في موضع دافئ ويحطّ تحته قليل تبن ويترك من العشاء إلى بكرة يصبح مثل القرص. تجعله في كيس وتصفيه يصير قنبريس تفرغه من الكيس. يعمل عليه ملح ويخدم ويشال إلى وقت الحاجة في وعاء ضاري نظيف.

١٩٠. صفة عمل زَعْتَر

ينظف ورقه ويغسل ويمسك بالملح ويعصر عليه زيت طيّب لكلّ عشرة أرطال منه رطل زيت طيّب ويعمل في برنية مدهونة ويكلس ويزاد ملح مصحون. فإذا أردت تتبيله تدقّ الثوم المقشور بقليل ملح وزيت حتّى يصير مثل المرهم ويدقّ له الجوز ويؤكل. وهو مليح في غاية.

أَلْبَابُ ٱلرَّابِعُ عَشَرُ

ٱلْمُخَلَّلات

١٩١. صفة عَمَل اللِفْت بالخَمِيرَة

تأخذ اللفت تقشّره وتقطّعه وتغلى عليه في دست فرد غلية وتأخذه يجعله في الإناء الذي تريد وتدوّب الخميرة والملح في الماء وتقلب عليه غمره. وتأخذ خردل تدقّه ناعمًا وتستحلبه من خرقة وتسكبه فوقه وتغطّى رأسه وتشيله ولا تلمسه حينًا وليكن الخمير والخردل على قدر ما يكون اللفت.

١٩٢. صفة لِفْت آخَر يُؤْكَل بَعْد يَوْم وَاحِد

وهو أن يقشّر ويصلق نصف صلقه ثمّ يخرج ويترك حتّى ينشف ماؤه ثمّ يجعل في القدر مع الخلّ ويصبغ بالعصفر قبل أن يجعل في القدر مع الخلّ إن أردته أحمر.

١٩٣. صفة مِن اللِفْت يُعْمَل السَّنَة كامِلَة

يؤخذ ويقشّر في إناء حتّى ينصل الماء ويذبل. بعد ذلك يشال. ويعمل عليه الخلّ

والخردل والحوائج وكذلك عمل سائر اللفوت.

١٩٤. صفة عَمَل الخَرْدَل لأَجْل اللِفْت وَغَيْره

يؤخذ الأبيض منه يدقّ بالملح اليسير حتّى لا يتمرّر ويستخرج اللفت وغيره والبندق أيضًا الذي يجعل في المخلّلات يحمّص ويترك <٢٦و> حتّى يبرد ويزول قشره ويبيض ويدقّ ناعمًا وكذلك الجوز ويخلط بالخردل. ويجعل على ما يختاره من أعمال المخلّلات من اللفت وغيره.

١٩٥. لِفْت يُقِيمُ شَهْر

يقطّع اللفت كما ذكرنا أوّلًا ويغلى الماء في دست حتّى يقلب ويرمى اللفت ويشال الدست ويجعل على مصفاة ويعصر باليد حتّى ينصل الماء ويذرّ عليه الخردل والحوائج كما ذكرناه. ومن أراده محلّى يقلب عليه خلّ خمر محلّى بالعسل أو سكّر وكذلك الذي ذكرنا أنّه لسنة وأطراف طيب غمره ويجعل عليه نعنع وسذاب ورق قلوب. ومن أراد بسكّر فعل ومنهم من يذرّ عليه أطراف طيب وسمسم مقشّر.

١٩٦. صفة لِفْت رُومِي

يؤخذ لفت صغار وكبار على قدر ما تريد تقطّع عروقه ويخلّى له من ورقه عقصه قدر أصبع وشيء بلا عروق ولا ورق يقشّر ويشقّق عن شقوق طولًا وعرضًا ويذرّ عليه ملح وماء ويترك يومين وليلتين. ثمّ يشال من الماء والملح ويحشى شقوقه خردلًا وملحًا ويقلب عليه خلّ خمر ويترك فإنّه يبقى سنة كاملة.

١٩٧. صفة لِفْت آخَر

يقطّع اللفت صغارًا ويصبغ بزعفران فإذا أخذ حدّه من الصبغ قلب عليه خلّ خمر محلّى بعسل أو سكّر أو دبس ونعنع ورق وخردل وأطراف طيب ومنهم من يدعك العصفر بقليل خلّ. ثمّ يصبغ ثمّ يلقى عليه الخلّ المحلّى والحوائج إذا أراده أحمر.

١٩٨. صفة لِفْت يُسَمَّى مَحْشِي

يؤخذ اللفت ويذبل كما ذكرنا ويذرّ عليه الخردل. ثمّ يؤخذ زبيب أسود يدقّ ناعمًا ويصفّى بخلّ خمر دفعات حتّى لا يبقى من الزبيب شيء بحيث يكون خاثرًا وإن كان حامضًا يحلّى. ويجعل فيه نعنع وسذاب وأطراف طيب وسمسم وشهدانق محمّص ويجعله على اللفت غمره.

١٩٩. صفة لِفْت عَجَمِي

يؤخذ اللفت ويقطّع ورقه من وسط وترمى العروق الطوال التي ليس فيه ورق كي يبقى على طول ثلاثة أصابع. ثمّ تشقّق الرؤوس أربع فلق ولا يبري بعضه من بعض وتخلّى العروق كما هي في العقصة. ثمّ يغلى لها الماء ويرمى فيه ويشال الدست كما هو من على النار ويصفّى عنه الماء ويذرّ <**٢٦ظ**> عليه الملح والخردل وهو سخن ويترك حتّى يبرد. ويؤخذ الخلّ يجعل فيه بندق محمّص مدقوق كما ذكرنا أوّلًا شيء جيّد وزيت طيّب وكسفرة يابسة محمّصة مدقوقة وكراوية وأطراف طيب وثوم مدقوق وسمسم مقشور وشهدانق ويقلب الجميع على ورق اللفت. ويشال في وعاء وكثر زيته ومن أراده لسنة لا يجعله في الماء المغلي ومن أراد

أكله بسرعة ينضجه على النار كما ذكرنا أوّلًا. ومن أراد أن يحلّيه بسكّر أو عسل فعل ويجعل فيه أفلاق جوز محمّص مقشور. وإيّاك أن تجعل فيه قلب جوز مدقوق فإنّه يزرق الخلّ والبندق أجود.

٢٠٠. صفة لِفْت بِحَبّ رُمّان

يدقّ الحبّ رمّان ويصفّى بخلّ خمر دفعات بحيث لا يبقى في الحبّ الرمّان شيء ويجعل فيه عسل أو سكّر ويشال على النار ويعقد عقدًا جيّدًا. ويجعل فيه نعنع وسذاب وأطراف طيب وفلفل وزنجبيل وخشخاش وسمسم وشهدانق وقطع جوز محمّص. فإذا عقد يؤخذ ثوم يقشّر بالسكّين قطعًا ويقلى في الشيرج إلى أن يحمر الثوم ويرمى عليه بعد ذلك قطع اللفت بعد أن يقشّر ويقطّع صغارًا ويذبل كما ذكرنا. ويسلق على قدر ما يريد ويجعله في الحبّ رمّان ويغلى عليه غليان فإنّه من خيار هذه.

٢٠١. صفة لِفْت عَجَمِي قَرِيب المَأْخَذ

يحتاج إلى لفت وكزبرة يابسة وكراوية وخردل مطحون بقدر الكفاية يسلق اللفت ويضاف إليه الكزبرة والكراوية والخردل بقدر الكفاية.

٢٠٢. صفة لِفْت آخَر

يقشّر ويخرّط قدر وتعمله في ماء وملح يومين ويشال ويعصر جيّد وتعمله في الخلّ الخمر والعسل النحل وأطراف طيب والنعنع ويتبّل ويشال.

٢٠٣. صفة لِفْت آخَر بِخَمِيرة

يؤخذ دقيق الشعير يعجن بخميرة وماء سخن ويسير ملح ويخلّى حتّى يحمض حمضًا جيّدًا فإذا أخذ حدّه يسلق اللفت نصف نضاجة ويعزل ماؤه تحلّ به الخميرة جيّدًا ويردّ على اللفت ويذرّ عليه الخردل. ويترك حتّى يبرد وينزل في المرقة بالخميرة ويكثر نعنعه وسذابه جدًّا وورق النارنج وأطراف الطيب. ويدقّ الخميرة التي فيها اللفت في مكان دافئ وتشيل منه ويؤكل. <٢٧و>

٢٠٤. صفة لِفْت آخَر لَذِيذ الطَعْم

يؤخذ نصف قنطار لفت يقشّر ويلقى في قدر غمره ماء ويوقد عليه حتّى يسخن الماء جيّدًا ولا يبلغ الغليان ثمّ ينزل ويصبّ عليه ماء باردًا حتّى يبرد ويجعل في دنّ. ويؤخذ رطلان ونصف خميرة عجين قمح فيحلّ بالماء البارد الذي يردّ به اللفت ويلقى على اللفت حتّى يغمره. وإن أعوزه من غمره صبّ عليه ماء باردًا من مائه المغسول به ويؤخذ نصف ثمن قدح خردل يستحلب بالماء حتّى يخرج قوّته فيلقى عليه ويمعك باليد حتّى يختلط ويردّ أعلاه أسفله ويترك إلى أن يصلح طعمه ويستعمل.

٢٠٥. صفة لِفْت آخَر

يقشّر ويقطّع ويغلى بماء وملح وفيه بعض قوّة وتؤخذ خلّ خمر وعسل نحل أبيض أو سكّر طبرزد أو خردل مسحوق. ويجعل في براني ويكون أي برنية شئت بأيّ لون وشدّ رؤوسها إلى أن يعلق الصبغ باللفت.

٢٠٦. صفة لِفْت آخَر

يقشّر اللفت ويقطّع صغارًا وكبارًا ويسلق بحيث يغلي غليتين ليخرج وفيه قوة ويتبّل بالخردل والملح ويجعل في حقّ ويخرّط عليه سذاب. ويؤخذ خميرة حامضة لها خمسة أيّام تحلّ بماء حارّ وتخلّيها حتّى تركد ويصفّى ماءها ويصفّى الماء الذي على اللفت ويترك أربعة أيّام ويستعمل.

٢٠٧. صفة لِفْت عَجَمِي

يؤخذ عقص اللفت يصلق نصف سلقه ويحطّ في خلّ وخردل وطحينة وبندق وقلب جوز وكزبرة يابسة وزيت طيّب ويذرّ عليه كراوية.

٢٠٨. صفة لِفْت آخَر

يؤخذ لفت يسلق وينشف من الماء ويعرك عركًا جيّدًا حتّى يدخل في جسمه. ثمّ يؤخذ له السكّر والخلّ الخمر والهال والزعفران الشعر يجعل عليه ويخمر ثلاثة أيّام. فإنّه يأتي أصفر كأنّه الذهب لون وطعم.

٢٠٩. صفة لِفْت أَحْمَر بِخَمِيرة

ينقع بياض اللفت المقشّر المقطّع مطاول ومدوّر في ماء وملح ثلاثة أيّام ثمّ يغسل وينقع في ماء حلو يومين. ثمّ تأخذ أربعة أرطال خميرة تذاب بالماء حتّى تبقى رقيقة جدًّا وتترك حتّى تركد تأخذ صافيها. ثمّ يرفع اللفت من الماء يلقى في برنية ويلقى عليه من ماء الخميرة الصافي وثلاث أوراق خردل مسحوق مغسول بالنطرون <٢٧ظ> وسذاب ونعنع ويسير زرّ ورد ويترك خمسة أيّام ويغيّر السذاب

والنعنع الأوّل بغيره ويجدّد له خميرة ويحرّك بسكّر أو عسل. وكلّما أراد تناوله يحرّك الوعاء فإنّه غاية.

٢١٠. صفة الزَّيْتُون المُكَلَّس

يؤخذ الزيتون المنقّى السالم من ضربة أو عاهة ويغسل له الخوابي ويعمل فيها. ويؤخذ الكلس يطفى ويبيت إلى الغد. ثمّ يؤخذ القلي فيدقّ جيّدًا وينخل ويجعل على كلّ مدّ من الزيتون أوقية من القلي وأوقية من[١٨] ووزن المُدّ الشامي عشرة أرطال مصري. ثمّ يؤخذ من الماء ما يغمر الزيتون فيطرح في قدر نحاس ويلقى عليه الكلس والقلي ويغلى الماء حتّى ينقص الثلث فإذا نقص الثلث أنزله عن النار يحطّ في وعاء من فخّار. ويبيّت تلك الليلة فيصبح رائقًا كلون لشيرج فيقلب من الماء الرائق على الزيتون غمره ويجعل على وجه الزيتون من أعلاه مهما كان من الورق الأخضر ويثقّل ويبقى في الخوابي ثلاثة أيّام. ثمّ يؤخذ منه زيتون ويكسر فإن وجدت نواتها قد اسودت وحلّى طعمها فيشال الزيتون ويوضع في قفة أو شيء من السلال ويغسل بالماء حتّى ينظّف. ثمّ يرفع لساعة لئلّا يسوّد فيوضع في ماء حلو بلا ملح ثلاثة أيّام. ثمّ يوضع في ماء وملح شيء جيّد ويؤخذ منه ويؤكل. جيّد.

٢١١. صفة زَيْتُون آخَر مُكَلَّس

يؤخذ الزيتون الجيّد الأخضر حين يصير فيه الزيت السالم من الضربات والخدوش. ينزل في إناء مدة يومين وعليه من الماء ما يغمره. ثمّ يخرج من الماء ويحطّ عليه ماء آخر وكلس لكلّ مدّ زيتون أوقيتان الدمشقي كلس. ويبقى في الكلس إلى حيث يطيّب فيرفع ويغسل ويترك في ماء وملح ويبقى إلى وقت الحاجة إليه فيستعمل.

١٨ هكذا في الأصل.

٢١٢. صفة أُخْرَى مِنْهُ

يؤخذ الزيتون الأخضر الذي يعصر منه الزيت السالم من الخدوش والضربات ويكون صلب ويحطّ في وعاء يصبّ عليه من الملح والماء ويترك أسبوعًا. ثمّ يغربل له الرماد ويطرح عليه بحيث يحبل به كالطين ويترك مقدار شهر أو أكثر فإذا أردت الأكل منه تخرج من الإناء مقدار الحاجة ويغسل ويؤكل. <٢٨و>

٢١٣. والزَّيْتُون المُمْكِن أَكْلَهُ

يخرج نواه فمنهم من يدقّ له الثوم بقدر ما يظهر فيه طعمه ويقلب عليه شيرج ولوز وقلب جوز وسمسم وسمّاق مدقوق منخول وصعتر ونعنع كما شئت ومنهم من يغيّر عليه المياه حتّى يحلّى. ويعصر عصرًا جيّدًا كلّ ذلك بعد نزع نواه. ويؤخذ له كراوية وكسفرة محمّصان بقدر الحاجة وأطراف طيب وقلب بندق وطحينة وخلّ خمر حادق ويعمل في إناء ثلاثة أيّام ويقلب عليه زيت طيّب ويستعمل.

٢١٤. هذا صَنْف مِن أَصْنَاف المُتَبَّل

ومنهم من يضيف إلى الحوائج سمّاق ومنهم من يسقيه بالشيرج وكلّما كثرت الحوائج كان أجود إلّا السمّاق يكون قليلًا والقلوبات تحمّص.

٢١٥. أمّا أعمال البصل

فإنّها ظاهرة وكلّ شيء يغيّر عليه الماء والملح ويكرّر ذلك ثمّ يكرّر عليه الماء فإنّه يحلو ثمّ تفعل ما شئت فلا يحتاج الحادق في أكثر الأمور إلى شيرج.

٢١٦. صفة عمل فِجْل بِخَلّ يمرئ الطَّعام وَهُوَ طَيِّب

يؤخذ الفجل الكبار يشقّق إلى[١٩] مثل الأصابع ويجعل في قارورة واسعة الفم ويصبّ عليه من الخلّ الخمر الجيّد ما يغمره ويطرح فيه أنجدان[٢٠] وشونيز وشيء من حمّص مدقوق وخردل مدقوق معمول قد أخرجت مرارته وصعتر مدقوق وملح. وليكن الأنجدان غالب عليه يدقّ قبل أن يجعل فيه ويؤكل فإنّه يمرئ الطعام.

٢١٧. صفة عمل كبَّاد

يقطّع الكبّاد شقّات ويؤخذ له الملح والكراوية المحمّصة والسذاب والزيت الطيّب وقطع زنجبيل صحاح وقطع قرفة وحطب قرنفل صحاح. يؤخذ الكبّاد بهذا الملح والكراوية المحمّصة والسذاب والزيت الطيّب ويحطّ في وعاء ويختم رأسه بزيت طيّب ويغطّى بغطاء وفوق الغطاء خرقة إلى وقت الحاجة. فهو يستوي في ثلاثة أيّام وهو يحبّ الخدمة والافتقاد. وإذا نقص الماء كمّله بزيت طيّب وحطّه في وعاء أصغر من ذلك الوعاء فإنّه عجيب.

٢١٨. صفة حُمَّاض الأُتْرُنْج

يؤخذ الحمّاض ويؤخذ شعيره ويؤخذ له سكّر وقلب فستق وقلب بندق محمّص وتأخذ له ورد مربّى مطبوخ مجهّز تنزله عليه مع الزعفران والمسك والماء ورد ويشال <**٢٨ظ**> على النار ويزاد ماء ورد. ويعقد على قوام الجلّاب ويبخر له برنية بعود وعنبر وينزل الحمّاض في البرنية ويعمل غطاءها جيّدًا بحيث لا تصعد منه

١٩ هكذا في الأصل.
٢٠ في الأصل: أبدنجان.

الرائحة. فإنّه غاية.

٢١٩. صفة تَخْلِيل الخِيار

يؤخذ خيار تشرين خصوصًا الصغار منه ينقع في ماء وملح يومين وليلتين. ثمّ يشال من الماء والملح ويجعل في قطرميز ويقلب عليه خلّ خمر ويرمى فيه قلوب كرفس ونعنع وسذاب ويكون السذاب أكثر من الكرفس ويشال أيّامًا ويستعمل.

٢٢٠. صفة القُبَّار بالخَلّ

يؤخذ القبّار المملوح فيغسل بالماء إلى أنّ لا يبقى فيه ملح وينقع في خلّ محلّى بسكّر أو عسل ويجعل شيء يسير ثوم مدقوق وكزبرة يابسة ويجعل فيه زيت طيّب.

٢٢١. صفة أُخْرَى بِسُمَّاق

يؤخذ القبّار المملوح ينقع إلى أن يزول ملحه ويؤخذ خلّ وماء ليمون يستخرج فيه السمّاق مدقوقًا من خرقة ويقلب عليه القبّار ويذرّ عليه يسير من سمّاق مدقوق ناعم وثوم وكزبرة يابسة وكراوية وصعتر يابس. ويقطّع فيه ليمون مالح صغارًا ويجعل على وجهه زيت طيّب.

٢٢٢. صفة الثُّم المُخَلَّل

تعمد إلى ما أردت منه فتجعله برؤوسه في إناء مزفّت ويلقى فيه من الماء ما يغمره

وكفّ ملح وكفّ شعير ويطيّن رأسه ويتركه حتّى يحمّض ويطيّب طعمه. وكذلك يعمل بالكراث الشامي والبصل الحرّيف الرقيق الأصفر.

٢٢٣. صفة لَيْمُون مالِح

يؤخذ ليمون مالح يقطّع صغار ويجعل في إناء ويعصر عليه ليمون أخضر ونارنج ويقلب عليه زيت طيّب وأطراف طيب وكسفرة يابسة محمّصة مدقوقة ومقدونس مخروط ونعنع وسذاب. فإنّه من أجود ما يكون وأطيبه ومنهم من يقلب عليه خلًّا محلّى بعسل نحل وزيت طيّب.

٢٢٤. صفة

إذا ملّحت ليمونًا فيجعل في كلّ إناء قبضة سذاب وقليل عسل نحل وزيت طيّب وزعفران ويكون من ليمون طوبة وامشير فإنّه يجيء غاية.

٢٢٥. صفة لَيْمُون

تشقّق الليمون وتحشيه ملح وتكسره بعد يومين وتعصره من مائه وتخرج حبّه منه وتعمل في كلّ ليمونة عرق زنجبيل وعود نعنع وسذاب وتردّه في وعائه وتعمل في الوعاء الذي له زعفران وعسل نحل تلقيه عليه وتختمه بزيت. <٢٩و>

٢٢٦. صفة أيضًا

يشقّق الليمون صليبًا ويحشى بملح ويرصّ في قصرية ويثقّل بحجر ويغطّى ويخلّى

ثلاثة أيّام. ثمّ تشيله تجعله في قطرميز وتشيل ماءه وتصبغه بزعفران وتصفيه من حبّه وإن عاز ماء ليمون زده. ثمّ أكبسه في المطرة كبسًا جيّدًا إلى أن يفيض عليه الماء وتختمه بزيت طيّب وتغطّيه وترفعه.

صفة المَنافِع وتَوَابِعها

اللبن: حارّ يابس.

الصحنة: حارّة يابسة معطّشة تفسد الدم وتولد الجرب.

كامخ الكبر: حارّ يابس ردئ للمعدة معطّش نهك للبدن.

كامخ الثوم: جيّد لصاحب البلغم والحمّى النافض ويذيب الحصاة.

كامخ المرزنجوش: جيّد للريح وبرد المعدة ويقلّ الرأس الذي يعرض من البرد والبلغم.

والكوامخ كلّها تكتسب من الخلّ فضل لطافة.

الكبر المخلّل: أقلّ حارًّا من المكبوس بالملح جيّد للسدد في الكبد والطحال.

البصل المخلّل: لا يسخن ولا يبرد ولا يعطّش ولا يبعث الشهوة.

مخلّلات الخيار والقثّاء: يبردان تبريدًا قويًا وهما مع ذلك لطيفان.

وكل الكوامخ المالحة والمخلّلات ضارّة لمن في حلقه خشونة والمالحة منها خاصّة رديئة لمن يعثر به حكّة وجرب وسائر الأمراض الكائنة عن احتراق الدم.

الزيتون الذي يعمل بالماء: حارّ يابس يطلق البطن إذا قدّم قبل الطعام ويقوّي فم المعدة.

وأمّا زيتون: فإنّه إسخانه كثير وتقويته لفم المعدة وإطلاقه للبطن أقلّ.

أَلْبَابُ ٱلخامِسُ عَشَرُ

خَزْنِ ٱلْفَوَاكِهَ وادِّخَارُها إلَى غَيْر أَوانِها

٢٢٧.

قالوا إن ماء السمّاق إذا طبخ حتّى يذهب ثلثه ثمّ يبرد ويجعل في إناء زجاج أو فخّار. ثمّ يطرح العنب في ذلك الوعاء ويسدّ رأسه بالجص فإذا أخرج منه العنب بعد ذلك في غير وقته وجد طريًا طعمه ورائحته كأنّه كما قطف والماء يصير بعد ذلك خلًّا جيّدًا.

٢٢٨.

والسفرجل يلفّ في ورق التين ويطلى بالطين ويجفّف في الشمس ويعلّق بعد ذلك في الموضع. وكذلك التفّاح وله أدوية أخرى غير هذه الصفة <**٢٩ظ**> اختصرناها فلم نذكرها.

٢٢٩. صفة الوَرْد

تأخذ صحفة جديدة وملأها طين القمح وحطّها في ماجور يكون فيه ماء وخلّيها

عائمة على وجه الماء ولا تقربها بماء ثمّ يؤخذ ورد عراقي أزرار فتغرسه في ذلك الطين واتركه يومين وغطّ المأجور. فإذا كان اليوم الثالث شيل الغطاء فإنك تجد ذلك الورد قد بقي على حالته الأولى وورقه الأحمر أحمر والأخضر أخضر. وتأخذ زرّ الورد اليابس الصحيح انقعه في ماء ورد ثلاثة أيّام فإنّه يفتح.

.٢٣٠

أو تأخذ زرّ الورد الصحيح تجعله في قصبة فارسية واحدة بعد واحدة صفًّا واحدًا وتشمّع رأس القصبة واربط في طرف القصبة خيط واجعلها في خزانة الحمّام على بخار الماء يومًا وليلة واخرجه فإنك تجده طريًا.

.٢٣١

وإذا أردت خزن الفواكه والحبوب والبزور والدقيق ففي المواضع الباردة النظيفة البعيدة من المطابخ والدخان والروائح القبيحة ولا تخزن مع حبّ السفرجل.

٢٣٢. صفة خَزْن العِنَب

قالوا إن حرق ورق التين وحطبه ونثر رماده على عناقيد العنب يبقى زمانًا وإن غمست عناقيده في البقلة الحمقاء بقى محفوظًا وإن غمست في ماء الشبتّ بقي سنة. وإن ضربت نشارة العاج أو الأرزّ أو رماد الكرم بالماء كضرب الخطمي وتغمس فيه العناقيد وترفع مفروشة أو معلقة في غرفة في مكان نظيف معتدل فإنّها تبقى. وإن أخذ العنب الشتوي الطيّب الغليظ القشر بعد نضجه واستحكام حلاوته في النصف الأخير من شهر نونبر او في آخره بحسب تبكير الأرض وتأخيرها وليقطف

بحديد قاطع إذا ارتفعت الشمس ونشف النداء في يوم مصبح. ويتوخّى نقصان الشهر ويزال ما فيه من حبّ غير نضيج أو فاسد ويفرش له الخوابي إلى أن يملأ الدنّ طاقة وطاقة فوقها من العنب وطاقة من التين ما يدفع عادته الهواء ويختم فمها بالطين بعد أن تجعل فوقه من التين ما يدفع عادته الهواء وتجعل الخابيه في مكان لا يصل إليه الشمس فإنّ العنب يبقى غضًا عامًا كاملًا. وقد تغمس العناقيد في ماء وملح. <٣٠و> وينضده متفرّقة على تبن الترمس أو تبن الباقلّاء أو تبن الشعير أيّها حضر وليكن في موضع بارد لا تشرق فيه الشمس ولا تستوقد فيه نار فيبقى زمانًا. وإن جعلت العنقود في ظرف فخّار وسدّدت رأسه بجلد سدًّا جيّدًا ودفنتها بالتراب أخرجته متى شئت صحيحًا. وإن جعلت الجرّة في الماء إلى حلقها فذلك وإن قطعت العنقود بقضيبه وورقه وغرست موضع القطع منه في قار مذاب ويعلق ولا يقرب العناقيد بعضها من بعض فإنّه لا يزال كذلك.

(أَلْبَابُ ٱلسَّادِسُ عَشَرُ)

(فِي ٱلْأَطْعِمَةِ)

٢٣٣. طَعام التَّمْرِيَّة

يؤخذ للتمرية اللحم يقطّع صغارًا ويغسل بماء سخن ثمّ ينضج ويقلى قليًا جيّدًا أو يؤخذ التمر المعجون المليح يشقّق نصفين ويرمى عجمه ويؤخذ اللوز يغلى له ماء ويقشّر ويحمّص ويعمل مكان عجم التمر. ويؤخذ ماء ورد مع قليل ماء مع أوقية شيرج يخلط الجميع ويحطّه في القدر. ثمّ يضيف إليه التمر ويحرّك قليلًا قليلًا. فإذا انتهى يستعمل.

٢٣٤. الرُّخاميَّة

يسلق اللحم إلى أن ينضج فإذا بقي عليه ماء كثير شيل منه وإن كان ماء يسير صبّ عليه اللبن ويؤخذ الأرزّ ويضاف إليه المصطكاء ودار صيني ويلقى مع اللبن الحليب على اللحم ويكون للرطل اللبن أرزّ. فإذا انتهى وشيل في إناء أكل بالعسل أو بالسكّر أو الجلّاب المحلّى. يقطّع اللحم صغارًا ويغسل بماء سخن وتغلى عليه إلى أن ينضج ثمّ يقلى. فإذا يقلى قليًا جيّدًا تعمل عليه العسل أو

السكّر المحلول أو الدبس ويدقّ للأرزّ وينخل ويرمى فيه اللوز مقشور أو قلب الجوز ويدقّ له الأبازير الحارّة ويتبّل بها.

٢٣٥. الخَيْطِيَّة

يؤخذ اللحم الأحمر الطيّب يقطّع ويسلق حتّى يتهرّأ فإذا نضج نضجًا جيّدًا نشف الماء عنه. ثمّ تنشل ما عليه شعرة شعرة ويغسل بالماء إلى أن يبيض اللحم والماء الذي غسل به ويحطّ اللبن على النار ويغسل الأرزّ ويضاف إليه. ثمّ يدقّ أرزّ آخر وينخل ويذرّ عليه قليل ويخبط ثمّ قليل ويخبط ويكون للرطل اللحم أربع أواق أرزًّا وثلاثة أرطال لبن أو رطلان لبن ورطل ماء <٣٠ظ> والأرزّ المدقوق أوقيتان. فإذا انتهى يؤكل بالجلّاب.

٢٣٦. الزِّيرْبَاج

يغسل اللحم وينضج ويقلى ثمّ يعمل عليه قليل ماء ويحطّ عليه الثلثين دبس والثلث خلّ ويدقّ أرزّ وينخل ويذوّب بماء ويضاف إلى الجميع. وإذا نضج الأرزّ حطّ عليه اللوز والعنّاب ويدقّ له الأبازير الحارّة ولا يزال يده في الأرزّ حتّى لا يلتصق. ويكون الخلّ بقدر إلى أن يعتدل ثمّ يهدّأ.

٢٣٧. الكَمُّونِيَّة

يغسل اللحم ويعمل عليه قليل ماء فإذا غلى غلية حطّ عليه قليل ملح فإذا نضج حطّ عليه الجبن والبصل ويدقّ له الجبن والكراويا والكسفرة والأبازير الحارّة ويخرّط له النعنع والكسفرة الخضراء والبقل والكرفس والبقدونس. وتجعلهم في

إناء يضاف إليه الأبازير ويفقش فوق الجميع البيض ويخبط ويصبّ في القدر ولا تمسكه حتّى يغلى. فإذا غلى ذوّب له الزعفران وتدفقه في القدر وتضيف الجبن ويكون قد ترك من الأبقال فتضيف الأبقال والجبن واللوز المقشور والعنّاب ويجعل في القدر إلى أن ينتهي.

٢٣٨. السِّكْبَاج

يغسل اللحم ثمّ ينضج ويقلى ويحطّ عليه قليل ماء ويقطّع الجزر واللفت والباذنجان والبصل والكرّاث ثمّ يحطّ على اللحم. فإذا غلى على الحوائج ثلاث غليات يصبّ عليه الخلّ والدبس الثلثين دبس والثلث خلّ ويذوّب له الزعفران ويتبّل بالأبازير الحارّة والثوم والكمّون. ثمّ يستعمل.

٢٣٩. المُلُوخِيَّة

يؤخذ اللحم بعد الغسل ينضج ويقلى ثمّ يحطّ عليه الماء ويذبل الملوخية في الشمس وتخرط خرطًا دقيقًا وإلّا فتخرط من غير أن تذبل إلّا أنّها إذا ذبلت كانت أجود. ثمّ يحطّ الملوخية على الماء في القدر ويدقّ الكسفرة والكراويا والأبازير الحارّة والملح والثوم يدقّ الجميع ويذوّب بالماء ويحطّ عليها. فإذا انتهت تؤكل.

٢٤٠. القَنْبَرِيسِيَّة

يغسل اللحم بماء سخن وينشف من الماء ويحطّ في إناء يذوب له القنبريس ويحطّ في القدر فإذا غلى حطّ عليه اللحم والدار صيني وقليل ملح ويستعمل.

٢٤١. التَّبَّالة

يغسل اللحم ويحطّ في القدر وغمره ماء فإذا غلى على الأرزّ غليتين ثلاثة يحطّ السلق فإذا نضج السلق حطّ الإطرية وإن شئت <٣١و> اقفش عليه بيض والّا فلا. فإذا نضج الجميع دقّ له جبن وكسفرة وكراويا ومصطكى ودار صيني ويتبّل به ثمّ يستعمل.

٢٤٢. الزَّبِيب وَالخَلّ

يغسل اللحم ويحطّ في القدر وغمره ماء فإذا نضج يقلى ثمّ يدقّ نصف رطل زبيب ويستخرج بثلاث أواق خلّ ويصفّى. فإذا صفّى يدقّ ثانية إلى أن تخرج خاصيته. فإذا فرغ الخلّ يصفّى بماء بحيث إنه إذا ذاقه يكون معتدلًا. ثمّ يقطّع السلق والجزر واللفت والبصل والباذنجان ويحطّ الجميع في القدر. فإذا نضج الحوائج يدقّ الأبازير الحارّة مع الكمّون والثوم وتذوّب الأبازير في إناء من مرقة الطبيخ ويحطّ في القدر وتحرّك الحوائج حتّى تختلط وبعد ذلك يهدأ. ثمّ يستعمل.

٢٤٣. الإِصْفَانَخِيَّة

إذا نضج اللحم حطّ من الأرزّ ثلاث أواق ومن اللحم نصف رطل ويؤخذ جرزة إصفانخ وينقّى ويغسل ويحطّ في القدر وتحرّك قليل حتّى لا يتحطّم وإن كانت كثرة الإصفانخ يسلق الإصفانخ ناحية ويصفّى. ثمّ يحطّ على الأرزّ وتكون لا سمجة ولا شديدة ويحطّ فيها مصطكى مفروك بين الكفّين ودار صيني مقطّع. فاذا انتهى يستعمل.

٢٤٤. اللَّبَنِيَّة

يؤخذ اللحم ويغسل ويشال في إناء ويحطّ اللبن في القدر الثلث ماء والثلثين لبنًا ولا تزال تحرّكه بالمغرفة حتّى يغلى فإذا غلى يحطّ عليه ثلاث أو أربع بصلات فاذا نضج اللبن واللحم يدقّ شعرتين كمّون مع ثوم وتحطّ في القدر ويرمى عليه مصطكى ودار صينى صحاح وتهدأ إلى أن تنتهي ويستعمل.

٢٤٥. المُهَلَّبِيَّة

يؤخذ اللحم يقطّع قطعًا لطافًا ويحطّ عليه قليل ماء فاذا نضج نصف نضاجة يقلى فإذا انقلى يحطّ عليه مقدار نصف رطل ماء ويغسل الأرزّ ويصبغ بالزعفران ويرمى في القدر حتّى ينضج ويصبّ عليه الدبس أو العسل وينشف حتّى يشرب العسل أو الدبس. فإذا انتهى تستعمله.

٢٤٦. قَلِيَّة الجَزَر

ينضج اللحم ويقلى فاذا انقلى ان بقى عليه ماء شيل منه في اناء ويضاف إلى اللحم الجزر مقطّع والبصل المخروط وينشف فإذا نضج تدقّ له الأبازير الحارّة والكسفرة والكراويا مع قليل ملح وتذرّ عليه وينشف. فإذا <٣١ظ> انتهت تستعمل.

٢٤٧. الكَمْأَة

تنقع الكمأة وتحتّ حتّى لا يبقى فيها تراب ولا وسخ ويكون اللحم قد انقلى وتحطّ عليه قليل ماء وتسلق الكمأة فإذا نضجت صفّى عنها الماء وتحطّ على اللحم

المقلي في القدر وينشف ويتبّل بالكسفرة والكراويا والأبازير الحارّة ويكون في قلبه الجزر والكمأة والكسفرة الخضراء.

٢٤٨. المَضِيرَة

يقلى البصل فإذا نضج حطّ اللبن والماء النصف والنصف فإذا نضج يحطّ عليه السلق والبصل والجزر والكرّاث بدل البصل فإذا نضج الحوائج تتبّل بالثوم والكمّون وقليل ملح وإن كانت بلحم إذا غلى اللبن ومثله ما حطّ عليه اللحم. فإذا يتبّل بهذه الحوائج يستعمل.

٢٤٩. طَبَاهَجَة الباقِلّاء

يدقّ اللحم بالبصل والأبازير الحارّة والكسفرة والكراويا وتقرص أقراصًا مدوّرة مبسوطة وتحطّ عليه قليل ماء ويغلى حتّى ينضج ويقلى. ثمّ يرمى عليه الباقلّاء الأخضر المفصّص من القشر فإذا نضج الباقلّاء افقش عليه البيض ويحيى من الأبقال إلى أن ينضج الجميع ثمّ تصفّ الأبقال على الوجه وتذرّ عليه أبازير المدقّقة.

٢٥٠. صفة طَبَاهَجَة

يغسل اللحم ويعمل عليه غمره ماء فإذا نضج إن كان الماء كثيرًا شيل وقلى اللحم فإذا انقلى ردَّ عليه الماء الذي أخذ منه ويكون الباقلّاء مفصّص من القشر الكثير وقد حطّ عليه البصل وحطّ في القدر ولا يزال ينشفه حتّى ينضج

الجميع. ثمّ تدقّ الكسفرة والكراويا والأبازير الحارّة يدق الجميع ويتبّل به مع الكسفرة الخضراء وينسف نسفين ثلاثة حتّى تختلط الأبازير بهذه الحوائج ويكون قد بقي من الأبازير شيء قليل يذرّ على الوجه وتستعمل.

٢٥١. صفة حَبّ رُمَّان بِزَبِيب

يقطّع اللحم ويغسل ويقلى من غير ماء ويدقّ له الحبّ رمّان والزبيب لرطل الزبيب نصف رطل حبّ رمّان ويدقّ كلّ واحد منهما منفردًا. ثمّ يصفّى ويضاف إلى اللحم ولا يزال يدقّ ويصفّى بماء إلى أن يعتدل الطعم ويقطّع السلق والبصل والجزر واللفت والباذنجان. فإذا نضج اللحم نصف نضاجه ألقي إليه الحوائج المذكورة أوّل الصفة ويدقّ له ثوم وكمّون ويتبّل <٣٢و> به ويستعمل.

٢٥٢. صفة القَمْحِيَّة

تبّل الحنطة وتدقّ وينشف ويغسل اللحم ويحطّ في القدر هو والحنطة جملة واحدة فإذا نضج الجميع وأرخت الحنطة النشا يرمى عليها المصطكى والدار صيني ويدقّ لها الكمّون والجبن ويتبّل به وتستعمل.

٢٥٣. صفة السُّمَّاقِيَّة

يسخن الماء حتّى يمزع ويدقّ لها السمّاق ويمرس ويصفّى ويغسل اللحم ويحطّ في القدر فإذا انقلى يضاف إليه السمّاق. فإذا غلى أربع خمس غليات ارم عليه الجزر واللفت والسلق والبصل والباذنجان فإذا نضج تبّل بالجوز والبقل مخروط والكرفس والثوم والكمّون. فإذا انتهى يستعمل.

٢٥٤. صفة طَباهَجَة العَجُّور

ينضج اللحم ويقلى عليه قليل بصل ويقشّر صغار العجّور ويحطّ في القدر مع البصل وينشف. فإذا نضج يتبّل بالكسفرة والكراويا والأبازير الحارّة ويكون اللحم سمين.

٢٥٥. صفة النَّرْجِسِيَّة

ينضج اللحم ويقلى ويحطّ عليه الجزر ويغلى غليتين ثلاثة ثمّ يغسل الأرزّ ويذرّ عليه وينشف. فإذا نضج الجميع يدقّ له المصطكى والدار صيني والأبازير الحارّة ويذرّ عليه ويحرّك. وإن شئت يصفّف على الوجه بيض والّا فلا.

٢٥٦. صفة أَرُزّ بِلَبَن حَلِيب

يغلى اللبن ويغسل الأرزّ ويحطّ عليه مع قليل مصطكى ودار صيني ويكون للرطل اللبن ثلاث أواق أرزّ وتكون تحته نار ليّنة فإذا نضج يحطّ في الأواني وتخلّيه إلى أن يبرد وتأكله بعسل أو دبس أو سكّر.

٢٥٧. صفة قَلِيَّة الجَزَر بِماء اللَيْمُون

ينضج اللحم ويقلى فإذا انقلى نصف قلية يخرط عليه البصل فإذا نضج الجميع يؤخذ ماء الليمون ويمزج بأكثر منه ماء ويحطّ في القدر ويغلى غليتين ثلاثة ويتبّل بالكسفرة والكراويا والأبازير الحارّة والملح ويستعمل.

الدجاج: قبل أن يذبح يكدّ كدًّا قويًا حتّى لا يقدر يطير ولا يمشي من التعب فعند ذلك يذبح ويشوي فإنّ لحمه ينعم.

٢٥٨. صفة

تؤخذ الفراريج ويسلق وليكن جميع الأعضاء مفصولة مقطّعة فإذا سلق ونضج تقلب عليه شيرج غمره ويطجّن الجميع وكلّ قليل يرشّ عليه كزبرة يابسة ويجعل في زبدية. <٣٢ظ>

٢٥٩. صفة لَيْمُونِيَّة

يؤخذ دجاج ويصلق فإذا نضج تأخذ مرقته وتعصر عليها ليمون أخضر ويجعل فيه سكّر وعرق نعنع وقرفة ومصطكاء ويقلب على الدجاج ويغلى غليتين ويغرف.

٢٦٠. نَوْع آخَر

يؤخذ دجاج يصلق ويجعل في مرقته لوز مقشور مدقوق ناعمًا ويستخرج من منخل صفيق ويرمى فيه قطع يقطين. عند عقده يقلب عليه ماء ليمون أخضر شيء يرضيك حمضه ويغلى على الدجاج.

٢٦١. نَوْع آخَر مِثْلُهُ

عوّض اللوز قرطم ويطبخ إلى أن يصير قوام القنبريسية.

٢٦٢. نوع أخر

يؤخذ الدجاج المسمن يصلق فإذا نضج نصف نضجه يقشّر لوز ويدقّ ناعمًا إلى

أن يلعب في دهنه. يقلب عليه مرقة الدجاج ويصفّى من منخل ضيّق وتعيده على الدجاج ويقلب عليه ستة سبعة دراهم من اللوز يحلّ في مرقة الدجاج ويجعل فيه السكّر ويعقّد على النار بحيث يشرب بالجمجة. فإذا أخذ حدّه يعصر له ليمون أخضر ويقلب عليه بعد تصفيته ويغلى غليتين ثلاثة ويجعل فيه فستق مسموط ونعنع وقرفة ومصطكاء ويغرف. وهو من أجود المأكولات. وإن شئت تعمل فيه قطع يقطين كبارًا فافعل. والله الموفّق.

٢٦٣. حَبّ رُمَّان

يدقّ ناعمًا ويصفّى ويختّر بقلب لوز ويعمل فيه سكّر وعرق نعنع وقرفة ومصطكاء ويعقّد على النار ويلقى فيه الدجاج مصلوقًا مطجّنًا ويغلى عليه. وإن أردت تعمل فيه يقطينًا افعل.

٢٦٤. صفة البُنْدُقِيَّة

ينضج الدجاج ويطجّن بالشيرج ويشال في إناء ثمّ يحطّ في القدر الماء والماء ورد والسكّر البياض. ثمّ يغلى إلى أن يصير جلّاب ويقشّر البندق بماء حار ويدقّ وينخل ويذرّ عليه. ثمّ يصبّ الجميع فوق الدجاج ويستعمل.

٢٦٥. صفة سِتّ النُّوبَة

يؤخذ الدجاج يسمط ثمّ يغلى ثلثي نضاجه ثمّ يطجّن بالشيرج ويشال في إناء. يؤخذ لوز مقشّر بماء حارّ يحمّص ثمّ يدقّ يصفّى مثل اللبن الحليب ويشال على النار ويضاف إليه سكّر بياض ثمّ يذوّب زعفران ويغلى على ماء اللوز والسكّر. ثمّ

يغلى إلى أن يأخذ قوام. ثمّ يؤخذ الدجاج يحطّ فوق الجميع ولوز وعنّاب وزبيب أسود ويكون منقوع بماء ورد ومسك يرمى على الجميع. ثمّ يؤخذ فستق يقشّر بماء حارّ ويشقق نصفين نصفين ويغلى على الجميع. ثمّ يعمل على الجميع دهن لوز محمّص ويستعمل.

٢٦٦. صفة الأَرُزّ المُفَلْفَل

<**٣٣و**> إذا نضج اللحم نقّى الأرزّ وغسل وحطّ عليه القرفة والمصطكى وقليل ملح ويكون عند حطّ الأرزّ غمر اللحم ماء وللنصف رطل لحم ثلاثة أواق أرزّ ويحطّ على رأس القدر قليل ماء حتّى يسخن فإن عازه شيء صبّ عليه ويستعمل.

٢٦٧. صفة السَّنْبُوسَك

يدقّ اللحم دقًّا ناعمًا ويسلق ولا تبرح يده فيه حتّى لا يتكتّل فإذا نضج ونشف وانقلى ولم يبق فيه ماءه يخرط له البقول الكرفس والبقدونس والكسفرة الخضراء والنعنع. وتدقّ الكسفرة والكراويا والأبازير الحارّة وتخلط باللحم والبقول ويدقّ الجوز واللوز ويخلط بالجميع وإمّا أن يرشّ عليه قليل ليمون بحيث لا يكون كثيرًا يتهرّأ الدقاق وقليل سمّاق بحيث لا يكون كثيرًا يتهرّأ الدقاق ويقلى بالشيرج أو الألية.

٢٦٨. فصل

وأمّا العجج فهي على صفة السنوسك ويضاف إليها البيض ويقلى بالزيت وإن كانت العجج بغير لحم يخرط لها البقول الكرفس والبقدونس والنعنع والكسفرة

الخضراء. ويدقّ الكسفرة اليابسة والكراويا والأبازير الحارّة والجبن والجوز ويخلط كلّ قليل من هذه الحوائج ببيضتين تصير عجّة ويقلى بالزيت وتستعمل.

٢٦٩. صفة المُتَوَكِّلِيَّة

ينضج اللحم ويقلى فإذا نضج دقّ له الكسفرة والكراويا والأبازير الحارّة وقليل كمّون وملء الكفّ ثوم مقشّر وملح. ويدقّ الجميع دقًّا ناعمًا ويخلط على اللحم المقلي ويقلى معه ويدقّ أقراص الترمس ويصفّى بالمنخل ويدقّ الجوز ناعمًا ويضاف إلى المصفّي ويكون سمج. ثمّ يصبّ على اللحم المقلي والأبازير إلى أن يغلى. ثمّ تهدّأ النار تحته ويستعمل.

٢٧٠. صفة المَفَرَّكَة

يسلق المعاليق من الخرفان فإذا نضجت يغلى نصف غلية ويخرط عليه البصل. ثمّ يقلى فإذا نضج الجميع يفقش عليه البيض ويحرّك فإذا استوى تبّل بالكسفرة والكراويا والأبازير الحارّة ويستعمل.

٢٧١. صفة

يغسل اللحم ثمّ ينضج فإذا نضج قطّع عليه البصل والسلق فإذا نضج افقش عليه البيض ويتبّل بالأبازير الحارّة.

٢٧٢. صفة المَغْمُومَة

ينضج اللحم ويقلى ثمّ يحطّ غمره <٣٣ظ> ماء ويؤخذ الباذنجان يشقّق أربعًا مع بصل ويحطّ في القدر وينشف حتّى ينضج الجميع ثمّ يتبّل بالكسفرة والكراويا والأبازير الحارّة.

٢٧٣. صفة البُورَانِيَّة

ينضج اللحم ويقلى فإذا انقلى نصف قلية حطّ عليه البصل فإذا نضج الجميع قلى له الباذنجان ناحية عن اللحم. ثمّ يضاف إلى اللحم في القدر. ثمّ يتبّل بالكسفرة والكراويا والملح.

٢٧٤. صفة المَحْشِي

يؤخذ السمك الطري ويقشّر فلوسه بالسكّين ويشقّق ويغسل وينشف من الماء. ثمّ يؤخذ البقول البقدونس والكرفس والنعنع والكسفرة الخضراء يخرط الجميع جيّدًا ويضاف إلى ماء الليمون وأوقية سمّاق منسوف ومثله جزر ومثله قنبريس ومثله طحينة. ثمّ يؤخذ كسفرة وثوم وكراويا وأبازير حارّة يدقّ الجميع مع قليل ملح ويضاف إلى الحوائج كلّها. ثمّ يحشى به السمك ويحطّ في مقلى ويحطّ عليه قليل زيت طيّب قليل الحرارة والا النصف شيرج والنصف زيت ويشوى في الفرن ويستعمل.

٢٧٥. وأمّا الدَّجَاج

فيسمط ويشقّ جوفه ويغسل ثمّ يحطّ في القدر وغمره ماء إلى أن ينضج نصف

نضاجه. ثمّ يحشى بهذه الحوائج على هذه الصفة ويحطّ في مقلى ويصبّ عليه شيرج بدل الزيت لأنّ الزيت يقطّع زفرة السمك والشيرج يطيّب الدجاج. ثمّ يشوى في الفرن ويستعمل.

٢٧٦. وإنْ كانَ المَحْشِي طَبِيخ بِلَحْمٍ

يقطّع اللحم قطعًا لطافًا ويغسل بماء سخن ثمّ يحطّ في القدر وغمره ماء ويطبخ إلى أن ينضج ويشال الماء عنه في إناء ويقلى قليًا جيّدًا ويقطّع عليه بصل ثمّ يضاف إليه الماء المشال عنه فإذا غلى شيل من الماء قليلًا يذوّب به الحوائج المحشي ويحطّ في القدر إلى أن يغلى ثمّ يهدّأ.

فائدة: إذا كان الطبخ قد لحقه حريق قليل يؤخذ الأشنان يصرّ في خرقة صرًا جيّدًا ويحطّ في الطبيخ ويغوص إلى أسفل القدر ويخلّي ساعة فإنّه يقلع منه الحراقة. **وإن كان الطبخ كثير الملح** يؤخذ قشر البطّيخ الأصفر اليابس يرمى في القدر ويغوص إلى أسفلها فإنّه يقلع الملوحة منه.

٢٧٧. صفة عَدَس مُصَفًّى بِالخَلّ وَالدِّبْس

يحتاج الرطل العدس المجروش المنسوف لثلاثة أرطال ماء ورطلين دبس وثلثي رطل خلّ واللوز والعنّاب والزعفران مهما أردت.

٢٧٨. صفة المُهَلَّبِيَّة بِغَيْر لَحْمِ

للرطل الأرزّ أربعة أرطال ماء ورطل عسل نحل أو رطلين دبس وأوقيتين شيرج وللعسل ثلاثة <٣٤و> دراهم زعفران وللدبس درهم زعفران والحرارات

بقدر الحاجة.

٢٧٩. حَبّ رُمَّان

وهذا النوع من أطيب ما يكون يؤخذ حبّ رمّان ويصفّى بعد دقّه وصلقه ويجعل فيه سكّر ونعنع وقرفة ويرمى فيه الدجاج مغسولًا إلى أن ينضج ويستعمل.

٢٨٠. نَوْع آخَر

يؤخذ حبّ رمّان ويصفّى ويحلّى بسكّر ويخثّر بقلب لوز ويستعمل فيه زنجبيل حارّ وقطع سفرجل وتفّاح فتحي ويقطّع الدجاج المسلوق ويطجّن ويلقى عليه.

٢٨١. كُزْبَرِيَّة

يؤخذ دجاج يصلق ويقطّع ويقلى ببصل وشيرج وأبازير حارّة وثوم مدقوق وكزبرة خضراء فإذا انقلى يدقّ ورق الكزبرة دقًّا ناعمًا. ثمّ يعيد المرقة عليها ويجعل الكزبرة فيها مثل الملوخية.

٢٨٢. نَوْع آخَر

يطبخ الدجاج كما ذكرنا ويقلى بثوم وبصل مخروط بالشيرج ودهن دجاج وأبازير حارّة فإذا انقلى يدقّ الكزبرة الخضراء دقًّا ناعمًا ويجعل في مرقه ويصفّى خاثرًا من منخل دفعات وتقليه على الدجاج ويجعل فيه دقيق أرزّ منخول جيّدًا فإنّه يخثّر ويبقى له طعم. وهو من الأطعمة الغريبة.

٢٨٣. صفة طَبْخ تَمْر هِنْدِي لِلصَّفْراء يُسَهِّل الطَّبْع

يصلق الدجاج ويطجّن ويمرس التمر هندي بمرقة الدجاج بعد أن يمرس دفعات ويجعل فيه سكّر ويعقّد على النار مثل حبّ الرمّان بنار ليّنة ويعمل فيه نعنع وقرفة.

٢٨٤. صِفَةُ طَبِيخِ أَمْبَرْبارِيس يَنْفَعُ الإِسْهالَ

يصلق الإمبرباريس ويصفي ويعقّد بالسكّر ويعمل فيه الدجاج وقليل نعنع.

٢٨٥. زِيرْبَاج

يؤخذ دجاج يصلق ويطجّن ويؤخذ مرقة الدجاج ويجعل فيها سكّر وخلّ وزعفران ويختّر بقلب لوز مسلوق مدقوق منزل من منخل وقليل نشا. ويعمل فيه قلب فستق ولوز فإذا أردت أن تعمل مع الخلّ ماء الليمون. فإنّه يجئ طيّب.

٢٨٦. صفة طبَيخ بَقْدُونِس

يؤخذ الدجاج يصلق ويطجّن ثمّ يؤخذ بقدونس من الورق ويدقّ ناعمًا ويسقى خلًّا ويدقّ إلى أن يخلط جميعه بالخلّ ويصير رقيقًا بحيث يرتفع على الخبز ويجعل فيه زنجبيل وفلفل وثوم وأطراف طيب ويوضع الدجاج فيه وهو سخن. فإنّه مليح.

٢٨٧. صفةٌ لَذِيذَة الطَّعْم

تؤخذ دجاجة سمينة تصلق وتطجّن حتّى تحمر وتهندم ويؤخذ بيض يقشّر بياضه بحيث يبقى الصفار وتؤخذ مرقة الدجاج ودهنه وتجعل على الدجاجة المطجّنة

المقطّعة وصفار البيض صحاح. ويلقى على المرقة ودهن الدجاج وقرفة ومصطكى وقليل <٣٤ظ> كزبرة يابسة وفلفل ويغلى غليانًا كثيرًا بحيث تنقص بعض المرقة ويغرف. فإنّها لذيذة.

٢٨٨. طَبْخ تُوت شَامِي

يؤخذ التوت يمرس ويصفّى ويعمل فيه سكّر ويعقّد ويجعل فيه نعنع وأطراف طيب ويجعل فيه دجاج مطجّن.

٢٨٩. طَبْخ قَرَاصِيَا بَلَدِيَّة نَاضِجَة

تؤخذ القراصيا تصلق بقليل ماء وتصفّى ويعقّد على النار وتجعل والدجاج المطجّن.

فائدة: إذا طبخ الدجاج السمين ووضع لكلّ دجاجة نصف أوقية ألية فإنّها تصير دهن دجاج.

٢٩٠. نَوْع مِن السَّنْبُوسَك

يؤخذ لحم الأفخاذ والتقاوير ويدقّ على قرمة بصاطور[٢١] ويصلق حتّى ينضج ثمّ يصفّى عنه الماء ويدقّ في الهاون حتّى ينعم. ثمّ يجعل في دست ويقلب عليه دهن ألية وكزبرة يابسة ودار صيني ومصطكى وفلفل ويحمّص ويجعل عليه بقدونس مخروطًا جزءين ونعنع جزء وسذاب نصف جزء ويغلى عليه. ثمّ يقلب عليه خلّ حادق ويغلى حتّى يصير الخلّ أبيض. ثمّ يقلب عليه ماء الليمون ويغلى

٢١ هكذا في النص.

غليات وبعد ذلك يحشى رقاق السنبوسك فإنّه أجود ما يعمل.

٢٩١. نوع آخر

يزاد في هذا الحشو سمّاق وقلب فستق وقلب جوز.

٢٩٢. نَوْع آخَر

يؤخذ لباب خبز يصبغ بزعفران وينزله من الغربال ويقلب عليه سكّر مدقوق وعسل نحل وشيرج ويعمل مثل الأسيوطية فإذا أستوى يعمل فيه خشخاش وقلب فستق ويحشى به السنبوسك.

٢٩٣. شَرَائح

يشرّح البشتمازك[٢٢] والتقاوير عراضًا ويجعل في سيخ ويدهن بشيرج وزيت وكزبرة يابسة وثوم مدقوق ويشوى في السيخ على نار هادئة.

٢٩٤. نَوْع آخَر

أحسن ما يكون البشتمازك يقطّع قطعًا ويقطّع مثله ألية ويغرز في السيخ قطعة ألية وقطعة لحم ويشوى على نار فحم وكلّما أراد الدهن ينقط يشال رأس السيخ حتّى ينقط الدهن على اللحم ويدهن بماء ورد وشيرج يفعل به كذلك دفعات حتّى يستوي ويرشّ عليه كزبرة يابسة ويؤكل.

٢٢ في الأصل: بستمارك.

٢٩٥.

يؤخذ اللحم يشرّح عريضًا ويعلّق في خطاف على رأس التنّور حتّى يقطر منه الدم والماء منه كما يفعل بالشرائح المدخّنة ويجعل في نعارة ومن الناس من يجعل على اللحم أوّل ما ينزل من النعارة ماء تفّاح وماء سفرجل. ومنهم من يجعل عليه الخلّ وماء الليمون ونعنع وأطراف طيب ومنهم من يزيده ماء حصرم. ومنهم من يعمل عليه ماء رمّان طري وسكّر. وسائر أنواع الشرائح التي في النعارة عندما <٣٥و> يحطّ اللحم في النعارة يقطر عليه زيت طيّب وماء ورد ومصطكاء وقرفة ويسدّ رأسها ويجعلها في الفرن ولا يكون عليها ماء.

٢٩٦.

يؤخذ كبد يصلق ويعمل فيه أبزار حارّ[٢٣] وأطراف طيب ويحشى السجق ويشوى. فإنّه طيّب.

٢٩٧.

يؤخذ أضلاع لحم وقصبة وتقويره يقطّع ويؤخذ قدر كبير يسدّ على رأسها مصفاة واسعة ويجعل اللحم عليه ويجعل في القدر نصفها ماء ويرمى فيه بصل وحمّص وقرفة ومصطكاء وشبتّ ويغطّى ويطيّن حافتها بعجين قويًا ويجعل على نار هادئة من العشاء إلى بكرة وعند الأكل يسقى بالمرقة لباب كماج ويجعل عليه اللحم فإنّه لذيذ جيّد.

٢٣ هكذا في الأصل.

٢٩٨. مُخّ مَصْنُوع

يعمل قصب نحاس مثل عظم الفخذ يكون مسدود الرأس الواحد ثمّ يؤخذ كبد يصلق ويعمل منه جزء ومن الألية جزءين ويدقّ دقًّا ناعمًا ويعمل في أنابيب النحاس ويسدّ رأسها بعجين ويجعل في ماء يغلى ويصلق إلى أن ينضج. ثمّ ينفض في زبدية. فإنّه يجئ مثل المخّ لونًا وطعمًا.

٢٩٩. مُلُوخِيَّة

يؤخذ اللحم ويقطّع صغارًا ثمّ يدقّ بعضه ببصل وكزبرة ويعمل فيه قرفة ومصطكاء ويصلق اللحم نصف نضاجه ويقلى ببصلة مخروطة وثوم مدقوق بكزبرة خضراء وفلفل وكزبرة يابسة وكراوية وملح. ويعمل على اللحم دهن ألية ويقلى حتّى يحمر ويجعل فيه المدقّقة وتغليه. فإذا أخذ حدّه تعيد عليه مرقة اللحم ويغلى عليه وتخرط ملوخية رفيعة وترمى عليه وتغلى بحيث لا تكون رقيقة ولا ظاهرة الحرارة.

٣٠٠. نَوْع آخَر

ومنهم من يقلب عليه ماء ليمون أخضر أو عتيق ويغلى غليات بعد القلي حتّى يدخل فيه الحمض وعند ذلك يعيد المرقة ويطجّنها على العادة.

٣٠١.

ومنهم من يكون قد شوى ستّ بصلات أو نحوها حتّى يصير مثل المخّ من النضاج ويدقّ في الهاون مع الكزبرة الخضراء أو اليابسة والثوم والفلفل دقًّا ناعمًا

ويلقى على الملوخية بعد نضاجها ويقلب عليها الدهن ويغرف. وفي غير أوان الملوخية تخرط خبيزة لكلّ زبدية <٣٥ظ> حزمة خبيزة وكفّ ملوخية يابسة تفركها باليد وتخلطه معها.

٣٠٢. البَاذِنْجَان

قبل أن يقلى ينبغي أن يغرز بسكّين وينقع في ماء وملح حتّى يخرج منه الماء الأسود ثمّ يغسله ويعصره ويصلق نصف صلقه ويعصر.

٣٠٣. بَاذِنْجَان مَحْشِي

يؤخذ باذنجان كبار يقطّع رأس الباذنجان من القمع ويقوّر إلى داخل ثمّ ينزع ما فيها من اللبّ ولا يحوّر على القشر ثمّ يؤخذ اللحم يدقّ مدقّقة. ثمّ يصلق فإذا نضج يدقّ في الهاون ثاني مرّة حتّى ينعم. ثمّ يجعل في دست ويقلب عليه كزبرة يابسة وكراوية وفلفل ودار صيني وكزبرة خضراء مخروطة وبقدونس مخروط مقدارًا كثيرًا ويقلى الجميع حتّى يتحمّص. ثمّ يطيّبه بالملح ويحشى الباذنجان. ثمّ يغطّى بالذي قطع من أقماعه ويغرز ثلاثة أسياخ خشب. ثمّ يحطّ في الدست ويقلى بدهن ألية حتّى يحمر ويعمل في زبدية ويذرّ عليه كزبرة يابسة وتقلع الأسياخ منه ويؤكل.

٣٠٤. قُلْقَاس مُتَوَكِّلِيَّة

يصلق اللحم ويعمل مدقّقة ويقلى بدهن ويقطّع له بصل ويقلى مع اللحم ويجعل عليه ثوم مدقوق وكزبرة خضراء ويابسة وأبازير حارّة إلى أن يأخذ

حدّه. ثمّ يقطّع القلقاس ويصلق حتّى تطلع منه الرغوة فإذا طلعت يصفّى عنه الماء ويعمل عليه قليل ملح ونقطة زيت طيّب ويعرك جيّدًا ويغسل دفعات حتّى ينظف من اللزوجة وبعد ذلك يجعل عليه اللحم ويغلى على نار هادئة حتّى ينضج ويغرف.

٣٠٥. الفُولِيَّة

لابدّ لها من الزعتر الأخضر وهو الأصل ويقلّل مرقها ويفقش عليها البيض والباقي معلوم.

٣٠٦. نَوْع مِن أَنْوَاع النَّرْجِسِيَّة

يقطّع اللحم صغارًا ويصلق ويعمل مدقّقة بأبزار وكزبرة خضراء ويكتل صغارًا ويقلى يدهن وينحت الجزر مثل النرجسية ويرمى على اللحم ويغطّى ولا يجعل على الجزر ماء ويترك حتّى ينضج في الدهن على نار هادئة فإنّه مليح.

٣٠٧. نَوْع مِن حِصْرِمِيَّة

يؤخذ الحصرم ويفرط ويصلق حتّى يتهرّأ ويصفّى ويشال <٣٦و> على النار ويجعل فيه لحم نيء ويصلق ومدقّقة كبار وحمّص مجروش وأرزّ وأضلاع سلق وبصل ونعنع ويقطين وباذنجان يقطّع نصفين وتفّاح حامض يقطّع نصفين ويخرج منه حبّه وعراميشه وشعير أخضر. فإن لم يجد فيابس ويختّر بالخبز وبالأرزّ المدقوق أحسن. فإنّها تجيء بيضاء وإذا نضج يدقّ له ثوم وكزبرة خضراء.

٣٠٨. طَعَام اللِفْت

يقدّم اللحم على العادة[٢٤]. فإذا احمر قليًا بلا ألية رمى عليه اللفت وغطاءه إلى أن يستوي يغرفه.

٣٠٩. لَوْنٌ مِن أَنْوَاعِ السُّمَّاق

يؤخذ السمّاق يدقّ وينسف زهرته ويؤخذ الحبّ وما بقى من الزهر ينقع في ماء ثمّ يخرط بقدونس ونعنع وسذاب ولباب خبز ينزل من منخل ويعرك مع البقول حتّى يذبل وينزل عليه زهرة السمّاق وأبزار وزعتر يابس ويكثر من الزعتر وأطراف طيب ويعجن بماء ليمون وطحينة وقليل من لبن وقلب جوز مدقوق محمّص. ويعمل منه حشو ويقطّع فيه ليمونًا مالحًا صغارًا. ثمّ يؤخذ الماء المنقوع فيه السمّاق ويجعل في القدر ويرمى فيه اللحم والكباب ويعمل في الكباب ليمون مالح مقطّع صغارًا ويصلق ويرمى فيه أضلاع سلق وباذنجان ويقطين وقطع سفرجل ورمّان وجزر ولفت. وإذا نضج الجميع يرمى فيه القرط مخروط وثوم مدقوق بكزبرة خضراء ويرمى في الحشو وحمّص مجروش في مرقة اللحم ويغلى غليتين ويحمّص على قدر ما تريد ولا يخلّيه يغلى كثيرًا يسوّد ولا تكثر من زهرته. وإن أردته يستخرج الزهر في ماء ليمون وكذلك في مرقة اللحم حتّى لا يجئ مكمد اللون وإن يرمى فيه البندق كثيرًا فهو أجود من الجزر.

---

٢٤ أي بالأبازير والحرارات كما يقدم من غير اللفت.

٣١٠. نَوْع آخَر

يؤخذ السمّاق يدقّ وينقع في ماء ويصفّى ويحطّ في القدر ويحلّى بسكّر ويخثّر بقلب لوز مسموط مدقوق مستخرج في ماء سمّاق ويعقّد على النار. ويؤخذ اللحم يصلق ويغرق بدهن وبصل ويجعله في السمّاق ويغلى عليه حتّى يدخل في اللحم الحموضة ويفتق بقليل ماء ليمون.

٣١١. تَمْرِيَّة تُسَمَّى المَعْشُوقَة

يؤخذ رطل لحم بلا عظم يقطّع صغارًا ويصلق نصف صلقه ويصفّى عنه الماء ويجعل في مقلاة ويؤخذ <٣٦ظ> ثلثي رطل ألية يقطّع صغارًا قدر اللحم ويضاف إلى اللحم ويجعل على نار هادئة ويغلى نصف غلية حتّى يحمر الدهن. يؤخذ رطلان تمر جيّد ينزع نواه ويحشى عوّضه قلب فستق مدقوق بسكّر معجون بماء ورد ومسك وتضيف التمر فوق اللحم والدهن ويجعل على نار هادئة حتّى ينضج التمر. ويجعل عليه أمقال بيض ويذرّ على أمقال البيض فستق صحاح مسموط ممسّك. فإنّه جيّد.

٣١٢. نَوْع مِن أَنْواع المَأْمُونِيَّة

تؤخذ الألية يصلق بماء حتّى ينضج وينهرئ ويصفّى عنها الماء وبعد ذلك يمرس وتخرج الألية من المنخل وتعمل في زبدية ويغسل لها أرزّ ويدقّه وينخله ويصحن له سكّر. ويجعله مع الألية في دست ويطبخ على نار هادئة حتّى يستوي ويبقى لها قوامّ ويبسط في صحن ويرمى فيها قلب فستق صحاح.

٣١٣. نَوْع آخَر

يؤخذ الأرزّ يغسل ويدقّ ناعمًا وينخل من المنخل ويؤخذ لبن حليب طيّب تغليه على النار ويجعل فيه سكّر حتّى يذوب ويلقى فيه الأرزّ ويطبخ عصيدة مرقة ويجعل عليها دهن الية مسلية شيئًا كثيرًا. فإنّها تشرب الدهن ولا تزال تطبخها على نار هادئة حتّى يخرج الدهن علامة طبخها أن يقذف الدهن ويحمر الأرزّ ويعمل فيه قلب فستق وحبّ رمّان وأقراص ليمون مصبّغات.

٣١٤. نَوْع آخَر وَهُو مَلِيح يُطْبَخ بِصُدُورِ الدَّجَاج

يؤخذ الدجاج السمان يصلق ويطجّن بالشيرج ويؤخذ صدورها يبرد وينسّل مثل الشعر فإذا فعلت ذلك خذ أرزًّا اغسله ودقّه وانخله ناعمًا واعمل لكلّ رطل أرزّ صدر دجاجتين منسولة والسكّر على قدر ما تريد من حلاوتها وخذ لبنًا حليبًا اغليه وحلّ فيه السكّر حتّى يصير شديد الحلاوة. فإذا ذاب السكّر اجعل فيه صدر الدجاجتين المنسولة واغل غليات. ثمّ ردّ الأرزّ وحرّكه حتّى لا يلتزق فإذا صار مثل العصيدة ألق عليه دهن ألية واطبخها على نار هادئة حتّى يقذف دهنها ويحمر لونها ولا ترفع يدك من تحريكها. فإذا صارت <٣٧و> تمدّ في الصحن أغرفها وارم في وسطها فستق مقشور فإنّها تجيء محيطة بصدور الدجاج. وهذه عملت في دار الملك الأشرف رحمة الله تعالى.

٣١٥. هَرِيسَة الفُستُق

يؤخذ الفستق يسمط وينشف ويحطّ على نار هادئة ويدقّ دقًّا ناعمًا ولكلّ رطل فستق صدر دجاجتين يصلق صدور الدجاج بلا ملح ويطجّن بزيت طيّب

وشيرج ويبرد. فإذا بردت ينزع منها العظام وينسّل اللحم ومهما نسلته تعمله على ورق سلق حتّى لا يزال رطبًا. ثمّ يعمل جلّاب دقيق يكون نصف عقاده. ثمّ ترمى فيه صدور الدجاج ويحرّك بنشّابة فإذا احمرت الصدور يرمى فيه الفستق المذكور أوّلًا ويضرب بالمغرفة ضربًا قويًا مثل الهريسة حتّى ينعقد ويجعل فيه لبنًا محلولًا بماء ورد لكلّ رطل فستق ربع أوقية ونصف الدهن . . . . . يعمل في . . . . قويًّا . . . . . [٢٥] العمق والصفر ويجعل فيه مسك وماء ورد ويبسط في الصحون ويزين بأقراص ليمون والسكّر المدقوق.

٣١٦. فُسْتُقِيَّة بِلا صُدُور دَجَاج

يؤخذ فستق يسمط ويحمّص ويدقّ حتّى يلعب في دهنه سياقة الهريسة ويعقّد الجلّاب ويرمى فيه الفستق والنشا ثمّ يطبخ حتّى ينعقد ويستعمل ويصبغ بورق السلق.

٣١٧. لَيْمُون مَالِح

يؤخذ ليمون مالح يقطّع صغارًا ويجعل في إناء ويعصر عليه ليمون أخضر ونارنج – فإنّه أوطأ من الليمون – غمره ويقلب عليه زيت طيّب وكزبرة يابسة محمّصة مدقوقة وبقدونس مخروط ونعنع وسذاب. فإنّه أجود ما يكون وأطيب.

٣١٨. نَوْع آخَر

يؤخذ الليمون يقشّر من قشره الخارج بحيث لا يخرج القشر الرقيق ويدهن بزعفران وسكّر مذوّب وتجعله في قطرميز ويقلب عليه ماء ليمون غمره وملح

٢٥ سطر مطموس في المخطوطة.

جيّد يحفظه من التلف ويختم بزيت فإنّه صنف آخر غريب جيّد مليح.

٣١٩. آخَر

<٣٧ظ> يؤخذ خلّ خمر يحلّى بسكّر أو عسل ويقلب عليه رطب ويجعل على الليمون المالح.

٣٢٠. بَقْسَمَاط

يؤخذ دقيق مثلّث ويعجن بلبن وسمن ويعمل صفة ركب وعيار كلّ أربعة أرطال دقيق رطل سمن. ثمّ يعجن باللبن الحليب ويعمل فيه الأبزار. ويقرّص طلم مدوّرة ويشقّ بالسكّين صليبًا ويخبز فإذا خبز يفصص بعضه من بعض. ثمّ يقمّره ثاني مرّة ويدهن وجهه بالعسل وبيض وماء ورد.

٣٢١. نَوْع

يؤخذ تمر ينزع نواة ويجعل فيه قلب فستق مسموط مدقوق معجون بالسكّر وماء يضاف إليه من المسك ويحشى به التمر. ثمّ يؤخذ عجين القطايف يضاف إليه نشا محلول بماء ورد ويضيفه للعجين مثل حلاوة المشبّك ويغطّس التمر في العجين ويقلى بالشيرج في الذي له قوام. ثمّ يغطّس مرّة ثانية بالخمير ويقلى ومرّة ثانية ويرمى في الجلّاب ويصفّ في الصحن ويذرّ عليه سكّر وقلب فستق ويرشّ عليه ماء ورد ومسك.

ٱلْبَابُ ٱلسَّابِعُ عَشَرُ

فِي شَيّء مِن عَمَل البَوَارِدَ

٣٢٢. صفة السِّلْق

يؤخذ السلق يقطّع صغارًا به كلّ ورقة قدر أصبع ويسلق ويعصر من مائه ويعمل عليه لبن مصفّى وثوم.

٣٢٣. صفة أُخْرَى مِنْهُ

يسلق ويقلى بشيرج ويؤخذ سمّاق منقوع في ماء مستحلب ويصفّى من خرقة ويدقّ الجوز ناعمًا ويصبّ عليه ماء الليمون ويزاد ماء ليمون وفلفل وثوم وزنجبيل وأطراف طيب ويجعل على السلق وعلى وجهه زيت طيّب ويعمل بقدونس ونعنع وسذاب. وإن أردت بماء حصرم فافعل.

٣٢٤. صفة العَجُّور

يؤخذ العجّور يقشر ويسلق ويعصر من مائه ويطجّن بزيت طيّب وشيرج وبعد أن

يشقّق ويخرط عليه بصل جيّد ويطجّن ويرمى عليه بقدونس مخروط ويقلى حتّى يذبل ويجعل الجميع على العجّور المقلي ويقلب عليه خلّ حادق ويغلى غليات ويجعل فيه أطراف طيب وكزبرة يابسة وعروق نعنع وفلفل. <٣٨و> ومنهم من يجعل يسير ثوم ومنهم من يجعله بسكّر ومنهم من يجعل قلب جوز مدقوق أمّا قلب الفستق فإنّه لذيذ في كلّ شيء.

٣٢٥. صفة القَرْع بِاللّبَن

يحتاج إلى يقطين ولبن حامض وثوم وزيت طيّب وكمّون أسود قليل يقطّع اليقطين على العادة رقيق ويسلق ويعصر من الماء ويدقّ الثوم بعد أن يقشّر ويضرب في اللبن ويعمل معه قليل زيت طيّب ويعمل اليقطين في اللبن ويعمل في الأوعية ويذرّ عليه الكمّون.

أَلْبَابُ ٱلثَّامِنُ عَشَرُ

الخِلال

.٣٢٦

كلّ بارد يابس من الأخشاب ينفع للخلال وهو أنفع من الحارّ اليابس وأجود ما استعمل الخلال في الفم بعد أن ينقع في الماء ليلة أو ليلتين ليعوج في التخليل ولئلّا ينكسر بين الأسنان فيحتاج إلى إخراجه بالمنقاش وهو يتخذ من الصفصاف وهو بارد يابس قليل الإضرار بالأسنان كبير النفع وهو أجود ما جعل لتنقية الأسنان.

أَلْبَابُ ٱلتَّاسِعُ عَشَرُ

الطِّيب

٣٢٧. صفة بُخُور

قشر ليمون وقشر نارنجة ومرسين وظفر وصندروس ومصطكاء وزعفران شعر وصندل وسكّر نبات يدقّ كلّ واحد على حدة ويوزن بالسوية ويعجن بماء ورد نصيبيني ويقرص وشال.

٣٢٨. صفة طِيب أَهْل اليَمَن

يؤخذ سكّر يذوب في ماء ورد ويسكب على المحكّة ويحكّ فيه كافور ويسير عنبر خام وصندل أبيض وعود طيّب يجمع الجميع في شيء ويخلط ويطيّب به.

٣٢٩. صفة ماء عَجِيب الرَّائِحَة يُصْلِح للمُلُوك

يؤخذ زهر ونبق وورد نصيبيني في وعاء ويستقطر ثمّ يعمل في ذلك المسك ويختم رأس الإناء فإنّه طيّب الرائحة.

٣٣٠. صفة أَقْرَاص

يؤخذ قشر أترنج ونارنج وكبّاد وقشر تفّاح وأس يدقّ الجميع ناعمًا وينخل ويؤخذ من كلّ واحد نصف درهم وسدس درهم عود قمارى وصندل مقاصيري من كلّ واحد مثقالان ولادن عنبري ومصطكى <٣٨ظ> وزعفران شعر مهرش ويجعل في قعر قدر ثانية والحوائج أجزاء متساوية ويجعل القدر الذي فيه القرص على رأسها مكبوبة ويطيّن بحيث لا تخرج منه الرائحة. ويجعل القدر التي فيها البخور على نار هادئة لينة ليدخن فإذا احترق البخور يفتح القدر ويخرج وينشف في الظل ويطحن ناعمًا ويجعل فيه العنبر هو والعود المسحوق وقليل مسك ويستعمل فيه قليل زباد على ما تريد.

٣٣١. صفة حَبٍّ يُطَيِّب النَّكْهَةَ ويُبَخِّر مِنْهُ

يؤخذ عود درهمان وثلث وقرنفل دانقين وزعفران قيراط جوزة ربع درهم ومسك قيراط ونصف سكّر دانقين ويحلّ له وزن دانق كثيراء بماء ورد نصيبيني ويعجن به وكبّب حبّ كالحمّص ويجفّف في الظلّ ويجعل في الفم من بكرة وعند النوم وإن أراد ببخر به فعل.

٣٣٢. صفة حَبّ طِيب النَّكْهَة

ويقوّي الأسنان ويهضم الطعام بعد الأكل ويجعل في الفم منه عند النوم فتبقى رائحة الفم طيّبة ويبخّر منه أيضًا وإن شئت يسحقها مثل الذريرة وتطيّب بها يابسة وإن صحنته في دهن بان يدهن به قام مقام الغالية وإن حلّلت الحبّ بماء ورد ومسحته على جسدك كان حسنًا يؤخذ من العود الهندي سبعة دراهم

ومن الكبّابة ثلاثة دراهم ومن القرنفل أربعة دراهم ومن البسباسة أربعة دراهم ومن السعد الأبيض الكوفي خمسة دراهم ومن الصندل مثله ومن القاقلّة ثلاثة دراهم ومن سك المسك نصف أوقية ومن المسك مثقال ومن الكافور نصف مثقال يسحق ذلك ويعجن بماء ورد فارسي والأجود نصيبيني ويصنع منه حبًّا كالحمّص أو أكبر قليلًا ويجفّف في الظلّ ويؤخذ منه بالغداة على الأكل ولا يزال يديرها في فمه حتّى تذوب ويبلع في ذوبانها ثمّ كذلك عند النوم.

تمّ والحمد للّه وحده وصلّى الله على سيّدنا محمّد وسلّم تكمله لنفسه الفقير إلى الله التعالى محمّد عبد الله العمري غفر الله له ولوالديه ولجميع المسلمين.

فهرس

ت

ث

ج

ح

خ

د

ر

ز

س

ش

ص

ض

ط

ظ

ع

غ

ف

ق

ك

ل

م

ن

هـ

و

ي